TEACHING ENGLISH LANGUAGE LEARNERS

TOOLS FOR TEACHING LITERACY

Donna Ogle and Camille Blachowicz, Series Editors

This highly practical series includes two kinds of books: (1) grade-specific titles for first-time teachers or those teaching a particular grade for the first time; (2) books on key literacy topics that cut across all grades, such as integrating literacy with technology and science, teaching literacy through the arts, and fluency. Written by outstanding educators who know what works based on extensive classroom experience, each research-based volume features hands-on activities, reproducibles, and best practices for promoting student achievement. These books are also suitable as texts for undergraduate- or graduate-level courses; preservice teachers will find them informative and accessible.

TEACHING LITERACY IN SIXTH GRADE
Karen Wood and Maryann Mraz

TEACHING LITERACY IN KINDERGARTEN
Lea M. McGee and Lesley Mandel Morrow

INTEGRATING INSTRUCTION: LITERACY AND SCIENCE
Judy McKee and Donna Ogle

TEACHING LITERACY IN SECOND GRADE
Jeanne R. Paratore and Rachel L. McCormack

TEACHING LITERACY IN FIRST GRADE
Diane Lapp, James Flood, Kelly Moore, and Maria Nichols

PARTNERING FOR FLUENCY
Mary Kay Moskal and Camille Blachowicz

TEACHING LITERACY THROUGH THE ARTS
Nan L. McDonald and Douglas Fisher

TEACHING LITERACY IN FIFTH GRADE
Susan I. McMahon and Jacqueline Wells

TEACHING LITERACY IN THIRD GRADE
Janice F. Almasi, Keli Garas-York, and Leigh-Ann Hildreth

INTEGRATING LITERACY AND TECHNOLOGY:
EFFECTIVE PRACTICE FOR GRADES K–6
Susan Watts Taffe and Carolyn B. Gwinn

DEVELOPING LITERACY IN PRESCHOOL
Lesley Mandel Morrow

TEACHING LITERACY IN FOURTH GRADE
Denise Johnson

INTEGRATING LITERACY AND MATH:
STRATEGIES FOR K–6 TEACHERS
Ellen Fogelberg, Carole Skalinder, Patti Satz, Barbara Hiller, Lisa Bernstein, and Sandra Vitantonio

A PRINCIPAL'S GUIDE TO LITERACY INSTRUCTION
Carol S. Beers, James W. Beers, and Jeffrey O. Smith

TEACHING ENGLISH LANGUAGE LEARNERS:
LITERACY STRATEGIES AND RESOURCES FOR K–6
Shelley Hong Xu

TEACHING ENGLISH LANGUAGE LEARNERS

LITERACY STRATEGIES AND RESOURCES FOR K–6

Shelley Hong Xu

Series Editors' Note by Donna Ogle and Camille Blachowicz

THE GUILFORD PRESS
New York   London

© 2010 The Guilford Press
A Division of Guilford Publications, Inc.
72 Spring Street, New York, NY 10012
www.guilford.com

Printed in the United States of America

This book is printed on acid-free paper.

Last digit is print number: 9   8   7   6   5   4   3   2   1

Library of Congress Cataloging-in-Publication Data

Xu, Shelley Hong, 1964–
    Teaching English language learners: literacy strategies and resources
for K–6 / Shelley Hong Xu.
        p. cm. — (Tools for teaching literacy)
    Includes bibliographical references and index.
    ISBN 978-1-60623-529-4 (pbk.: alk. paper) — ISBN 978-1-60623-530-0
(hardcover: alk. paper)
    1. English language—Study and teaching—Foreign speakers.   2. English
language—Study and teaching (Elementary)   3. Bilingualism.   4. Language
acquisition.   I. Title.
    PE1128.A2X8 2010
    428.2′4—dc22
                                                            2009046494

ABOUT THE AUTHOR

Shelley Hong Xu, EdD, is Professor of Teacher Education at California State University, Long Beach, where she teaches literacy courses in a graduate reading program and a teaching credential program and a research course in the educational leadership doctoral program. She previously taught English as a foreign language and as a second language. Her research interests include preparing teachers for teaching English language learners and integrating multimedia texts into the literacy curriculum. Dr. Xu's work has appeared in literacy journals and edited books. She is coauthor of *Teaching Early Literacy: Development, Assessment, and Instruction* (with Diane M. Barone and Marla H. Mallette); *Literacy Instruction for English Language Learners Pre-K–2* (with Diane M. Barone); and *Trading Cards to Comic Strips: Popular Culture Texts and Literacy Learning in Grades K–8* (with Rachael Sawyer Perkins and Lark O. Zunich). She was formerly the Essay Book Review Editor for *Reading Research Quarterly* and Chair of the Publications Committee of the National Reading Conference.

SERIES EDITORS' NOTE

This is an exciting time to be involved in literacy education. Across the United States, thoughtful practitioners and teacher educators are developing and fine-tuning their instructional practices to maximize learning opportunities for children. These cutting-edge practices deserve to be shared more broadly. Because of these changes, we have become aware of the need for a series of books for thoughtful practitioners who want a practical, research-based overview of current topics in literacy instruction. We also collaborate with staff developers and study group directors who want effective inservice materials that they can use with professionals and colleagues at many different levels and that provide specific insights about literacy instruction. Thus the Tools for Teaching Literacy series was created.

This series is distinguished by having each volume written by outstanding educators who are noted for their knowledge and contributions to research, theory, and best practices in literacy education. They are also well-known staff developers who spend time in real classrooms working alongside teachers applying these insights. We think the series authors are unparalleled in these qualifications.

This volume, *Teaching English Language Learners: Literacy Strategies and Resources for K–6*, is written for the literacy teacher of this century—the teacher whose classroom contains a yeasty variety of students whose first language is not English, often with many different language groups represented in a single cohort. Shelley Hong Xu proposes eight guiding principles to help teachers in such situations do the best possible job. They begin with becoming knowledgeable about the characteristics of students' native languages and move toward preparing English language learners to become independent and strategic learners. By providing a strong research base; a thoughtful compendium of instructional, assessment, and content integration strategies; and family engagement ideas, Xu leads the reader through an organized process of translating and implementing best practices for linguistically diverse classrooms. Each instructional chapter (Chapters 3–8) ends with a section titled "Voice from the Classroom," where a classroom teacher shares her experience of teaching the component of literacy discussed in the chapter.

We are delighted to include *Teaching English Language Learners* in the Tools for Teaching Literacy series.

DONNA OGLE
CAMILLE BLACHOWICZ

PREFACE

Many years ago, I had an opportunity to teach in a summer English program for refugee children from all over the world. I was excited about this opportunity and felt confident that I would do a great job with teaching, as I was equipped with the second-language acquisition theories and pedagogies I had learned in my graduate program. One week later, Arash, an Iranian 10-year-old boy, reminded me that my approach to teaching was not effective. Arash, speaking no English at all, had a keen interest in the environmental print (grocery store ads) I brought to each class session. Every time I went to his table during a group activity, he would circle pictures of various fruits and vegetables and point at the pictures. Often my response was to say the words while pointing at the words and the pictures. One Monday, when Arash was pointing at the picture of tomatoes on a grocery ad, I immediately assumed my role as a teacher by saying the word *tomatoes* to him. He did not repeat after me. Instead, he repeatedly tapped his index finger on the picture and then pointed at his mouth. I said, "Tomatoes, yes, you can eat them." Again, Arash did not repeat the word, but showed me a frustrated look. During the following several class sessions, Arash continued doing the same thing. It was not until Friday that it dawned on me that Arash probably wanted to taste a tomato. On the following Monday, I went to Arash's table and put a tomato next to a picture of a tomato while saying the word *tomato* again; he immediately grabbed the tomato and took a big bite of it. Before I realized what had happened, the tomato juice had already splattered over my shirt. Shocked, but happy, I said to myself that I now knew what Arash wanted.

After the tomato incident, I thought a lot about what went wrong with my teaching. I felt that I failed as a teacher of the refugee children because I perceived Arash only as a student learning English and did not consider him as a child who was curious about things in his environment and had a desire to experience and learn about these things. I wish that I could have known about his desire sooner so that he had not felt so frustrated about not being understood. Since this incident, I started teaching English with an integration of content that was meaningful, important, and relevant to the children. For example, the children used their five senses to explore the apples I brought to the class and learned about describing words related to their experience with the apples. The approach of considering students' interests and needs and of integrating content into language teaching lowered the children's anxiety level and enhanced their experience in this summer English program.

This approach is what I am advocating in this book about teaching literacy to English language learners (ELLs). This book is written to share instructional strategies and materials adapted from those used with native English-speaking children. The modifications of strategies and materials, as illustrated in teaching examples, reflect teachers' consideration of individual students' strengths and needs in instruction and assessment. Throughout the book, you will read about how a set of strategies and materials used with non-ELLs can be used, with appropriate modifications, to address similar needs of students from various grade levels and native language backgrounds. For example, instructional strategies and materials for developing oral English would be appropriate for both a fifth-grade newcomer literate in a first language (L1) and a first-grade newcomer. In order for the strategies and materials to be effective, teachers do need to consider the strengths each student brings to learning. The fifth grader probably has more knowledge about a language than the first grader. Thus, the modifications for the strategies and materials for each student will be different.

ORGANIZATION OF THE BOOK

This book has eight chapters, each of which focuses on one component of literacy instruction. Chapter 1, "Guiding Principles of Teaching Literacy to English Language Learners," discusses guiding principles serving as an overarching framework for the subsequent chapters in this book. The guiding principles highlight the importance of (1) becoming knowledgeable of students' native languages and cultures; (2) engaging families in supporting their children's learning; (3) treating each child as a person and as a student; (4) becoming knowledgeable of research, theory, and pedagogies; (5) contextualizing teaching through comprehensible input, experience with L1, and content integration; (6) teaching everyday and academic English; (7) becoming skillful at conducting classroom-based assessment; and (8) preparing ELLs to become independent and strategic learners.

Chapter 2, "Language Acquisition and Linguistic Interferences," provides an overview of language acquisition theories and concepts, and language components (writing system, phonology, orthography, semantics, syntax, and morphology). This chapter also discusses language interferences from L1s in various areas and presents strategies to address the interferences.

Chapter 3, "Instruction for Oral Language Development," focuses on instructional strategies and activities for oral language development of students at various grade and proficiency levels. The strategies address the oral language for everyday communication and academic tasks.

Chapter 4, "Instruction for Phonological and Orthographic Knowledge and Fluency Development," shares instructional strategies, activities, and materials for teaching phonemic awareness, phonics, spelling, sight vocabulary, and fluency. Modifications for different age groups and proficiency levels are discussed.

Chapter 5, "Instruction for Vocabulary Development," focuses on academic vocabulary development. The instructional strategies, activities, and materials and teaching examples highlight an important role of academic vocabulary in oral and written language.

Chapter 6, "Instruction for Reading Comprehension Development," provides an overview of the comprehension process and discusses instructional strategies, activities, and materials for facilitating comprehension of both narrative and expository texts. This chapter emphasizes students' active participation in the comprehension process.

Chapter 7, "Instruction for Writing Development," centers on instructional strategies, activities, and materials for teaching ELLs to write for meaningful daily and academic communication. A reading–writing connection is highlighted throughout this chapter.

Chapter 8, "Instruction for Grammar," tackles the issue of teaching grammar as an isolated skill. From the perspective of teaching grammar as a resource model, this chapter presents instructional strategies, activities, and materials that integrate all components of language and literacy.

Despite the differences in content presented in each chapter, all chapters share several common features. Each chapter begins with a classroom scenario that reflects a reality of teaching ELLs. Questions based on the scenario are included to serve as a tool to stimulate your thinking about teaching before, during, and after reading the chapter. Throughout each chapter, teaching examples are presented to illustrate instructional strategies, activities, and materials and differentiated instruction for students with different needs. Various forms for assessment and instruction are illustrated with classroom examples within their respective chapters and appear again as reproducible forms in the Appendices. Additionally, Chapters 3–8 have some unique features:

> A presentation of strategies, activities, materials, and teaching examples illustrates the integration of all components of language and literacy in teaching ELLs one particular component (e.g., teaching grammar during the editing stage of the writing process).

> Each chapter focuses on classroom-based assessment and a connection between assessment and instruction.

> Each chapter provides examples of teaching language through content and

differentiating instruction for students at different grade and proficiency levels.

➤ Children's literature and everyday texts (e.g., environmental print and students' popular culture texts) are discussed and presented as instructional materials.

➤ Each chapter concludes with a section, "Voice from the Classroom," where a classroom teacher shares her experience of teaching the component(s) of literacy as discussed in the chapter.

Like many researchers, teacher educators, and classroom teachers, I believe in the power that teachers, not programs, have in making an impact on the success of ELLs' language and literacy development. It is my hope that this book will be helpful to you in your continued endeavors to effectively teach language and literacy to your ELLs.

ACKNOWLEDGMENTS

Many people have contributed to making the completion of this book a reality. First of all, my appreciation goes to California State University, Long Beach (CSULB), for its generous research funds from the Scholarly and Creative Activities Committee awards in the past years and for the 2008–2009 sabbatical leave award. The support made it possible for me to conduct research on exemplary literacy instruction for ELLs and to complete this book. My colleagues and students at CSULB deserve my recognition as well. I am also grateful to many dedicated classroom teachers and their students who welcomed me to their classrooms and allowed me to experience firsthand the excitement of teaching and learning!

I especially wish to acknowledge the valuable support from this special group of people:

Renee Gonzalez-Gomez, Maritza Magana, Olivia Martinez, Sarah Serrano, Hilary Shuler, and Camille Wilson, whose unique contributions to the "Voice from the Classroom" sections in Chapters 3–8 of this book showcase innovative, quality approaches to literacy instruction for ELLs.

Laura Barlow, Ana Cervantez-Cea, Rosio Dominguez, and Rachael Sawyer Perkins for allowing me to witness their exemplary teaching in their classrooms and their commitment to providing ELLs with a wide range of quality, meaningful learning experiences.

Christopher Jennison, Publisher, Education, at The Guilford Press, for his extraordinary encouragement and confidence.

Craig Thomas, Editor at The Guilford Press, for his guidance and his vision that this book must be accessible to classroom teachers and written for the purpose of enhancing their teaching with ELLs.

Natalie Graham, Associate Editor at The Guilford Press, for her patience, attention to details, and guidance throughout the production of this book.

Anna Nelson, Senior Production Editor at The Guilford Press, and her colleagues for their diligence, attention to details, and patience throughout the production of the book.

Donna Ogle and Camille Blachowicz, Series Editors of Tools for Teaching Literacy, for the constructive feedback that has strengthened this book.

Spencer, my husband, and Charlie, my son, for their patience, understanding, and support that have helped bring this book to fruition.

CONTENTS

CHAPTER 1

GUIDING PRINCIPLES OF TEACHING LITERACY TO ENGLISH LANGUAGE LEARNERS

Mrs. Smith, who spoke Spanish, was teaching first grade in Sunshine Elementary School. Every year, half of her students were identified as English language learners (ELLs), most of whom were Spanish-speaking. Before school started, Mrs. Smith had anticipated that the composition of this year's class would be similar to that of last year's. On the first day of school, Mrs. Smith was in for a big surprise. Although most of her ELLs were Spanish-speaking, she now had one Chinese boy (Ming) and one Vietnamese girl (Phung) whose English language proficiency level was at the very beginning. With no knowledge of Chinese or Vietnamese, Mrs. Smith became worried about how to communicate with these students and how to teach them. During lunch time, Mrs. Smith shared her concern with her colleagues and was happy to learn from Ms. Ravel, a fifth-grade teacher, that one of her students (Wei) spoke Chinese. During a lunch recess, Ms. Ravel introduced Wei to Mrs. Smith, who asked Wei to talk in Chinese to Ming. The more Wei talked, the more puzzled Ming looked. Mrs. Smith's brief talk with Wei revealed that Wei and Ming spoke different dialects of Chinese, not a shared dialect, Mandarin, needed for them to communicate with each other. Mrs. Smith now became frustrated. To make matters worse, she could not find one single child in her school who spoke Vietnamese. Like all dedicated teachers, Mrs. Smith was determined to find ways to help her students. During dismissal time, Mrs. Smith talked to Ming's and Phung's parents. She greeted them and told them that their children had done well on the first day of school. The only responses she got from both parents were smiles, nodding, and occasional utterances of "Okay" and "Thank you." Mrs. Smith did not get much information regarding Ming and Phung. During the rest of the first week, she continued talking to Ming's and Phung's parents, hoping to get to know them. But she continued to receive only smiles, nodding, and a few utterances of "Thank you" and "Okay."

The preceding scenario looks very familiar to many teachers of ELLs in elementary school classrooms. It reflects the diversity of ELLs and the challenges

1

their teachers face. If you were Mrs. Smith, you would probably ask questions about how to work with ELLs like Ming and Phung:

1. What do I need to know about teaching ELLs?
2. What does literature say about enhanced, modified literacy instruction for ELLs?
3. How important is my role as a teacher in the successful learning experiences of my students from diverse cultural, linguistic, and academic backgrounds?
4. How important is it for me to conduct classroom-based assessment (CBA)?
5. How can I invite parents to participate in their children's literacy learning at school and outside school?

Answering these questions is not an easy task, as working with ELLs and their families is a complicated and an ongoing process. In this chapter, I first briefly discuss the diversity of ELLs and the challenges of teaching ELLs. The primary focus of this chapter is guiding principles for teaching ELLs.

ELLs IN YOUR CLASSROOM

Before thinking about a plan to help ELLs, teachers of ELLs must first understand the diversity of ELLs. While Spanish-speaking ELLs compose a large number of ELLs, the number of ELLs with other first languages (L1s) has increased in recent years. In California, for example, between 2005 and 2006, the top 10 languages spoken by ELLs were Spanish, Vietnamese, Cantonese, Hmong, Filipino, Korean, Mandarin, Punjabi, Armenian, and Khmer (Cambodian) (California Department of Education, 2006). In other large states, such as Texas and New York, ELLs also speak a wide range of L1s.

The diversity of ELLs is further evidenced in their language and literacy experiences in L1, life experiences in general, length of U.S. residence, and parental educational levels (Freeman, Freeman, & Mercuri, 2002). Some ELLs coming to the United States as young children are in the process of developing L1 language and literacy. Others, before immigrating to the United States, have developed a solid foundation of language and literacy in L1. Still others born in the United States have used L1 as a dominant language and have little experience with English before coming to school. There are also ELLs who have experienced limited literacy in L1 and English (Rea & Mercuri, 2006). Immigrants from Singapore or Hong Kong, for example, have been exposed to English as a dominant medium of instruction during schooling (not necessarily a first language of children) (Mallozzi & Malloy, 2007). The life experience of an ELL from a developed country is different from that of an ELL from a war-torn or a poverty-stricken country. In addition, two ELLs from the same country, but with parents at different educational levels, have many differences in terms of language and literacy experiences in L1 and life experiences in general.

The diversity of ELLs presents an overwhelming set of challenges to teachers. Among the challenges, the following stand out: (1) developing knowledge of L1s and students' language and literacy experiences in L1 and life experiences; (2) developing knowledge of the differences between English and L1s and considering the differences in teaching; (3) working with ELLs' families; and (4) addressing needs of ELLs with diverse L1s and life experiences.

The diversity of ELLs and the challenges of teaching ELLs make working with ELLs a complex process (August & Shanahan, 2006; Rea & Mercuri, 2006; TESOL, 2001). This book does not provide "one-size-fits-all" solutions to addressing the challenges. Rather, it focuses on ways to identify and address specific needs of an ELL who is at a specific language and literacy proficiency level. Unlike a traditional way of identifying an ELL's needs solely by his or her English language proficiency level, in this book I take into consideration an ELL's language and literacy experiences in L1 and in English, and the impact of one variable on the other and on the student's overall English language and literacy development. I suggest that teachers not *just* identify an ELL as a child at a specific English proficiency level (e.g., English language development level 2, or beginning English proficiency level), but *also* as a child who has emotional needs, is eager to learn about the world around him or her, and exhibits a set of language and literacy behaviors (e.g., speaking fluently in L1, but not being literate in L1, and needing to strengthen L1 oracy and develop both language and literacy in English and in L1).

The advantage of identifying an ELL by their language and literacy behaviors in L1 and English is that it allows teachers to go beyond a grade and proficiency level and focus on addressing specific needs. It is not always effective to present strategies and materials for teaching ELLs by a grade level because of the complexity of strengths and needs ELLs bring to the classroom. Suppose you have two fourth-grade ELLs: one has developed L1 literacy while the other has limited language and literacy skills in L1. The needs of each ELL would be very different. Your lesson would incorporate a different set of strategies and materials for each of them or would use the same set, but with needed modifications.

GUIDING PRINCIPLES

Given the complexity of teaching ELLs, a set of principles is necessary in guiding us during planning and delivering instruction and assessment. In this section, I focus on these guiding principles for teaching literacy to ELLs (see Figure 1.1). Each principle is supported by research and/or position statements from professional organizations, including International Reading Association (IRA), National Council of Teachers of English (NCTE), Teachers of English to Speakers of Other Languages (TESOL), and National Association for Bilingual Education (NABE). All principles stress the importance of teachers—not programs—in ELLs' language and literacy learning (IRA, 2000; NCTE, 2006). No matter how well a program is designed to help ELLs, it is you, the teacher, who makes the program work for students.

Principle 1: Becoming Knowledgeable of an ELL's L1 and Culture
Knowledge of L1
Knowledge of a Native Culture

Principle 2: Engaging Families in ELLs' Literacy Learning
Rationales for Engaging Families
Benefits of Engaging Families

Principle 3: Treating an ELL as a Person and as a Student
Understanding ELLs' Emotional Experiences
Valuing ELLs' "Funds of Knowledge"
Focusing on ELLs' Strengths

Principle 4: Becoming Knowledgeable of Research, Theory, and Pedagogies
Becoming Familiar with Research and Theory
Developing Pedagogical Knowledge

Principle 5: Contextualizing Teaching through Comprehensible Input, Experience with L1, and Content Integration
Providing Comprehensible Input
Capitalizing on ELLs' Experiences in L1
Teaching through Content Integration

Principle 6: Teaching Everyday English and Academic English
Basic Personal Communicative Skills (BICS) and Cognitive Academic Language
*   Proficiency (CALP)*
Everyday English and Academic English

Principle 7: Becoming Skillful at Conducting Classroom-Based Assessment (CBA)
Identifying Assessment Foci
Considering Students' Interests and Life Experiences
Selecting Appropriate Assessment Materials

Principle 8: Preparing ELLs to Become Independent and Strategic Learners
Learning Contexts
Learning Tasks
Learning Materials

FIGURE 1.1. Guiding principles.

Principle 1: Becoming Knowledgeable of an ELL's L1 and Culture

Knowledge of L1

It is not new to understand that teaching ELLs would not be successful if teachers had little or no knowledge of an ELL's L1 and culture. The importance of this principle lies in the benefit of such knowledge for teachers in enhancing instruction (Barone & Xu, 2008; Dutro & Moran, 2003; Fillmore & Snow, 2000; Rea & Mercuri, 2006) and in gaining an understanding of the challenges and frustration an ELL may experience (Collier, 2008). For example, if you know about Vietnamese, you would have a better chance of identifying a source of confusion that a Vietnamese-speaking ELL has experienced while pronouncing the word *thing* as *ting*. The letter *t* in Vietnamese is pronounced as the sound of the English digraph *th*, while the letter combination *th* in Vietnamese is pronounced as the sound of the letter *t* in English. After the source of such a confusion has been identified, you can help the child overcome this difficulty. (See Chapter 2 for a more detailed discussion on addressing interferences.) If you do not know about this interference from Vietnamese, you might assume that the child's repeated mistake in pronouncing *thing* as *ting* results from his or her inability to pronounce /th/.

Knowledge of a Native Culture

Knowledge of a native culture can play a crucial role in ELLs' successful literacy learning (TESOL, 2006a). When you are familiar with a native culture, you are more likely to know how to approach an ELL and understand how an ELL participates in classroom activities. Asian children, for example, may not always volunteer their opinions in class discussions, but may prefer to be called on to share their thinking. The children's behavior reflects one aspect of many Asian cultures, the one that considers modesty as a virtue. If you are unfamiliar with this aspect of culture, you may mistake children's reluctance to participate in discussions as a sign of a lack of English language proficiency.

Unfamiliarity with a native culture can also cause difficulty for both you and students to develop a mutual, respectful relationship, which is essential for effective teaching and learning. For example, you may get upset when your Spanish-speaking children address you using the word *teacher* rather than a title (*Mrs.*, *Ms.*, *Miss*, or *Mr.*) and your last name. In an Hispanic culture, addressing you with the word *teacher* is a way for students to show a respect for you. Similarly, when a boy from a Middle Eastern country exhibits unwillingness to follow your instruction (if you are a female), you should not automatically assume that the boy is showing no respect for you. Rather, you need to understand a possible reason for such a behavior, that is, the boy's life experiences in his home country (e.g., growing up in a male-dominated society and knowing about the inferior status of women in the society).

Figure 1.2 provides a list of resources from which you can learn about L1s and native cultures of your ELLs. It is always helpful to gain knowledge of L1 and cultures directly from ELLs' families, community members, and others who speak L1 (e.g., school staff, students in your class or school, university students majoring in L1, and international students and scholars).

Principle 2: Engaging Families in ELLs' Literacy Learning

Rationales for Engaging Families

Children in American public schools usually go to school for between 180 and 185 days in a year (roughly half a year). For each 6-hour school day, about 5 hours

- Sundem, G., Krieger, J., & Pikiewicz, K. (2008). *10 languages you'll need most in the classroom.* Thousand Oaks, CA: Corwin Press.

This book focuses on 10 languages: Spanish, Vietnamese, Hmong, Chinese, Korean, Haitian Creole, Arabic, Russian, Tagalog, and Navajo. The authors provide cultural facts about each country, useful phrases (for communicating with families and students, and for student–student communications), and picture dictionaries (with a pronunciation guide) of school-related vocabulary (e.g., words for classroom supplies) and content-area vocabulary. Sample parent letters written in English and translated in a language vary from welcoming students to the classroom to informing parents about students' performance to scheduling a parent–teacher meeting.

- Feder, J. (1995). *Table, chair, bear: A book in many languages.* New York: Houghton Mifflin.

This picture book presents each common word (e.g., *table, window*) in 13 languages (English, Korean, French, Arabic, Vietnamese, Japanese, Portuguese, Lao, Spanish, Chinese, Tagalog, Cambodian, and Navajo).

- De Zutterm H. (1993). *Who says a dog goes bow-bow?* New York: Doubleday.

This picture book provides each word for a sound an animal makes in different languages (Chinese, Dutch, English, Farsi, Greek, Hebrew, Japanese, Korean, Spanish, and Thai).

- *Interactive Language Lessons in English and Other Languages* (web-books.com/Language)

This is a site for independent work on English and for teachers to learn about other languages.

- *CAL Discover Languages* (www.cal.org/resources/discoverlanguages/spotlight.html)

This site of the Center for Applied Linguistics spotlights a new language each quarter. Past languages included Arabic, Chinese, Spanish, and Russian.

- *Languages by Countries* (www.infoplease.com/ipa/A0855611.html)

This site provides information about languages spoken in one particular country. For example, in Cambodia, Khmer is an official language, and French and English are also used. In Iran, in addition to Persian and Persian dialects, other languages and dialects include Turkic and Turkic dialects, Kurdish, Luri, Balochi, Arabic, and Turkish.

- *I Love Languages* (www.ilovelanguages.com/index.php?category=Languages|By+Language)

This site provides useful information about many languages.

FIGURE 1.2. Resources for learning about L1s and cultures.

is for instruction. ELLs may get different types of instruction (e.g., pullout ESL lessons, English language development [ELD] lessons) in addition to the instruction they get from their home room teacher. Within the 5-hour instructional time, ELLs are pressured to accomplish more than their native English-speaking peers. For example, they need to learn about how to interact with peers and teachers and how to understand, speak, read, and write in English. Obviously, 5-hour-per-day instruction is insufficient for ELLs to learn about the culture and school language. It is not surprising that many ELLs either "sink or swim" in a classroom.

Given the limited instructional time ELLs receive at school, it is important to invite ELLs' families to be part of ELLs' learning experiences. Families, including extended families (grandparents, aunts, uncles, cousins), can contribute to ELLs' learning more than they have been credited for (Delgado-Gaitan, 2001; Edwards, 2004; Paratore, Melzi, & Krol-Sinclair, 2003). In particular, the household studies by Moll and his associates (Gonzáles & Moll, 1995; Gonzáles, Moll, & Amanti, 2005; Moll, 1998) describe valuable resources and experiences families offer their children. Engaging families is about making families partners in their children's literacy experiences (Li, 2004). Most families do care about their children's education but often lack ideas about how to get involved. Some family members feel reluctant to get involved for fear of their own lack of English language proficiency. Thus, it is more likely to be your job to invite families to participate in their children's learning experiences.

Benefits of Engaging Families

The benefits of engaging families are many. For example, since parents are able to communicate with ELLs in L1, they can supply you with valuable information, such as how a child feels about school, what type of literacy activities a child does outside school, and what literacy, linguistic, and content-specific concepts a child already knows. This type of information becomes handy in your planning of assessment and instruction. In addition, family members are able to use L1 to strengthen and help ELLs develop concepts related to content areas and language in general (e.g., story grammar). ELLs' foundation in these concepts developed via L1 helps lessen the process of learning and mastering these concepts in English. You can even engage family members with limited English proficiency. For example, you can ask (via a translator) an ELL's family member to bring to class some artifacts representative of the student's native culture and L1 print materials. The presence of these items helps make the ELL's classroom a little bit more familiar. In Chapters 3 to 8, I present specific ideas related to engaging families.

Principle 3: Treating an ELL as a Person and as a Student

Understanding ELLs' Emotional Experiences

A first way to treat ELLs as persons is for teachers to understand the frustration, fear, self-esteem, and self-confidence they experience in learning English, and to become sympathetic with them. Just think back on your own experience of learning a foreign language in high school or in college. How did you feel when you were asked to say in front of the whole class a word or phrase that you did not think you had mastered in the foreign language? Did you wish that your teacher had not done this to you? Did you feel that your self-esteem was hurt, that you were not smart, or that you could not learn the language well? Also remember that you were an adolescent or adult during that time and that you had developed a relatively solid foundation in English. You could draw from your literacy knowledge, skills, and strategies in English to help you learn the foreign language. Unlike you, many ELLs in elementary schools have not fully developed their L1 language and literacy and are virtually learning English and their L1 simultaneously. Now you can understand how ELLs would feel given a situation similar to what you experienced as an adolescent or adult.

Valuing ELLs' "Funds of Knowledge"

As teachers, we all respect our students and want the best for them. We, however, at times forget that each student is first a human being with various experiences, feelings, and knowledge, among other things, and then a student who needs to accomplish many language and literacy goals during the school year. Treating ELLs as persons also means that you value the rich experiences and resources they bring to class. Moll and his associates' notion of "funds of knowledge" frequently reminds us of the importance of recognizing and utilizing the resources ELLs bring to school (Gonzáles & Moll, 1995; Gonzáles, Moll, & Amanti, 2005; Moll, 1998). In Moll's (1998) study about Mexican children's funds of knowledge, the children brought candies from Mexico back to the U.S. and sold them to their friends and classmates. During this process, the children were applying language and critical thinking skills (e.g., persuasion, negotiation), math skills (e.g., addition), and knowledge of money (e.g., value of a bill, a quarter). These skills and knowledge, related closely to what the children were learning about language and literacy and content area subjects (e.g., math), are what teachers should capitalize on during teaching.

Focusing on ELLs' Strengths

Another way to treat ELLs as persons and students is for teachers to recognize their strengths. It often seems easy for us to identify what ELLs cannot do and overlook what they can do. A deficit perspective of perceiving ELLs leads us to provide instruction with a focus on correcting and remediating student problems rather than engaging students in learning how to use language and literacy for everyday and academic communication, a critical skill for survival in a modern society (August & Shanahan, 2006; Peregoy & Boyle, 2009). The danger of this perspective is the discouragement it brings to students and teachers. If we do not point out for our students what they can do, students may feel discouraged to continue trying to reach an expected goal.

For example, when Spanish-speaking Maria is repeating after her teacher the sentence "My chair is here, and Jose's chair is over there," Maria repeatedly says *share* for *chair.* Maria's teacher can take two different approaches to addressing Maria's error in her oral language. If Maria's teacher focuses on correcting her substitution error (*share* for *chair*), the teacher would insist that Maria correct the pronunciation of the word *chair.* If you were Maria, you would probably feel that you lack an ability to repeat after your teacher even though you have said the whole sentence correctly except for the word *chair.* You would probably feel frustrated, less confident, and discouraged. Similarly, Maria's teacher would feel frustrated, as Maria cannot correctly repeat a simple sentence. On the other hand, Maria's teacher could say something like this: "Wow, you said the sentence. That's right (*emphasizing the strength*). Now, I am going to say the word *chair* again, and then you say it. Listen. /ch/ *chair.*" After the teacher has said the word and Maria repeats it, the teacher would say, "Do you hear my word and your word? Are they the same? I said, /ch/ *chair.* You said, /sh/ *share.* Can you now try to say *chair*?" By saying this, the teacher makes Maria realize that she is able to repeat the whole sentence and also points out for Maria what she needs to work on. The modeling the teacher provides through repeating "/ch/ *chair*, /sh/ *share*" serves as a scaffold for Maria. The second approach recognizes Maria's strength (which gives the teacher and Maria hope) and identifies Maria's needs.

Principle 4: Becoming Knowledgeable of Research, Theory, and Pedagogies

Becoming Familiar with Research and Theory

Research and theory about the developmental process of L1 and English language and literacy and instruction in language and literacy is a vital set of knowledge for every teacher with ELLs (Fillmore & Snow, 2000). This knowledge enables teachers to gain a better understanding of many whys and hows regarding teaching ELLs. Equipped with this knowledge, teachers will become skillful at orchestrating instructional strategies and materials tailored to address specific needs of each particular ELL or group of ELLs. One source of information about research, theories, and pedagogies is journals published by professional organizations such as Teachers of English for Speakers of Other Languages (TESOL; *www.tesol.org*), National Association of Bilingual Education (NABE; *www.nabe.org*), International Reading Association (IRA; *www.reading.org*), National Council of Teachers of English (NCTE; *www.ncte.org*), and National Reading Conference (NRC; *www.nrconline. org*). The websites of these organizations also list valuable resources on teaching ELLs.

Developing Pedagogical Knowledge

Many scholars have considered it vital that teachers of ELLs develop a body of knowledge of instructional strategies and materials and an ability to skillfully orchestrate strategies and materials to address curriculum standards (IRA, 2001; Rea & Mercuri, 2006; TESOL, 2001). Although there are some strategies and materials designed particularly for ELLs (e.g., TPR [total physical response], Sheltered

Instruction, bilingual materials), most instructional strategies and materials that have been effective for teaching non-ELLs can be effective for ELLs as well (Fitzgerald & Graves, 2004; Rea & Mercuri, 2006; Shanahan & Beck, 2006).

The crucial difference in using a similar set of strategies and materials with ELLs and with non-ELLs is that teachers of ELLs should focus on scaffolding (Echevarria, Vogt, & Short, 2008; Fitzgerald & Graves, 2004; Peregoy & Boyle, 2009; Rea & Mercuri, 2006). For example, reading aloud is a useful strategy for teaching young ELLs concepts about print, sight words, phonics, and comprehension. When you are pointing at each word while reading aloud a book to non-ELLs, you are teaching print directionality in English. If you have a student whose L1 print directionality is different from English (e.g., in Japanese, print is read vertically from right to left; in Farsi, print is read horizontally as in English, but from right to left), you need to take one extra step in reading aloud. You may bring a book or a text (e.g., a newspaper article) written in L1 and lay it side by side with an English book to draw the student's attention to the difference in print directionality between English and L1. This extra step serves as a meaningful scaffold to help the ELL become aware of the difference in print directionality. The strategy of reading aloud can also be modified for older ELLs who are literate in L1 but have limited English oral proficiency and need to develop speech-to-print match. You build on ELLs' strengths in L1 literacy by using content-related picture books whose illustrations provide contextual clues for the concepts.

Most instructional strategies and materials discussed throughout this book are not much different from those used with non-ELLs. The teaching examples with these strategies and materials do show that modifications and scaffolding are necessary to ensure the effectiveness of these strategies and materials. It is important for teachers to constantly reflect on modifications and seek improvement for future use of a set of strategies and material (see Appendix A at the back of this book for a reproducible form).

The latest research has redefined what is considered instructional materials. For example, a new literacies perspective (Dyson, 2003; New London Group, 1996; Street, 1995) recognizes, among other things, a wide range of texts (print, digital, visual, and oral) through which students construct meaning by reading, writing, speaking, and performing, and the important role these texts play in students' becoming literate in the 21st century. When playing a video game, for instance, a student has to make sense of the positional relationship among the characters before he or she is able to decide which action button to push (Gee, 2003). The latest information related to various types of texts has an important implication for teaching ELLs. Print texts are no long the only dominant instructional materials useful for teaching ELLs. Due to the globalization of popular culture, many ELL newcomers from Asian countries, for example, have as much experience with Japanese anime (a visual and oral text) and manga (comic books based on Japanese anime) as other ELLs and non-ELLs in American schools. If teachers understand that instructional materials are not just limited to print texts and recognize ELL newcomers' experiences with visual and print texts, they are able to find additional material to make a connection between ELLs' prior experiences and new concepts.

You, for instance, can help ELL newcomers realize that understanding a story in English is similar to what they have been doing when reading manga (e.g., getting information from pictures, drawing inferences, and understanding a story setting). This type of connection provides a layer of scaffolding for ELLs.

Principle 5: Contextualizing Teaching through Comprehensible Input, Experience with L1, and Content Integration

The goal of literacy instruction should be more than just teaching children how to decode and spell words; it should focus on helping students learn how to make sense of a text that is being read or heard and how to convey ideas when composing a text (e.g., Block, Gambrell, & Pressley, 2002; Graham, MacArthur, & Fitzgerald, 2006). Similarly, teaching English language and literacy to ELLs aims to assist them in extracting meaning from oral and written language. When language and literacy teaching is contextualized, students have a better chance to understand what is being said and read (Cummins, 1986; IRA, 2001; NCTE, 2006; Shanahan & Beck 2006). Just imagine which way is better for you to understand an instructional manual on assembling a piece furniture: (1) just reading the steps of instruction; (2) reading the steps of instruction and the illustrations of the steps; or (3) reading the steps of instruction and the illustrations of the steps and watching a video showing the steps. Obviously, the third way helps you better understand the words in each step of the instructions. There are three *interrelated* ways to contextualize teaching to maximize opportunities for ELLs to construct meaning: (1) providing comprehensible input, (2) capitalizing on ELLs' experiences in L1, and (3) teaching through content integration.

Providing Comprehensible Input

Comprehensible input, a phrase coined by Krashen (1985), refers to language input at the level an ELL can comprehend (see Chapter 2 for a more detailed discussion). For example, the sentence *Would you please sit down?* is less comprehensible to beginning ELLs than the sentence *Please sit down*. The first sentence with an interrogative sentence structure and the intended purpose of a formal request would mislead the ELLs to answer the question with a *yes* or *no* rather than actually sitting down. The sentence *Please sit down*, a straightforward command, makes it easier for ELLs to comprehend. Similarly, in teaching a literary concept, one way you can provide ELLs with comprehensible input is to relate a concept to a similar concept familiar to ELLs. For instance, in teaching the concept of event sequence in a story, you can begin by asking students about a series of things they do after getting up. In so doing, you are providing comprehensible input related to the concept of sequence by reminding students of their prior experience with it.

Capitalizing on ELLs' Experiences in L1

A second way to contextualize teaching is for teachers to capitalize on ELLs' experiences with L1 (Dressler & Kamil, 2006; Geva & Genesee, 2006; IRA, 2001).

Some examples of such experiences include (1) general knowledge about language (e.g., functions of language [instruct, inform, entertain, etc.] and conventions of language [concepts of print, sound–symbol relationship, etc.]); (2) language and literacy strategies and skills; and (3) content-area concepts acquired through L1 (e.g., math and science concepts). For example, if you are teaching Spanish-speaking ELLs how to map each letter of an English word into a sound, you begin with a common Spanish word (e.g., *casa*) to show students how to look at each letter, come up with its sound, and blend all sounds together to say the word. For upper grade ELLs who have already mastered specific content concepts in L1, all they need is a review of the concepts and the English equivalent for these concepts. Figure 1.3 shows an example of the English equivalent of a math concept.

Teaching through Content Integration

A third way to contextualize teaching is to teach the English language and literacy through content (Freeman & Freeman, 2009; Freeman, Freeman, & Mercuri, 2002; Houk, 2005; Mansukhani, 2002) (see Figures 1.4 and 1.5). Many language and literacy concepts (e.g., sounds and words), relatively abstract, are embedded in specific content (e.g., sentences about different types of clouds). Even when one is reading a story, the story is about something. When language and literacy are taught with an integration of content, linguistic concepts become relatively concrete and meaningful. Furthermore, teaching language and literacy through content makes it possible and easier for ELLs to bring what they already know (acquired through their life experience and L1) to the task of learning something new. For example, in teaching the word *hand*, if you hold up your hand and say the word *hand*, and then write the word on the board with a line under *and* to indicate that the word belongs to the *-and* family, the word *hand* is not a totally new word to ELLs. They just need to learn a new layer of information related to this word;

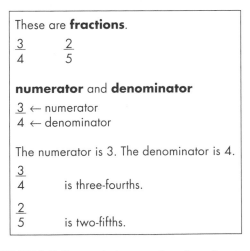

FIGURE 1.3. English equivalent for a fraction.

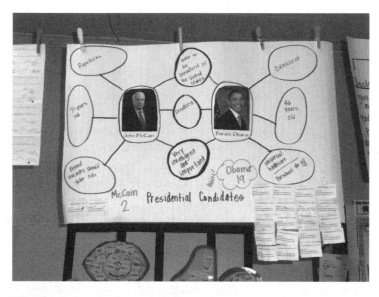

FIGURE 1.4. Mock election in Mrs. Dominguez's third-grade class.

FIGURE 1.5. A chart about matter in Mrs. Martinez's first-grade class.

that is, the word *hand* belongs to the *-and* family. When you are teaching the word *hand* as an *-and* family word as well as a word representing a body part, the word becomes less abstract to ELLs.

Furthermore, content integration allows students to practice listening, speaking, reading, and writing skills simultaneously. The task of writing a book review, for example, requires students to first read the book. When they share their review with the class or a group, students practice speaking using a set of academic language related to literary terms (e.g., characterization, setting, and plot) and practice offering comments on the book. The students listening to the book review and asking questions are practicing their listening and speaking skills.

Principle 6: Teaching Everyday English and Academic English

Basic Personal Communicative Skills and Cognitive Academic Language Proficiency

As early as 1979, Cummins distinguished 2 different types of linguistic skills ELLs need to learn and master in order to survive in American schools: *basic personal communicative skills* (BICS), and *cognitive academic language proficiency* (CALP). BICS are often used for daily, interpersonal communications in contextualized settings with cues (e.g., gestures, pictures) for learners to construct meanings. CALP is necessary for ELLs to complete academic tasks in often decontextualized settings that lack cues to assist learners. For instance, while reading, readers cannot ask an author about questions related to the text, as opposed to the situation in which a listener can ask a speaker to clarify some confusion. Collier (1995) and Cummins (1989) further state that it usually takes ELLs 2 to 3 years to develop BICS and 5 to 7 years to master CALP. In addition, both BICS and CALP can be cognitively demanding. For example, a beginner's show-and-tell about a picture can present a heavy cognitive and linguistic load similar to the task of sharing a book report by a third grader at an intermediate level. Scarcella (2003) further points out that development of BICS and CALP can occur simultaneously. For example, "Rudimentary phonemic awareness (sensitivity to sounds in spoken words) may facilitate the development of beginning oral proficiency (BICS), but it may also facilitate the development of advanced reading proficiency (CALP), since it aids learners in accessing difficult academic words when reading" (p. 6).

Everyday English and Academic English

In the past decade, Cummins' concepts of BICS and CALP have been expanded to mean, respectively, everyday English and academic English. There is a growing focus on teaching ELLs academic English as early as possible (Scarcella, 2003; Schleppegrell & Colombi, 2002; Zwiers, 2008) (see Table 1.1 for the differences between everyday English and academic English). Among various definitions for academic English, I have found the one by Scarcella (2003) to capture the essence of academic language:

TABLE 1.1. Differences between Everyday English and Academic English

Category	Everyday English	Academic English
Forms	Informal	Formal
Diction	• High-frequency • Single- or two-syllable words • From Anglo-Saxon lexicon (e.g., *pull together*)	• Low-frequency • Multisyllabic, discipline-specific words (e.g., math, science) • Many derivational words (e.g., *illustrate, illustration, illustrative, illustrated, illustrating*) • From Greek or Latin roots (e.g., *assemble*)
Structure	• Mostly simple sentences • Some compound and complex sentences • Acceptable fragments (e.g., *quickly, quickly*) • Basic use of punctuation marks	• Mostly compound and complex sentences • Frequent presence of phrasal structures (e.g., present and past participles, infinitive) • Advanced use of punctuation marks (e.g., : , ; , —)
Contextual cues	• Gestures • Body language (e.g., facial expressions, pitch and tone of voice) • Opportunities for a listener to ask a speaker for clarification, explanations, etc.	• Words in the previous or following sections of texts • Readers' knowledge of the topic • No opportunities for a reader to ask an author for clarification, explanations, etc.
Setting	• Less formal (e.g., playground, school cafeteria, parking lot)	• More formal (e.g., classroom, science lab)
Task	• Interpersonal communications (e.g., asking for directions, telling a joke)	• Academic communications (e.g., presenting a book report, conducting an interview)

Academic English is a variety or a register of English used in professional books and characterized by the specific linguistic features associated with academic disciplines. The term "register" refers to a constellation of linguistic features that are used in particular situational contexts (Halliday & Hasan, 1976; Martin, 1992). (p. 9)

First, academic English encompasses a wide range of genres (Saville-Troike, 1984; Swales, 1990) (e.g., instructional manual for conducting a science experiment; an argumentative essay). Each genre uses one or a combination of several expository text structures (e.g., description, compare and contrast). In addition, academic English has its own unique linguistic features different from everyday English (e.g., diction). One pair of words provided by Scarcella (2003) illustrates well the difference in diction between everyday English and academic English. The phrase *find out* is used in everyday English, whereas the word *investigate* is used in academic English. Further, academic English has its own grammatical rules different from those for everyday English. Scarcella (2003), for example, refers to "the grammatical features (morphological and syntactic) associated with argumentative composition, procedural description, definition, and analysis"; "the grammatical co-occurrence restrictions governing words"; and "more complex rules of punctuation" (p. 12). Helping students develop an ability to understand and use these features in the reading and writing of academic texts should be an instructional focus for ELLs, as academic language directly affects how well students comprehend academic texts.

Academic English has its unique functions: describing complexity, higher-order thinking, and abstraction (Zwiers, 2008). Academic English is a tool for explicitly describing and explaining complicated concepts and conceptual relationships (Schleppegrell, 2004). Take the concept of tornadoes as an example. It involves such concepts as storm, wind, atmospheric pressure, diameter, and season, and the cause–effect relationship related to winds and atmosphere. Another function of academic language is its use in expressing higher-order thinking related to concepts and their relationships. For example, in a research paper on the American Revolution, students are expected to describe the events, explain the cause(s) of the events, compare the Revolution with other historical events, and evaluate the Revolution. All of these tasks requiring higher-order thinking skills cannot be completed without academic language (Valdez-Pierce & O'Malley, 1992).

A description of abstraction, a third function of academic language, involves the use of language beyond everyday communication, which is not familiar to students and not easy and automatic to learn (Snow & Brinton, 1997). Zwiers (2008) explains that an understanding of the academic language used to describe abstraction requires students to identify the cue words in an expressed concept and the relationship between the words. In the example of the expression *A force causing an object not to slide is called friction*, students need to understand that an explanation of the concept of friction is expressed in the phrase before the verb *is*. Within that phrase are three related concepts (*a force, an object*, and the actions of *causing* and *to slide*) and one cause–effect relationship. Additionally, students need to understand that this expression in a passive voice has the same meaning as the expression in an active voice: *Friction is a force causing an object not to slide*. If they cannot grasp these cue words representing concepts and the relationship between the concepts, students will fail to understand the meaning of this definition.

The components of academic English include academic vocabulary (see Chapter 5), academic text structures (see Chapter 6), academic grammar (see Chapter 8), and academic tasks (see Figure 1.6). Academic tasks are characterized as higher-order thinking, context-reduced, and content-specific. For example, in sharing a research report with the class, an ELL uses the content-specific vocabulary and follows a specific way of conveying the content of the report to the class. The sharing may include a statement of the rationale for the selection of the topic, an overview of the report, a highlight of the research outcome, and an invitation for questions from the audience. In tasks involving more than one student, everyday English for interpersonal communication is also used. As Scarcella (2003) puts it,

Academic English builds on and extends the learners' developing competence in the sociolinguistic component. This component includes an increased number of language functions. The functions include the general ones of everyday English such as apologizing, complaining, and making requests as well as the more academic ones, such as signaling cause and effect, hypothesizing, generalizing, comparing, contrasting, explaining, describing, defining, justifying, giving examples, sequencing, and evaluating. (p. 18)

Some examples of academic tasks include designing, performing, and reporting an experiment; explaining the steps for solving a math problem; and comparing and contrasting the American Revolution and the Civil War. It is important to be aware that academic language exists in both oral and written language. To master academic language, students must be engaged in listening to, talking about, reading, and writing about academic texts. Given the complexity of academic English, it presents a special challenge to ELLs, including those literate in L1. Scarecella (2003) and Collier (2008) offer some suggestions on teaching academic language:

1. Providing scaffolded and planned instruction during which you model the use of academic language and students have many opportunities to practice academic language.

2. Building instruction on students' prior experience and knowledge with L1 and English (e.g., using cognates).

3. Offering explicit instruction and explanations on the specific features of academic language.

Academic Vocabulary and Concepts (see Chapter 5)
  Discipline-Related Words
  Words Used across Disciplines
  Morphological, Phonological, and Grammatical Features of Words
  Modal Auxiliaries

Academic Text Structures (see Chapter 6)
  Description
  Sequence
  Compare and Contrast
  Cause and Effect
  Problem and Solution
  A Combination of Two or More

Academic Grammar (see Chapter 8)
  Phrasal Structure
  Sentence Structure
  Punctuation

Academic Tasks

FIGURE 1.6. Components of academic language.

4. Motivating and engaging students in learning and applying academic language with accessible texts, media texts, and hands-on projects.

5. Conducting assessment to inform instruction and to provide feedback on students' learning and application of academic English.

Principle 7: Becoming Skillful at Conducting Classroom-Based Assessment

Given that the performance of ELLs on standardized tests are counted in a school's adequate yearly progress (AYP) calculation (TESOL, 2005), teachers are pressured to make sure that their students pass state tests, possibly failing to consider various factors involved in assessing ELLs. García, McKoon, and August (2006) remind us that assessing ELLs involves a complex process with many compounding factors that would affect students' performance. They recommend that teachers "need to understand the linguistic and psychological structures he or she [an ELL] has in both minority and majority language and how they interact" (p. 593). Other factors that teachers are advised to take into consideration include students' prior knowledge on the topic, their culture, and the process and outcome of language and literacy learning (García, McKoon, & August, 2006; TESOL, 2003). Further, test biases would make standardized assessment less valid in providing teachers with accurate information about ELLs' language and literacy proficiency (Au, 2002; García, McKoon, & August, 2006). One bias, associated with assessing ELLs' content and linguistic abilities (Short, 1993), makes it difficult for teachers to decide whether ELLs' poor performance on a test is due to their lack of linguistic abilities or their lack of content knowledge embedded in the test. In "Position Paper on High-Stakes Testing for K–12 English-Language Learners in the United States of America," TESOL (2003) further explains the frustration ELLs experience while taking a test measuring both linguistic abilities and content knowledge:

> English language learners cannot demonstrate their mastery of content without having already attained a high degree of English fluency. Many English language learners come to this country with significant content knowledge; however, they often cannot express this knowledge because they lack academic proficiency in English (LaCelle-Peterson & Rivera, 1994). (p. 1)

Given the complexity of assessing ELLs, a standardized test often fails to provide a holistic view of an ELL's linguistic and literacy knowledge, skills, and strategies. Furthermore, teachers are not informed of the assessment results before the end of the school year, which makes it impossible for them to modify their instruction to address specific individual needs during the school year. Classroom-based assessment (CBA) provides relatively current, accurate, and specific information about an ELL's linguistic and literacy knowledge (Lenski, Ehlers-Zavala, Daniel, & Sun-Irminger, 2006). With the ongoing, teacher-controlled, and curriculum-embedded nature of CBA, it is possible for teachers to tailor assessment to identify specific strengths and needs and implement the assessment more frequently throughout a school year. Figure 1.7 shows an example a record of a student's basic literacy skills and strategies observed during assessment. In Chapters 3–8, I discuss specific ideas of CBA tailored to ELLs with specific needs. As Barone and Xu (2008) state, CBA maximizes the possibility for teachers to identify assessment foci, consider students' interests and life experiences, and select appropriate assessment materials.

Identifying Assessment Foci

Before identifying an assessment focus, you read about an ELL's assessment results from the previous year to develop some knowledge of what an ELL can and cannot

---

Name: Dan Tran

Text Title for Reading: The section "Did All People Come to the New World to Get Rich?" (p. 17) from Davis's (2003) *Don't Know Much about American History*

Decoding	Reading fluency	Vocabulary used in retelling	Comprehension	Use of strategies
No problem	Failed to pay attention to commas in long sentences	Used 50% of content words from the text; substituted the content words with common words (e.g., *groups* for *communities*)	Was able to retell most content	Self-monitored and self-corrected during the retelling; related the text to self and other texts

Needs:
1. Learning about the use of the commas in long sentences
2. Uderstanding the content words
3. Identifying all important details

Topic for Writing: Getting Rich (based on the section "Did All People Come to the New World to Get Rich?" [p. 17]) from Davis's (2003) *Don't Know Much about American History*

Content	Organization	Diction	Grammar	Use of strategies
Included 75% of the content from the text	Followed a descriptive structure	Used 60% of the content words from the text	Failed to use most complex sentences and some verbal phrases correctly; most sentences had the subject–verb–object pattern.	Rephrased some sentences; sed an outline for planning

Needs:
1. Listing details to be included before writing
2. Listing content words to be included
3. Learning more about complex sentences
4. Using a variety of sentences

FIGURE 1.7. Record of basic skills and strategies (fifth grade).

perform. This knowledge, coupled with curriculum standards, helps you identify an assessment focus. For example, Adar, a third-grade Iranian boy, demonstrated comprehension skills at the beginning level as evidenced in his second-grade standardized reading test. His teacher, Mrs. Taylor, after reviewing the second-grade test results, realized that Adar's great need was inferential comprehension. She also wondered if content and cultural knowledge had some impact on Adar's performance on inferential comprehension. Based on third-grade standards for comprehension, Adar should work on comprehending texts with complex plot and characterization at an inferential level. Equipped with this type of background knowledge, Mrs. Taylor selected two assessment foci for Adar: One focus is to assess Adar's inferential comprehension of a text with background knowledge familiar to Adar; the other focus is to assess the same inferential comprehension of a text with content/culture background knowledge unfamiliar to Adar. The purpose of both assessment foci is for Mrs. Taylor to learn if Adar's limited inferential comprehension was due to his lack of ability and experience in this area, or due to his lack of background information on the topic of a text.

If a student is a newcomer, or if no assessment data from previous years are available, you select assessment foci based on the student's language and literacy experiences with L1 and English and on the grade-level standards. For example, if one fifth grader is from a country where English is used often (but not an official or a second language), this student would have relatively more knowledge about English. By contrast, another fifth grader who has never learned English would need to learn many basic concepts related to English (e.g., concepts about print).

It is possible that some basic literacy skills and strategies are not listed in the curriculum standards at the students' current grade. If this is the case, it is necessary for you to conduct differentiated assessment and instruction with small groups or individual students based on one or more standards from a previous grade. For example, before teaching grammar based on the sixth-grade standard 1.2, "Identify and properly use indefinite pronouns and present perfect, past perfect, and future perfect verb tenses; ensure that verbs agree with compound subjects" (California State Board of Education, 2007, p. 171), you need to make sure that students already know how to use verbs and pronouns. Thus, an assessment based on the fifth-grade grammar standard 1.2, "Identify and correctly use verbs that are often misused (e.g., lie/lay, sit/set, rise/raise), modifiers, and pronouns" (California State Board of Education, 2007, p. 151), seems to be necessary.

Considering Students' Interests and Life Experiences

It is well known that a student's life experiences affect the student's performance on assessment (Cummins, 1989; TESOL, 2003). Jiménez (2004) suggests that teachers should begin with becoming familiar with students' non-school-based literacy practices in order to understand their literacy knowledge. In support of Jiménez's suggestion, Barone and Xu (2008) provide one example of a kindergartner at a beginning language proficiency level who was able to demonstrate her decoding skills on the vocabulary test based on her popular culture interest (a

TV show, *Kim Possible*). She explained five out of six words on the test (*Kim, doll, girl, Barbie, clothes*, and *pretty*). For example, for the word *girl*, she said, "A person, she's a girl (*points to Destiny*)." This same child, however, could recognize only one word, *like*, from a preprimer word list (Johns, 2005). As illustrated in this example, when ELLs' interests and life experiences are considered in CBA, they are given an opportunity to demonstrate what they know. If you know that an ELL came from a country where no supermarkets exist, you would avoid a text with a supermarket as a setting. In so doing, you have a better chance of assessing the student's reading comprehension rather than assessing the student's background knowledge on supermarkets.

Selecting Appropriate Assessment Materials

Once you have identified assessment foci and considered students' interests and life experiences in selecting CBA, the last step—choosing appropriate materials—cannot be overlooked. Material selection must be based on the assessment foci. If you want to assess an ELL's ability to segment a group of words, you should select words from the student's receptive language (i.e., either from the books familiar to the student or from the student's oral vocabulary). Otherwise, the student would be puzzled by the unfamiliar words, not to mention performing the task of segmenting each of these words. The student's unfamiliarity with these words would possibly compound the assessment outcome.

In a similar way, the factor of students' interests and life experiences need to be considered in material selection. As discussed earlier in the example of a kindergartner's ability to decode words from her popular culture interest, when the factor of personal interest is considered in the assessment, the ELL was given an additional opportunity to demonstrate what she knew about words. To learn more about whether students' interests or life experiences have some effect on student performance, you can vary the assessment materials. You can use one text with a topic interesting to an ELL and another text with a topic unfamiliar to the student.

In addition, you need to withhold your emotional attachment to a certain text (e.g., children's books) so that you do not choose a text simply because you have enjoyed the text, thus overlooking the above-mentioned factors. Before choosing CBA materials, it is always helpful to ask questions such as "What do I want to get from this assessment?"; "Would this chosen material help me get what I want?"; "What compounding variables would this chosen material cause?"; and "What is the effect of these variables on the assessment outcome?"

In identifying students' strengths and needs, instead of relying solely on a worksheet format for assessment, you may consider adopting a think-aloud approach that enables you to assess students' application of literacy skills and strategies and oral language. For example, to check on a student's decoding and fluency, you have the student first read aloud a short text and then explain to you any mistakes or difficulties he or she experienced. In assessing comprehension and vocabulary, you have the student retell the text while you measure his or her use of specific vocabulary and knowledge of text structure. In addition, you may have the student explain the meaning of some words in the text and the way the meaning is extracted. This type of think-aloud provides you with valuable information about a student's vocabulary knowledge and other relevant knowledge (e.g., background knowledge; using strategies). Similarly, for writing, having a student write on the topic of his or her choice allows you to assess the student's skills and strategies related to writing a coherent and focused piece. A student's think-aloud about the written piece (e.g., choice of the topic, diction, and content focus) can shed light on the student's thinking process about composing. This think-aloud format, indeed time consuming, does allow you to gain more information than you could get from a worksheet. You may make an audio recording of a think-aloud for both reading and writing for future use.

Principle 8: Preparing ELLs to Become Independent and Strategic Learners

Similar to teaching native English-speaking children, the goal of language and literacy instruction for ELLs is to prepare them to become independent and strategic learners (Block & Pressley, 2007; National Reading Panel, 2000; Palincsar & Brown, 1984). To achieve this goal, instruction needs to focus on teaching learner strategies and providing opportunities for ELLs to apply the strategies in order to internalize them (Chamot & O'Malley, 1994; García, 2000; Jiménez, 1997; Peregoy & Boyle, 2009). I use the term *learner strategies* to refer to strategies ELLs use (e.g., self-monitoring), and the term *instructional strategies* to refer to strategies teachers use to facilitate students' use of learner strategies (e.g., read-aloud). When ELLs become strategic, they are more likely to be able to deal with oral and written language on their own, which makes becoming independent learners an attainable goal. Throughout this book, you will read examples in which teachers prepare ELLs to use these learner strategies in various contexts and for various purposes. The key to successfully preparing ELLs to become independent and strategic learners is to scaffold their learning process (Chamot & O'Malley, 1994; Echevarria, Vogt, & Short, 2008; Fitzgerald, & Graves, 2004). Scaffolding can be achieved through varied learning contexts, learning tasks, and learning materials.

Learning Contexts

Broadly speaking, a learning context is a classroom environment. A supportive environment is language- and print-rich in English and L1, low-anxiety, and full of meaningful, authentic opportunities for ELLs to learn and practice skills and strategies. Your students can contribute to building an environment conducive to their success. For example, you can encourage them to share their knowledge of L1 and culture and to bring in artifacts and print materials in L1 and related to their native culture. Another way to help build classroom community as soon as the school year starts is to have students form committees. A classroom decoration committee, for instance, can be responsible for what needs to be posted on the walls and how often the content needs to be changed (e.g., a bulletin board of book reviews of narrative and expository texts read in and out of class). A sixth-grade teacher I know had every student participate on the committee of book selections for reading. She first introduced the books, allowed students to leaf through them, and then had the committee work with the rest of class to select a book of the month for the whole class to read in a literature circle. The committee's choice of books was often surprisingly similar to the teacher's. The teacher shared with me, "This sounds so cliché. But I have learned never to underestimate my students." Another advantage of the committee work is an opportunity for meaningful oral communications among students.

As a teacher, you build your classroom community by creating specific learning contexts (teaching or learning situation within a setting of the whole class, a small group, or a pair) that maximize opportunities for ELLs to practice learner strategies and specific concepts. For example, after having read aloud a pattern book to a first-grade class, you can use this book for daily group guided reading. The context has been changed from a whole-class setting to a small-group setting, and you can pay special attention to individual students. While listening to each ELL read aloud, you are able to check on students' fluency, decoding, comprehension, and use of learner strategies (e.g., rereading to correct an error). You also can prompt students to become aware of their own errors or learner strategies. This type of semi-independent practice with your guidance offers students a meaningful context to practice skills and strategies.

Learning Tasks

In addition to a learning context, a learning task also plays a crucial role in teacher scaffolding. In the preceding example, students take a turn reading aloud independently the same book that you have read aloud to them several times. The new task pushes students to a higher level of learning where, with your support, they practice what they have learned during your read-aloud. Similarly, after you have modeled a think-aloud for your fifth graders using the first paragraph of Chapter 1 in a novel, you can ask students to work in groups to repeat the same set of steps with the second paragraph as you modeled with the first paragraph. Each student in a group begins with sharing his or her think-aloud. Then, you call on each group to share their think-alouds. Before the end of the lesson, you assign each student to write out his or her think-aloud about reading the third paragraph of Chapter 1. On the following day, each student would share his or her think-aloud in a group. In this example, the learning context changes from a whole class to a small group to individuals, and the learning task also varies from listening to the teacher model a think-aloud with the first paragraph to doing an individual think-aloud with the second paragraph and to sharing this think-aloud in a group setting, and finally, to doing an individual think-aloud with a third paragraph.

Learning Materials

Variations in instructional materials are also an important component of scaffolding. In the preceding fifth-grade example, the students have read three different paragraphs from Chapter 1. The related content across the three paragraphs provides some level of support for students' independent practice. Another way for you to vary materials and provide support is to have students apply a concept to a new set of materials. For example, after having taught three different spelling patterns for the long-*a* sound (CVCe as in *cake*, *-ai* as in *rain*, *-ay* as in *play*), you have students look for words in environmental print that fit each of the three spelling patterns. In so doing, students strengthen their understanding of the three spelling patterns through identifying words outside their school-related materials.

CONCLUSION

In this chapter, I discussed eight guiding principles for teaching ELLs. These principles serve as an overarching framework for the subsequent chapters. The essence of these guiding principles emphasizes your role as a teacher, not a program, in ELLs' language and literacy development; advocates treating ELLs as knowledgeable human beings; and stresses the importance of teaching all components of language and literacy, integrating assessment into instruction and content into language and literacy instruction, and making ELLs' families partners. I hope that these principles will guide your own reflections while reading this book.

CHAPTER 2

LANGUAGE ACQUISITION AND LINGUISTIC INTERFERENCES

During a staff meeting at Horizon Elementary School, where there were 15 different languages spoken, teachers shared their experience of teaching ELLs whose languages were unfamiliar to them. Mr. Robinson, a kindergarten teacher, told a story of a Spanish-speaking girl who kept saying *book* as *vook*, *that* as *dat*, and *boy* as *voy*. Ms. Puchelski, a second-grade teacher, shared a similar observation of a Latino girl who often put an adjective after the noun in her writing (e.g., *house my*). A group of teachers who worked with students who spoke Chinese, Vietnamese, Korean, and Japanese all found that students often forgot to write articles (*the, a,* or *an*) in front of countable nouns. In addition, several upper-grade teachers shared their frustration about not knowing why their students kept making the same type of errors even after they had discussed them with the students numerous times. For example, a fifth-grade teacher stated that several Latino students who had large vocabularies in Spanish and English repeatedly wrote multisyllabic words in partial English and partial Spanish (e.g., *necesario* for *necessary, opportunidad* for *opportunity, situación* for *situation*). A sixth-grade teacher found that Asian students often omitted auxiliary verbs in sentences (e.g., *In the near future, the scientist invent a new device.*).

The preceding scenario could occur at a staff meeting in many elementary schools. It is common for teachers to feel at a loss as to how to address L1 interferences, largely due to their unfamiliarity with ELLs' L1s. If you were one of the teachers who shared their frustration, you might ask:

1. Why does an ELL repeatedly make the same type of mistake even after many hours of instruction related to that linguistic point?

2. Why is the concept of articles so hard for ELLs whose L1 is an Asian language?

3. Why does an ELL at an advanced level write a word with a Spanish spelling pattern?

25

4. What do I need to know in order to identify my students' source of confusion about English?

5. What can I do in my teaching to help my ELLs overcome interferences from their L1?

There is no simple response to each of these questions, because addressing language interferences involves several steps. In this chapter, I first discuss the importance of mastering linguistic knowledge and understanding language acquisition, which can prepare teachers to effectively explore and identify sources of ELLs' linguistic confusion and lay a foundation for effectively teaching ELLs. Next, I highlight interferences in the areas of writing system, phonology, orthography, semantics, syntax, and morphology. I conclude this chapter with a focus on strategies for addressing interferences. Focusing only on linguistic interferences in this chapter does not mean that I overlook the interferences due to the factor of limited background knowledge. This factor is discussed throughout the rest of this book.

THE IMPORTANCE OF LINGUISTIC KNOWLEDGE

In the section on Guiding principle 1, *Becoming Knowledgeable of an ELL's L1 and Culture*, presented in Chapter 1, I briefly discussed the importance of learning about L1s. In *What Elementary Teachers Need to Know about Language*, Fillmore and Snow (2000) present the rationale for teachers' linguistic knowledge and describe *teacher as communicator, teacher as educator, teacher as evaluator, teacher as educated human being*, and *teacher as agent of socialization*. In the following sections, I explain each role with classroom examples.

Teacher as Communicator

You communicate with students during instruction, when you monitor small group and individual work, and during daily routines (e.g., tallying lunch choices). When you are equipped with linguistic knowledge, you are better at understanding various linguistic forms ELLs produce during communication and thus become more skillful at communicating with ELLs. In addition, you become less likely to correct ELLs' errors in communication. Rather, you accept and value what students have produced and highlight what is understood. When Mrs. Flores, a first-grade teacher, was commenting on Maria's show-and-tell about a family photo, she did not point out Maria's grammatical and lexical errors (*mi* for *my, familia* for *family, Mi familia and me at party* for *My family and I were at a party*). Instead, she said to Maria and the class, "Maria told us a lot of things about this photo. We now know the answers to these questions. Who is in the photo? Where was the photo taken? What is the photo about? Why is this photo important to Maria? Who can remember the answer to the first question, Who is in the photo? . . . "

Teacher as Educator

Linguistic knowledge helps you lay a solid foundation for teaching ELLs to become skillful at communicating with others in oral and written language. For example, knowing that some languages cannot be analyzed at a phoneme level, you might allow more time for young ELLs speaking Chinese and Japanese (a syllabic language) to participate in phoneme segmentation activities to develop their understanding of the concept of phoneme segmentation and their ability to segment words into phonemes. For upper-grade teachers, their knowledge of expository text structures is essential. It is hard to imagine that you can teach academic language effectively to ELLs without a good body of knowledge about expository text structures.

Teacher as Evaluator

The role of *teacher as evaluator*, is closely related to *teacher as communicator* and *teacher as educator* because while communicating with and teaching students, you are constantly evaluating them. In an example of Maria's show-and-tell of her photo, Mrs. Flores did not point out Maria's mistakes, but did write down in her notebook the linguistic points she would need to address with Maria (e.g., Spanish interferences on sentence structure). Notes of this nature enable you to focus on the needs unique to one particular group of students. Further, when you are knowledgeable about L1 and culture, you are more likely to understand students' behaviors exhibited along with their literacy performance. Fillmore and Snow (2000) share one example: "In some cultures, for example, children are encouraged to listen rather than to ask questions of adults. Only rude and poorly reared children would chatter away in the presence of an authority figure like the teacher" (p. 9). If some ELLs do not ask questions in a lesson, you should not assume this behavior as a sign of an inability to ask questions or participate in a class activity.

Teacher as Educated Human Being

As educated human beings, teachers must develop a good body of knowledge about language. As Fillmore and Snow (2000) explain,

> Understanding the basics of how one's own language works contributes to skillful reading and writing. Recognizing the difference between nouns and verbs, consonants and vowels, oral and literate forms is as basic for the liberally educated human being as is knowledge about addition and subtraction, evolution, or the solar system. (p. 10)

In support of Fillmore and Snow, I may add that while it is impossible to learn the languages of all ELLs and their native cultures, it is possible to learn *about* these languages and cultures. Knowing the differences between English and L1 will make it a little easier for you to identify sources of difficulty or confusion ELLs experience and to plan or modify instruction to address the difficulty and confusion (see Figure 1.2 in Chapter 1 for resources for learning about L1s and cultures).

Teacher as Agent of Socialization

Fillmore and Snow (2000) define the role of teacher as agent of socialization as follows:

> Teachers play a unique role as agents of socialization—the process by which individuals learn the everyday practices, the system of values and beliefs, and the means and manners of communication of their cultural communities. . . . Socialization begins in the home and continues at school. When the cultures of home and school match, the process is generally continuous. . . . When there is a mismatch between the cultures of home and school, the process can be disrupted. . . . In fact, what teachers say and do can determine how successfully children make the crucial transition from home to school. (p. 11)

For ELLs, the transition between home culture and language to school culture and language needs to be as smooth as possible. This cannot happen without your efforts to understand how second language proficiency develops, how a person from another culture accommodates and assimilates to a new culture, and how a person maintains L1 and culture while learning a new language and culture (Schmidt & Finkbeiner, 2006). Further, in your teaching, you model appropriate school language and academic language and provide ample opportunities for ELLs to practice different types of language.

After arguing for the rationale for linguistic knowledge, Fillmore and Snow (2000) raise 10 questions for teachers, which I invite you to think about while reading the rest of this book.

1. What are the basic units of language?
2. What is regular, and what isn't? How do forms relate to each other?
3. How is the lexicon (vocabulary) acquired and structured?
4. Are vernacular dialects different from "bad English" and if so, how?
5. What is academic English?
6. Why has the acquisition of English by non-English speaking children not been more universally successful?
7. Why is English spelling so complicated?
8. Why do students have trouble with narrative and expository writing?
9. How should the quality and correctness of a piece of writing be judged?
10. What makes a sentence or text difficult to understand? (pp. 13–30)

THEORIES AND CONCEPTS OF LANGUAGE ACQUISITION

In this section, I highlight some second language acquisition theories and concepts and their implications for teaching ELLs. The theories and concepts include

Krashen's (1981) five hypotheses, Cummins's (1979) concept of common underlying proficiency, and Halliday's (1975) functions of language.

Krashen's Five Hypotheses

The Acquisition–Learning Hypothesis

Krashen differentiates acquisition and learning by describing acquisition as an unconscious process of learning a language just as young children acquire their first language, and learning as a conscious process in which learners master a formal set of knowledge about a language. The implication of this hypothesis for classroom teaching is that you need to create a native-like language environment, that is, a language-rich environment, in which learners are exposed to the language. Meanwhile, you also have the responsibility to formally instruct students about the elements of English (e.g., letter–sound correspondence in English, the comprehension process).

The Monitor Hypothesis

Krashen states that as learners are developing their language proficiency, they also learn to use a monitor or an editor that helps them detect errors in their communication. Three conditions are necessary for learners to use the monitor: (1) explicit knowledge of linguistic rules, (2) a focus on grammatical form, and (3) adequate wait time. For example, a learner may not be able to correct his or her error while talking with others, as there is not enough time to do so. The same learner may be able to correct his or her oral reading error during a read-aloud, given that he or she has time and has developed adequate phonics knowledge and comprehension strategies and skills. The implication of this hypothesis is that teachers need to prepare students to be metacognitive learners who always monitor their own learning.

The Nature Order Hypothesis

Krashen points out a predictable order of acquisition of language forms and rules. Some linguistic components, such as inflectional endings (e.g., -ing in playing), are acquired earlier than others, such as possessives (e.g., John's book, theirs). Another example of nature order is the acquisition of negation in a sentence. Learners go through putting a negation in the beginning of the sentence (e.g., No I like games.) to inserting a negation in front of a verb (e.g., I no like books.) to having a correct negation marker (e.g., I don't like games.). This hypothesis is consistent with the claim made by scholars on second language learners (August & Shanahan, 2006) that ELLs follow a path of language and literacy development similar to the path that non-ELLs have taken. The implication of this hypothesis is that ELLs need to be exposed to a language-rich environment in the same way that their non-ELL peers do, and that instruction should focus on meaning rather than rote memory about language rules.

The Input Hypothesis

Krashen stresses that when learners understand a message (written or oral), learning the language of the message is not as difficult. As discussed in Chapter 1, the understandable message is referred to as "comprehensible input." Krashen further states that the grammatical structure of a message needs to be at an $i + 1$ level, where i stands for the input at the student's current proficiency level, and +1 stands for a level that the student needs to reach in language learning. The implication of this hypothesis is that comprehensible input, at the i level achieved through visual aids and multimodalities, is needed for comprehension. Meanwhile, the input at the i level should present something new for a student to learn. For example, you might use a book familiar to students (which is at an i level) to teach story elements students need to learn (which are at a +1 level). If you use a book unfamiliar to students to teach story elements, they would receive no language input at an i level, but all input at a +1 level. That is, students would need to comprehend the story *and* learn about story elements from this book, thus increasing the cognitive and linguistic load for students.

The Affective Filter Hypothesis

Krashen points out the affective and social–emotional factors in second language acquisition (anxiety, motivation, and self-confidence). He explains that a learner's affective filter can block language input necessary for language acquisition if the above mentioned factors are not considered. The implication of this hypothesis is that teachers need to provide a lower-anxiety learning environment filled with learning experiences and activities that motivate students, that are meaningful and authentic, and that support students to become successful. When you ask a newcomer at a beginning level to produce error-free and fluent sentences as other ELLs at the intermediate level, you fail to consider the affective filter. On the other hand, when you encourage this same newcomer to use pictures or gesture to express meaning, you are striving to lower the anxiety level and to provide an opportunity for the learner to experience a sense of success, which helps build self-confidence.

Cummins's Concept of Common Underlying Proficiency

A proponent of bilingualism, Cummins (1979) argues that a bilingual child has a *common underlying proficiency* (CUP). That is, what a child has learned about language and literacy in L1 shares some commonalities with L2 that the child is learning. The notion of CUP recognizes the shared, underlying characteristics of two languages, even though they do not appear very similar at the surface level. For example, unlike English, Chinese is a nonalphabetic language. At the surface level, both languages seem to share few features. At the deep level, many linguistic features are similar. Both languages have the components of a writing system, phonology, orthography, semantics, syntax, and morphology. A Chinese-speaker uses a rising tone for a question in the same way that an English speaker does.

The implication of the CUP concept is the importance of recognizing that students even at the very beginning level of proficiency know something about a language. This recognition assists teachers in identifying a starting point for instruction. If a Korean child has some concepts of print in Korean, you can begin with the concepts of print in English.

Halliday's Functions of Language

Halliday (1975) identifies seven functions of language. Each function can be used by itself or in combination with other functions during oral and written communication.

1. *Instrumental.* Satisfying personal needs: "I want that book."

2. *Regulatory.* Controlling others' actions, behaviors, and feelings: "Read the book quickly."

3. *Interactional.* Interacting with others: "Can we read the book together?"

4. *Personal.* Expressing feelings and self awareness: "I am sharing my favorite book."

5. *Imaginative.* Making believe: "If I were the first little pig in this story, I would trick the wolf."

6. *Heuristic.* Seeking explanations: "Tell me why you don't like this book."

7. *Representational.* Communicating information to others: "Here is what I learned from this book."

The implication of these functions of language is that the instructional goal for ELLs should be geared toward developing proficiency in these functions. For example, learning activities that exclude group or paired interactions would deprive ELLs of opportunities to develop language skills needed for regulatory, interpersonal, and representational functions.

Factors Affecting Second-Language Learning

TESOL (undated) states that "Since English language learners are a heterogeneous group of children, a variety of factors can affect the success of each student's achievement of oral and written proficiency." For example,

a. The relationship between English and the child's first language;
b. Individual learning rates and styles, age of learner, and each learner's linguistic and cognitive abilities;
c. Age at arrival and length of time in the United States;
d. Entering level of English oral proficiency;
e. The child's literacy achievement in the first language, which provides a foundation for learning a second language;
f. Socio-economic status and educational background of families; and
g. The quality of the child's previous schooling and current instruction in supporting English language learners. (n. p.)

The above mentioned factors interweave with the quality of teaching and learning (i.e., learning contexts, learning tasks, and learning materials) ELLs experience in a classroom. They also remind teachers of the complexity and diversity of ELLs and of what they bring to school, which teachers, in planning assessment and instruction, cannot overlook. Hence, differentiated, individualized instruction becomes vital to ELLs. Lastly, teachers' knowledge of L1s and native cultures, and treating ELLs as human beings, should be an important part of successful teaching of ELLs.

LANGUAGE COMPONENTS AND LINGUISTIC INTERFERENCES FROM L1

All languages, alphabetic or nonalphabetic, have the components of writing system, phonology, orthography, semantics, syntax, and morphology. The complexity of each component, however, varies from language to language. Shared similarities with English range from many (e.g., Spanish) to few (e.g., Chinese). In this section, I briefly explain each language component and provide some examples of linguistic interferences from L1.

Writing System

There are two writing systems for languages: alphabetic and nonalphabetic. An alphabetic language (e.g., English, Spanish, German, and Korean) uses alphabetic letters to represent sounds. The alphabetic letters of some languages, such as Korean, look more like symbols. A nonalphabetic language has symbols to represent sounds (e.g., Chinese and Japanese) (see Table 2.1). Closely related to a writing system are concepts about print (book orientation, print directionality, punctuation marks, word space, and capitalization). While many languages share the commonalities of the English concepts about print (CAP), there are some CAP features unique to English and different from other languages (Barone & Xu, 2008).

TABLE 2.1. Examples of Writing Systems			
Alphabetic languages		**Nonalphabetic languages**	
English	I have a book.	Chinese	我有一本书(書)。
Spanish	Tengo un libro.	Japanese	私は、本を持っています。
Vietnamese	tôi có một sách.		
Korean	나는 책을 읽었다.		
	나는 책을 합니다.		

Interferences for ELLs

There are several areas of interferences for ELLs with different L1s (Barone & Xu, 2008). Book orientation and print directionality is one area of interference. ELLs speaking Chinese (including those from Taiwan and Hong Kong), Farsi, Hebrew, or Japanese may open a book from a back cover and start reading it from right to left and top to bottom. Punctuation marks can be another area of interference for speakers of certain languages. Spanish-speaking ELLs may put an exclamation point or a question mark at both the beginning and the end of an English sentence or question. Farsi-speaking students may begin a sentence with a punctuation mark as if they were writing from right to left in Farsi. Chinese ELLs may use a tiny circle for a period in an English sentence. Additionally, word space can pose some challenges to speakers of Chinese, Japanese, and Korean, as the square shape of each word/character in their respective native languages provides a clue to a word space (i.e., after each square, there is a space) (see also Table 2.1). Each English word, varied in its length, makes it hard for an ELL to decide where to insert a space between words. A final possible area of interference is capitalization in English. In Chinese, Korean, and Japanese, no words or characters are capitalized. In Spanish, Romanian, Russian, or Portuguese, the proper noun of a nationality is not capitalized (Gregory & Kuzmich, 2005).

Phonology

Phonology is the sound system of a language, including how and where each sound is articulated and the way that phonemes are combined to form a word (see Figure 2.1 for phonological concepts). The articulation of the English consonant sounds involves the lips, tongue, teeth, and other parts of the mouth. For example, stop consonants can be produced between the lips (e.g., /p/), with the tongue behind teeth (e.g., /t/), or from the back of mouth (e.g., /k/). Consonant sounds can be voiced when vocal cords vibrate (e.g., /v/) or voiceless when vocal cords do not vibrate (e.g., /f/). The articulation of the English vowel sounds is related to the tongue position (front, mid, back) and tongue height (high to low). The sound of /ē/ in *meat* is the highest, front vowel sound while /ŏ/ in *bottle* is the lowest, middle sound (Moats, 2000).

In English, the smallest unit of sound is a phoneme, and 26 letters represent about 44 phonemes. Although English is an alphabetic language, the letter–sound correspondence is not as consistent as in other alphabetic languages (e.g., Spanish and Korean). One letter can be used for multiple sounds (e.g., the letter *i* for /i/ in *pit*, /ī/ in *bite*, /ə/ in *possible*, /ē/ in *ski*). Inconsistency is also evident in some letters representing a sound in some words, but not in other words. For instance, the letter *c* is usually pronounced as /k/ as in the word *cat*, or as /s/ as in the word *city*. But it is silent when combined with the letter *a* before the letter *q* (e.g., *acquire, acquaint*). Some letters are not pronounced (e.g., *gh* in *night*, *b* in *comb*, *e* in *cake*). Another example of inconsistency is that a sound in a word can be changed with a shift in stress. For example, the stress for the word *produce* when used as a verb

Phoneme:	/k/, /a/, /t/ in *cat*	
Grapheme:	*c* for /k/, *a* for /a/, and *t* for /t/	
Consonant:	/t/ in *cat*	
	Blend:	/bl/ in *blend*
	Cluster:	/str/ in *street*
	Digraph:	/f/ for *ph* in *digraph*
Vowel:		
	Short vowel:	/a/ in *cat*
	Long vowel:	/ā/ in *lake*
	Diphthong:	/oi/ in *oil*
	Schwa:	/ə/ unstressed vowel sound as the first *a* in *awake*, *e* in *system*, *i* in *possible*, *o* in *gallop*, and *u* in *circus*
	R-controlled Vowel:	/ar/ in *car*
Onset:	/k/ in *cat*, /sh/ in *sheep*	
Rime:	/at/ in *cat*, /ep/ in *sheep*	
Syllable:	/ba/, /be/ in *baby*	
Open syllable:	a syllable that ends in a vowel sound as in *me*, *soda*	
Closed syllable:	a syllable that ends in a consonant sound as in *stop*, *begin*	

FIGURE 2.1. Phonological concepts.

is at the second syllable, and the stress is at the first syllable when it is used as a noun. The words *fast* and *break* each receive a stress when used alone, but when they are combined into the compound word *breakfast* only *break* has a stress, thus weakening the vowel sound of *a* in *fast* to a schwa sound (/ə/). Sound change also occurs when a suffix is added to a base word. Consider the sound change for the first letter *e* in *compete* from a long-*e* sound to a short-*i* sound when the suffix *-tion* is added to the base word to form *competition*.

Phonemic Awareness

Phonemic awareness is an awareness of the smallest units of sounds in words (phonemes). Students with phonemic awareness are able to manipulate sounds. There are different types of sound manipulation (Yopp & Yopp, 2000):

> *Phoneme identification*: identifying beginning, middle, and ending sounds
> *Phoneme matching*: matching words with a same phoneme (e.g., *feet*, *hat*, and *hot* have the same phoneme, /t/)

➤ *Phoneme substitution*: substituting one phoneme in a word with another phoneme (e.g., substituting /th/ with /t/ in the word *thing*)

➤ *Phoneme blending*: blending individual sounds to make a word (e.g., blending /b/, /oo/, and /k/ to say the word *book*)

➤ *Phoneme segmentation*: segmenting a word into individual sounds (e.g., segmenting the word *feet*, into /f/, /ē/, and /t/)

➤ *Phoneme deletion*: deleting a phoneme from a word (e.g., deleting the sound /h/ from the word *hit*)

➤ *Phoneme addition*: adding a phoneme to a word (e.g., adding the sound, /ə/ to the word *teach* to form the word *teacher*)

Interferences for ELLs

Barone and Xu (2008) identify several areas of interferences for ELLs. The first area is that some sounds do not exist in ELLs' L1, and ELLs may try to articulate these sounds in a similar way that they do for other sounds in L1. Ninety-nine percent of English speakers pronounce my last name as the sound for *shoe, Sue*, or *zoo* as a result of their way of pronouncing the letter *x*. Spanish-speaking ELLs would confuse /sh/ with /th/, saying *chair* for *share* and vice versa. Many Asian languages do not have the voiced and voiceless sounds for *th*, and ELLs speaking an Asian language may produce /ð/ or /θ/ as /s/. Table 2.2 lists some difficult sounds for students speaking Arabic, Chinese, Spanish, and Vietnamese (Barone & Xu, 2008; Kress, 2008; Sundem, Krieger, & Pikiewicz, 2008).

A second area of interference is the level of sounds that can be analyzed. Sounds in English are broken down into the phoneme level, whereas for other languages (e.g., Chinese, Japanese, Vietnamese), a syllable is the smallest unit of sound. ELLs speaking one of these Asian languages would become confused about breaking a word (e.g., *baby*) at the syllable level (/ba/, /bē/) and at the phoneme level (/b/, /a/, /b/, /ē/). Even in an alphabetic language, such as Korean, the letters representing all phonemes of a word are not displayed in the horizontal way as in English. The Korean word for *book*, 책`, is separated into the top part where there are two let-

TABLE 2.2. Difficult Sounds

L1	Difficult sounds
Arabic	k, h, i, u, w, y, z
Chinese	b, ch, g, q, sh, th, v, x, y, l-clusters, r-clusters
Spanish	b, c, ch, g, h, j, k, q, th, v, w, wh, y, z, s-clusters, final consonant blends (e.g., ft, mp, nd, ng, nk, nt, st, and rl)
Vietnamese	ā, ē, c, k, ng, s, sh, th, t, tr, l-clusters, end clusters

ters, and the bottom part where there is only one letter. Given this, the way that English sounds in a word are mapped into the letters in the positions of the beginning, middle, and end becomes very confusing to Korean-speaking ELLs.

Letter–sound correspondence can become another area of interference for ELLs speaking L1 in which letter–sound relation is relatively consistent (e.g., Spanish and Vietnamese). ELLs speaking these L1s take a long time to learn that the sound of a letter may change based on its position in a single-syllable or a multi-syllable word (e.g., *y* as /ī/ in *try* and *y* as /ē/ in *sunny*), and based on its combination with other letters (e.g., *a* as /ā/ in *wait* and *a* as /ō/ in *coat*). ELLs may pronounce every letter in a word where some letters are silent (e.g., *gh* in *night*, *e* in *cake*, *b* in *comb*).

Orthography

Orthography is a spelling system of a language. Bear, Helman, Templeton, Invernizzi, and Johnston (2007) explain three layers of English orthography. The first layer is the sound or alphabet layer, where a sound is mapped into a letter (e.g., *t* for /t/). This layer can become complicated when long or short vowel sounds are involved (e.g., *i* is /i/ as in *sit*, *i* is /ī/ as in *site*, *i* is /ē/ as in *ski*) and when a neighboring sound has some influence on a sound (e.g., *a* is /a/ in *cat* vs. *a* is /ar/ in *car*). In the example of the word *classify*, with a stress in the first syllable, when the suffix, *-tion*, is added to it, the long-*i* sound for the letter *y* becomes a short-*i* sound.

The second layer, the pattern layer, is about the ways that English letters are arranged in a word. The syllable structures reflect the pattern layer. For single-syllable words, there are 13 patterns: "V (*I*), CV (*me*), VC (*ice*), VCC (*ask*), CVC (*sack*), CCV (*ski*), CCVC (*skin*), CVCC (*cans*), CCVCC (*stops*), CCCVC (*scream*), CCCVCC (*squeaks*), CCVCCC (*starts*), and CCCVCCC (*scrimped*)" (Moats, 2000, p. 52). For two-syllable and multisyllabic words, there are patterns associated with how the syllables are combined. For example, *o* in *hotel* as a long *o* is in an open syllable, and *o* in *nodding* as a short *o* is in a closed syllable.

The third layer is the meaning layer, and it is closely related to the morphology of a language, or is "a deep orthography" as Moats (2000) describes (p. 83). As Bear et al. (2007) explain, there are inflectional and derivational morphologies. Inflectional morphology is about adding a suffix (e.g., *-ed*, *-s*, or *-es*) to a base word to indicate its tense or number (e.g., *walked, boxes*). Derivational morphology is about adding an affix (prefix or suffix) to a base word or a Greek or Latin root to signify a change in part of speech and a slight or considerable change in meaning. For example, when *-ly* is added to the word *mother*, *motherly* becomes an adjective and its meaning (like a mother) is different from its base word but is still related to the base word. When *-im* is added to *possible*, the change in meaning from *possible* to *impossible* is significant, but the part of speech of *impossible* remains an adjective. For the meaning layer of English spelling of multisyllabic words, a base word and its derivational word may have a different pronunciation, but the spelling of certain letters remains the same (e.g., *compete, competition*) because the base word and the derived word share a similar meaning.

Interferences for ELLs

Differences in spelling patterns between English and L1 can cause interferences. For example, some Spanish words begin with an *es* letter combination (e.g., *esa* [that], *Español* [*Spanish*], *especial* [special]). Spanish-speaking ELLs tend to put an *e* in front of an *s* in the spelling of English words (e.g., *eschool*). They also experience difficulty identifying rhyming words ending in a consonant sound, as most Spanish words end in a vowel sound (e.g., *casa, libro*). They may be able to identify *he* and *me* as a pair of rhyming words, but fail to group *net* and *met* under the *-et* word family due mostly to their limited exposure to rhyming words ending in a consonant sound. An change in spelling when an inflectional or a derivational morpheme is added to a base word or a root is a challenge to ELLs whose L1 is a nonalphabetic language that does not have this type of rule. As a result, ELLs may not, for example, drop the *e* before adding *-ing* to *hope*, or double the *p* before adding *-ing* to *hop*. Furthermore, a change in pronunciation of some letters in a base word after a suffix is added would lead some ELLs to change the spelling of these letters (e.g., *compitition* for *competition*).

Semantics

Semantics is the meaning system of a language. Moats (2000) identifies three types of semantics: lexical semantics (the study of word meanings), sentential semantics (the study of sentence meanings), and pragmatics (the study of sociocultural context and its impact on meaning construction).

Lexical Semantics

One characteristic of English words is that each word can have multiple meanings. Consider the common word *house* in the following sentences:

> They lived in a small <u>house</u>. The squirrels stored food in their new <u>house</u>. We had a full <u>house</u> at yesterday's show. Let's meet at the fraternity <u>house</u>. The golden statue was <u>housed</u> in a secured room of the museum. The <u>House</u> of Representatives passed the bill. Your birthday dinner is on the <u>house</u>. She has a <u>dollhouse</u> for Barbies. The kindergartners were playing <u>house</u>.

Further, the meaning of some commonly used words in English resides in their respective contexts. Consider the meaning of *good* in each of the following sentences:

> He is a <u>good</u> student. Possible meanings: hard-working, high-achieving, attentive to rules.

> He is a <u>good</u> child. Possible meanings: obedient to parents, having a good sibling relationship, not making trouble, doing well at school.

> He is a <u>good</u> neighbor. Possible meanings: being courteous to neighbors, willing to help others, not playing loud music.

> He is a <u>good</u> colleague. Possible meanings: collegial, hardworking, willing to help, not engaging in gossip.

In addition to multiple meanings of a word, other semantic features of words include: synonyms, antonyms, content words with a specific meaning (e.g., *I am singing happily*); function words serving grammatical functions with no specific meaning (e.g., *am* in *I am singing happily.*); superordinate words that are inclusive of other words on a related concept (e.g., *vehicle* includes *cars, bikes, vans,* and *trucks*), subordinate words that belong to a subgroup of words on a related concept (e.g., *car* is a subordinate word under the concept of *vehicle*); and parts of speech (the nature of the specific grammatical functions that words serve [e.g., *house* as a noun in *He has a house* and as a verb in *The new machine is housed in a big building*]).

Sentential Semantics

Sentence meaning relies on the noun and verb phrases and the position of these phrases in a sentence. As Moats (2000) puts it, "Sentence meaning is governed by underlying, hierarchical structures that allows us to interpret the clusters of words (phrases) that convey sense" (p. 137). The meaning of *I gave my friend a new book* is different from that of *My friend gave me a new book*, although the surface structure of both sentences is the same, subject + indirect object + direct object.

The sentence meaning cannot be literally interpreted when figurative language is used. One cannot interpret the expression *pull over the car* as *pulling the car over the sidewalk*. The English language is full of idioms. Consider the idioms using the word *dog*: *rain cats and dogs*; *led a dog's life*; *Every dog has his day*; and *Let sleeping dogs lie*. Many idioms do not make much sense, such as *easy as pie*, and *a piece of cake* (Barone & Xu, 2008). Similes and metaphors, commonly used in oral and written language, make constructing sentence meaning more challenging as they are often based on cultural knowledge and life experience, which ELLs may lack. Consider the following sentence from *Maniac Magee* (Spinelli, 1990). "They say Maniac Magee was born in the dump. They say his stomach was a cereal box and his heart a sofa spring" (p. 1). ELLs' limited life experience and/or cultural knowledge related to "a cereal box" and "a sofa spring" would make it much harder for them to get the point that Spinelli intended to convey in the sentence (i.e., Maniac Magee is not an ordinary child.).

Pragmatics

Pragmatics is about how a language is used in socially and culturally accepted ways. The ways words are used in the same language can vary across subcultures and geographic regions. We all know that people in some parts of the United States use the word *soda* to refer to any carbon dioxide drinks, whereas some in other parts of the United States specify a type of carbonated drink as *Pepsi, Cola,* or *Sprite*. Communication can turn rocky if what is said or written does not seem to follow the accepted cultural and social practices in a particular geographic region. For example, when a New Yorker who just moved to California called Pizza Hut to order her "pie", she was immediately told to call Maria Callender's (a famous restaurant and bakery) for her pie.

Interferences for ELLs

As stated above, words, phrases, sentences, and context play an important role in a reader's process of constructing meaning from a piece of written text. At the word level, multiple meanings of a word pose one of the challenges for ELLs. While all languages have words with multiple meanings, the nature of multiple meanings may be different in English than in L1. For example, the character 房 in Chinese only means house. The different meanings derived from this character only occur when it is combined with other characters, not when it is used in different contexts, as in English: 房客 (tenant), 房东 (landlord), 房产 (real estate), and 房舱 (cabin). ELLs' confusion about a meaning of a word may also be caused by the interference from L1. For instance, the Spanish word for *spend* is *gastar*, which includes other meanings, such as "waste," and "use up." A Spanish-speaking ELL may say or write a sentence like, "I wasted $10 on this book," even if he or she does not intend to convey the English meaning of *waste*. A third source of interference comes from cognates. Not all words similar in pronunciation and spelling to English words are actually cognates. Table 2.3 lists some examples of false cognates in Spanish. (See Figure 5.12 for some examples of positive English–Spanish cognates.)

At the sentence level, the meaning interferences may be due to differences in sentence structures between English and L1 (which I will discuss in the following section on syntax) and a lack of cultural and general knowledge about expressions, including a linguistic context for the sentences (refer to the previous examples about the word *good*) and a general social context (refer to the example about pizza pie). I have observed newly arrived college students from foreign countries use the expression *go Dutch* while dining out with American students. While it does mean that each person pays for his or her bill, the expression is seldom used in contemporary America. This example shows that knowing only expressions, but not the ways with words, is not enough for successful communication between native English speakers and people learning English.

TABLE 2.3. Some Examples of False Cognates

Spanish word	Meaning in Spanish	Intended English word	Spanish word for the intended English word
carpeta	folder	*carpet*	*alfombra*
complexión	physiological build	*complexion*	*tez* or *cutis*
contestar	answer	*contest*	*contender*
éxito	success	*exit*	*salida*
fábrica	factory	*fabric*	*tejido* or *tela*
largo	long	*large*	*grande*
once	eleven	*once*	*una vez*
tuna	cactus	*tuna*	*atún*

Syntax

The importance of English syntax in supporting reading and writing is well stated in this sentence: "Understanding of sentence structure supports reading comprehension, and construction of sentences is elementary to written expression" (Moats, 2000, p. 131). Moats (2000) defines syntactic processing as "a level of language use that depends on recognition of permissible word sequences, interpretation of the meaning of word sequences, and generation of novel word sequences that conform to the structure of an underlying system" (p. 132).

At the word level, syntax means a grammatical category of a word and its position in a phrase or a sentence. For example, the word *happy* belongs to the category of adjective and comes before a countable noun (e.g., *a happy student*) or after a linking verb (e.g., *He is happy.*). The word *a* (an article) cannot be positioned between the word *happy* and a noun. A phrase belongs to one of the lexical grammatical categories: *a happy student* (a noun phrase), *read quickly* (a verb phrase), and *in the classroom* (a prepositional phrase).

At the sentence level, syntax means that different types of sentences are formed when words are grouped into an underlying structure. The order of words in a sentence determines the sentence meaning and the functions of different words. The sentence *The man chased the dog* is different in meaning and functions of words from another sentence, *The dog chased the man.*

In English, there are three types of sentence structure. A simple sentence (*The student read one book*) contains a subject (the noun phrase *the student*) and a predicate (the verb phrase *read one book*). This same simple sentence can be elaborated to include other components (*The hardworking student read at least one book each week during the summer break*). A compound sentence is formed when two simple sentences (independent clauses) are joined together by such conjunctions as *and, but, or, nor, yet*, or *so* (e.g., *He likes reading, but his sister enjoys surfing the Internet*). A complex sentence is composed of one independent clause and one or more dependent clauses—for example, *When I was young* (a dependent clause), *I often visited my grandma during the summer break* (an independent clause).

Another feature of English syntax is transformation—moving phrases around within a sentence structure governed by certain syntactic rules. Table 2.4 lists some examples of transformation. After the transformation, the new meaning for two out of three sentences is different from their respective original sentences. The transformed sentences, however, are still grammatically correct, because the transformation has followed the syntactic rules. If transformation is not done by a rule, the new sentence will not be understood. For example, if the word *not* is put between the words *good* and *student*, as in *He is a good not student*, the meaning will be confusing and ambiguous: *Is he not a good student?* or *Is he not a student?*

Interferences for ELLs

The challenges the English syntax poses vary greatly among ELLs speaking different L1s. At the word level, it is common for Spanish-speaking ELLs to put an adjective after a noun, as in *a book red* (*un libro rojo*) and for Korean-speaking ELLs

TABLE 2.4. Some Examples of Transformation

Type of transformation	Example	Any meaning change after transformation
Active voice → passive voice	*John gave Jane a new book.* *Jane was given a new book* by John.	No
Positive → negative	*He is a good student.* *He is not a good student.*	Yes
Statement → interrogative	*He attended the meeting.* *Did he attend the meeting?*	Yes

and Japanese-speaking ELLs to put a verb after a noun, as in *a book read* (Korean: 책을읽었다; Japanese: 本を読みなさい). Barone and Xu (2008) point out that English articles, nonexistent in some L1s, are very difficult for many ELLs speaking an Asian language (e.g., Chinese, Korean, Japanese, and Vietnamese) to master. Mistakes like *I have apple* are common in speaking and writing. Distinguishing the use of *a* and *the* is even harder.

At the sentence level, the concept of compound and complex sentences may mean different things to ELLs speaking different L1s. For example, there are compound sentences in Korean, but they are not expressed in the same way as English compound sentences. Conjunctions may not be used in a sentence: *He likes rice, she likes bread,* 그는 밥을 좋아하고, 그녀는 빵을 좋아한다. Another source of interference comes from the change of verb tenses in English, a concept that does not exist in every L1. Barone and Xu (2008) share several examples. A verb tense in Chinese or Khmer is not indicated in a change of verb. Rather, the time phrase implies the verb tense. The sentence *I went to school yesterday* is *I go to school yesterday* in Chinese. In Japanese, a verb tense is indicated by a fixed phrase added to the verb. The phrase した indicates a past tense, and the phrase ている indicates a present progressive tense. The third-person singular present verb tense (*she runs*) does not exist in many L1s.

Interferences related to sentence transformation can be caused by the following:

> ➢ The use of an auxiliary verb (e.g., *do, does, did*) when a sentence is changed from a statement to an interrogative (e.g., *Ms. Tran likes writing. Does Ms. Tran like writing?*)

> ➢ The use and position of negation when a sentence is changed from a positive statement to one with negation (e.g., *He has a lot of books. He does not have a lot of books.*)

> ➢ The order of phrases and possible verb change when a sentence is changed from active voice to passive voice (e.g., *He received a special gift from his grandmother. He was given a special gift by his grandmother.*)

While most languages have a similar set of sentences as English (e.g., statement, interrogative), the rules governing the sentence structures in L1 may be different from those in English. For example, the subject–verb–object sentence pattern in English does not exist in such languages as Arabic, Japanese, and Korean. The Arabic language has a verb–subject–object sentence pattern, and a subject-object-verb sentence pattern exists in both Japanese and Korean.

Another common interference among ELLs is the transformation between an active and a passive voice. When the sentence with an active voice *He gave me a book* is changed into one with a passive voice, *I was given a book by him*, the changes include verb tense from past tense (*gave*) to past participle (*was given*), subject in the active voice from *he* to *by him*, and the indirect object in the active voice *me* to *I*. In Spanish, the only change from an active voice (*Él me dio un libro*) to a passive voice (*Él me di un libro*) is the verb *dar*. In Chinese, a passive voice is less common. Instead, the verb phrase 受到 (*receive*) indicates a passive voice while the verb 给 (*give*) indicates an active voice. In Japanese, the indirect object 彼 (*him*) in a passive voice sentence, 私は彼によって本を与えられた (*I was given a book by him*), is next to the subject 私は (*I*). This structure holds true for an active voice of the same sentence 彼は私に本を与えた (*He gave me a book*).

Morphology

Morphology focuses on the word parts (prefixes, suffixes, base words, and roots), and their meanings. Mastery of morphological knowledge enables students to understand words well in reading and listening and use words effectively in speaking and writing. Table 2.5 lists morphological concepts as discussed in Moats's (2000) book.

English morphology has several characteristics. The first one is the complexity in the relationship between form and meaning. One example Moats (2000) uses to illustrate the complexity is the prefix *con-* in *contract*. It may be mistaken as having a similar meaning to the prefix *con-* in *contrary* (meaning "against"). *Con-* in *contract* is actually a varied form of the prefix *com-* (meaning "with" and "together"). Some suffixes can mislead students when they're determining the part of speech of a new word after a suffix is added. The suffix *-ly* usually marks a word as an adverb, as in *quickly*, but sometimes as an adjective, as in *brotherly*.

A second characteristic is associated with the meaning layer of English spelling. Words sharing a same morpheme are related in meaning, although the spelling and pronunciation of these words may vary. For example, words derived from the Latin root *viv* (meaning "live" and "alive") include *vivid, vivify, vivacity, revive, survive, vivacious*, and *vivisection*. The first letter *i* has a short-*i* sound in *vivid, vivify*, and *vivisection*, a long-*i* sound in *revive* and *survive*, and a schwa sound in *vivacity* and *vivacious*.

Another characteristic involves the phonological changes that occur when a derivational suffix is added to a base word. These changes include syllable regrouping, vowel alternation, consonant alternation, and stress alternation. Moats (2000) explains:

TABLE 2.5. Morphological Concepts

Concept	Explanation	Example
Morpheme	Smallest linguistic unit with a meaning	*book, pre-* (*preview*), *-ly* (*friendly*)
Free morpheme	Morphemes that can stand alone	*the, cat, nation*
Content words	Words that have content meaning	adjectives (*excellent*) adverbs (*quickly*) nouns (*school*) verbs (*jump*)
Function words	Words that serve grammatical functions	articles (*a, an, the*) auxiliary verbs (*do, does, did*) conjunctions (*but, and*) prepositions (*inside, over*) pronouns (*she, we, it*)
Compound words	Words composed of two free morphemes	*afternoon, basketball*
Bound morpheme	Morphemes that become meaningful when combined with other morphemes	prefixes (e.g., <u>*im*</u>*possible*) suffixes (e.g., *book<u>s</u>*)
Prefix	A bound morpheme that is added to the beginning of a base word or a root	*im-* in *impossible*, *ab-* in *abrupt* (Latin root: *rupt*)
Suffix	A bound morpheme that is added to the end of a base word or a root	*-ure* in *rupture* (Latin root: *rupt*)
	Inflectional suffixes serve grammatical functions and do not change the part of the speech of the base words.	*-s/-es* in *books/boxes*, *-ed* in *worked*, *-ing* in *reading*, *-er/est* in *harder/hardest*
	Derivational suffixes are added to a root or base word to form words and change the part of speech of the base word.	For the root *litera* *-cy* in *literacy* (n.) *-ate* in *literate* (adj.) *-al* in *literal* (adj.) *-ary* in *literary* (adj.) *-ion* in *alliteration* (n.) *-ure* in *literature* (n.)
Root	A bound morpheme from which a new word with related meaning can be derived when a prefix and/or a suffix is added to it	For the root *ject* add *pro-* to form *project* add *pro-* and *-ion* to form *projection*
	Many derivational words are from Latin roots, and more academic content-specific words (e.g., mathematical and scientific terms) are from Greek roots.	For the Latin root *vis* *visual, vision, visible, invisible, television, envision* For the Greek root *meter* *diameter, barometer, odometer, speedometer*

Syllable regrouping describes what happens when *differ* become *different*, vowel alternation describes what happens when *sane* is changed to *sanity*, vowel alternation explains the difference between *electric* and *electricity*, and stress alternation describes the changes that occur between *philosophy* and *philosophical* and is a common result of derivational word building. (p. 69)

Interferences for ELLs

Again the morphology interferences for ELLs vary across different L1s. For ELLs speaking an L1 that cannot be analyzed at the morpheme level for smallest units with meaning in a word (e.g., Chinese, Japanese, Thai, and Vietnamese), the concept of a morpheme poses a special challenge. For example, for the word *excited*, the Chinese equivalent is 激动. Unlike the word *excited*, which can be analyzed at the morpheme level (*excite* + *ed*), the two-character phrase loses its meaning if one character is taken away from the phrase. When this happens, each character means something different from the meaning of *excited*.

The English morphology presents a different type of challenge to ELLs whose L1 does share some similarities with English. For example, in Spanish, verbs, adjectives, nouns, and even articles are inflected. In particular, Spanish verbs are considerably inflected, providing information about gender, tense, and number. Spanish-speaking ELLs may add additional letters to an English word to reflect gender, tense, and/or number. Although Japanese is a syllabic language, its verbs are highly inflected, but in a way different from English verb inflection. As discussed earlier, verb inflection in Japanese is done by a fixed phrase added to a verb.

Regardless of the L1, rules governing English morphology that are nonexistent in some L1s and not consistent across all the words are hard for most ELLs to master. These include (1) the rules about the changes in spelling and pronunciation of a new word formed by a suffix added to a base word (e.g., *wild* → *wilderness*), (2) the rules about adding inflectional suffixes (e.g., *hope* → *hoping* vs. *hop* → *hopping*), and (3) the rules about the change in pronunciation of the suffix *-ed* (e.g., *worked*, *planned*, and *planted*). In addition, the change in irregular verb tenses (i.e., present tense [*go*], past tense [*went*], and past perfect tense [*gone*]) causes confusion.

STRATEGIES FOR ADDRESSING INTERFERENCES

Before describing strategies for addressing interferences, I want to share the advice Peregoy and Boyle (2005) offer teachers when it comes to correcting students' errors:

The way you treat English learner errors will depend on your own judgment, taking into consideration the student's English language developmental level, the prevalence of the error type, the importance of the error type for communication, and your specific goals for the student in terms of English language development. (p. 70)

Following Peregoy and Boyle's advice, I will focus on these strategies: learning about a native language, identifying the sources of interferences, modeling a correct version of output, helping students note the differences, using the writing process, and teaching linguistic concepts explicitly and systematically.

Learning about a Native Language

I cannot emphasize enough the importance of learning *about* L1s, a point discussed in Chapter 1's *Principle 1: Becoming Knowledgeable of an ELLs L1 and Culture*. I believe that this is a critical strategy for teachers to use before addressing any interferences. The other strategies to be discussed would be effective if you have applied this strategy first. The valuable resources for you to learn about a native language are parents (if they speak English), community members, older siblings of ELLs, international students and scholars, books, and the Internet. Barone and Xu (2008) suggest that while studying about native languages teachers keep a record about each language (see Appendix B for a reproducible form), which comes in handy when you want to identify the sources of interferences.

Identifying the Sources of Interferences

Many teachers feel frustrated about the repeated interferences in ELLs' oral and written language output. To address the interferences, you first identify the sources of interferences. This strategy becomes possible when used in conjunction with the strategy of learning about L1s. Only when you are familiar with L1s is it possible to identify the sources and address effectively and explicitly the interferences. For example, if you know there are no articles in Chinese, Japanese, Korean, and Vietnamese, you would understand why articles are difficult for ELLs speaking one of these L1s. Consequently, you would group students experiencing similar difficulties with English articles for a focused lesson. Figure 2.2 lists some examples of student errors in oral and written English derived from the L1 interferences (see Appendix C for a reproducible form). I encourage you to use this form to document the interferences and identify patterns of errors to focus in instruction. See Figure 2.3 and Appendix D for a reproducible form for planning instruction.

Modeling a Correct Version of Output

Directly correcting students' errors is not always helpful to ELLs, partly because some errors are developmental, and students will master the correct forms after they have had ample linguistic input and practice. In addition to teaching minilessons to a certain group of ELLs who speak the same L1 and have a similar interference, you can model a correct version of linguistic output. In an example mentioned earlier in this chapter, Mrs. Flores, a first-grade teacher, did not point out Maria's grammatical and lexical errors (*mi* for *my, familia* for *family, Mi familia and me at party* for *My family and I were at a party*). Instead, she focused on what Maria told the class about the family photo and recognized her effort for the show-and-tell. For the next show-and-tell, if Maria makes a similar set of errors, Mrs. Flores

Student error	L1s	Possible explanation for the error
I have a car red.	Spanish	An adjective comes after a noun.
Rhyming words: he—she net—met???	Spanish	Most Spanish words end in a vowel sound.
I have book. He has three book.	Chinese, Japanese, Korean, Vietnamese	No articles exist in L1. Quantity is expressed in a different way.
T: What's the beginning sound in the word book? S: book?	Chinese, Japanese, Korean	A native language can not be analyzed at the phoneme level. One character in Chinese (书) or in Japanese (本) is a single syllable unit. Phonemes are not arranged in the order of beginning, middle and end. The Korean word for "book" (책) has a sound in the upper left, upper right, and bottom of the word.
I a book have. I a book write.	Korean, Japanese	A sentence ends in a verb. 나는책을읽었다. (I have a book.) 나는책을쓴다. (I write a book.)
ting for thing thing for ting	Vietnamese, Chinese	/th/ in English is pronounced as /t/ in Vietnamese; /t/ in English is pronounced as /th/ in Vietnamese. No /th/ sound exists in Chinese.
three-two for two-thirds	Chinese, Japanese, Vietnamese	A denominator is said and written before a numerator (e.g., 三分之二; 3分の2).

FIGURE 2.2. Samples of student errors and possible explanations for the errors.

Student Name	L1	Interference	Instructional Focus
Jin Chen Beibei Pei Ming Sheng Shuaje Zhao	Chinese	No articles in Chinese; misuse and/or no use of English articles in oral and written language	1. Highlighting articles in a book during small group read-aloud 2. Highlighting articles in a text produced through language experience approach, interactive writing, or morning messages 3. Including an article for a noun displayed on the word wall

FIGURE 2.3. Instructional focus based on L1 interference.

would model the correct way of talking about the photo by repeating Maria's talk with correct words and grammatical structure: "Maria told us about this photo. My family and I were at a party." It would be more supportive for Maria if Mrs. Flores wrote down the sentence on a sticky note or an index card and gave to Maria to take home to practice with a family member. This example reflects a heavy focus on meaning while addressing a student's errors (Diaz-Rico & Weed, 2006; Peregoy & Boyle, 2005). For older ELLs, you can withhold saying back to a student a correct version of what he or she has said. Instead, you can use a combination of questioning and repeating with more complicated sentence structures. Table 2.6 shows one example of such scaffolding in a sixth-grade history class (Zwiers, 2008) and includes my analysis of the scaffolding.

Helping Students Note the Differences

Another strategy to address interferences is for you to guide students to note the differences between English and L1. Of course, the usefulness of this strategy depends on how much you know about L1s and about the sources of interferences. This strategy can be used with young and older ELLs. For ELLs at beginning English proficiency, highlighting the new linguistic concepts that are different from L1s' via visual aids seems to be effective. For example, for a group of students who

TABLE 2.6. Modeling through Questioning and Scaffolding

Teacher–student conversation[a]	Analysis of the teacher question and scaffolding
TEACHER: So, what's the topic?	
STUDENT E: People lookin' at daily life things?	
TEACHER: Yes, how archaeologists study . . . let's use the word *artifacts*. How archaeologists study artifacts to . . .	• Using the sentence structure, "how archaeologists study . . . " • Using the word *archaeologists* • Telling the student to use the word *artifacts* • Expanding the sentence structure to include the word *artifacts*: "How archaeologists study artifacts to . . . "
STUDENT E: Find out.	
TEACHER: What's a better word? What do you do in school?	• Encouraging the student to use a more appropriate word • Providing a clue to the appropriate word
STUDENT E: Learn?	
TEACHER: Let's put that for the topic. "How archaeologists study artifacts in order to learn about daily life in the past." Why do they study artifacts? In order . . .	• Stating a complete sentence with the intended sentence structure and words • Checking the student's understanding of the later part of the sentence by questioning, "Why do they study artifacts?" • Providing a clue to the answer to the question: "In order . . . "
STUDENT E: In order to learn about the past?	

[a]From Zwiers (2008, p. 60).

have had difficulty with articles, you can use a highlighter in one color to note all the articles in a book or a text that you and students coproduced during a language experience approach interactive writing, shared writing, or morning message (see Chapter 7 for a description of each activity). The nouns after all the articles can then be highlighted in a different color. In so doing, you direct students' attention to an English linguistic concept new to them and teach them a rule regarding this concept (i.e., an article comes before a countable noun).

After they become familiar with this strategy, ELLs should be encouraged to highlight English linguistic concepts in the books they read and in their own writing. It is not recommended and should be avoided to have ELLs highlight a linguistic concept in a text that is unfamiliar to them (e.g., highlighting all adjectives in a worksheet). Language is best learned through meaningful content (Freeman, Freeman, & Mercuri, 2002; Houk, 2005; Mansukhani, 2002; Peregoy & Boyle, 2009). If we let ELLs identify a new linguistic concept without understanding the meaning of the text, students would later balk at words, but not understand the meaning of the words and their relation to other words in the sentence.

For older ELLs whose language proficiency is at least at an intermediate level, directing their attention to the interferences can foster the development of their metalinguistic awareness (i.e., explicit knowledge about a language) of the differences between English and L1. The following example shows how a fourth-grade teacher talked with a group of ELLs speaking Japanese who frequently made an error of verb–object inversion in oral and written output.

> "I have noticed some of you sometimes say or write an object before a verb in a sentence. You would say, 'We books like.' We have talked about the structure of a simple sentence in English. [Writing on a chart paper: Subject + Verb + Object: We like books.] I know this sentence structure is very different from the sentence structure in Japanese. In Japanese, you say or write an object before a verb. After today's mini-lesson, every time you say or write a sentence with an object, I want you to first think about SVO and say or write the sentence in this order. Can you please identify one sentence from your talk or your writing that has the correct verb–object order? Can you also find another sentence with the wrong order and correct it? Once you are done with that, please come to talk to me and tell me how you have corrected the sentence."

Using the Writing Process

The writing process, which has been used with non-ELLs, can be an effective strategy to address interferences. Peregoy and Boyle (2009) explain that unlike errors in speech that cannot be retrieved after the speech has been produced, errors in writing can be preserved for later analysis, and they are visible to students. Analyzing the errors, explaining sources of errors, and teaching the correct way to convey an intended meaning become more effective within a context of a text meaningful to and written by students. Table 2.7 shows a piece of writing with some errors and possible foci for instruction. For this example, while working with the student,

---

TABLE 2.7. An Example of Using the Writing Process

Writing example	Instructional focus
The weather was cold. I yesterday goed to my swimming lesson. Water is cold. Wind is big. I cold. Teacher asked me to should relax. That was hard.	• Having the student clarify what is meant by "That was hard." • Verb tenses (having student list verbs, identify their tenses, and supply correct verb tenses) • Adjectives (e.g., *big*) • Word order within a sentence (e.g., *I yesterday goed swimming.*) • Sentence order (i.e., the order of the first and second sentence in the sample)

---

you would begin with having the student share the content and then confirm the correct use of English. Next, you would question the student to clarify the unclear content. During the process, you would show the student about the importance of meaning in writing. Then, you would direct the student's attention to the instructional foci as outlined in the Table 2.7.

Addressing interferences can also be done within a whole-class setting if the interferences are common across the class. After identifying the interferences in students' writing of various types, you can select each of them for a daily mini-lesson, which may include the following steps:

1. Having students identify errors in the sentences from their writing;

2. Having students provide the correction for each error and an explanation for each correction;

3. Making a comment on students' corrections and explanations;

4. Offering comments on the corrections;

5. Explaining the errors students have failed to identify and the corrections for the errors; and

6. Having students write down the errors and corrections in their workbooks.

During the mini-lesson, student participation needs to be maximized. It is amazing that ELLs, when given opportunities and encouragement, can notice and even correct their own errors.

Teaching Linguistic Concepts Explicitly and Systematically

In conjunction with other strategies, the explicit and systematic teaching of linguistic concepts should be part of instruction throughout the school year. In addition to the concepts stated in the grade level standards and standards for ELLs, it is best that you identify additional concepts that cause interferences for certain linguistic groups or that may have been targeted in a previous grade but not mastered by ELLs. For instance, a group of second-grade newcomers speaking Farsi may need instruction on English concepts about print, in particular print directionality.

Teaching concepts seems to be more effective when combined with students' rich and frequent exposure to English. It would be very difficult to teach a concept causing interference if students have no or little knowledge about the correct application of the concept. Furthermore, concepts need to be taught after students understand the meaning of the text where a concept appears. For example, it would be less effective to teach the structure of a complex sentence and the use of a conjunction in the sentence *After he chased away the cat, the dog asked his owner for a reward by wagging his tail* before you are sure students understand the meaning. After students understand the meaning of each clause, it becomes easier for you to help them learn about the relationship between these two clauses (subordinate clause and independent clause, and the use of the subordinating conjunction *after*).

The following are some ways to teach concepts causing interferences:

➢ Highlighting a concept in a written text (e.g., noun plurals for ELLs whose L1 does not have the concept)

➢ Having a metalinguistic talk about a concept and its related interferences (e.g., word order reversion for ELLs whose L1 has a different set of rules governing word order)

➢ Using sentence frames (e.g., a subordinating clause, an independent clause: *When _____, _____*) (see Figure 2.4 for an example of linguistic patterns for visualizing)

➢ Using a word wall to display the differences between English and L1 (e.g., word order: *a red book, un libro rojo*)

➢ Providing each student with a language concept journal where he or she

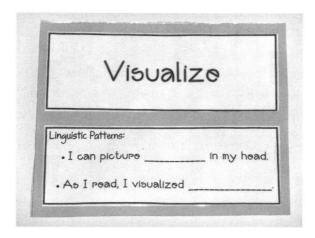

FIGURE 2.4. Linguistic patterns for visualizing (Mrs. Dominguez's third-grade class).

records the interferences related to the concept and the correct application of the concept (e.g., *Wes reads a book red. Wes read a red book.*)

In conjunction with the above-mentioned ways of teaching linguistic concept, optimal opportunities for ELLs to listen to and read authentic texts at their interest and proficiency levels and to speak and write about meaningful content are critical for ELLs to master English linguistic concepts.

CONCLUSION

In this chapter, I discussed the importance of teachers developing their linguistic knowledge and presented theories and concepts of language acquisition and English language components (writing system, phonology, orthography, semantics, syntax, and morphology). I also shared strategies for addressing interferences. In each of the following chapters, I continue to illustrate ways to address linguistic interferences within the specific context of teaching one particular component of literacy.

CHAPTER 3

INSTRUCTION FOR ORAL LANGUAGE DEVELOPMENT

During a class session on oral language development, five teachers of ELL at High Mountain Elementary School shared with me their experiences of teaching oral language. Mrs. Lee began by saying, "My first graders repeatedly make the same mistakes even after I have said back to them with a corrected version. I feel I may have overdone it with saying the corrected version. I don't know what to do with their oral mistakes." In agreement with Mrs. Lee, Ms. Taylor added, "I have fifth graders in my room who would repeat the same mistakes again and again. I have them write down the linguistic patterns in their journal, hoping that they would remember." Later, Mr. Solomon brought up another issue. "I have a hard time understanding what some of my third graders were saying. I am able to understand most of my Spanish-speaking students. I guess that I am used to their accent, but not the accent caused by other languages, like Chinese, Farsi, and Vietnamese." Ms. Hamm reminded her colleagues: "Sometimes, it is not just the accent, but the wrong sentence structure as well." Ms. Chen expressed her frustration: "I have some students who do not even say anything during class. I, however, do hear them talk one or two words in English on the playground and during lunch time."

What the five teachers have said here may reflect what you are experiencing in your teaching. Like these five teachers (and many others), you may wonder about how your teaching can facilitate your ELLs' development in oral language. For example, you might wonder:

1. How do ELLs develop English oral language?
2. How do I conduct classroom-based assessment to evaluate ELLs' English oral proficiency?
3. What strategies can I use to facilitate ELLs' oral language development?

4. How can I handle my students' oral mistakes so that I do not hurt their feelings or make them feel discouraged?

5. How can I engage families to support their children's oral language development?

These questions are common among teachers of ELLs. In this chapter, I begin with a discussion on oral language development of ELLs, highlighting areas of strengths and difficulties for them. Then I discuss ways to assess students' oral English. The next section focuses on various strategies and activities for facilitating oral language development. In presenting the strategies, I highlight those appropriate for young ELLs, for older ELLs, and for those who are literate in L1. This is followed by a section about engaging families in supporting their children's oral language development. To conclude this chapter, Mrs. Serrano, who taught kindergarten, second, and fourth grade, shares her experience of teaching oral language.

DEVELOPMENT OF ORAL LANGUAGE

Scholars of second language acquisition (e.g., Collier, 1995; Cummins, 1979; Krashen, 1985) remind us to become aware of the similarities and differences in first- and second-language acquisition. When students of L1 reach age 5, they have not yet mastered the complex system of oral language. Throughout elementary and middle school, students continue to develop and fine-tune their oral language proficiency. Specifically, they learn to deal with subtle distinctions and complexity in phonology, morphology, semantics, syntax, and pragmatics. This process of learning is fostered by a language rich environment at school and outside school, by interactions with others for communicative purposes, by their cognitive development, and by their expanded knowledge of the world and of language and literacy.

Although ELLs go through a process of acquiring English similar to that of their non-ELL peers, their process is complicated by some unique factors. One factor is the pressure of learning and mastering English within a short period of time. Native English-speakers had the period from birth to age 5 to develop basic oral language before starting school, whereas ELLs are pressured to speak English and communicate in it as soon as they enter a classroom (Collier, 1995). In addition, ELLs are pressured to develop literacy skills while they are just beginning to learn about English oracy (Meier, 2004; Peregoy, & Boyle, 2009). Another factor is the English input. ELLs may have only their teachers and native English-speaking peers as language models (Herrera & Murry, 2005). Their school and classroom are the primary environment for them to receive English input.

Areas of Strengths and Difficulties

The recognition of strengths ELLs bring to their learning allows teachers to build instruction on what students already know and can do. Herrera and Murry (2005) identify the following strengths:

- Second language learners already have a language for communication and thoughts.
- Second language learners can transfer knowledge about language (metalinguistic awareness) and thought process from the first to the second language.
- Second language learners have a greater repertoire of language learning strategies.
- Second language learners can use cognates to comprehend new words in a second language.
- Second language learners have greater prior knowledge and experience to rely on as they acquire the second language. (p. 63)

The difficulties of oral language development for ELLs result from three areas: (1) knowledge of English, (2) linguistic interferences from L1, and (3) content knowledge. As to knowledge of English, the difference between formal and informal registers can make oral production challenging. If an ELL uses an informal, everyday English for an oral report on a science project, the student's oral language is not acceptable. Another element of knowledge of English is associated with diction. When a word used does not best fit the context of a sentence, an ELL may fail to convey the meaning. For example, a Chinese-speaking ELL may translate the word *want* from Chinese into English as *think to want*. The sentence produced, *I think to want a cookie*, may confuse a listener. This situation occurs frequently among ELLs at the beginning and intermediate levels because they are in the process of developing their vocabulary knowledge. A third element of knowledge of English is related to the English linguistic patterns. If an ELL is unfamiliar with the request function of the linguistic pattern *Would you please* in the sentence *Would you please pass the book to me?* the student might respond with a "yes," but not grant the request by passing the book to the speaker. In this case, the student fails to communicate with the speaker.

A second area of difficulty in oral language development is linguistic interferences from students' L1 (Herrera & Murry, 2005). Interferences may be evident in the use of the L1 linguistic pattern in the production of English sentences. For example, a Japanese-speaking ELL might forget the inflectional ending *-ed* for a verb intended for an action in the past. Another element of interferences is related to collocation. ELLs may produce a sentence with an awkward collocation. For example, an ELL may say, "We eated a fast lunch," which reflects a transfer of the word *fast* from the phrase *fast food*. Evidently, the phrase *fast lunch* has a wrong collocation, thus making the phrase an awkward one. The accent in oral language production as influenced by L1 may make an ELL less understood. Next time you listen to ELLs speak, pay attention to the wide range of accents derived from different L1s. This means that phonology differences in L1s can affect the production of oral English in different ways. ELLs speaking one L1 may have difficulty with certain sounds in English which may be easy for another group of ELLs who speak a different L1. Helping students reduce accent calls for different foci for ELLs speaking different L1s. For students at the beginning and intermediate levels, code switching between English and L1 in oral output is common, largely due to a lack of knowledge of English in general and of vocabulary and sentence structures in particular. Some code-switching does not interfere with communications if it occurs with less important words, while others would make linguistic output difficult to understand if the major part of a sentence has words in L1.

A third area of difficulty in oral language development comes from ELLs' limited knowledge about content. For example, the sentence *School starts at 8 a.m.* is about the operation hours of a school. If an ELL states, "School starts at 8 p.m.," the student would confuse a listener.

Goals of Instruction

ELLs' proficiency in oral language is closely related to their literacy and other aspects of language development (Genesee, Lindholm-Leary, Saunders, & Christian, 2006). As August and Shanahan (2006) put it, "It is not enough to teach language-minority students reading skills alone. Extensive oral English development must be incorporated into successful literacy instruction" (p. 5). In order to deliver effective instruction, teachers' knowledge of stages of oral language development is imperative. Table 3.1 summarizes the oral language behaviors of students

TABLE 3.1. Stages of Oral Language Development

Stage	Oral language behaviors
Silent period/preproduction (starting)	• Having limited or no understanding of English • Responding nonverbally to simple commands and questions • Listening to English and observing its use • Using simple words or phrases in imitated responses • Producing many errors that hinder communication
Early production (emerging)	• Understanding phrases and short sentences • Using memorized phrases and formulaic language in communication • Beginning to use familiar everyday English and general academic vocabulary • Producing errors, most of which hinder communication
Speech emergence (developing)	• Understanding more complex speech, some of which needs to be repeated • Having limited vocabulary and language structure • Being able to express most thoughts • Using simple sentences • Producing errors, many of which hinder communication
Intermediate fluency (expanding)	• Having adequate language skills for most daily communication • Having difficulty with complex structures and abstract academic concepts • Producing errors, some of which hinder communication
Advanced fluency (bridging)	• Expressing themselves for everyday communication and academic purposes in a way similar to native English speakers • Producing speech with varied linguistic complexity • Having minimal errors and being able to correct them

at different stages, which are based on the classifications of language proficiency in the work of Krashen (1982), Krashen and Terrell, (1983), and TESOL (2006b).

The goal of instruction for oral language is to enable students to be proficient in receptive and expressive language for both social and academic functions (Collier, 1995; Cummins, 1979, 1986; Krashen, 1982; Krashen & Terrell, 1983). Receptive language (listening and reading) is what students can understand, and expressive language (speaking and writing) is what students can produce in their oral and written communication. People speaking any language are usually better at receptive language than at expressive language. For example, we are able to understand the news on TV. However, even if we know the news content and related vocabulary, we are not proficient in producing a piece of news with eloquent language that would catch viewers' attention. ELLs may develop their receptive language faster than expressive language largely due to their observations through listening and watching and through rehearsing in their mind what they have observed during the silent period and early production stages (Tabors & Snow, 2001).

Receptive and expressive language serve both social and academic functions. ELLs proficient in oral language are able to use both types of language for everyday and academic communication. Some examples of language serving various social functions are "asking permission, asking assistance, asking directions, promising, requesting, suggesting, and wishing/hoping." Academic functions include "classifying, comparing, giving/following directions, describing, questioning, evaluating, expressing position, explaining, hypothesizing, planning/predicting, reporting, and sequencing" (Herrell, 2000, p. 102).

ASSESSING ORAL PROFICIENCY AND FLUENCY

In this section, I focus on classroom-based assessment, which is beneficial to both you and students. The assessment data provides you with immediate feedback specifically related to what you want to know about a student's oral language. In addition, you can choose one particular assessment over another for one student, or use a same assessment for a group of students. Classroom-based assessment includes explicit assessment, where a student is asked to produce oral language for you to assess (see the following sections on Say Something, Oral Retelling of a Wordless Book, and Having a Conversation), and embedded assessment, where you observe and keep anecdotal records of a student's oral production in various settings.

Explicit Assessment

Say Something

In the assessment of Say Something, you ask a student say something about a topic of his or her choice and about a topic you have chosen. The purpose of this assessment is to measure how well a student can express ideas related to a topic. The reason for the two choices is for you to see if familiarity with a topic has some impact on how well the student can produce oral English. For students at the preproduction and early production levels, you can show students a picture and have them say something about it. Here are the steps:

1. Say to the student, "Choose a topic you know. A topic can be your family, your friends, your favorite game, your books, or your home country. Tell me about the topic."

2. Record what the student says.

3. Say to the student, "Now, I am going to give you a topic. Please tell me what you know about _____." When selecting topics, make sure they are relatively universal, such as the first day of school, eating with families, and playing a game.

4. Repeat Step 2.

5. Transcribe the tapes (if there is time) or listen to the recorded talks numerous times.

6. Complete the Oral Language Assessment Chart (Appendix E) (see Figure 3.1 for a completed example).

Oral Retelling of a Wordless Book

Oral retelling, which has been used as a way to measure students' comprehension of a text, can be used with ELLs to assess oral fluency—how well a student can construct a story in oral language (Hadaway, Vardell, & Young, 2004; Peregoy & Boyle, 2009). In this assessment, a student reads a wordless book and retells what is being read. The advantage of using a wordless book is that ELLs, even at the early production level, are encouraged to tell a story based on their understanding of the pictures, not words that are unfamiliar to them, thus possibly intimidating them. Even if an ELL is not ready to produce a connected text in English, words and phrases in English used in retelling become a source of assessment data. This holds true for older ELLs who are at the early production and speech emerging levels. They would not feel embarrassed by reading a wordless book! Wordless books further encourage students to use their imagination and activate their prior knowledge in retelling. Figure 3.2 provides a list of wordless books, and Figure 3.1 is a completed Oral Language Assessment Chart of an oral retelling of *Pancakes for Breakfast* (dePaola, 1978) by a second grader at an intermediate proficiency level. Here are the steps:

1. Say to the student, "I have read this book without words. Can you read it? First, look at the pictures in the book. Take your time. You can look at the pictures again when you are telling me your story."

2. Have the student retell the story.

3. Record the retelling.

4. Transcribe the tapes (if there is time) or listen to the recorded retelling numerous times.

5. Complete the Oral Language Assessment Chart (Appendix E).

Student Name: Lydia	Date: November 12, 2008

Book Title: *Pancakes for Breakfast (dePaola, 1978)*

Oral Retelling

This story is about a lady that wants to make pancakes. Then she walks up and thinks about pancakes. She gets all the things she needs to make pancakes. Then she forgot something. Then she went to the house of the chicken to get some eggs. Next, she goes to her house and then she needed some milk and went to the store to buy some milk and the man said, "Your welcome." to the lady. Finally, she went back home and she threw the milk because the cat and the dog made a mess in the house.

Expressed Ideas

The oral retelling resembles a story with connected ideas and includes many important details of the book.

Linguistic Patterns Used

Effective or Acceptable Ones	Less Effective or Unacceptable Ones
• subject + *be* predicate with a relative clause (*This story is about a lady that wants to make pancakes.*) • subject + verb predicate (2 verbs) (*She walks up and thinks about pancakes.*) • subject + verb predicate with a relative clause (*She gets all the things she needs to make pancakes.*) • subject + verb predicate with an infinitive (*She went to the house of the chicken to get some eggs.*) • a complex sentence with a *because* clause (*She went back home and she threw the milk because the cat and the dog made a mess in the house.*)	• too many ideas expressed in one sentence (*She goes to her house and then she needed some milk and went to the store to buy some milk and the man said, "Your welcome." to the lady.*) • the second *she* can be deleted (*Finally, she went back home and she threw the milk . . .*) • a mixture of present and past tenses throughout the retelling

Diction

Effective or Acceptable Ones	Less Effective or Unacceptable Ones
• most verbs • transitional words (*then, next, finally*)	• unclear phrases (*walks up, threw the milk*) • too many *then* throughout the retelling

Average Length of a Sentence

There are 7 sentences. The shortest one has 4 words, and the longest one has 30 words. The average length of a sentence is 14 words per sentence.

Plan for Instruction

• verb tenses (present and past)
• words to precisely express the ideas
• sentence structure with one idea per sentence
• transitional words

FIGURE 3.1. Oral language assessment chart of an oral retelling of *Pancakes for Breakfast* (dePaola, 1978).

Baker, J. (1991). *Window*. New York: Greenwillow Books.
Baker, J. (2004). *Home*. New York: Greenwillow Books.
Banyai, I. (1995). *Zoom*. New York: Viking.
Blake, Q. (1996). *Clown*. New York: Holt.
Briggs, R. (1978). *The snowman*. New York: Random House.
Carle, E. (1973). *I see a song*. New York: Crowell.
Carle, E. (1976). *Do you want to be my friend?* New York: Harper Collins.
Crews, D. (1980). *Truck*. New York: Greenwillow Books.
dePaola, T. (1978). *Pancakes for breakfast*. New York: Harcourt Brace.
Drescher, H. (1987). *The yellow umbrella*. New York: Bradbury Press.
Fleischman, P. (2004). *Sidewalk circus*. Cambridge, MA: Candlewick Press.
Lehman, B. (2004). *The red book*. Boston: Houghton Mifflin.
Liu, J. S. (2002). *Yellow umbrella*. La Jolla, CA: Kane/Miller.
McCully, E. A. (1987). *School*. New York: Harper & Row.
Rohmann, E. (1994). *Time flies*. New York: Crown.
Spier, P. (1983). *Christmas*. Garden City, NY: Doubleday.
Spier, P. (1997). *Rain*. Garden City, NY: Doubleday.
Weitzman, J. P. (1998). *You can't take a balloon into the metropolitan museum*. New York: Dial Books for Young Readers.
Weitzman, J. P. (2000). *You can't take a balloon into the national gallery*. New York: Dial Books for Young Readers.
Wiesner, D. (1991). *Tuesday*. New York: Clarion Books.
Wiesner, D. (1998). *Fire fall*. New York: Lothrop, Lee & Shepard Books.
Wiesner, D. (1999). *Sector 7*. New York: Clarion Books.
Wiesner, D. (2006). *Flotsam*. New York: Clarion Books.
Wilson, A. (1999). *Magpie magic: A tale of colorful mischief*. New York: Dial Books.

FIGURE 3.2. Wordless books.

Having a Conversation

The assessment of Having a Conversation intends to measure how well a student can communicate effectively with another person, an ability that resembles interpersonal communication. Here are the steps:

1. Start the conversation by sharing or asking a specific question or asking a general question.

   a. Sharing and asking a specific question

   ➤ "I read a new book. It is about _____. Did you read a book? What is it?"

   ➤ "I met a friend yesterday." Say something about the meeting [e.g., "We were happy to see each other. We talked and laughed."]. "How often do you and your friends get together?"

   b. Asking a general question

   ➤ "What did you do this weekend? What book are you reading? What did you do for the holiday?"

2. Record the conversation.

3. Prompt the student and/or add something to keep the conversation going.

> ➤ "That's very interesting. Now tell me more about it."

> ➤ "So you read the book and liked it. Can you tell me why you liked it? Is the book like the one you read [the movie you saw] before? How?"

4. Provide positive feedback throughout the conversation.

> ➤ "This is an excellent point!"

> ➤ "You made an interesting comparison between this book and the book you read. I have never thought of comparing two books like the way you did."

> ➤ "I like the way you used the expression/words/phrases [list them] in here."

5. Transcribe the tape (if there is time) or listen to the recorded conversation numerous times.

6. Complete the Conversation Assessment Chart (Appendix F).

Embedded Assessment

We cannot overlook the importance of embedded assessment, in which you observe and document a student's oral production in an authentic context (e.g., talking during recess, lunch, or during group work). Some students may demonstrate a higher level of oral language proficiency in a nonassessment setting because they are not under stress and they are using English for a real purpose. You would also learn about the peers with whom a student feels comfortable to interact. The knowledge of peers helps you group students in a way that maximizes student interaction.

One way to collect and document data from embedded assessment is to keep anecdotal records of students' oral production (Appendix G). Boyd-Batstone (2004) offers teachers some tips on using anecdotal records that are relevant to teachers of ELLs. One tip is to identify a curricular standard before an observation, focus on it during observation, and analyze a student's strengths and needs based on the standard. Boyd-Batstone suggests that in writing down information, teachers use action verbs (e.g., *identified, stated*), document a specific example for each record (e.g., Jose talked in a sentence: "I want ball."), use abbreviation to speed up note taking (e.g., *ID* for *identified*), and avoid the use of the word "can't." You analyze the records when you have cumulative details related to the standard.

STRATEGIES AND ACTIVITIES FOR PROMOTING ORAL LANGUAGE

In delivering instruction for oral language, you need to keep in mind a set of guidelines. The strategies and activities presented in this chapter (see Table 3.2) reflect the guidelines. First, it is important for you to understand the different foci for

TABLE 3.2. Proficiency Levels, Instructional Foci, and Strategies and Activities for Oral Language Development

Proficiency level	Instructional foci	Strategies and activities
Beginning Silent period/ preproduction (starting) Early production (emerging)	• Providing exposure to English input • Providing continued exposure to L1 input • Lowering anxiety level and making the learning environment and language activities inviting and engaging • Using verbal and nonverbal responses to commands and questions • Understanding and using simple, memorized, and formulaic classroom language for interpersonal communication and for academic purposes • Understanding and using basic interpersonal communication in noninstructional settings	• Read-aloud • Listening to books on tape • Watching TV and videos • Total physical response (TPR) • Literacy play • Echo reading • Shared reading • Show-and-tell • Think–pair–share • Group work • Promoting the use of linguistic patterns • Teaching pronunciation
Intermediate Speech emergence (developing) Intermediate fluency (expanding)	• Providing exposure to English input • Providing continued exposure to L1 input • Understanding all simple and most complex speech • Expressing most thoughts in daily communication • Expanding knowledge of vocabulary and language structure • Becoming aware of errors in communication	• Read-aloud • Listening to books on tape • Watching TV and videos • Literacy play • Role play • Buddy reading • Paired reading • Independent reading • Sharing a book • Sharing a piece of writing • Think–pair–share • Group work • Promoting the use of linguistic patterns • Teaching pronunciation
Advanced Advanced fluency (bridging)	• Providing exposure to English input • Providing continued exposure to L1 input • Expressing themselves for everyday communication and academic purposes in a way similar to native English speakers • Producing speech with varied linguistic complexity • Having minimal errors and being able to correct them	• Listening to books on tape • Watching TV and videos • Role play • Buddy reading • Paired reading • Independent reading • Sharing a book • Sharing a piece of writing • Sharing a project (oral report) • Think–pair–share • Group work • Promoting the use of linguistic patterns • Comparing and contrasting English and L1

younger and older ELLs respectively. For example, for young ones, the instructional foci are geared more toward basic linguistic patterns and interpersonal communication (at school and outside school). Older ELLs who have not mastered the basic linguistic patterns and interpersonal communicative skills need to develop oral language for daily communication and for academic purposes.

It is imperative that you provide students with many opportunities to be exposed to English, use it in communicating with others for authentic, meaningful purposes, and learn language through content (Cummins, 1986; Freeman, & Freeman, 2009; Freeman, Freeman, & Mercuri, 2002; Herrera & Murry, 2005; Houk, 2005; Krashen, 1985; Rothenberg & Fisher, 2007). The strategies and activities presented in the rest of this chapter aim to address the instructional foci and areas of difficulties for ELLs and to maximize interactions among students and between you and students.

Another guideline is providing comprehensible input as a way to differentiate and scaffold instruction (Echevarria, Vogt, & Short, 2008; Freeman & Freeman, 2002; Herrera & Murry, 2005; Krashen & Terrell, 1983; Soltero, 2004). For example:

> Slow down speech (but keep the natural rate) and pronounce every sound of a word clearly. Pause often if needed.

> Simplify language by using common, familiar words (e.g., *woman* for *female*); easily pronounced words (e.g., *teach* for *instruct*); or cognates (e.g., *bote* for *boat*).

> Use fewer idioms, slang, and pronouns.

> Use more familiar linguistic patterns (e.g., *Please pass the book to me.* for *Could you please pass me the book?*), simple sentences, and fewer clauses.

> Repeat and paraphrase what is being said if necessary.

> Provide visual aids along with speech (e.g., pictures, gestures, actions, realia [objects])

> Include concrete, familiar, and specific examples in an explanation of something new.

> Explain and display key vocabulary using expressions students can understand.

> Teach new linguistic patterns and vocabulary for something students have known (e.g., *Could you please* + verb _____? as another way to make a request; *instruct* for *teach*).

A third guideline is related to whether or not you should correct students' errors in oral production. It is important to remember that comprehension and fluency are more important than accuracy, especially during the early stages of oral language development (Diaz-Rico & Weed, 2006; Horwitz, 2008; Peregoy, & Boyle, 2009). Correcting students' errors would increase their anxiety level, which would lead to a possible decrease in their participation and speech production. You, however, can model a correct way by paraphrasing a student's sentence. For example, when a student says, "I read three book," you can respond, "Good! You read three books" (stressing the /s/ in the word *books*). Before correcting the errors, you should consider students' proficiency levels and the purpose of the communication. If students' errors make a message difficult to understand, you can ask clarifying questions to guide students to possibly self-correct the errors. For example, when a student says, "I want tis piksh [this picture], you could ask, "What do you want? You want this picture?" If the error is difficult for you to detect, you can request, "Say it again." When a student code switches between L1 and English, it is better not to treat words in L1 as errors. Rather, code switching needs to be considered as evidence of a student's resourcefulness. If the code switch affects meaning, you can ask questions to help the student clarify or have the student use visual aids to replace the words. No matter whether you do not correct or gently correct students' errors, you should document commonly made errors by individual students as another source of assessment data.

Maximizing Language Input

Before students are able to produce any oral language, they need to have much exposure to English. The exposure enables them to get acquainted with English and thus later become familiar with various aspects of English, including rhythm, linguistic patterns, diction, and tone. Language input during school days provides an important linguistic experience for students who usually do not get much exposure outside of school. These students may have family members who speak no or little English, live in an environment where English is not often spoken (e.g., a Persian neighborhood), and have limited access to English media (e.g., TV shows, newspapers in English). Reading aloud, listening to books on tape, and watching TV or videos are just three common ways to provide students with language input. While students participate in other activities requiring interactions with you and peers, they also receive language input.

Reading Aloud

Teachers in primary grades read aloud a book to students for oral language development (listening and language input) and for comprehension (Snow, Burns, & Griffin, 1998; Strickland & Morrow, 1989; Teale, 1984, 2003). Read-alouds for ELLs further promote language exposure, expansion, and production (Roberts, 2008). When using read-alouds with ELLs, you need to focus more on the scaffolding process (Gibbons, 2002). The first step in the process is to consider certain factors in selecting appropriate books. The factors listed in Appendix H help you choose appropriate books for read-alouds. If a book is interesting to students but has difficult linguistic patterns and vocabulary and the pictures do not always support words, students may not benefit much from the read-aloud, mostly because they may be frustrated with the language. Older ELLs at a beginning level may find books with many pictures and repetitive linguistic patterns embarrassing for them to read. In this case, teachers should find books with a strong focus on content related to what students are learning, but still with easy language.

A second step in the scaffolding process is to read aloud a core book multiple times. A read-aloud book can be a core book of the week that is related to the unit under study. During the first reading, you should focus students' attention on the content by having students browse the pictures, pay attention to new or key words explained by you, ask questions and make comments, and listen to the book read aloud once or more. During the second and third read-aloud session, you should emphasize some linguistic points and/or interesting expressions and show how these points and expressions can be used in daily communication. During the fourth read-aloud, students should be encouraged to do shared reading with you. During the fifth read-aloud, you should invite students to choral read the book. Table 3.3 shows an example of a multiple read-aloud with *How Kids Grow* (Marzollo, 1998). After a week's read-aloud of the same book, some students may benefit from additional exposure to the book. You can read aloud the book again to them. Reading aloud a core book multiple times does not mean that you should read only one book per week; it is necessary for you to read aloud other books related to the core book in content or with similar language patterns so that students would have additional exposure to the content or language patterns.

A third step in the scaffolding process is to vary the way that a book is read aloud to address the needs of students. For young ELLs, multiple readings of the whole book are necessary. For older ELLs not literate in L1 and English, the language and content (in particular, subject-area content) of the book should be stressed. After several readings, you can focus on specific language patterns and vocabulary in the book and explain the subject-area content. In so doing, reading aloud helps students expand their vocabulary and knowledge of a specific content area. For ELLs who are literate in L1 and have developed some content-area knowledge, the focus of a read-aloud is to help them learn about English linguistic patterns and vocabulary representing content-area concepts already familiar to them.

Listening to Books on Tape

Books on tape provide another source of language input for students. Students can listen to books that you have read aloud to them, that are related to the content under study, and/or that are interesting to them. While listening, it is best that students have a copy of the book for following along. Some examples of a follow-up activity include sharing with peers the story or content knowledge and interesting expressions and vocabulary. It would be helpful for you to talk with students after listening to the book to learn about what students gained from the listening, what difficulties they experienced, and what was easy for them. This type of talk provides valuable information about students' listening experiences.

Books on tape are usually part of a basal reader program for primary grades. Books on tape for upper grades can be obtained from a local public library. The

TABLE 3.3. Read-Aloud of *How Kids Grow* (Marzollo, 1998)

First reading

1. Show the pictures of the book and briefly talk about the content of the book.
2. Show the pictures of the book and encourage students to make comments or connections.
3. Write key words and/or difficult words on the board and explain these words in simple speech aided by pictures and realias [objects].
4. Read the book, pointing at each word and referring to a picture or parts of a picture (e.g., referring to the phrase *big wooden beads* and the action *string big wooden beads* after reading the sentence *Alex likes to string big wooden beads*)
5. Read the book and ask students questions and/or invite students to ask questions and make comments.

Second and third readings

1. Identify a repetitive linguistic pattern and record sentences representing the pattern on a chart paper or on the board.
   "I see some sentences that look alike. For example, *He can do many things. James can hold his sister's fingers. She can lie on her tummy and lift her head up.*" (Underline the subject of each sentence with one color and the verb with another color and write the word *can* in a color different from the other colors used.)
   "All these sentences have the pattern: _____ (*He, She, James*) can (*do many things, hold his sister's fingers, lie on her tummy and lift her head up*). This is our first pattern sentence."
2. Invite students to find more sentences with this pattern.
   "How can we find other sentences? What key word should we look for?"
3. Record the identified sentences, using different colors to highlight the subject and verb of each sentence and the word *can*.
4. Direct students' attention to different subjects in the identified sentences.
   "In the book, the author uses *he, she, James, Adeline, Mark, Noël, Alex, Olivia, Annie*, and *Adrienne* at the beginning of the pattern sentence.
   What else can we use? Can we say *I*? *I can do many things.* Can we say, *Jose*? *Jose can do many things.* Can we say *we*? Can we say *they*?
   I want you to try to use different names for the beginning of the sentence. First I am going to say *I* (to replace *Mark*) *can build a tower of blocks.* Now you try."
5. Repeat the above steps in directing students' attention to action verbs of the identified sentences.
6. Have students think–pair–share a sentence with the pattern.
7. Invite students to share their sentences and make comments on the sentences.
8. Repeat steps 1 to 7 with another sentence pattern in this book.
   _____ *likes to* _____ (*James likes to look at faces.*)

Fourth reading

1. Invite students to do shared reading.
   "We have learned two sentence patterns. I am going to read this book again. When I get to the sentence patterns we are learning, I want you to read aloud with me. Of course, if you want to read aloud with me other sentences, that would be great!"
2. Refer to the picture related to a sentence pattern as a way to support students.

Fifth reading

1. Invite students to do choral reading or, for some students, shared reading.
2. Refer to the picture related to a sentence pattern as a way to support students.

Internet offers electronic books with sound and animation effects. For example, Raz-kids (*www.raz-kids.com/main/ViewPage/name/sample*) has free samples of interactive books. Reading Rainbow (*pbskids.org/readingrainbow/books/index.html*) provides a list of books featured on the PBS television show *Reading Rainbow*. For the synopsis of each book, a reader can click on the "Listen" button to hear the synopsis read aloud.

Watching TV and Videos

Another source of language input are TV programs and videos, which are often directly related to students' interests and/or current events (Farrell, 2006). When the videos are about current events, students are learning not just the English language, but also culturally and socially specific content knowledge. While showing a TV show or a video related to a content area, display the closed captions if they are available. Major broadcasting companies (e.g., ABC) have shows and videos accessible on the Internet. Students can view the videos as many times as they want. You can stop the video and discuss with students the content and answer students' questions. The PBS Kids website (*pbskids.org/video/index.html*) offers video clips of popular TV shows. The website for the NOVA program on PBS (*www.pbs.org/wgbh/nova/programs/*) houses videos with closed captions on a wide range of content topics, from history to nature to technology. The closed captions support ELLs at various levels of English proficiency during their listening to English and learning about the content. A sharing or discussion activity can follow the reviewing of the video.

Total Physical Response

In total physical response (TPR), you model acting out a command for students, and then students act out the command (e.g., *stand up*). For students at the preproduction and early production levels, TPR is an approach focusing on comprehension of language input rather than language output. As Krashen and Terrell (1983) explain, when students are not forced to produce English they are still learning, their attention focuses on understanding what is being said. TPR can be used to teach action verbs (e.g., *smile*), body parts (e.g., *touch your nose*), and classroom language (e.g., *open your book*). After students become familiar with this approach, you can have students at a more advanced level give out commands for students at the beginning level to act out.

Literacy Play

Literacy play (e.g., playing house) is an effective way to develop oral language, and in particular the forms and functions of language for young native English-speaking students (Neuman & Roskos, 1990; Vukelich, Christie, & Enz, 2007). In a classroom with ELLs, literacy play has an even more important role for several reasons. First of all, literacy play allows students to listen to and speak English for an authentic purpose, thus learn about the forms and functions of English. For example, in a play about a neighborhood park (with a mini-set of a slide and swing or a picture of a swing set), children would negotiate a turn to play on a swing, ask another child to push the swing, and warn other children to stay away from the moving swing. Literacy play also brings to the classroom the outside school world unfamiliar to children, thus making it possible for students to expand their background knowledge.

In order for your students to experience different settings during literacy play, you can rotate each setting once a month or even less frequently depending on students' knowledge about the context and the language related to a chosen setting. Literacy play is not free play, but guided play. Before having students participate in a literacy play setting, you teach students about the common language used in that particular setting and explain the print usually present in the setting. Table 3.4 lists some sample language and print used in the common settings. To create a setting, you can ask business establishments (e.g., a supermarket) to donate relevant props, download photos related to a particular setting and post them in the center area, or take a photo of each needed item and post the photo in the play area. While students are interacting in a literacy play setting, you can take anecdotal notes about their language use, noting students' strengths and needs (see Appendix G).

Role Play

Similar to literacy play, in a role play a student assumes a role. Unlike literacy play, the student has a range of choices for roles, and the activity can be less structured to support students to use oral language (Anthony, 2008). A student can assume the role of a character from a book and act as if he or she were the character (see Chapter 4 for a discussion of Readers' Theater). This type of role play connects comprehension of the book to oral language practices. In a similar vein, a student can assume the role of a news reporter presenting information gathered from print and nonprint sources. This type of role play encourages students to talk like a scholar in one particular discipline using content-specific academic language.

Read-Aloud

Student read-alouds help with building oral fluency and practicing oral English. For students who are afraid of opening their mouth to speak English, you can use these ideas to ease students' anxiety:

> ➢ Have a student read aloud a book to a stuffed animal who would never criticize.

> ➢ Have a student read aloud a book with a puppet in hand. The student will feel less discouraged when the puppet not the student, seems to be the one who makes mistakes in oral reading.

> ➢ Have a student read aloud a book to a tape recorder. Most students are curious about how their own voice sounds on a tape.

(text resumes on page 70)

TABLE 3.4. Oral Language and Print for Literacy Plays

Setting	Sample oral language	Sample print
House	**In the kitchen** What's for dinner? I am thinking of . . . What are you cooking? I am cooking . . . Can you wash . . . ? Can you pass the plate? Hello. This is . . . . May I speak to . . . ?	calendar recipes/cookbooks food containers grocery ads coupons words on the appliances decorative magnets phonebook
	At the dining table This . . . tastes yummy (good, delicious, too salty, too sweet). Can you pass the salt? I am going to try . . . again.	newspaper
	In the living room (watching TV) Can you switch to . . . channel? This . . . is funny (sad). Oh, my goodness. I don't believe this. This reminds me of . . . Hello. This is . . . . May I speak to . . . ?	TV guide newspaper books magazines phonebook
Neighborhood park/ playground	Can I play with you? What are you playing? You can go down the slide first. Let's play . . . Can you catch me? Are you hurt (okay)? This is so fun! Please push me (on the swing). I am going to swing. Please stay away from it. I am going home. See you tomorrow. Thank you.	name of the park regulations posed by a city (e.g., *Don't Litter*) street names print on a trash can
Fast food restaurant	Can I help you? What would you like to order? One order of. . . , two orders of. . . A total of . . . (price). Please wait for a few minutes. Here is your change. Here is your order. Thank you.	ads menu signs (e.g., *Order, Pick-up, Exit*) labels of condiments

(continued)

TABLE 3.4. *(continued)*

Setting	Sample oral language	Sample print
Supermarket	I want to buy . . . Is this going to be expensive (cheap)? I am going to get . . . Oops, I forgot to get . . . Let me see, what else do I need? Hello/thank you (to cashier) Where can I find . . . ? This tastes . . . (yummy, delicious). I am going to get some. Make a decision. Which type of . . . (ice cream) do you want? Have a great day! Thank you.	store name store signs (e.g., *Express Check-out*) price tags container labels checkbook money grocery ads coupons newspapers books magazines
Doctor's office	How do you feel today? I feel . . . What's wrong? My . . . hurts. I . . . (cough a lot, have a headache, hurt my foot). Let me take a look at . . . Does it hurt when I am touching . . . ? I'll see you again in a week. Breathe in and breathe out. Get rest and drink a lot of water. Take this medicine . . . (once a day with food). Thank you.	appointment book books magazines pamphlets signs (e.g., *No Smoking, Turn Off Cell Phones*) business cards prescription pad
Library	Can I help the next one in line? The . . . (books, tapes) are due on . . . Your . . . are overdue. There is a fine of . . . How would you like to pay the fine? The book is checked out. Would you like us to call you when the book is checked in? I need to renew these . . . Thank you for visiting us.	books magazines tapes (DVD, VHS, CD) posters information sheets/pamphlets computers library cards

> ➢ Have a student read aloud a book to a best friend with whom the student feels comfortable.

> ➢ Have a student read aloud a book to a small group of friends with whom the student has worked and played.

> ➢ Have a student read aloud a book to you when the student feels confident and comfortable with you.

> ➢ Have a student read aloud a book to the whole class. By this time, the student should have a relatively lower level of anxiety.

One form of read-aloud, round robin reading, tends to hurt the self-esteem and self-confidence of many ELLs and struggling students. I would suggest an alternative to round robin reading, an alternative that supports students in their practice of oral fluency and connecting oracy with comprehension. After students have read a book and become familiar with the content and language, they choose a short paragraph or several paragraphs to practice oral reading. On the day of the read-aloud, each student shares his or her selected paragraph or paragraphs and explains to the group or the whole class the rationale for the choice. During the process, students enjoy reading aloud their favorite parts of the book and sharing their responses to the selection, and they learn from peers about how others have selected and responded to the paragraph(s). As a teacher, imagine how much you can learn about students' understanding of a text from the following responses: "This paragraph reminds me of my dog. He was very brave." (Making a text–self connection.) "These two paragraphs show readers a problem Jason faces." (Identifying a story problem.) "The big word *unfolding* has a prefix, *un*, and a suffix, *ing*." (Conducting a morphemic analysis.)

Read-aloud can take other forms. The descriptions that follow are presented in an order that reflects a decrease in teacher support and an increase in student responsibility.

Echo Reading

When a teacher is echo reading a text, he or she reads each sentence from the text and the students repeat it. The text appropriate for echo reading is the one with sentence structures and words that are easy for students to follow and pronounce. Of course, it is important that the text has been read to students multiple times and that students have a good understanding of it.

Shared Reading

You and students share the responsibility of reading aloud a book (often a predictable book). Choose a text that you have read to students multiple times so they have become familiar with some expressions in the text. When you come to these expressions, invite students to read.

Buddy Reading

A student chooses a buddy to read to and listens to the buddy read. These two students may read the same book or different books. If they read the same book, buddy reading allows a student to hear and observe how the other student reads. If different books are read, buddy reading provides an opportunity for both students to learn about the other book. Many teachers also implement cross-age buddy reading. This is a common practice where an older student reads aloud a book to a young one. This practice, however, sends a subtle message to young students that they may not be able to read until they reach the grade level of their buddies who read to them. This message could be detrimental to ELLs' self-confidence. Given that, younger ELLs should also read aloud a book to their older buddies, regardless of how well they can read.

Paired Reading

Traditionally, one student is paired with another based solely on the difference in reading ability of the two students. For paired reading used with ELLs, other factors need to be considered. For example, two students who speak the same L1 can be paired together, even if both are at the same English proficiency and reading levels. One student who has a good knowledge of text content can be paired with another who has little or limited knowledge. Other factors to consider for pairing include motivation, interest, and personality.

Independent Reading

Students read various texts for independent reading and document the text titles in a log. Have a conversation with a student once a week or biweekly to learn about the types of books read and the number of times a book is read. This type of conversation gives each student another chance to practice oral language and prepares the student for sharing his or her book with the class.

Sharing

Different types of sharing help students develop oral language for everyday and academic communication. Horwitz (2008) suggests that a sharing activity should begin with students' talking about themselves. This type of sharing helps build a class community, provides an opportunity for students to use the formulaic language (e.g., *My name is* _____. *I am* _____ [ethnic identity]. I was born in _____.), and allows you to learn about students. Younger ELLs, older newcomers, and those unfamiliar with different types of sharing benefit from a teacher's guidance in terms of the structure of sharing and the language used in sharing. You can provide some linguistic patterns for students to use, which can be posted on the classroom walls for students (see Table 3.5). Focus on one type of sharing at a time, and move onto another one with an increased difficulty level after students have mastered the previous, less difficult one.

TABLE 3.5. Structure and Language Used for Sharing

Type of sharing	Structure	Sample linguistic patterns
Show and tell	Tell about the object.	This is . . .
	Tell how you got the object.	I got . . . (name of the object) from . . . (a person's name) on . . . (time).
	Tell how you feel about the object.	I like/love . . . because . . . It is important to me because . . .
	Tell how you use the object.	I use this object for . . .
	Invite the audience to ask questions.	What questions do you have about this object?
Sharing a book	Tell about the title, author, and genre of the book.	The title of the book is . . . It is written by . . . and illustrated by . . . The genre of the book is . . .
	Give a summary of the book.	This book is about . . . (try to cover who, when, where, what, how, and why)
	Tell about your favorite part of the book.	My favorite part of the book is . . . It is my favorite because . . .
	Tell a lesson learned from the book.	From this book I learned . . .
	Tell interesting language (expressions, words) learned from the book.	The expression . . . is something new I learned. It means . . .
	Invite the audience to ask questions.	What questions do you have about this book?
Sharing a piece of writing	Tell the title of your writing.	My writing is titled . . .
	Read your writing with expression *or* give a summary of your writing.	My writing is about . . . [Read the writing.]
	Tell how you came up with the topic.	I got the idea for my writing from . . . After reading . . . , I felt that I could rewrite the story.
	Tell how you added creativity and imagination to your writing.	I wrote . . . to create . . .
	Tell what difficulty you experienced and how you overcame it.	The difficulty I had is . . . I overcame the difficulty by . . .
	Invite the audience to ask questions.	What questions do you have about my writing?
Sharing a project (oral report)	Tell the title and main idea of the project.	My project, [insert title], is about . . .
	Share the project.	[Showcase the visuals, products, and/or PowerPoint presentation.]
	Tell how you came up with the idea for the project.	I got the idea for this project from . . . (when I was reading/when I was surfing the Internet).
	Tell what difficulty you experienced and how you overcame it.	The difficulty I had is . . . I overcame the difficulty by . . .
	Invite the audience to ask questions.	What questions do you have about my project?

Think–Pair–Share

Think–pair–share, a less structured type of sharing, can be used across various grade and proficiency levels (Echevarria, Vogt, & Short, 2008). Mrs. Barlow, a kindergarten teacher with ELLs at early production and speech emerging levels, often used think–pair–share. She had her students practice a linguistic pattern or a word with a peer, and then regrouped the class so that each student practiced the pattern or the word with at least four or five different peers. She also varied her way of giving her students the directions. In the beginning of the practice, she gave students step-by-step directions, and later, general directions were given. In the following excerpt, Mrs. Barlow reviewed the concept of setting she taught on the previous day. She passed out a picture card of a different setting (e.g., a park, a house) to each student and wanted students to practice saying, "The setting is _____."

MRS. BARLOW: Let me hear again what we are learning.

STUDENTS: Setting.

MRS. BARLOW: Tell your partner again what a setting is.

(*Students share with each other a definition of setting.*)

MRS. BARLOW: Here is what I want you to do now. Each of you is going to get a brand new setting picture. I want you to tell your partner what setting you get.

(*Mrs. Barlow writes* The setting is _____. *on the board.*)

MRS. BARLOW: If you have a picture of Disneyland, you would say, "The setting is Disneyland." (*She points at each word of the pattern* The setting is _____, *and puts the picture of Disneyland next to the word* is *when saying the word* Disneyland.)

(*Mrs. Barlow passes out the pictures.*)

MRS. BARLOW: Do not forget to use the sentence "The setting is _____." Do not just tell me, "Disneyland." I don't know what that is. Say "Good morning" to your partner.

STUDENTS: Good morning!

MRS. BARLOW: Tell your partner, "The setting is _____."

STUDENTS: The setting is Disneyland (school, airplane, castle).

MRS. BARLOW: Tell your partner, "Thank you."

STUDENTS: Thank you.
(*Mrs. Barlow regroups the class.*)

MRS. BARLOW: Now you have a brand new partner. Tell your partner "Good morning!" Tell your partner what we are learning. Tell your partner what a setting is and then tell your partner what your sentence is.

Mrs. Barlow regrouped the class and repeated the same activity another four times. Think–pair–share, if used with students at a higher proficiency level, can be done quickly and integrated into another activity (e.g., asking students to think–pair–share their prediction in a prereading activity).

Group Work

Group work offers students authentic opportunities to engage in a dialogue or discussion with their peers in a context of solving problems related to content (Gibbons, 2002; Horwitz, 2008; Houk, 2005; Rothenberg & Fisher, 2007). Such collaborative conversations help students learn English for everyday communication (e.g., negotiating turn taking and responsibility) and for academic purposes (Cazden, 2001; Herrera & Murry, 2005; Swain, 2005). For example, in a literature circle, each student assumes a role (e.g., vocabulary picker, summarizer, responder, discussion director, and questioner) and shares the content from a book. In addition to practicing everyday oral language and academic language, students learn from their peers and develop thinking skills that are crucially needed for literacy and language development.

Houk (2005) advises teachers to consider opportunities and constraints when grouping ELLs with non-ELLs, ELLs with a same L1, and ELLs with different L1s. For example, in a heterogeneous group where non-ELLs serve as a language model for ELLs, ELLs are forced to communicate in English with non-ELLs. Teachers need to provide comprehensible input for the group while not lowering the quality of instruction. In a homogeneous group with L1, ELLs are given an opportunity to use L1 and experience at a lower anxiety level. However, they lose the opportunity to learn from their non-ELL peers. The challenge for teachers is to find instructional materials in L1 and to be minimally proficient in oral L1. In a homogeneous group of ELLs with different L1s, ELLs receive instruction at their level and tend to take more risks as they are not competing with their non-ELL peers. However, they do not have peers as a language model. While grouping ELLs, teachers strive to strike a balance between these three types of grouping for optimal learning opportunities for ELLs.

Promoting the Use of Linguistic Patterns

Students will not internalize any linguistic patterns just by listening to a teacher's explanation and modeling and then memorizing them. Having students use these patterns in oral production contributes to their growth in mastery of English. For example, students learn that the sentence *May (or Can) I help you?* is acceptable while the sentence *Will I help you?* is not. Here are ways that you can encourage students to use linguistic patterns in daily activities:

➢ Have students use each linguistic pattern in a small-group activity (see the example of Mrs. Barlow teaching the sentence structure *The setting is _____*) after the guided practice.

➢ Post the linguistic patterns on the wall so that students can refer to them if needed in their oral and written communication (see Figure 3.3 for an example from Mrs. Dominguez's third-grade class).

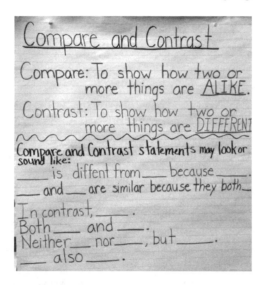

FIGURE 3.3. Linguistic patterns for compare and contrast.

➤ Have students use linguistic patterns for interpersonal communication (e.g., *Thank you! Thank you for _____. May I have your book?*).

➤ Reinforce the use of linguistic patterns during sharing (see Table 3.5).

Teaching Pronunciation

Read-aloud is a great way for teachers to model the correct way to pronounce English words. Having students listen to books on tape and watch TV and videos are also helpful for students to be exposed to pronunciation of English words. But for some ELLs, and in particular those at the beginning level, these ways may be not enough for them to learn how to pronounce English words correctly. Students may need more opportunities in and out of class.

Using an Online Dictionary

Both the Merriam-Webster Dictionary (*www.merriam-webster.com*) and The Free Dictionary (*www.thefreedictionary.com*) provide a pronunciation feature allowing a student to click a button and listen to a word pronounced.

Using Internet Resources

Learn English with Pictures and Audio (*www.my-english-dictionary.com*) has pictures of commonly used words and pronunciation of the words. Language Guide (*www.languageguide.org/english/*) offers categories of words and concepts and expressions (e.g., greetings). Every word and expression can be read aloud. Native language translation includes Dutch, Greek, Arabic, Spanish, Polish, Chinese, Japanese, Korean, Italian, French, Portuguese, Russian, and German.

Creating a Narrated PowerPoint Presentation of Words

The online dictionaries and the Internet resources may not be appropriate for all of your students. At times, it is necessary for you to create a narrated PowerPoint Presentation featuring the target words. An appropriate picture (downloadable from the Internet or clip art) representing the word will assist students in understanding it (see Figure 3.4 for a sample slide). Individual students can go through the slides at their own pace as many times as needed to learn the pronunciation and meaning of the words. Here are the steps for creating a PowerPoint presentation:

1. Type the word.

2. Add a photo, an animated image, or a clip art picture representing the word. Photos and animated images can be downloaded from the clip art of Microsoft Office Online (*office.microsoft.com/en-us/clipart/FX101321031033. aspx?pid=CL100570201033*)

3. Go to the menu in PowerPoint. Under "Slide Show," click on "Record Narration," and follow the onscreen instructions to record yourself saying the word.

4. Save your slide.

If there are students at the intermediate and advanced level, they can help with creating slides for words which they have mastered. You just record the pronunciation for each word. If there are native English-speaking students in the class, they can create each narrated PowerPoint slide by following steps 1–4.

FIGURE 3.4. A sample slide of the word *bridge*.

DIFFERENTIATED INSTRUCTION FOR ELLs LITERATE IN L1

Comparing and Contrasting English and L1

For ELLs literate in L1, an activity of comparing and contrasting L1 and English is good for practicing oral English and developing some level of metalinguistic awareness about L1 and English. You provide students with a focus for the comparison, such as sentence structure, tone of a sentence, idiomatic expression, diction, and formal versus informal expressions. It is helpful for students to discuss their areas of difficulty in English. Students may write up a paper on the comparison or develop a PowerPoint presentation to share with the class. This task can be completed as an individual activity when L1 is not shared by other students or as a collaborative activity when a group of students speak the same L1. The essays or PowerPoint presentations can be compiled into a class book on languages. During the process of comparing and contrasting, students get to practice oral language, research, reading, and composing skills. Similarly, you have a chance to learn about L1s and similarities and differences between English and L1s. When you invite students to participate in this activity, you send a powerful message to them that you respect and are interested in students' L1s and that you want students to be proud of their native language and maintain it.

ENGAGING FAMILIES

It is important for students to have opportunities beyond the classroom walls to learn more about English oral language and practice it to hone their proficiency. Students' families can help them achieve this goal. The role of families in students' oral language development is very significant, as they are with the students most times outside school. For family members speaking English, students can benefit from interacting with them. Family members speaking limited or some English can be listeners and "students" when ELLs are sharing and teaching what they have just learned at school about English. Additionally, the exchanges in L1 between the student and his or her family members help strengthen the L1 foundation, which in turn promote students' linguistic awareness about a language (Fillmore, 2000). Therefore, regardless of the English proficiency of family members, students' families can contribute to students' oral language development. Here are some ideas that you can share with students' families:

> ➢ Family members continue communicating with the student in L1, in addition to English.

> ➢ Students share with their family a new linguistic pattern learned at school (e.g., *I have _____. As soon as _____, I _____.*) by using the pattern and by having family members use the pattern. You can send home the pattern on an index card.

> ➤ A student shares with his or her family about a day at school. You can provide each family with a daily schedule and the student can fill in the details.

> ➤ The student and family members play a game of I Spy and take turns saying "I spy." In the beginning, the sentence is kept short and simple (e.g., *I spy a tree*). Gradually, the student and the family members can expand the sentence to include more details (e.g., *I spy a tall willow tree behind the small house*).

> ➤ Watch a TV show with the captions on. It is better to record the show. After the show, the student and his or her family can discuss new words and new linguistic patterns from the show.

> ➤ Discuss a TV show by commenting on the favorite and the least favorite part. You can send home a discussion guide (e.g., *Say something about your favorite part* [the part you like most]. *Why? Say something about your least favorite part* [the part you do not like]. *Why?*)

> ➤ A student and his or her family role play in a context familiar to them (e.g., supermarket, church, neighborhood park, family gathering) or in a context with which students have had a second hand experience (e.g., news broadcast, singing on *American Idol*). You provide the students and families with sample expressions used in the context (Table 3.4).

VOICE FROM THE CLASSROOM

Sarah Serrano
State Street Elementary School, South Gate, California

Teaching ELLs for 4 years at K, second, and fourth grades has opened my eyes to the incredible strengths and needs students bring into the classroom. Many decisions made in the classroom stem from what we believe about teaching and learning. I believe that all children have the ability to learn and that education should be accessible for all children. It is my job as a teacher to discover the knowledge, strengths, gifts, and talents that exist in each student and to encourage their innate curiosity through the discussion and exploration that arise from their natural interests. This philosophy is the underlying foundation for my decisions in teaching. Although there are some decisions regarding instructional programs that I cannot make, there are many scaffolds and instructional strategies that I can add to the required programs.

I supplement the mandated reading/language arts programs (Open Court and Into English!) with the strategies mainly taken from specially designed academic instruction in English (SDAIE), experience, and collaboration with colleagues. When planning, assessing, and teaching oral language development, I separate students' oral English level into listening and speaking, as I am aware that students understand much more English than they speak. When I differentiate instruction,

I look at their current level of both speaking and listening knowledge in English and instruct them individually, in a small group, and in a whole-class settings to meet them at their level, pushing them a step further using strategies and techniques such as realia, visuals, and manipulatives.

When developing oral English lessons for my ELL students, I use as much realia as possible. If the lesson discusses corn, I bring in a cob of corn and discuss the husk and how we take it off to get to the corn cob. Students would take turns holding the corn in order to feel, smell, and try tearing off the husk while discussing it with their neighbor. Using realia helps to bring the vocabulary to the concrete level. Another technique I incorporate is cooperative groups. During a read-aloud, we discuss the content of the book and review vocabulary, allowing students to interact with each other and with me about the content comprehensible to them. At the end of the book, student continue to have an opportunity to practice oral language through summarizing and acting out the story or by writing scripts with an alternative ending (in an language experience approach activity or during interactive writing) and acting them out.

When instructing about specific vocabulary or concepts, I make sure to speak slowly so that students can hear all of the sounds in the words that I am saying. Another strategy that I use often is repetition. I repeat the words, phrases, or concepts often in order to increase comprehension. When I am teaching a new word, phrase, or concept that a student does not quite understand, I repeat whenever I can in addition to describing and explaining it. The more I repeat, the greater the chance my students have of understanding and using that word. For example, during a read-aloud with kindergartners, I noted confused looks on many students when I got to the word *drip*. So I explained:

T: *Drip* is when water falls very slowly, when we try to turn off the water from the faucet and we didn't turn the handle tight enough. When we look at it, there is water still coming from the faucet very slowly and so the water is dripping. (I directed students' attention to the dripping water from the faucet in our classroom.) Say "drip."

Ss: Drip.

Later in the day, before recess, I reminded students to wash their hands. I went over to the sink and I demonstrated washing my hands.

T: Oh, look, I didn't turn off the faucet all the way so the water is dripping. Can you say "dripping"?

Ss: Dripping.

T: I'd better turn the faucet off all the way so the water doesn't drip. Good, the water is not dripping anymore. Let's line up to wash hands.

At the end of the day, during the rereading of the book, when I came to the page with the word *drip*, I gave the class another opportunity to discuss and share the meaning of the word *drip*.

T: Turn to your neighbor and tell them what the word *drip* means. Now, can some-one tell me what *drip* means?

Ss: It means when the water is coming down.

T: Thank you. Can someone tell me more about the word *drip*?

Ss: It is when the water is still coming but really slow like rain sometimes.

T: Very good. When you go home, go to the sink and show your mom or dad or grandma how the water can drip from the faucet and tell them what the word *drip* is.

The next day it rained, and I referred to the word *drip* throughout the day. At the end of the day, I asked students to draw a picture that showed the word *drip*. Some students drew a faucet with a little water coming out, others drew a slow rain, and one little boy drew spilled milk dripping off the table onto the floor and labeled it "drip."

Another strategy to encourage oral English language development is peer/group collaboration, which gives students an opportunity to develop their English language within the context of a lesson with contextual words that are written and/or drawn on the board, shown through realia, and spoken by myself throughout the lesson. Oftentimes if a student has trouble with a particular word or thought he or she wants to get across, a peer supplies the needed information. This gives both students a feeling of success and safety, a needed opportunity to speak English orally, and a chance to reinforce the concepts of the lesson.

For example, while teaching my second graders a math lesson on bar graphs, I invented a partner game to supplement the math worksheet. During the game, I walked by one peer group and heard the following conversation:

S1: Hey, you spinned blue so you got to color in the square on this side of the bar graph. That way it shows what you did, you know?

S2: Oh yeah. You're right. Now it's your turn to spin.

I walked to another pair of students and listened in.

S3: Look. We had more red spins than blue or yellow.

S4: How do you know?

S3: Because see here. The red has more boxes colored in on the bar graph than the blue or yellow. That means that red won. You get it?

S4: Oh yes. Now I get it.

I think the most important tip for teaching ELLs is to remember that they comprehend more English than they speak. This helps me to remember not to hold back higher level vocabulary during teaching, but just to explain, describe, illustrate, and repeat. It is equally important to continue instruction that pushes students one step further than where they currently are. I strive to achieve this by differentiating instruction through repetition, peer/group collaboration, individual and small group instruction, SDAIE strategies, and read-alouds.

CONCLUSION

In this chapter, I discussed ELLs' oral language development, the strengths they bring to learning, and difficulties they may experience. For identifying students' strengths and needs, I presented several classroom-based assessment tools. The strategies and activities, consistent with the overarching framework (the eight principles discussed in Chapter 1) and goals of instruction for oral language development, are geared toward preparing students to communicate in English for interpersonal and academic purposes. Mrs. Serrano's account about teaching oral language to ELLs reflects the importance of valuing what students have brought to school, scaffolding the learning process, and setting high expectations for ELLs at various proficiency levels. I hope that her sharing, along with the classroom examples presented, will enhance your understanding of ways of teaching ELLs oral language development.

CHAPTER 4

INSTRUCTION FOR PHONOLOGICAL AND ORTHOGRAPHIC KNOWLEDGE AND FLUENCY DEVELOPMENT

During a midyear staff meeting, teachers of ELLs at Magnificent View Elementary School gathered to discuss what they had observed about their students' development in phonemic awareness, phonics, spelling, and fluency. Ms. Gunn shared, "I have noted my fifth graders who are literate in Spanish or Vietnamese did much better in decoding and spelling than those who are not illiterate in their L1." Mr. White added, "I completely agree! I have been trying to help my fourth graders note the connection between phonics and spelling, and decoding and fluency. I have tried to teach these areas in an integrated way." Mrs. Le commented, "That's great! But that would be hard for me to do with my kindergartners. They are learning everything—the alphabet, phonemic awareness, phonics, and sight words. I have been feeling overwhelmed with the standards I need to cover." Ms. Sanchez raised another issue, "I thought that my second graders should have a good foundation in all these areas. But some of them don't. So I am always helping these students to catch up. Most of time, this process is frustrating for me and for the students."

It is common to hear what the teachers at Magnificent View Elementary school shared. Yes, it is difficult to teach very abstract elements of English to ELLs who are lacking in an oral language foundation. You probably would ask many questions, too:

1. How can I make teaching the abstract elements of English more interesting and connected to students' experience with and knowledge of L1?

2. How can I conduct classroom-based assessment to evaluate ELLs' development in phonemic awareness, phonics, spelling, and fluency?

3. How can I integrate phonemic awareness, phonics, spelling, and fluency in my teaching so that my students understand the interconnectedness of these elements?

4. How can I integrate the teaching of phonemic awareness, phonics, spelling, and fluency into reading and writing?

5. How can I teach older students with limited knowledge in phonics and spelling?

In this chapter, I provide an overview of ELLs' development in phonemic awareness, phonics, spelling, and fluency, highlighting the areas of strengths and difficulties ELLs possess. Then, I discuss different types of classroom-based assessment for identifying student strengths and needs in each area. The next section focuses on strategies and activities for teaching phonemic awareness, phonics, spelling, and fluency. The following section is about engaging families in supporting their children in these areas. To conclude this chapter, Mrs. Olivia Martinez, a first-grade teacher, shares her experience of teaching these areas.

DEVELOPMENT OF PHONOLOGICAL AND ORTHOGRAPHIC KNOWLEDGE AND FLUENCY

Phonological knowledge includes phonemic awareness and phonics. Orthographic knowledge is associated with how sounds are mapped into letters. (Refer to Chapter 2 for a detailed discussion of phonological and orthographic knowledge.) A student with phonemic awareness is able to identify the sounds in a word. This ability is crucial to the spelling process, where the student maps each sound in a word to its written form (a letter or letters). Meanwhile, the student's knowledge about spelling patterns makes this encoding process successful. For example, a student needs to know the rule of silent *e* after a long vowel in most English words in order to map the sounds /c/, /ā/, and /k/ and spell the word *cake*. In addition, orthographic knowledge assists students in decoding words quickly and efficiently. For example, in decoding the word *swing*, a student knowing the *-ing* pattern and the consonant cluster *sw* would have a much fast speed for decoding the word than a student who lacks orthographic and phonics knowledge and perceives the word as a group of individual letters, *s-w-i-n-g*. Just imagine how much time the second student loses in decoding a sentence and how laborious the decoding process is. Hence, interrelated knowledge of phonology and orthography is a key component of literacy development. Furthermore, an ability to recognize sight words and decode high-frequency words fast and automatically is closely related to reading fluency (Adams, 1990; National Reading Panel, 2000; Snow, Burns, & Griffin, 1998).

After reviewing research on developing literacy in ELLs in the past decades, August and Shanahan (2006) conclude that phonological and orthographic knowledge are important to ELLs in their literacy development. Along with existing research (Fitzgerald & Noblit, 2000; Lesaux & Siegel, 2003; Manis, Lindsey, & Bailey, 2004), a recent two-year study on Spanish-speaking students shows that Spanish-speaking ELLs' development of phonological awareness is similar to that of their native English-speaking peers, albeit with some differences (Fitzgerald,

Amendum, & Guthrie, 2008). Furthermore, phonemic awareness is an important predictor of reading success for young children (Adams, 1990; Juel, Griffith, & Gough, 1986; Stanovich, 1986). The research Yopp and Stapleton (2008) cited to support this close relationship between phonemic awareness and reading acquisition holds true for second language learners (e.g., Alegria, Pignot, & Morais, 1982; Carrillo, 1994; Naslund, 1990). Furthermore, phonemic awareness in one language (e.g., Spanish) can be transferred to another one (e.g., English) (Manis, Lindsey, & Bailey, 2004).

Similarly, based on the work with ELLs with different L1s, Bear, Helman, Templeton, Invernizzi, and Johnston (2007) conclude that ELLs go through similar stages of spelling development as their native English-speaking peers, though variations may exist:

> *Emergent*: Students use pictures, numbers, and letter-like writing to convey an idea. The writing may be in a horizontal or vertical order (e.g., a picture for an idea).

> *Letter name*: Students spell easily heard beginning and end sounds and experiment with short vowel sounds (e.g., *ct* for *cat*; *bad* for *bed*).

> *Within word*: Students experiment with long vowel sounds (e.g., *cot* for *coat*; *pae* for *pay*).

> *Syllables and affixes*: Students experiment with spelling multisyllabic words (e.g., *litel* for *little*).

> *Derivational*: Students experiment with spelling words derived from their base words (e.g., *plesure* for *pleasure*).

Related to phonological and orthographic knowledge is the development of sight vocabulary, which contributes to fluency and comprehension (August & Shanahan, 2006). When a student stumbles over many words in a text, a sign that the student cannot decode fast enough and does not possess a large sight vocabulary, the student has to devote more time and energy to decoding, leaving little time and energy for comprehending what is being read. Mastery of sight vocabulary and decoding strategies lessens a linguistic and cognitive load during reading so that students can focus on constructing meanings.

Areas of Strengths and Difficulties

One salient strength for ELLs is that they bring to English learning strategies they have used with L1 (e.g., generating a phonics rule inductively, experimenting with the rule, modifying it, and experimenting with the modified rule). While developing phonological and orthographic knowledge, ELLs use such strategies to help them cope with the learning process. The number of learner strategies that can be transferred from learning L1 to learning English vary from student to student, depending on their experiences with L1 and the nature of L1. For example, older ELLs literate in L1 may have more strategies to reply on if their L1 is similar to

English. Another strength is that some specific aspects of L1 may become useful in helping students learn English. For example, ELLs speaking an alphabetic L1 have more advantages than their peers speaking a nonalphabetic L1 in learning phonemic awareness, letter–sound relationship, and spelling patterns. Another interesting strength is that children learning a second language seem be more attuned to sounds in a second language than their monolingual peers (August, Calderón, & Carlo, 2000).

As discussed in Chapter 2, the areas of difficulty for phonology and orthography are derived from several sources. One source is the sounds that do not exist in L1 and/or the sounds pronounced differently in L1 and in English. Different letter combinations and their corresponding sounds may confuse students (e.g., the sounds for the letter *o* when it is combined with another letter in English: *oa* in *coat*; *oi* in *oil*; *oy* in *boy*; *ou* in *tough*; *ow* in *how*). The three layers of English spelling (alphabet, pattern, and meaning) may not exist in L1 or may not be as transparent as in English (Bear, Helman, Templeton, Invernizzi, & Johnston, 2007). Furthermore, for students whose L1 cannot be analyzed at the phoneme level (e.g., Chinese), it is extremely difficult to understand individual phonemes in an English word. Another source of difficulty comes from the concept of less consistent letter–sound relationships in English (e.g., unlike Spanish).

Goals of Instruction

Table 4.1 summarizes the characteristics of ELLs' different proficiency levels in the areas of phonemic awareness, phonics, spelling, and fluency (Bear, Helman, Templeton, Invernizzi, & Johnston, 2007; California State Board of Education, 2006; TESOL, 2006). Be aware that the characteristics are not inclusive, and a student can be at different levels for different areas. For example, an ELL can be at an intermediate level for spelling due to some experience with English spelling, but at a beginning level for fluency.

One ultimate instructional goal is to help students understand the interconnectedness of phonological and orthographic knowledge and fluency in reading and writing. To achieve this goal, daily instruction should highlight such a connection (Cummins, 2003; Peregoy & Boyle, 2009). For example, after discussing the rule that only one sound is pronounced for double consonants (e.g., *tt* in *little* and *ss* in *class*), you can ask students to find other words fitting the pattern that they have heard and/or read from such language input as books and daily conversation. In so doing, you help students understand that what they are learning about phonics has practical applications with language they hear and read and that the rules exist in books and other print. As Cummins (2003) emphasizes, it is important to provide "explicit instruction in phonemic awareness, letter knowledge, and concepts about print, together with a significant instructional focus on actual reading" (p. 175).

Another instructional goal is to contextualize the process of learning the abstract concepts in phonological and orthographic knowledge through students' direct application in their reading and writing (August & Shanahan, 2006;

TABLE 4.1. Student Proficiency Levels and Characteristics for Phonological and Orthographic Knowledge and Fluency Development

Level	Characteristics
Beginning	• Recognizing and producing easily audible English phonemes that are similar to those in L1 and that are nonexistent in L1 • Recognizing some sight and high-frequency words • Making attempts to decode unknown words • Spelling or copying words with symbols (letter-like or not), environmental print, words posted in the classroom environment, and/or sight or high-frequency words; invented spelling evident in most words. • Having a choppy fluency
Intermediate	• Recognizing and producing not easily audible English phonemes similar or dissimilar to those in L1 • Recognizing a large group of sight and high-frequency words • Applying letter–sound correspondence to decoding unknown words • Spelling correctly most words with regularities, and using invented spelling mostly in multisyllabic words and those with irregularity • Having an average fluency
Advanced	• Recognizing and producing most English phonemes similar or dissimilar to those in L1 • Mastering most sight and high-frequency words • Applying decoding strategies for multisyllabic words with regularities and irregularities • Making fewer spelling errors for words with regularities, and spelling multisyllabic and derivational words with regularities and irregularities with some errors • Having a higher level of fluency

Bear, Helman, Templeton, Invernizzi, & Johnston, 2007). It seems to be easy to adopt an isolated approach to teaching phonological and orthographic knowledge, as such knowledge deals with the smallest units of sound (phoneme) and the smallest units with meaning (affixes, roots, and words) in English. The detrimental effect of such an approach is the production of word callers who can decode (or bark at) words without understanding the meaning of each word, not to mention the meaning of the phrase and the sentence where the word is present. To avoid this, it is necessary to strike a balance between an integrated approach and direct instruction. For instance, it is not enough for you to deliver direct instruction on the CVCe pattern (e.g., *take*) during which students identify words that fit the pattern. You must continue to observe students' spelling and reading of CVCe words. Students may treat the word *come*, when they encounter it in reading, as the one fitting the pattern. If this happens, you should first praise the student for applying the rule and then conduct a mini-lesson about the exception to the rule.

A final instructional goal is to encourage students to continue developing L1 (August & Shanahan, 2006; Genesee, Geva, Dressler, & Kamil, 2006; Yopp & Stapleton, 2008). Further development in a language with which students have some foundations would contribute to students' growth in knowledge about English. As discussed in Chapter 2, all languages have a system of phonology and orthography, albeit with some differences. If a student whose L1 is an alphabetic language understands the concept that words are made up of individual sounds, the student would transfer this knowledge to learning letter–sound relationship in English. For ELLs whose L1 is a nonalphabetic language, the transfer, though minimal, is still possible. For example, a student with Chinese as L1, in which there are not transparent character–sound relationships, may still understand the concept of rhyming in English. This concept is similar in English and Chinese, though in Chinese, a same ending sound in a pair of rhyming words does not have the same strokes (spelling of a character).

ASSESSING PHONEMIC AWARENESS, PHONICS, SPELLING, AND FLUENCY

While data from standardized assessments provide teachers with some information, the information can be misleading or incomplete, thus making the assessment data less valuable and less accurate. Imagine how accurate the data would be from a phoneme segmentation assessment administered to a newcomer who has been exposed to English mostly in school for a month! To remedy this shortcoming of assessments, you or someone who speaks L1 can conduct a phoneme segmentation assessment in L1 (if it can be analyzed at the phoneme level). Classroom-based assessment (explicit or embedded) can provide additional information about your students. For example, in an explicit assessment, to find out if a student pays attention to a vowel sound in the middle of a word, you may use a group of words with different vowel sounds (e.g., *hit/hat*; *coat/bat*), and have the student tell whether the middle sounds are the same or different. In an embedded assessment, you observe and document students' strengths and needs in applying phonological and orthographic knowledge (e.g., recognizing and using sight words in reading and writing). The value of this type of implicit assessment is the data informing you how well students transfer knowledge learned from direct instruction to the real contexts of reading and writing.

Explicit Assessment

Using Words Familiar to Students

Barone and Xu (2008) provide an excellent example of how student interest and familiarity offer an advantage for students (feeling a sense of success) and for teachers (learning about both strengths and needs). As shared in Chapter 1, a kindergartner at a late-beginning proficiency level was able to recognize and demonstrate her understanding in more words on a word list created by her teacher based on her favorite TV show, *Kim Possible*, than the words on a word list from a reading inventory. Here are some ideas for using words familiar to students.

➢ Use words in L1 (if an alphabetic language) to assess phonemic awareness and phonics.

➢ Use familiar English words from students' oral language, books, and other texts (e.g., classroom labels) to measure students' phonemic awareness and phonics and orthographic knowledge.

➢ Use English words from students' interests to assess their sight words.

Using Spelling Inventories

Bear, Templeton, Invernizzi, and Johnston (2008) offer spelling inventories for students at different grade levels. Each spelling inventory assists teachers to pinpoint the strengths and needs for specific letters and sounds. As shown in Figure 4.1, the student has mastered beginning and final consonants, short vowels, consonant digraphs and blends, and long vowels, but has shown difficulty in spelling words with complex vowel patterns and two-syllable words. For example, the student misspelled *fright* as *frite*, *chewing* as *choowing*, *shouted* as *showted*, *spoil* as *spoyolle*, and *riding* as *wriding*. This type of detailed, specific information regarding student's strengths and needs in spelling may be not available at all in a traditional, more formal spelling assessment. Bear, Helman, Templeton, Invernizzi, and Johnston (2007) also offer spelling inventories in Spanish, Chinese, and Korean.

FIGURE 4.1. Spelling inventory.

Oral Reading

Oral reading has been used with non-ELLs as a way to measure oral fluency. When used with ELLs, teachers must pay attention to several issues. One issue is the linguistic load of the passage for oral reading. It is important to select a passage with words and linguistic patterns at an *i* + 1 level as Krashen (1981) suggests (*i* stands for the input at the student's current proficiency level, and +1 stands for a level that the student needs to reach in language learning). Otherwise, the assessment would yield only what the student is lacking.

Another issue to consider is whether to select a text that the student has not read, or a text that the student has read or that has been read to the student. In making a sound decision, you should consider such factors as the students' proficiency level, grade level, and personality. For example, a young ELL who is a risk taker probably can handle a text that has been never read to him or her. An older ELL at the minimum of the early production level can probably read this type of text as well. On the contrary, for an older ELL who is often conscious of oral mistakes, it is best to allow the student to read a text that has been read to him or her before. If a student has done oral reading of familiar texts for several assessment sessions, in the near future, you can phase out the familiar texts and introduce texts the student has not read. Here are the step for oral reading:

1. Have the student read aloud a text of 100 words (texts for beginning readers with pictures may have fewer than 100 words).

2. Record and time the oral reading.

3. Transcribe the tape (if there is time) or listen to the recorded oral reading numerous times.

4. Calculate words per minute (wpm) to check the oral fluency.

5. Complete the Fluency Assessment Chart (see Appendix I).

6. Have the student read the same text a few weeks later and complete the Fluency Assessment Chart to see if there is any improvement.

7. Document the second reading of the same text.

8. Repeats steps 6 and 7 with the same text for the subsequent readings.

Matching a Target Sound or a Spelling Pattern

At the end of a lesson on a target sound (e.g., long-*a* sound) or a spelling pattern (e.g., *-dge* as in *judge, fudge, pledge*), you can ask individual students to tell or write down known words that contain the target sound or spelling pattern. If there is a rule regarding the sound or spelling pattern, students should explain it to you. For example, after a student has come up with a list of words containing *-dge* at the end of each word, you can ask the student why this group of words does not fit the pattern of CVCe. If the student can explain that *-dge*, not CVCe, is the pattern, he or she has demonstrated a good understanding of the letter combination, *-dge*. This assessment can be done quickly in a few minutes to inform you if the students have mastered the target sound or spelling pattern.

Embedded Assessment

In order to know how students apply phonological and orthographic knowledge in real contexts of reading and writing, teachers can practice "kid watching" (Goodman, 1985). That is, you observe students' literacy behaviors and explore their work samples. If you often hear a student say a sound for each letter in an unknown or difficult word and then blend the sounds together to say the word, you have learned something about this student's decoding ability. In a similar situation, another student, however, might look around the classroom trying to find a clue to an unknown word (e.g., a picture for the word on the word wall). This behavior informs you that this student may lack an appropriate decoding strategy, but that the student is resourceful and strategic as he or she tries to capitalize on available resources.

Furthermore, students' writing samples shed light on their knowledge of sight words and orthography. As the spelling inventory indicates (see Figure 4.2), the spelling stages of a fourth grader are between the middle- and late-within word pattern and the early syllable juncture. The student's writing sample reveals another spelling need, that is, the spelling of common words ("whith" for *with*, "Saterday" for *Saturday*, "wath" for *watch*, "freind" for *friend*, and "Afrecan" for *African*). Armed with this new discovery, the fourth-grade teacher can provide additional assistance to help the student master sight and high-frequency words.

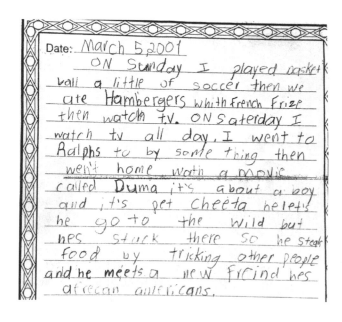

FIGURE 4.2. Spelling inventory and writing sample.

STRATEGIES AND ACTIVITIES FOR PROMOTING PHONOLOGICAL AND ORTHOGRAPHIC KNOWLEDGE AND FLUENCY

Given that students' phonemic awareness and knowledge of phonics, orthography, sight words, and fluency are interrelated, all the strategies and activities presented here (see Table 4.2) facilitate students' development of proficiency not in just one area, but in other related areas. For example, the use of alphabet books is not limited only to developing students' alphabetic knowledge. Teachers can use these books to teach sight vocabulary and different spelling patterns. When one book is used for multiple purposes, you provide students—especially those at the beginning level—with the advantage of familiarity with the content and language. Knowing the book well enables students to concentrate on the instructional focus of the lesson.

Phonological and orthographic knowledge is abstract. Having students perform tasks related to this type of knowledge requires students to develop metalinguistic awareness, a higher level of knowledge about a language. This task is challenging for non-ELLs, and even more for ELLs (Peregoy & Boyle, 2009). Most of us probably still remember the experience of learning this type of knowledge when we were in a reading methods course. Just imagine how difficult it would be for ELLs to analyze the oral and written units of a language unfamiliar to them. Thus, it is important to contextualize their learning process as a way of scaffolding so that students can go through it in a manageable way (Yopp & Stapleton, 2008).

Direct instruction is important, as it helps students to take a focused exploration of a phonological or an orthographic concept or a new word through first observing a teacher demonstration and modeling and then engaging in guided and independent practice. However, ELLs, like non-ELLs, cannot grow in their knowledge by relying only on direct instruction. ELLs must hear and read common and content-related words repeatedly. When students possess words with various sound and spelling patterns in their repertoire, they will do better with direct instruction and other activities (e.g., word sorting). Otherwise, words for instruction seem abstract to them as they cannot make any connection to them. It is important for ELLs to have opportunities to *discover* and *experiment* with, not memorize, phonological and orthographic patterns and sight vocabulary during reading and writing (August & Shanahan, 2006; Bear et al., 2007; Moats, 2000; Yopp & Yopp, 2000). If L1 is similar to English, teachers engage students in examining the similarities and differences in sounds, letter–sound correspondence, and spelling patterns. This practice nudges students to observe patterns and formulate rules about decoding or spelling patterns.

Additionally, teachable moments and on-the-spot mini-lessons provide valuable instruction for ELLs. For example, while teaching some common spelling patterns for the long-*e* sound (i.e., *e* as in *me, ee* as in *feet, ea* as in *meat*), some students may mention the word *key*, which has a less common spelling pattern, *ey*, for the long-*e* sound. You can seize this teachable moment to expand students' knowledge

TABLE 4.2. Proficiency Levels, Instructional Foci, and Strategies and Activities for Phonological and Orthographic Knowledge and Fluency Development

Proficiency level	Instructional foci	Strategies and activities
Beginning	• Providing oral and written comprehensible input • Teaching English phonemes first that are similar to those in L1 and then those that are nonexistent in L1 • Teaching phoneme manipulation • Teaching sight and high-frequency words • Teaching common word families and spelling patterns • Providing reading and writing opportunities • Encouraging invented spelling for experimenting with simple letter–sound correspondence	• Teaching phonemic awareness • Teaching difficult sounds • Using alphabet, rhyming and pattern, and concept books, and books about collecting words • Using environmental print • Using media texts • Teaching decoding strategies • Word sorting • Using a word wall • Repeated reading • Using Readers' Theater
Intermediate	• Providing oral and written comprehensible input • Mapping phonemes onto print during spelling and decoding letters during read-aloud • Strengthening sight and high-frequency words • Teaching complex word families • Applying various decoding strategies to unknown single-syllable or multisyllabic words • Spelling multisyllabic words with irregularities • Providing reading and writing opportunities • Encouraging invented spelling for experimenting with complex letter–sound correspondence	• Teaching phonemic awareness • Teaching difficult sounds • Using alphabet, rhyming and pattern, and concept books, and books about collecting words • Using environmental print • Using media texts • Teaching decoding strategies • Word sorting • Using a word wall • Repeated reading • Using Readers' Theater
Advanced	• Mastering most sight and high-frequency words • Applying decoding strategies for multisyllabic words with irregularities • Understanding the relation of derivational words • Spelling multisyllabic and derivational words with regularities and irregularities with fewer errors • Providing reading and writing opportunities	• Teaching difficult sounds • Using concept books and books about collecting words • Using environmental print • Using media texts • Teaching decoding strategies • Word sorting • Using a word wall • Repeated reading • Readers' Theater

about the spelling patterns for the long-*e* sound. In so doing, you have accomplished more than the planned lesson on spelling patterns for the long-*e* sound.

Teaching Phonemic Awareness

Yopp and Yopp (2000) suggest a sequence for phonemic awareness instruction, beginning with a focus on rhyme and moving onto a focus on syllable units, onset and rime, and finally phonemes. The sequence is appropriate for ELLs, because it begins with a bigger unit (rhyme) that is easier for students to hear in a word and ends with the smallest unit of sound that can only be heard if students can break a word into individual sounds. Further, this sequence lowers the difficulty level of developing phonemic awareness for ELLs whose L1 cannot be analyzed at a phoneme level. Yopp and Yopp's guidelines have direct implications for phonemic awareness instruction for ELLs.

1. Activities for phonemic awareness should be age appropriate. For ELLs, appropriate content and tasks are also important. If students do not know the words they hear, they may feel anxious and try to understand the words rather than participating in an activity. Similarly, if a student whose L1 can only be analyzed at a syllable level, it would take more practices for the student to learn segmenting a word into individual sounds.

2. Teachers should provide students with specific, focused, direct, and purposeful phonemic awareness instruction. ELLs benefit from a lesson that focuses on one concept at a time and that gives students a sense of the utility of the concept so that it can be applied quickly. For example, in teaching word families containing the short-*a* sound, you can focus on one or two patterns familiar to students (e.g., -*at*: *hat*; -*an*: *can*). After modeling how to segment the -*at* and -*an* family words by onset and rime, you can ask students to think of other words they know that fit one of the patterns and segment them into onset and rime. This narrow focus enables students to concentrate on mastering these two patterns and experience some level of success.

3. Phonemic awareness instruction is only one part of a comprehensive literacy program. This point is important for ELLs in that they are playing a catch-up game with their native English-speaking peers in all aspects of English language and literacy. If a focus of instruction is only on phonemic awareness, students would not receive appropriate and adequate instruction in other areas. Further, teachers should allocate the amount of time (usually 10 to 30 minutes per session) based on their students' needs and curricular standards. Apart from direct instruction, teachers can integrate practices of phonemic awareness into a daily class routine. For example, before recess, lunch, or dismissal, you could say, "If you have one syllable in your name, you can line up first at the door." You change the criterion every few days, weekly, or after the class has mastered the task. This activity can be applied to other concepts (e.g., number of phonemes in students' names).

In addition to the preceding three points, some modifications are needed. Gesture can be used as a support for students to remember what they are supposed to do. For example, for blending three sounds into a word, you can say each sound while putting your right hand on the upper, middle, and lower part of your left arm respectively. Then, you can move your right hand across your left arm from the upper to the lower part to indicate blending. For segmenting, you can move one hand in front of your chest up and down once for each segmented sound. Similarly, visual aids, such as an Elkonin box (Figure 4.3), help students see the number of sounds and each letter or letters representing each sound. Older ELLs lacking in phonemic awareness would benefit from focused instruction on phonics rules. For example, during teaching a decoding rule for words with a prefix or suffix (a prefix or a suffix itself is a syllable), you have students segment words with affixes first from their respective base words. If needed, conduct a discussion on the meaning of each prefix or suffix. In so doing, you combine instruction for phonemic awareness, phonics, and vocabulary development. A final modification is that some groups of students speaking a certain L1 (e.g., syllabic L1) may require more time with certain aspects of phonemic awareness than those with L1 similar to English.

Teaching Difficult Sounds

Some English sounds do not exist in L1 or are pronounced differently than similar sounds in L1. In order to help students learn these sounds and map them into print, teachers first need to identify the difficult sounds (See Table 2.2). One way to do so is to learn about an L1 (see Chapter 1 and Chapter 2), and the other is to observe students' oral output during various settings (e.g., a focused lesson or a small-group activity). Here are some ideas for teaching difficult sounds:

➢ Pronounce clearly each sound that does not exist in L1 or that is a little bit different from the one in L1. For example, the sound /b/, confusing to Spanish-speaking ELLs, should be pronounced as a stop sound, without an added /ə/ at its end as /bə/.

➢ Although consonant sounds are relatively stable in their pronunciation, phonetic variations, largely due to the vowel sound the consonant precedes, are common (Moats, 2000). Consider the slight difference in the sound /b/ in these words: *bat, book*, and *bake*. Given that, when teaching the sound /b/, teachers

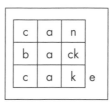

FIGURE 4.3. An Elkonin box.

should include words illustrating slight variations in the sounds for the letter *b*. In so doing, students are exposed to the variations.

➢ If a sound is easily confused with a sound in L1, it might be helpful to compare and contrast these two sounds. For example, the letters *ng* in Tagalog are pronounced like the letters *nk* in the word *bank*. When teaching the sound of the rime *-ing* you can direct students' attention to considering the letters, *-ing* as one unit of sound /iŋ/ rather than /ink/ as if the sound /i/ were added to the sound of the letters *ng*, which would be /nk/ in Tagalog. Other examples of comparison include: *chair–share, chip–ship* (for Spanish-speaking ELLs); *thing–ting, thin–tin* (for Chinese-, Japanese-, and Vietnamese-speaking ELLs). Sometimes it is necessary for you to discuss with students the sound and spelling patterns of a group of letters in L1 and in English. For example, you can begin a discussion on the letter *s* in the beginning of most English words (e.g., *school, slow, sleep*) and the letters *es* in the beginning of most Spanish words (e.g., *escoba* [*broom*], *escrito* [*writing*], *escuchar* [*listen*]).

➢ Lastly, when it comes to helping students master difficult or confusing sounds, it is appropriate to deliver small-group instruction on the same set of difficult sounds experienced by a group of ELLs.

Using Children's Books

Children's books are a valuable source of language input for ELLs. Although each instructional program comes with a collection of children's books, teachers always need to supplement the books at their students' levels of proficiency and background knowledge. Barone and Xu (2008) suggest that in selecting additional books for instruction, teachers should consider the factors of vocabulary, familiarity, and interest. The vocabulary of a written text may contain multisyllabic, formal, and content words that are not part of students' receptive language. Too much difficult vocabulary in a book lowers the possibility of students' successful experience with comprehending and enjoying it, which may increase their anxiety level.

Books that bring to students a sense of familiarity include bilingual books, books on native culture, books on life experiences students have encountered, books related to students' popular culture interests, books related to the same concept or to a theme under study, books written by the same authors, and book series (see p. 166, Chapter 6 for sample books). Interesting books often relate well to students through a familiar topic and playful language. Figure 4.4 lists some examples of alphabet books, rhyming books, pattern books, and concept books. From all types of books, students can word hunt based on a criterion set by you. The criteria can range from easy ones like finding words beginning with a target letter/letters or sound in one book (e.g., the letter *b*, or /b/; *sh* or /sh/) to difficult ones for which students have to go through different books (e.g., words containing the letters *gh* in the beginning as in *ghost*, middle as in *night*, or end as in *sigh*). Then you can have students sort these words into different groups of sounds the letters *gh* make or do not make.

(text resumes on page 98)

Sample Books	How to Use the Books
ALPHABET BOOKS	
Ada, A. F. (1997). *Gathering the sun: An alphabet in Spanish and English*. New York: Lothrop, Lee & Shepard. Baker, A. (1994). *Black and white rabbit's ABC*. New York: Larousse, Kingfisher, Chambers. Calmenson, S. (1993). *It begins with an A*. New York: Hyperion Books for Children. Carlson, N. (1997). *ABC, I like me*. New York: Viking. Ehlert, L. (1989). *Eating the alphabet: Fruits and vegetables from A to Z*. San Diego, CA: Harcourt. Lobel, A. (1981). *On market street*. New York: Greenwillow Books. Lyne, A. (1997). *My name is . . . A*. Dallas, TX: Whispering Coyote Press. Martin, B., Jr., & Archambault, J. (1989). *Chicka chicka boom boom*. New York: Simon & Schuster. McGinley, P. (1948). *All around the town*. Philadelphia: J. B. Lippincott. McPhail, D. (1989). *Animals A to Z*. New York: Scholastic. Pallotta, J. (1998). *The flower alphabet book*. Watertown, MA: Charlesbridge. Shannon, G. (1995). *Tomorrow's alphabet*. New York: Greenwillow Books. Slate, J. (1996). *Miss Bindergarten gets ready for kindergarten*. New York: Dutton. Wood, A. (2001). *Alphabet adventure*. New York: Scholastic.	• Preview the book (browsing or showing the picture, activating prior knowledge on content of the book, and talking about key vocabulary if needed). • Read the book and talk about each letter and the words beginning with the letter. • Talk about other information related to the word representing a letter. • Have students supply words beginning with a target letter. • Post the alphabet words on the word wall. • Have students follow the pattern of the book to make a class alphabet book on a topic.
RHYMING BOOKS	
Hopkins, L. B. (1990). *Good books, good times*. New York: HarperCollins. Rogasky, B. (1994). *Winter poems*. New York: Scholastic. Root, P. (1998). *One duck stuck*. Cambridge, MA: Candlewick Press. Seuss, Dr. (1957). *The cat in the hat*. New York: Random House. Seuss, Dr. (1968). *The foot book*. New York: Random House. Seuss, Dr. (1986). *The cat in the hat comes back*. New York: Beginner Books. Shaw, N. (1991). *Sheep in a shop*. Boston: Houghton Mifflin. Shaw, N. (1992). *Sheep out to eat*. Boston: Houghton Mifflin.	• Preview the book (browsing or showing the picture, activating prior knowledge on content of the book, and talking about key vocabulary if needed). • Read the book and discuss with the class the book content. • Read the book again if needed. Have students pay attention to the rhymes. • Have students identify pairs of rhyming words. • Have students sort words into groups of rimes (rhyming words).

(continued)

FIGURE 4.4. Children's books.

Sample Books	How to Use the Books
RHYMING BOOKS *(continued)*	
Shaw, N. (1997). *Sheep trick or treat.* Boston: Houghton Mifflin. Sierra, J. (2000). *There's a zoo in room 22.* Orlando, FL: Harcourt Brace.	• Have students supply rhyming words under each rime group. • Have students use a pair or more of rhyming words in an oral or written sentence or sentences. • Post the rhyming words on the word wall.
PATTERN BOOKS	
Carle, E. (1997). *From head to toe.* New York: HarperCollins. Kalan, R. (1981). *Jump, frog, jump.* New York: Greenwillow Books. Martin, B., Jr. (1983). *Brown bear, brown bear, what do you see?* New York: Holt, Rinehart & Winston. Martin, B., Jr. (1991). *Polar bear, polar bear, what do you hear?* New York: Holt, Rinehart & Winston. Miranda, A. (1997). *To market, to market.* San Diego: Harcourt. Numberoff, L. (1985). *If you give a mouse a cookie.* New York: Harper & Row. Numberoff, L. (1991). *If you give a moose a muffin.* New York: HarperCollins. Numberoff, L. (1998). *If you give a pig a pancake.* New York: HarperCollins. Numberoff, L. (2000). *If you take a mouse to a movie.* New York: HarperCollins. Numberoff, L. (2002). *If you take a mouse to school.* New York: HarperCollins. Taback, S. (1997). *There was an old lady who swallowed a fly.* New York: Viking. Williams, L. (1986). *The little old lady who was not afraid of anything.* New York: HarperCollins.	• Preview the book (browsing or showing the picture, activating prior knowledge on content of the book, and talking about key vocabulary if needed). • Read the book and discuss with the class the book content. • Read the book again if needed. Have students pay attention to the words, phrases, or sentences repeated throughout the book. • Have students identify repeated words, phrases, or sentences. • Have students imitate the words, phrases, or sentences in their oral or written expression. • Post repeated words on the word wall.
CONCEPT BOOKS	
Carle, E. (1993). *Today is Monday.* New York: Scholastic. Crews, D. (1984). *School bus.* New York: Greenwillow Books. Garza, C. L. (1996). *In my family/En mi familia.* Danbury, CT: Children's Press. Hoban, T. (1986). *Shapes, shapes, shapes.* New York: Morrow. Hoban, T. (1987). *26 letters and 99 cents.* New York: Greenwillow Books.	• Preview the book (browsing or showing the picture, activating prior knowledge about the concept if needed). • Read the book and discuss with the class the book content. • Read the book again and have students pay attention to the words representing the concept.

(continued)

FIGURE 4.4. *(continued)*

Sample Books	How to Use the Books
CONCEPT BOOKS *(continued)*	
Hoban, T. (1990). *Exactly the opposite*. New York: Greenwillow Books. Kalan, R. (1978). *Rain*. New York: Greenwillow Books. Kightley, R. (1986). *Opposites*. New York: Little, Brown. Lillie, P. (1993). *When this box is full*. New York: Greenwillow Books. Simon, N. (1954). *Wet world*. New York: Candlewick Press. Walsh, E. S. (1989). *Mouse paint*. San Diego, CA: Harcourt Brace.	• Discuss words representing the concept (if needed, using a graphic organizer to illustrate the relationship among the words). • Have students use the words in an oral or a written sentence or sentences. • Post the words on the word wall.

FIGURE 4.4. *(continued)*

Alphabet Books

Alphabet books help students learn about the name and sound of each letter of the English alphabet. Many alphabet books go beyond listing a letter and a word beginning with that letter. Some weave the alphabet words into an interesting story. For example, *Old Black Fly* by Aylesworth (1992) describes the troubles that an old black fly is making in his journey. "He ate on the crust of the Apple pie. He bothered the Baby and made her cry" (n. p.). Many other books present rich content knowledge associated with concepts (e.g., *The Boat Alphabet Book* [Pallotta, 1998]). There are bilingual books with both the English and Spanish alphabets. A variety of alphabet books provides a useful set of resources for students at various levels in the same class. For example, an alphabet book with each letter and one or several words on each page is more suitable for young ELLs. An alphabet book with a storyline or one specific content topic would help older ELLs learn the English alphabet while learning the content. This type of book would not make older ELLs feel embarrassed, as they are not just reading simple alphabet books for young ELLs. Rather, they are also learning about content-specific concepts whose labels begin with letters of the alphabet.

Further, teachers can vary the ways they use alphabet books. For young ELLs, you can initially focus on a picture for each label and then move on to the label itself and the letter in the label. If there is more text about the label, you may or may not share it with the class until later, depending on how well students are understanding the letters. For older ELLs, you may choose to share and discuss with students the content concepts in an alphabet book, and then introduce each letter by presenting a label related to each concept.

Rhyming and Pattern Books

In order for students to learn about rimes (word families, phonograms) and sight words, they must encounter as many words and as often as possible. Rhyming books and pattern books provide this type of language input that fosters ELLs' memorization of words (Meier, 2004). High-quality children's books with rhyming patterns should be used to supplement decodable texts from a mandated basal program. These books, full of live, authentic language, often tell an interesting story and make learning about rimes and sight words less boring. Some rhyming books with a complicated storyline may be suitable for older ELLs. The predictability in pattern books helps lower students' anxiety and increase their participation. Some books repeat only a phrase or a sentence (e.g., the sentence, "I can do it," in Carle's [1997] *From Head to Toe*). Others repeat a key phrase or a sentence across pages (e.g., Taback's [1997] *There was an Old Lady Who Swallowed A fly*). Still others repeat not the exact words, but a linguistic pattern (e.g., If _____, _____. in Numberoff's (1985) *If You Give a Mouse a Cookie*).

Concept Books

Scholars have advocated teaching language through content and teaching content through language (Collier, 1995; Freeman & Freeman, 2009; Freeman, Freeman, & Mercuri, 2002; Krashen & Terrell, 1983; Peregoy & Boyle, 2009). Concept books not only inform students of subject-area content, but also offer a rich set of language input (meaning, pronunciation, and spelling pattern of sight words and content vocabulary). Variations in topics and language difficulty levels support students at the diverse levels of language proficiency, experiences with L1 and English, and content and general world knowledge. Concept books are helpful even for older ELLs who may have mastered the concepts but need to learn an English equivalent for each known concept.

Books about Collecting Words

A key step for students' active participation in learning about the sounds, spelling, and meanings of different words is to encourage students to collect interesting words from their reading texts and their environment (Barone & Xu, 2008). Teachers may explain to students how to collect words, but that is not enough. Reading books about collecting words to and with students helps them understand the process and purpose of collecting words. In *Max's Words* (Banks, 2006), Max develops a hobby of word collection by cutting out words from newspapers and magazines. Max collects "small words" (e.g., *the*), "bigger words" (e.g., *hungry*), words "that made him feel good" (e.g., *baseball*), words related to food (e.g., *pancakes*), and words of "his favorite colors" (e.g., *brown*). The word collection leads Max to use a dictionary. Finally, Max uses the collected words to make a story. After reading this book, you can encourage students to collect their words related to a phonological concept (e.g., words containing a long vowel sound in the middle), an orthographical concept (e.g., spelling patterns of the long-i sound), a specific group of words (e.g., verbs), or content-specific words (e.g., words related to weather). The words collected by students from their receptive language become relevant, age- and proficiency-appropriate texts for teaching. In this way, students save their teacher a great deal of time searching for materials that are comprehensible, relevant, and interesting to students. Other books about collecting, learning, and using words include: *Bunny Cakes* (Wells, 1997), *Buz Words: Discover Words in Pairs* (Kelley, 2006), *Donavan's Word Jar* (DeGross, 1994), *Max's First Word* (Wells, 2004), *The Boy Who Loved Words* (Schotter, 2006), and *Word Wizard* (Falwell, 1998).

Using Environmental Print

In a recent study on environmental print (EP), Xu (2008b) examined 600 EP collected from eight culturally and linguistically diverse cities in southern California. She found that EP in cities with a higher population of immigrants is more visible and accessible in the surroundings of schools and residential areas than in cities with a lower population of immigrants. Bilingual EP were present in all cities. There is a wide range of words in EP related to different content categories (e.g., food) and linguistic categories (e.g., regular nouns). For example, there are more than 100 different types of EP related to traffic signs on the freeways and streets (e.g., *yield, right turn only*). Given the diversity and accessibility of EP, integrating it into teaching brings to ELLs something familiar and meaningful and assists students to become more aware of English and L1 in their environment (Diaz-Rico & Weed, 2006). Figure 4.5 shows an example of alphabetizing the circled words from environmental print in English and Chinese. Further, students should be encouraged to observe and interact with EP (e.g., including EP in their writing). It is important for teachers to have students bring to class their EP (see Xu & Rutledge, 2003, for details).

Students' names are a meaningful source of print in a classroom environment. Many teachers alphabetize them on a list and post the list on the classroom wall as a way to help students learn the alphabet. Mrs. Barlow, a kindergarten teacher of ELLs at the beginning and early intermediate levels, used her students' names, in what she called three cycles with names, to teach phonics, sight words, and sentence structure. In the first cycle (see Figure 4.6), Mrs. Barlow chose a student's name and guided her students to locate the beginning, middle, and ending letters in the name. Then Mrs. Barlow and the students counted the syllables in the name, and Mrs. Barlow recorded the name by syllables. Finally, Mrs. Barlow and the students came up with real and nonsense words that rhyme with the name.

During the second cycle (see Figure 4.7), Mrs. Barlow engaged her students in comparing and contrasting two names at a time. In writing the names on chart paper, Mrs. Barlow used a red color for vowel letters and a black color for consonant letters. She then guided her students in reviewing the beginning, middle, and end letters and number of syllables in each name. Finally, Mrs. Barlow prompted her students to identify the letters shared by both names and drew a Venn diagram to show this.

During the last cycle (see Figure 4.8), Mrs. Barlow focused again on individual names. She had students produce a sentence following each of the three linguistic patterns: _____ has _____; _____ likes _____; can _____. She first brainstormed with a student whose name was a focus of a discussion and wrote down what the student had done, liked to do, and could do. Then she had the student complete each sentence pattern. Finally, Mrs. Barlow and the class choral-read the written sentences.

FIGURE 4.5. Alphabetizing environmental print.

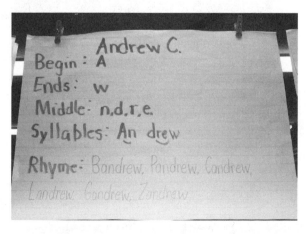

FIGURE 4.6. First cycle with names.

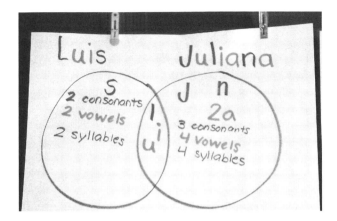

FIGURE 4.7. Second cycle with names.

During the activities of three cycles with names, the kindergartners learned many linguistic concepts associated with their names and developed a sense of pride in their own names. Furthermore, Mrs. Barlow's way of customizing the third cycle reflects that she values each student as a person with varied experiences and illustrates well how to tap into students' funds of knowledge (Moll, Amanti, Neff, & Gonzalez, 1992). These activities would be also appropriate for older ELLs who are lacking in basic English literacy skills. They most likely will not be embarrassed by a discussion of their own name. Such a discussion may prompt students literate in L1 to notice the similarities and differences in letter sounds and spelling patterns in L1 and English and to share their discoveries with you and the class. Hence, an opportunity of comparison of two languages might emerge naturally through a meaningful discussion about names.

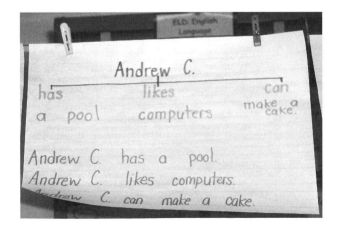

FIGURE 4.8. Third cycle with names.

Using Media Texts

Media texts with images, sounds, and animation provide visual and contextual support for ELLs' comprehension. Teachers can integrate media texts into teaching. These texts can be part of center activities. The websites for the television programs *Between the Lions* and *Sesame Street* feature games (e.g., Play Elmo Rhymes [*pbskids. org/sesame/index.html*] and Blending Bowl [*pbskids.org/lions/games/blending.html*]). Scholastic has a website for Clifford where there are phonics and alphabet games (*teacher.scholastic.com/clifford1*). Having students play games or complete activities reduces the cognitive load that unfamiliarity may otherwise cause.

Here are two interesting websites with a focus on the English alphabet: Star Falls (*www.starfall.com*) and Julia's Rainbow Corner (*www.juliasrainbowcorner.com/ html/letters.html*). Alphabet Photograph (*www.alphabetphotography.ca*), appealing to older ELLs, displays photos of everyday objects resembling the alphabet letters, and students can make any word using the photos. Little Explorer: Picture Dictionary with Links (*www.enchantedlearning.com/Dictionary.html*) lists many content-specific words for each English letter. For each word, there is a picture and a link offering more information about the word. There are seven different language versions of the dictionary (e.g., English–Spanish).

Online dictionaries are valuable for students to learn English alphabet and sight vocabulary. Internet Picture Dictionary (*www.pdictionary.com*) has words organized in categories (e.g., animals) in five languages (English, French, German, Italian, and Spanish) and activities for practicing and reviewing words (e.g., word scramble). Chinese Picture Dictionary (*classes.yale.edu/chns130/Dictionary/ index.html*) and Free Dictionaries Project (*www.dicts.info*) provide pictures for bilingual words. Yiddish-Hebrew-English-German-Russian-French Picture Dictionary (*www.ibiblio.org/yiddish/Vort/vort-m_files/error.htm*) shows a picture with a label in multiple languages. Another good example is Korean Multimedia Dictionary (*www.indiana.edu/~koreanrs/kordic.html*). Learn English with Pictures and Audio (*www.my-english-dictionary.com*) presents words with pictures and pronunciation.

Teaching Decoding Strategies

During explicit teaching of decoding strategies, ELLs observe teacher modeling of the steps of each strategy, practice the strategy with teacher guidance and immediate feedback (guided practice), and participate in independent practices. Phonic analysis is a strategy in which a student identifies the sound for each letter in a word and then blends the sounds together to say the word. In teaching this strategy, it is better to choose words with each letter or letter combination representing a sound (e.g., *hat, desk, stop*). Words with a silent *e* at the end, for example, would confuse students, and especially those whose L1 has a relative consistency in letter–sound correspondence. Students might come up with a sound for the letter *e*. This strategy, however, slows down decoding speed as a student has to think about a sound for each letter or set of letters. Decoding by analogy can remedy the problem. In decoding by analogy, a student uses his or her knowledge of rimes to decode another word sharing the same rime. For example, the student uses the rime *-atch* from *watch* to decode the word *match*. Obviously, when breaking a word into an onset and a rime, the student can decode it quickly.

Phonics analysis and decoding by analogy do not generally work well with multisyllabic words. One reason is that it takes a student some time to blend all the sounds. The letters in a multisyllabic word may be silent or have sounds very different from those when represented in isolation (e.g., the sound of *-tion* vs. the sound of each letter in *-tion*). Further, rimes are easily identified in single-syllable words, but not in multisyllabic words. Given that, syllabic analysis becomes a better strategy, particularly for older ELLs who are expected to read content-area texts with many multisyllabic words. With this strategy, students use one or more generalization rule about syllabication to decode a multisyllabic word. For example, according to the rule that an affix is a syllable, the word *teaching* is broken down into two syllables, *teach* and *ing*. While a teacher's manual might specify which rule to teach and supplies examples of words for instruction and practice of the rule, you need to make sure that the supplied words are familiar to students. Otherwise, a phonics lesson loses its focus as you have to spend time explaining the words. If the supplied words are unfamiliar to students, it is necessary for you to identify other words familiar to them.

All three strategies—phonics analysis, decoding by analogy, and syllabic analysis—do not help students understand the meaning of a word. Morphemic analysis is a decoding and vocabulary strategy in which students decode a word not by a rime, sounds, or syllables, but by morphemes. With this strategy, while decoding a word, students have already gotten the meaning of the word (providing that they know the meaning of the morphemes). This strategy is helpful for older ELLs when decoding content-area words.

In teaching decoding strategies, it is important that one strategy is focused, practiced, and reinforced before a new strategy is introduced. You may diverge a little bit away from a pacing chart of your school district, which does not really support ELLs' mastery of each strategy. It is also appropriate to deliver differentiated instruction to different groups of students with different needs. Lastly, a discussion is a critical part of strategy instruction. Irregularities in English letter–sound correspondence call for teachable moments. Discussing irregularities with students encourages them to explore the effective use of strategies and phonological and orthographic aspects of words. For example, when a student uses his or her knowledge of the word *sign* to decode the word *signature* the student may miss the sound of /g/. A mini-lesson can be conducted on the spot or later about derivational words like *signature*. You would explain to the student (and to others with a similar need) that a letter (or letters) in a derivational word can be pronounced differently than when in the base word. You then list other pairs, such as *please* and *pleasure*. This lesson can be easily connected to spelling instruction about how meaning-related words are spelled similarly even though they may be pronounced differently.

Word Sorting

Sorting pictures and words based on sounds, spelling patterns, or other linguistic features (e.g., parts of speech) has long been an instructional strategy with non-ELLs (Bear et al., 2008; Cunningham, 2008; Ganske, 2006). Bear et al. (2007) remind us that ELLs at various spelling stages would benefit from word sorting to increase their orthographic knowledge and sight vocabulary. I might add that learning to sort is an opportunity for young ELLs to develop concepts of classifying, comparing and contrasting, and labeling. Keep in mind that materials for word sorting (either pictures or words) should be familiar to students, and it is better to have students collect pictures and words from environmental print, books, and other texts they have read or have been read to and comprehend. When students are asked to find words from an unfamiliar text (e.g., highlighting the letter combination of *th* in words in a newspaper), it disconnects a word study and sorting activity from actual reading.

Although picture sorting is more common with young ELLs, older ELLs lacking in alphabet and orthographic knowledge and sight vocabulary would benefit from it (see Figure 4.5). Students will be clear about how to sort words if they are provided with a guide word for each group into which they can sort words (Bear et al., 2007). For example, the guide words in Figure 4.9 are *cap, pig,* and *hat.* There are many ways to sort pictures or words (see the list that follows). You can choose and combine several ways of sorting to best support your students. For example, you may have a group of beginning students first alphabetize words and then group the words by the beginning sounds. The first activity makes the second one a little bit easier. For a group of students who are confused about the short-*a* and long-*a* sounds, they can first participate in an activity of sorting the words into a group of long-*a* and a group of short-*a* sounds. Students can further sort words in each group into different spelling patterns. It is possible that students with certain L1s should participate in some sorting activities more often than another group of

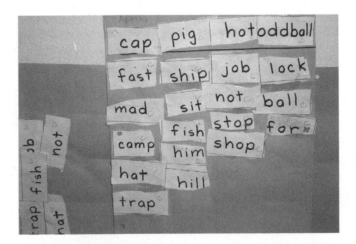

FIGURE 4.9. Sorting short-vowel sounds.

students speaking a different L1. For example, students speaking Chinese, Korean, or Japanese may be engaged in more word sorting related to affixes, as the concept does not exist in their respective L1s.

➢ *Sorting by alphabetical order*

Example: *blue, green, orange, purple, red, white, yellow* (*Mouse Paint* [Walsh, 1989])

➢ *Sorting by the number of letters*

Example: three-letter word (*red*); four-letter word (*blue*); five-letter words (*green, white*); six-letter words (*orange, purple, yellow*) (*Mouse Paint* [Walsh, 1989])

➢ *Sorting by a beginning or an ending letter or letters*

Example: *there, three, the, they, then* (*Mouse Paint* [Walsh, 1989])

➢ *Sorting by a beginning or an ending sound*

Example: *piece, paper, paint, puddles, purple, part* (*Mouse Paint* [Walsh, 1989])

➢ *Sorting by rimes (word family)*

Example: *-oor* (*floor, door*), *-ail* (*tail, pail, wail*), *-old* (*hold, told*), *-ink* (*drink, sink, stink, think*), *-est* (*rest, best*), *-ight* (*fight, night*) (*How Do Dinosaurs Get Well Soon?* [Yolen, 2003])

➢ *Sorting by a short or long vowel sound*

Example 1: words with long-*o* sound: *casserole, doze, drove, grocery, old, rode, stole* (*Old Black Fly* [Aylesworth, 1992])

Example 2: sorting short-vowel sounds (see Figure 4.9)

Example 3: a comparison of long-*a* and long-*e* sounds (see Figure 4.10)

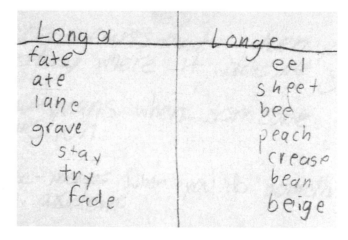

FIGURE 4.10. A comparison of long-*a* and long-*e* sounds.

➤ *Sorting by spelling patterns*

Example: the long-*e* sound for the letter *y* in two-syllable words: *sunny, windy, cloudy* (*Weather Words and What They Mean* [Gibbons, 1990]); the long-*i* sound for the letter *y* in one-syllable words: *dry, try, fly, fry*

➤ *Sorting by the number of syllables*

Example: one-syllable words (*hot, snow, wind*); two-syllable words (*sunny, windy, cloudy, humid, raining*); three-syllable words (*cumulus, snowflurries, nimbostraus*); four-syllable words (*temperature, evaporate, humidity*); five-syllable words (*cirrocumulus, stratocumulus*) (*Weather Words and What They Mean* [Gibbons, 1990])

➤ *Sorting by affixes*

Example: words with affixes (see Figure 4.11)

➤ *Sorting by spelling rules*

Example: spelling rules for adding a suffix (see Figure 4.12)

➤ *Sorting by parts of speech*

Example: words from Figures 4.11 and 4.12: nouns (*sellers, savings, retailer, transaction, competition, spoonful*); adjectives (*continuous, adjustable, biggest, continuous*); adverb (*wonderfully*); verb (present and past participles used as adjectives) (*sleeping, participating, delivered, reinvented, unlimited*)

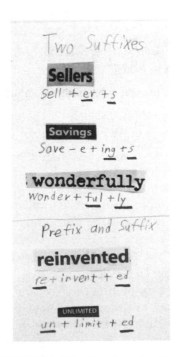

FIGURE 4.11. Words with affixes.

FIGURE 4.12. Spelling rules for adding a suffix.

➢ *Sorting by grammatical rules*

Example: past tense of regular and irregular verbs (*Old Black Fly* [Aylesworth, 1992])

<u>Regular verbs</u>: *bothered, buzzed, coughed, crawled, danced, dozed, frolicked, landed, lapped, licked, nibbled, pestered, played, sliced, sniffed, snoozed*

<u>Irregular verbs</u>: *ate, drove, got, hid, lit, made, ran, rode, slept, stole*

➢ *Sorting by easily confused sounds*

Example: different sounds for the letters *ou*: short-*u* sound (*tough, rough, thorough*); long-*o* sound (*dough, although, though*); diphthong (*about, house*); short-*o* sound (*should, could*)

Whether students are sorting words and pictures independently, within a group, or during a lesson's guided or independent practice, it is important for you to observe carefully students' performance and identify teachable moments. In Figure 4.9, the student put the word *fast* incorrectly under the *cap* column and the word *ball* correctly under the *oddball* column. After noticing the error, the teacher first praised the student for putting the word *ball* correctly under the *oddball* column and then explained to the student about the word *fast*. "You are right. The word *fast* has the letter *a*. But it does not say the short-*a* sound. Do you hear a short-*a* sound in /fəst/. Say the word yourself. Is the word *fast* just like the word *ball*? It does not say a short-*a* sound."

During the process of each sorting, you should find a few minutes to talk with students about the process of sorting and about the words. You may begin with praise or encouragement and then proceed to ask questions. For example:

> ➤ "What are your groups for the words? Why did you sort your words this way?"

> ➤ "How is your way of sorting different from how we were sorting the other day?"

> ➤ "I wonder if this word should stay in this group."

> ➤ "Can you think of another group for this word (or these words)? Do you think these words belong to this group? If not, what is a group for them?"

> ➤ "Do you know these words? All right, tell me what this word [saying the word] means."

This kind of talk is similar to a think-aloud, which helps you understand how a student sorts words and why the student makes a mistake. For example, some Spanish-speaking students at the beginning level may tend to group rhyming words mostly based on an ending sound, not a rime (e.g., *hit-feet, can-sun*). After talking with the students, you might learn that in Spanish, most rhyming words ending in a vowel sound (e.g., *cueva-activa* [*cave-active*]). The students transfer their understanding of the concept of rhyming words in Spanish (rhyming words share the same ending sound) to sorting words in English. Once the source of confusion is identified, a focused mini-lesson can be planned.

Word Wall

The use of a word wall is important for ELLs as they develop phonological and orthographic knowledge and sight vocabulary. The words displayed by categories provide support for students' understanding of the relationships among the words and the concepts illustrated by these words. For example, when two groups of words, the group beginning with the letter *b* (e.g., *book, ball, baby, bat*) and the group beginning with the letter *v* (e.g., *visit, van, verb, vegetable, vacation*), are on display, Spanish-speaking students obtain reinforcement about the difference in sound between /b/ and /v/, which is often confusing to them.

Several modifications are necessary for the use of a word wall for ELLs. For beginning ELLs in all grade levels, pictures are necessary to accompany each word on a word wall. If necessary, you can outline the shape of each word so that students will see the differences in letter formations (e.g., the letters *h* and *l* in *help* are taller than the letters *e* and *p*). This simple extra step benefits students whose nonalphabetic language's written form does not differ much from word to word (e.g., all Chinese characters are in a square shape). For older ELLs with limited sight vocabulary, a personal word book is a good alternative. In a word book, as in a personal dictionary, a student writes words that are difficult to spell or confusing in meaning that he or she has encountered during lessons and personal reading and writing. The student may include a pronunciation key, definition, and/or picture for each word. You can encourage the student to refer to the book for words during writing and talks with their peers.

Another modification is a more frequent visit with the words on the word wall. You can direct students' attention to the words by prompting them to make a connection. For example, before introducing another spelling pattern for the long-*a* sound, *ea* as in *great*, you can review the patterns displayed on the word wall. "We have learned CVCe as in *lake*, *ai* as in *wait*, and *ay* as in *play*. Who can give us more words other than those listed on the wall?" You can then write each word given by students on a card and place the cards under the appropriate pattern. A word wall becomes handy when you need to address a possible L1 interference in a specific area. For example, you can ask a student speaking an L1 that does not have articles (i.e., *the*, *a*, and *an*) to put an article in front of a noun in a linguistic pattern. Holding up a book, you would say, "This is my book. I can say, *I have book*. Ming [a Chinese student], can you find a word from the word wall [pointing to the word wall] that goes before the word *book*?"

Here are types of words that can be displayed on a word wall:

➢ Consonant blends and clusters (e.g., *bl-*: *black, blend, blind, blow*; *spl-*: *splash, split*)

➢ Consonant digraphs (e.g., *th-*: *thing, the, think*; *ph-*: *photo, phone, phonics*)

➢ Rimes (word family) (e.g., *-ock*: *sock, clock, block, rock, knock*)

➢ Short-vowel patterns (e.g., *-at*: *cat, hat, sat*; *-ad*: *dad, had, glad*; *-and*: *and, hand, sand*)

➢ Long-vowel patterns (e.g., CVCe: *lake, made, cake*; *-ai*: *wait, rain, train*; *-ay*: *day, play, say*; *-ey*: *they, whey*; *-ei*: *weigh, eight*; *-ea*: *great, steak*; *-a*: *flavor, favor*)

➢ High-frequency words (e.g., *the, a, an, desk, table, book, teacher, student, clock, whiteboard*)

➢ Oddball words (e.g., silent *b*: *doubt, subtle, comb, thumb*; exception to CVCe: *love, come*)

➢ Synonyms and antonyms (e.g., *happy-glad*; *big-small*; *long-short*)

➢ Key words from a book (e.g., from the "Three Little Pigs": *the, house, pig, wolf, straw, stick, brick, blow down, huff, puff, chimney*)

➢ Words related to a concept (e.g., order words [see Figure 4.13])

Teaching Fluency

Repeated Reading

When repeated reading is used with ELLs, one modification is crucial. A book for repeated reading cannot be too difficult due to many words that students cannot decode and understand on their own. If a book is too difficult in this way, repeated

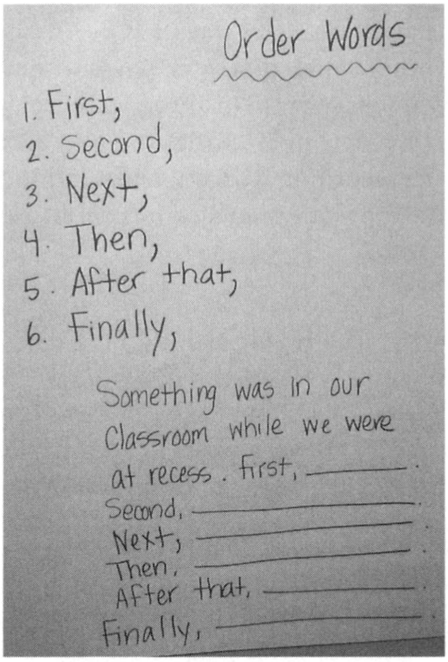

FIGURE 4.13. Word wall.

reading would not improve students' fluency. Rather, it would make students feel less competent and increase their anxiety level. A general rule is that if there are more than five words on each page that students cannot decode on their own, even if the book has been read aloud, the book is too hard, thus not appropriate for repeated reading. Sentence structures is another factor to consider in selecting a book for repeated reading. When a student's fluency does not improve after repeated readings of a text in terms of word per minute and number of miscues (mistakes that occurred in oral reading), you need to investigate a possible reason. At times, a student may be paying too much attention to illustrations, a visual cue for decoding. If this is the case, you may let the student read the book with illustrations and the typed text from the book without illustrations. Through a comparison, you may find out the reason for unimproved fluency, and a focused lesson targeting fluency can be planned.

Readers' Theater

Readers' Theater is appropriate with ELLs across language proficiency and grade levels as long as you select an appropriate script and assign a manageable role for each student. ELLs at a beginning level may just say a word or a phrase from a book with a repetitive pattern; ELLs at an intermediate or advanced level can play a narrator or a character who would say more words. Although there are many Readers' Theater scripts available for your immediate use, I strongly recommend that you choose books with a lot of dialogue that students have read or that have been read to them and that they have enjoyed. Let each student choose his or her part and then practice the part for several days before the performance. For picture and chapter books with not much dialogue, you can guide students in rewriting one section of the book into a script. This process serves as a great exercise for practicing reading comprehension and writing. You may record a Readers' Theater performance and share the recording with students and their families, who would enjoy a sense of pride. The recording can also be part of assessment data for fluency.

DIFFERENTIATED INSTRUCTION FOR ELLS LITERATE IN L1

It is very likely that students literate in L1 possess limited phonological and orthographic knowledge and sight vocabulary in English. Tapping into students' literacy strengths in L1 can help facilitate their development and knowledge in English.

> ➤ Have students sort words in English and in L1 and compare the similarities and differences in sorted groups. Have them share the comparisons with the class and with you.

> ➤ Have students compare and contrast sounds similar and dissimilar to those in L1. In particular, have them explore sounds represented by different letters or letter combinations. Have them share the comparisons with the class and with you.

> ➤ Use bilingual books to teach phonological and orthographic knowledge and sight vocabulary.

> ➤ Encourage students to collect bilingual words from environmental print, and use them in various activities related to sounds and spelling patterns.

> ➤ Have students compare and contrast decoding strategies used for English and L1. Have them share the comparisons with the class and with you.

ENGAGING FAMILIES

Phonological and orthographic knowledge, related to students' metalinguistic awareness, is abstract, and requires prolonged exposure to language in and outside school. Family members can contribute to ELLs' development of such knowledge:

> ➤ Students and their families sing in L1 or in English and recite poems or nursery rhymes with a component of sound manipulation (Yopp & Stapleton, 2008).

> ➤ Students and their families play games in L1 or English involving sound manipulation and identifying a target letter/letters, or sound.

> ➤ Family members read to and with students books in L1 or in English that illustrate language play (e.g., rhyming books, books with tongue twisters).

- ➤ Students and their families watch together—and sing or say along while watching—*Sesame Street* and *Between the Lions* (with captions on).
- ➤ Students and their families collect words from environmental print and other texts (e.g., books, Internet texts) related to a phonological or an orthographic concept.
- ➤ Students and their families sort collected words and discuss words.
- ➤ Students read aloud a favorite book to their family as fluency practice.

VOICE FROM THE CLASSROOM

Olivia Martinez
Glassell Park Elementary, Los Angeles, California

I am currently in my ninth year of teaching, and the majority of my students in grades 1 to 4 have been ELLs. I have always taught in English but have provided support by using SDAIE strategies and the students' L1s when possible. Although I primarily work with native Spanish speakers, I have also worked with ELLs speaking Armenian, Mandarin, and Tagalog.

Over the past nine years, my philosophy of teaching ELLs has been molded by my experiences with students. Cummins's concepts of BICS and CALP have helped me to better understand my students' various stages of language acquisition. Krashen's concept of affective filter is also an important part of how I work with ELLs. It is a necessity to create an environment where children feel safe to take risks and make mistakes. I also value Krashen's concept of comprehensible input and try to imbed this idea in all of my interactions and lessons with children. Furthermore, I believe that all of my students bring into the classroom certain funds of knowledge including their L1s. I make sure that my students know that I value their funds of knowledge by encouraging them to express themselves, read, and write in their L1.

I currently teach in a first-grade English immersion classroom with sixteen ELLs and two students mainstreamed from a special education class. About half of my students are ELLs at ELD (English language development) levels 2 and 3 (level 4 is the highest), who typically speak Spanish at home and English in the classroom. The materials from Open Court are typically at my ELL students' frustration level. I supplement this program with more "authentic" learning experiences such as Readers' and Writers' Workshops. During Readers' Workshop, students read meaningful material at their instructional and independent levels, enabling them to develop their phonics skills and build fluency. I teach guided reading lessons and do word sorts with struggling readers. These activities allow me to focus on specific sound/spelling patterns while helping my students become more fluent readers.

I also often modify the Open Court curriculum by rewriting at least one of the reading selections as a Readers' Theater piece, which is used to build fluency and discuss story elements. I also use repeated reading to develop fluency and monitor progress to assure that these interventions are effective. I approach this goal of developing fluency through sight word development, decoding skills, and authentic reading opportunities. For example, when working with small groups, I use decodable and/or sight word books such as *The Tug* (High Noon Books) to reinforce sight words and decode CVC words. We blend words that are in the story as well as nonsense words that focus on the particular sound the story highlights. When I have found that nonsense words are confusing for ELLs with very limited English proficiency, I have used real words to teach phonics and vocabulary. As their vocabularies increase, I begin to use nonsense words to assess their ability to decode. We also practice the sight words featured in the story by reading them and then finding them in the text, and then reading the story together again and independently throughout the week.

This year I have started using word sorts to develop word recognition and spelling skills. These sorts have been helpful for all levels of my students. Lately, I have asked the students to do sorts in pairs. ELLs at a lower level get paired with students with higher language and reading abilities. This leads to some beneficial language experiences for my ELLs. As I walk around and listen to the pairs, I realize that they are discussing the sorts and often using more language than I have originally anticipated or than when they had done the sorting alone. For example:

S1: Put it right there.

S2: Where does the card go?

S1: "Sit"—it goes with the "-it" words.

S2: Okay. Now it's your turn. Did you read your card?

S1: Yeah, "kit" . . . "-it." It goes right there.

S2: My turn. "Shot" . . . "-op" . . . "lot" . . . "shot."

S1: No, it doesn't say "-op," it says "-ot." See "shot" . . . "-ot."

S2: Oh yeah, you're right.

I also used interactive writing to integrate phonics, spelling, and fluency. I typically use this strategy during ELD, science, social studies, or art. For example, in an integrated unit on Diego Rivera we were able to create sentences about concepts such as color and self-portraits. We first come up with a sentence that we want to write and then students come up one at a time and write a word. As each student comes up, the class helps the student sound out the word. Interactive writing is a great opportunity to remind students about word boundaries, capitals, and periods. When the sentence is completed, we read it aloud. The sentence is then placed on a bulletin board where students can see it (see Figure 4.14). I feel that interactive writing is an authentic way to teach all three components. We often read the sentences for fluency building. Students feel a sense of pride for having written part of a sentence.

I feel that learning has to be meaningful to the learner. For ELLs this poses a particular challenge since their understanding of new concepts and vocabulary

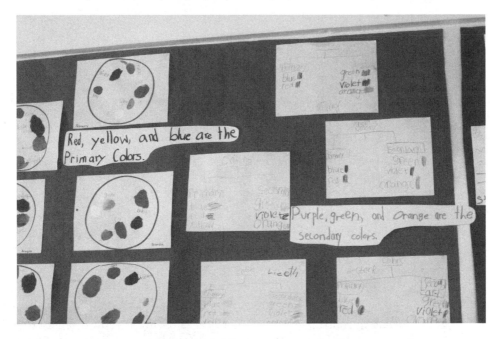

FIGURE 4.14. Interactive writing.

may be limited. It is therefore our job as teachers to make content as comprehensible as possible. Literature should be used for phonics lessons when possible, which helps connect phonics to something concrete. All too often we isolate the skills associated with learning to read. This may be necessary at times. However, whenever possible I believe that we should imbed lessons on skills in more authentic reading and writing experiences.

CONCLUSION

This chapter dealt with abstract aspects of language learning (phonological and orthographic knowledge and fluency), which pose special difficulties for ELLs. In presenting classroom-based assessment and strategies and activities, I stressed the importance of contextualizing assessing and teaching abstract phonological and orthographic concepts within meaningful, authentic reading and writing activities. All the classroom examples shared in this chapter and Mrs. Martinez's account of her experience of teaching reflect such importance. Furthermore, I directed your attention to the selection of instruction materials and differentiated instruction for students at various proficiency and grade levels. It is my hope that this chapter offered you ideas for teaching phonological and orthographic knowledge and fluency that you would integrate into your own teaching.

CHAPTER 5

INSTRUCTION FOR VOCABULARY DEVELOPMENT

Prior to the beginning of the school year, the teachers of ELLs at the fifth and sixth grades in Beachfront Elementary School gathered together to discuss vocabulary instruction. Ms. Tran stated that the content-area curriculum for her fifth graders was not modified for addressing the needs of her students. Mr. Johnston shared that his sixth graders had problems with academic vocabulary, and the textbooks did not have many activities to focus on vocabulary. As one sixth-grade teacher put it, "ELLs are constantly in the position of catching up in language and literacy development with their English-speaking-only peers, and how can they do well with mastering academic vocabulary?" Mrs. Goodman shared her interest in building her teaching on her sixth graders' literacy in L1.

The preceding scenario reflects teachers' view on the importance of academic vocabulary in ELLs' literacy development and their efforts and challenges in teaching academic vocabulary to ELLs. If you were one of the teachers at this school, you might ask these questions:

1. How do ELLs develop their vocabulary knowledge?
2. How can I conduct classroom-based assessment to evaluate ELLs' vocabulary knowledge?
3. What instructional strategies and materials can I use in teaching academic vocabulary?
4. How can I integrate vocabulary instruction into other components of literacy instruction?
5. How can I build my vocabulary instruction on students' literacy in L1?

These questions are just a few examples of teachers' concerns about how to best teach vocabulary to ELLs. In this chapter, I begin with an overview of ELLs' vocabulary development, with a focus on academic vocabulary, highlighting areas of strengths and difficulties for ELLs. Next, I discuss different types of classroom-based assessments for students' vocabulary development. The subsequent section centers around strategies and activities for vocabulary development. The following section is about engaging families in supporting their children's vocabulary development. I conclude this chapter with account of teaching ELLs vocabulary shared by Ms. Renee Gonzalez-Gomez, a reading specialist.

VOCABULARY DEVELOPMENT

Vocabulary development is an ongoing and complex process. Oral language development in the early years helps build children's receptive knowledge about words. After entering school, their vocabulary knowledge continues to expand (Anderson & Nagy, 1992; Graves, 1987). Evidently, ELLs are at a disadvantage to begin with. Often, they are pressured to develop vocabulary knowledge that should have been developed before schooling and to expand their vocabulary knowledge while expanding their knowledge about English. Goldenberg, Rezaei, and Fletcher (2005) remind us that even for ELLs equipped with a good body of vocabulary knowledge in L1, their reading performance still lags behind their native English-speaking peers.

The process of vocabulary development is ongoing because there are so many words to learn. Further, there are so many dimensions of a word that a student needs to master. Nagy and Scott (2000) identify five components of vocabulary knowledge: incrementality, polysemy, multidimensionality, interrelatedness, and heterogeneity. *Incrementality* of vocabulary knowledge means that children's mastery of each word results from multiple exposure to it over a long period of time. The *polysemy* aspect requires a learner to know different shades of meanings (e.g., different meanings of the word *run*). Upon mastery of *multidimensionality*, a learner knows how to say the word, how to use the word within an appropriate context, what other words are related to it (e.g., the words *jog, dash, dart*, and *scurry* are related to the word *run*), and what are the morphemic features of the word (e.g., the suffix *-er* in *runner* and the prefix *re-* in *rerun*). When a learner understands the *interrelatedness* of vocabulary, he or she has a good knowledge of how one word is related to another (e.g., *cumulus, cirrus*, and *stratus* are related to the word *cloud*). When a learner has developed the *heterogeneity* aspect of vocabulary knowledge, he or she has a large amount of vocabulary from which to choose words to use when needed. For example, a student with academic vocabulary would talk and write like a content authority by using a specific set of subject-area words (e.g., words used by a biologist).

The complexity of vocabulary development is further evident in its close relationship with speaking, listening, reading, and writing. A strong relationship between reading and vocabulary knowledge is well researched (e.g., Blachowicz & Fisher, 2006, 2007; Davis, 1944, 1972) This relationship is no exception to ELLs' vocabulary development. If an ELL has limited sight vocabulary, the student will experience a hard time learning new words by using contextual clues provided by sight words that the student may not know. For ELLs, oral proficiency also affects vocabulary development. For example, an ability to understand what is being said provides an ELL an opportunity to learn about new words or new meanings of known words and to try to communicate with the speaker using these words. Furthermore, the more an ELL communicates with others in oral and written language for a meaningful purpose, the more vocabulary the student gains through incidental learning, and the more chances the student has to be successful in literacy development (Carlo, August, & Snow, 2005; Folse, 2004; Nation, 2001).

Academic Vocabulary

Academic vocabulary are *discipline-related words* that are often abstract and concept-related. For example, when students are learning the two words *Venus* and *Mercury*, it is not enough to know just their spelling and pronunciation and understand that they are the labels for two planets in the solar system. More important, students must understand the characteristics of Venus and Mercury and their relationship to other planets in the solar system. *Words used across disciplines* are shared by different fields. The verbs *solve* and *analyze*, for instance, appear in texts on math, science, and social studies. The noun *system* can be found in *the solar system, the digestive system, the ecosystem, the judicial system, the political system*, and *the school system*. Furthermore, some academic words have their equivalents in everyday English. For example, everyday English words for the academic words *discuss* and *convention* are *talk about* and *meeting*, respectively. Some common words possess a meaning specific to disciplines. Consider the words *table* and *plane* in the following two sentences: *This table lists the changes in temperature across two seasons. Geometric shapes with plane surfaces include circle, square, triangle, rectangle, trapezoid, rhombus, and parallelogram.*

Academic vocabulary has *morphological and phonological features* different from those for most words in everyday English. Academic vocabulary are usually derivational words comprised of a prefix and/or a suffix (e.g., *evolution, metamorphosis*). Unlike everyday words, which often have an Anglo-Saxon and/or a Latin base, academic vocabulary is often composed of Greek roots and is thus relatively unfamiliar to students. For example, words derived from the Greek root *cracy* ("government") include *aristocracy, autocracy, bureaucracy, democracy*, and *plutocracy*. The phonological feature of academic words includes stress, sound patterns, and intonation (Scarcella, 2003). Specifically, derivational words sharing a common meaning may exhibit different patterns in stress, sound, and intonation. Consider the words *evolve* and *evolution*. When *-tion* is added to the base word *evolve*, the short-*o* sound in *evolve* becomes a schwa sound in *evolution*, and the stress is shifted from /vo/ in *evolve* to /lu/ in *evolution*.

Learning academic vocabulary includes understanding its own grammatical features. When students learn that the part of speech of the word *bacterium* is a noun, they also need to remember that the word is singular not plural (Scarcella, 2003). Learning grammatical features of an academic word further means to know all derivational forms of a base word or a root and their respective parts of speech and usage. For example, these words share the same root, *pend/pens* (meaning "hang"), but have different parts of speech: *append* (v.), *appendix* (n.), *pendant* (n.), *impending* (adj.), *pending* (adj.), *suspend* (v.), and *suspense* (n.). Even for the words with the same part of speech (e.g., *append* and *suspend*), their usage can be different. The word *append* is often directly followed by an object (e.g., *append a thank-you card*) while the word *suspend*, used with an object or not, is often followed by the preposition *from* (e.g., *suspend the lamp from the ceiling*).

Modal auxiliaries—*can, could, have to, may, might, must, will, would, shall,* and *should*—are very common in academic English and play an important role in conveying complex meanings of sentences (Scarcella, 2003; Zwiers, 2008). The strong tone in the sentence *The scientists will invent a space shuttle that can transport humans to Mars* would be weakened if the modal *would* is used instead. Another feature of modal auxiliaries is its extensive use in conditional (indicative and subjunctive) clauses. Consider the indicative condition in the sentence *If you provoke an animal, even a most gentle one, like sheep, it would attack you as a way to protect itself.* The sentence means that attacking is more likely to happen. In the sentence with a subjective condition, *If the American Revolution had not happened, we still would have been ruled by the British*, our being ruled by the British did not actually happen. Students not only need to understand the tone and meaning of sentences conveyed with modals in academic reading, but also develop an ability to use the modals correctly in academic writing.

Areas of Strengths and Difficulties

A salient strength in vocabulary development is ELLs' prior knowledge on some general and specific concepts acquired in L1 (e.g., a table has a flat surface and three or four legs). This knowledge varies greatly across ages, schooling, and life experiences. For example, older ELLs generally are equipped with more vocabulary knowledge. This assumption, however, can be misleading. An ELL from an isolated village would not know as much about establishments in a city (e.g., shops) as an ELL of the same age living in a city. Another strength is the transfer of students' knowledge about morphological and grammatical characteristics of words acquired in L1 (Nagy, McClure, & Mir, 1997). For example, derivational words exist in languages like Spanish, French, and German. Even for ELLs whose L1 shares limited characteristics with English, some level of L1 vocabulary knowledge can facilitate learning English vocabulary. For example, many words have multiple meanings, and all words belong to at least one part of speech. An understanding of collocation in L1 words would benefit ELLs in learning about word collocation in English.

The areas of difficulties for vocabulary developments come from three sources. First, students who may not have prior knowledge about the concepts represented in English (e.g., the Internet) are learning the words and concepts simultaneously. Second, students whose L1 does not share much commonality with English may have limited L1 resources to tap into (e.g., concepts of affixes and derivational words for speakers of Chinese or Japanese). Third, students whose L1 share cognates with English would experience another type of difficulty. For example, false cognates (see Table 2.3) may confuse Spanish-speaking children (García, 1991), and they have to unlearn a possible association between a false cognate and an English word and learn the English word as a brand new word. In identifying students' sources of vocabulary difficulties, Blachowicz and Fisher (2006) remind us to make sure that the difficulties are truly related to vocabulary (meaning of words) and not to decoding problems. This point is extremely important to teachers of ELLs, as ELLs are developing their decoding and vocabulary skills simultaneously. It is possible that an inability to decode a word may lead you to believe that a student does not understand it. There is also a high possibility that a student understands the concept acquired in L1 that a word represents, but that the student has a hard time pronouncing the word (see Table 5.1 for the characteristics of ELLs' vocabulary knowledge).

Goals of Instruction

One goal of vocabulary instruction is to provide direct, systematic vocabulary instruction and allow students to be exposed to a wide range of vocabulary (everyday and academic) through reading and listening and to apply the learned vocabulary through speaking and writing (Lesaux & Siegel, 2003; Peregoy & Boyle, 2009). This goal is important to ELLs because they are pressured to develop all

---

TABLE 5.1. Proficiency Levels and Characteristics of Vocabulary Development

Level	Characteristics
Beginning	• Understanding some common words, simple phrases, or short sentences predominantly in oral communication and some in written communication • Using with many errors some common words, simple phrases, or short sentences predominantly in oral communication and some in written communication • Learning words used in daily classroom routine • Having limited understanding of academic vocabulary
Intermediate	• Understanding more words with simple or multiple meanings, simple and complex phrases, or longer sentences mostly in oral communication and more in written communication • Using mostly appropriately words with or without multiple meanings, simple and complex phrases, or longer sentences mostly in oral communication and more in written communication • Mastering most words used in daily classroom routine • Expanding sight vocabulary • Having some understanding of academic vocabulary
Advanced	• Understanding and using appropriately most vocabulary used in oral and written communication • Expanding knowledge of commonly known words • Expanding understanding and use of academic vocabulary

four areas of language and literacy (listening, speaking, reading, and writing) simultaneously within a short period of time. Limited vocabulary and possible limited background knowledge may make vocabulary learning challenging. But when all areas of literacy are integrated in teaching, students are able to make a better sense of the words, which helps lessen the linguistic and cognitive load. Further, this approach enables students to experience the utility of learned vocabulary across four areas.

Related to this goal is providing a language- and word-rich environment for students who are "filled with curiosity and excitement about new words and opportunities to have fun with words" (Blachowicz & Fisher, 2006; Blachowicz, Fisher, Ogle, & Watts-Taffe, 2006, p. 527; Cunningham, 2005; Nation, 2001). This is one of the characteristics of strong vocabulary instruction that applies to vocabulary instruction for ELLs. This characteristic seems to be more important for ELLs, and specially for those who are not strong in general vocabulary and who are now expected to learn academic vocabulary. Teachers cultivate a language- and word-rch environment by providing many meaningful and authentic vocabulary activities (e.g., identifying key words from a newspaper article on a community event). Similarly, students contribute to the development of such an environment by participating actively in vocabulary activities.

A final goal, more important to ELLs, is to foster students' love for words (Blachowicz et al., 2006; Graves & Watts-Taffe, 2002). When students take an interest in words, they pay more attention to words in oral and written language. Further, motivation is a drive for ELLs to overcome difficulties in learning. Teachers can foster students' love for words through accomplishing the first two goals.

ASSESSING VOCABULARY DEVELOPMENT

Explicit Assessment

Free Recall

Free recall (Holmes & Roser, 1987) is a fast way to assess students' receptive knowledge about target words. You choose content-area words related to a unit of study (e.g., weather) or everyday words (e.g., for a daily classroom routine). You simply ask the student, "Tell me about the word _____," and write down student's responses. For ELLs who are developing their oral language, you model first by writing down a word with a picture and then draw pictures related to the word to illustrate what you know about the word. Then you have the student do the same. Or you have the student act out a word if possible (e.g., verbs and adjectives). If there is a bilingual student in your classroom or in your school, or a bilingual adult who can assist you with assessment, the student can tell you about the word in L1. In that case, you need to be aware that the meaning of a word, if it exists in L1, may vary due to cultural differences. In analyzing students' responses, you look for the richness in meaning (i.e., multiple layer of meanings) and for confusion in meaning (e.g., *home* and *house*).

Using a Word in a Sentence

An indirect way to assess expressive word knowledge is to have the student write at least one sentence using a target word, if the student has developed some literacy skills in English. If the student is lacking in literacy skills, he or she can tell you at least one sentence using a target word. Of course, sentences in L1 are acceptable if a bilingual child or adult is available to translate the sentences. In analyzing the sentences, you should look for richness in meaning from multiple sentences, word collocation, and meaning confusion.

Word Sorting

Word sorting, an instructional strategy for teaching phonics, spelling, and sight vocabulary, can be used as an assessment tool as well. Word sorting can be closed or open-ended (Bear et al., 2007). In a closed sort, you provide the student with a criterion, such as sorting words by meaning (e.g., derivational words) or by content (e.g., words about community). In an open-ended sort, the student groups the words in his or her own way. At the end of the sorting, you ask the student to explain each group. In analyzing how the student has sorted the words, you assess whether the student has a good understanding about a relationship between the words in a same group.

Embedded Assessment

Due to the close relationship between vocabulary and speaking and writing, data from embedded assessment of oral language and writing is a valuable source of information about students' strengths and needs in vocabulary development. You can observe how students use vocabulary during oral communication for daily routines (e.g., during recess time) and during literacy activities (e.g., a book discussion). Writing samples can shed light on students' expressive ability with words. The following questions may guide you to focus on what to look for in your observations: Does the student use newly learned words? Does the student use appropriate words in a correct way? Does the student overuse a few words in communication (e.g., *you know*)? Does the student use a wide range of words to express a similar idea?

STRATEGIES AND ACTIVITIES FOR PROMOTING VOCABULARY DEVELOPMENT

While there is limited research on vocabulary instruction for ELLs (Blachowicz et al., 2006; Dressler & Kamil, 2006), literature has indicated that sound vocabulary instruction for non-ELLs can be adapted for enhanced and modified instruction for ELLs (August & Shanahan, 2006; Fitzgerald, 1995; Slavin & Cheung, 2003). In Carlo et al.'s (2004) study, when vocabulary instruction for fifth-grade Spanish-speaking ELLs and English-only students focused on the elements of word knowledge, form, meaning, and use (Nation, 2001), ELLs improved in word knowledge, the depth of word knowledge, and reading comprehension. Teachers can provide ELLs with direct, scaffolded instruction on academic vocabulary for students to master various aspects of word knowledge (e.g., Carlo et al., 2004; Scarcella, 2003). The strategies and activities in this section (see Table 5.2) reflect the guidelines by Blachowicz et al. (2006):

- It takes place in a language- and word-rich environment that fosters what has been referred to as "word consciousness" (see Blachowicz & Fisher, 2006; Graves, 2006).
- It includes intentional teaching of selected words, providing multiple types of information about each new word as well as opportunities for repeated exposure, use, and practice.
- It includes teaching generative elements of words and word-learning strategies in ways that give students the ability to learn new words independently. (p. 527)

Providing a Language- and Word-Rich Environment

Blachowicz et al. (2006) identify one of the characteristics of strong vocabulary instruction as a language- and word-rich environment, which includes a display of various genres of texts, teacher modeling of the use of new and complex words, and teacher reinforcement of key words in discussion and in read-aloud. The following example illustrates how a fifth-grade teacher explained the meaning of the concept *chemical reaction*, modeled the use of the phrase, and invited the students to use the phrase.

"Today, we are going to talk about chemical reaction. Actually, part of this concept is not new at all. You have already had some experience with the concept *reaction*. For example, what is your reaction when you hear that we are going to dissect a pig heart? Your reaction can be excitement about this lab activity and curiosity about the similarities and differences between a pig heart and a human heart. Other words having a similar meaning with the word *reaction* are *response* and *effect*. So your reaction to dissecting a pig heart is an emotional response. Who can give me more examples of *reaction*? [Students give out examples (reaction to passing the tests, to going on a vacation, to reading an interesting book, and to watching a new movie).] Good. You have a good understanding of the concept *reaction*. Now let's talk about chemical reaction, the concept we are learning today. Chemical reaction is chemical change in one type of substance as a result of its reaction to something. That is, one type of substance changes into a new type of substance. [Writes on the board the following.]

chemical reaction = chemical change

chemically

Substance ⟶ New Substance

TABLE 5.2. Instructional Foci and Strategies and Activities for Vocabulary Development

Level	Instructional Foci	Strategies and Activities
Beginning	• Providing a language- and word-rich environment • Reading to/with students a wide range of books and other texts of different genres and interests • Providing opportunities for speaking and writing • Developing basic sight vocabulary • Introducing academic vocabulary on concepts familiar to students (e.g., body parts) • Encouraging students to make connections to prior knowledge of a concept	• Providing a language- and word-rich environment • Selecting words for instruction • Providing comprehensible input • Teaching word-learning strategies (using context clues) • Focusing on concepts (list-group-label) • Teaching dictionary use • Focusing on students' interests and independent learning (collecting words from texts of interests, personal vocabulary journal)
Intermediate	• Providing a language- and word-rich environment • Providing opportunities for listening, speaking, reading, and writing of narrative and expository texts • Expanding sight vocabulary • Mastering words used in daily classroom routine • Developing polysemy, multidimensionality, interrelatedness, and heterogeneity aspects of word knowledge • Mastering academic vocabulary of more complex concepts familiar to students (e.g., precipitation) • Encouraging students to make word/concept connections in English and L1 (if literate in L1) and prior knowledge and concept connections	• Providing a language- and word-rich environment • Selecting words for instruction • Providing comprehensible input • Teaching word-learning strategies (conducting self-assessment, using associations, using context clues) • Focusing on concepts (list-group-label, using analogies, concept circle) • Focusing on procedural vocabulary • Paraphrasing • Teaching definition • Teaching dictionary use • Focusing on students' interests and independent learning (collecting words from texts of interests, personal vocabulary journal)
Advanced	• Providing a language- and word-rich environment • Providing opportunities for listening, speaking, reading, and writing of narrative and expository texts • Expanding polysemy, multidimensionality, interrelatedness, and heterogeneity aspects of word knowledge • Mastering academic vocabulary on more complex concepts familiar or unfamiliar to students (e.g., American Civil War) • Encouraging students to make a connection between English and L1 cognates (if literate in L1)	• Providing a language- and word-rich environment • Selecting words for instruction • Providing comprehensible input • Teaching word-learning strategies (conducting self-assessment, using associations, using context clues, using morphemic analysis, using morphemic mapping) • Focusing on concepts (list-group-label, using analogies, concept circle and concept of a definition map) • Focusing on procedural vocabulary • Paraphrasing • Teaching definition • Teaching dictionary use • Focusing on students' interests and independent learning (issue log, collecting words from texts of interests, personal vocabulary journal) • Using cognates • Translating words on a word wall • Making a bilingual dictionary

"Now I am going to give you some examples of chemical reaction. When your food is mixed with the acid in your stomach, your food's reaction to the acid is to change into something different. That is a chemical reaction. Whatever food you put in your mouth earlier has broken down into something like mushy soup. That is a new substance ready to be further processed by your small intestines. There are no longer such things as tomatoes and McDonald's burgers. A chain of chemical reactions occurred to the food we ate. I can use the concept *chemical reaction* like this in a sentence: *When food is mixed with acid in the stomach, a chemical reaction occurs.* Respiration and photosynthesis (writing down both words on the board) are another two examples of chemical reactions. I'd like to hear from you some examples of chemical reactions."

In a language- and word-rich environment, students play an active role by applying words they've just learned. In a fifth-grade class, Ms. Cohen required her students to talk like social scientists by using words specific to a discipline. For example, in explaining how a bill becomes a law, she wanted her students to use these words: *bill, law, house/houses, committee, vote, veto, President, sign, unsigned, pass,* and *majority.* Here is one example of how a student explained the process.

"First, a bill is introduced into one of the houses, where it is voted on. If that passes, it is sent to the house's committee. If it passes, then it is voted on in the same house. After that, if it passes, it goes to the opposite house where it is discussed and voted on. If that passes, the bill is sent to a conference where the differences are worked out. It is then sent to the house for a final vote and if that passes, it is sent to the President. If he signs the bill or leaves it unsigned or does not veto it for 10 days, then the bill becomes a law. If he vetoes it, it is sent to the houses, and if there is a two-thirds majority in both houses, the bill still becomes a law."

Selecting Words for Instruction

A first factor to consider in selecting words for instruction is the importance of the words to ELLs. For beginners and newcomers, words related to classroom routines are most relevant (e.g., *raise your hands; open your book to page _____*). (See Kress's [2008] *The ESL/ELL Teacher's Book of Lists* for examples of expressions of classroom routines.) Understanding these words makes ELLs' daily experience in the classroom a little bit less frustrating, a little more pleasant and successful. For intermediate and advanced learners, you need to strike a balance between their needs in vocabulary knowledge and the curricular standards. In addition to words listed in your curricular guides, you can look for words in the glossaries of the textbooks and other materials, select italicized or bolded words in texts, and identify the words in sidebar texts explaining concepts or in captions describing visual representations.

Another factor to consider is students' prior knowledge of the concept learned in L1. For concepts familiar to students, you can focus instruction on reviewing the concepts and providing English equivalents. Besides the content-specific words, you can select to teach words used across content areas (e.g., *analyze/analysis*, *argue/argument*, *categorize/category*, *clarify/clarification*, *classify/classification*, *document/documentation*). Mastering these words early on supports students in navigating texts across different content areas and producing written output with academic vocabulary.

A third factor to consider is whether a particular expression representing a concept may be confusing, misleading, or different in L1 and in English. For example, while students literate in L1 may have mastered the concept of fractions, the way the concept is expressed differs across English and other Asian languages. The fraction three-fourths (¾), is said as 四分之三 in Chinese (四 means 4, 分 means *parts*, 之 means *of*, and 三 means 3), and 4分の3 in Japanese (分 means *parts*, の means *of*). In cases like this, just teaching the word *fraction* is not enough. You need to direct students' attention to the difference in the expression of the same concept in L1 and English. If possible, have a bilingual student explain the difference to the class.

A last factor to consider is who will select words for instruction. Traditionally, teachers are the ones who complete this task. Literature about English-only students and vocabulary instruction in general has indicated that having students select words for studying is an effective and motivating tool (e.g., Jimenez, García, & Pearson, 1996). The strategies of vocabulary self-collection (Haggard, 1986) and reciprocal teaching are primarily composed of having students select the words and talk about the words. Having students select words to study is doable especially for those who are literate in L1 and whose L1 shares the same roots (e.g., Spanish, French). If students are invited to select the words, you can present a visual display of the words in relation to the concept and a short text explaining the concept. The display facilitates students in identifying the known and new words and in learning about the concept the words represent. You can also refer to online visual dictionaries to locate pictures and labels for a concept. My favorite sites include Visual Dictionary (*www.infovisual.info/04/pano_en.html*), Merriam-Webster Visual Dictionary Online (*visual.merriam-webster.com*), and NASA Picture Dictionary (*www.nasa.gov/audience/forstudents/k-4/dictionary/index.html*).

Providing Comprehensible Input

It is important for students to receive comprehensible input during the process of vocabulary development (Freeman & Freeman, 2004). One way for students to receive comprehensible input in lessons on academic vocabulary is for you to control other elements of academic language. That is, the grammar and text structures cannot be too hard, and the task students are asked to perform should be familiar to them. If other elements of the academic language are not controlled, students will be like a juggler who has to pay attention to different objects (i.e., figuring out the grammar and text structures while learning new words).

For example, in teaching vocabulary related to the human body, you may supplement the science curriculum with children's books written at a student's proficiency level, such as *DK Eye Wonder Human Body* (Bingham, 2003). Terminology words in this book are introduced in very simple English. The subsection *What Are Germs* states, "Germs fall into two main groups: bacteria and viruses. Your body is good at keeping them out, but they are clever at finding ways in" (Bingham, 2003, p. 24). This two-sentence paragraph, with a simple sentence structure and everyday vocabulary, introduces three key words—*germs*, *bacteria*, and *viruses*—and the hierarchical relationship among them: the word *germs* is an overarching category for the words *bacteria* and *viruses*. In other words, the word *germs* is a hyponym for the words *bacteria* and *viruses*, or *bacteria* and *viruses* are subordinating words for the word *germs*. After introducing these three words, you can have students read the other two paragraphs written in a similar fashion explaining in detail what bacteria and viruses are. Later, you can talk about the form of each word. The word *bacteria* for example, is often used in its plural form. I strongly encourage you to make books like *DK Eye Wonder Human Body* available in your classroom library.

A second way to provide comprehensible input is glossing for unfamiliar words to facilitate comprehension. Some unfamiliar content words are crucial to comprehension of the content. Consider these two sentences about the flying ability of dragonflies: "They can also hover—useful while they seek out prey with their sharp eyes—and can dart in different directions. They do all this in spite of having a primitive wing design that has not changed for millions of years" (Dalby, 2003, p. 29). Four words, *hover, sharp, dart*, and *primitive*, may be unfamiliar to some students. Although only the word *primitive* is more content related, the other three words can cause difficulty as well. The words *hover* and *dart* are not as common as their respective synonyms, *fly* and *dash/rush*, and the word *sharp* has a meaning different from the one commonly used (e.g., *a sharp knife*).

Nation (2001) describes glossing as a way to provide a brief definition or a synonym in L1 or English for an unfamiliar word. The advantages of glossing include (1) allowing students to read an original text, (2) having students learn about the accurate meaning for an unfamiliar word as used in the text being read, (3) making the reading process flow smoothly without an interruption to consult a dictionary for an unfamiliar word, and (4) encouraging students to pay attention to the glossed words (Nation, 2001). Glossing can be done in two ways. One way is to attach to the end of a text a glossary of unknown words marked in the text. This is a relatively easy method, but students may choose not to consult the glossary. The other way is to make available a brief definition or a synonym in the text where an unknown word appears. This way is useful when a chosen text is from outside the curriculum and may contain some words not yet covered by the curriculum. In this case, you type up a brief definition or a synonym for each unknown word, print it out, and paste it next to the line where the word appears in a photocopy of a text passed out to your students (see Figure 5.1). You can also just write a brief definition or a synonym next to the line.

A third way to enhance comprehensible input during instruction of academic vocabulary is to provide a sentence frame for each content word students are asked to use. Mrs. Sawyer-Perkins, a fourth-grade teacher, required her students to use each key word in a sentence after she had explained and discussed it. To facilitate

Something like oil to make a surface smooth	People have hunted whales for their meat, oil, and bones. Whale oil, for example, was used as *lubricants, and in foods, soap, and candles.
Large scale, large quantities killing	The number of whales have been significantly reduced due to commercial whalers' *whole-sale *slaughter.

FIGURE 5.1. An example of glossing.

the success of this activity, she always created and wrote down on chart paper a sentence frame for each word (see Figure 5.2 for sentence frames for words related to medicine). For the word *suture* Mrs. Sawyer-Perkins included its verb and noun forms. The sentence frames invited students to apply their knowledge of sentence structures, along with their vocabulary knowledge. For example, for the sentence frame *During the fatal accident . . .* , a complete sentence is needed. To complete another sentence, *The doctor used sutures to . . .* , an infinitive verb is acceptable.

Teaching Word-Learning Strategies

While vocabulary instruction plays a crucial role in students' mastery of academic vocabulary, independent learning (e.g., incidental learning and extensive reading) is important to the growth of vocabulary knowledge. Given that, students must master a set of word learning strategies that will assist them to figure out unknown words in reading and even during standardized testing. In teaching strategies, you should explain the strategy with some examples, model the steps, provide guided

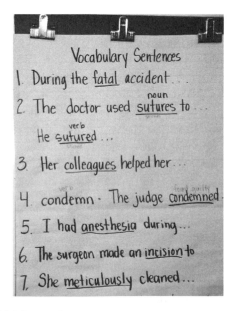

FIGURE 5.2. Sentence frames for vocabulary.

practice, assess and provide feedback, reteach if needed, provide independent practice, and conduct final assessment.

Conducting Self-Assessment

Becoming aware of one's own word knowledge is an important word learning strategy, as it is the first step in setting a goal for oneself for expanding vocabulary. Blachowicz and Fisher (2006) suggest using a Knowledge Rating Chart where students indicate their level of knowledge about a given set of words. Their chart includes these three levels: "Know Well," "Seen/Heard It," and "Don't Know" (p. 97) or "Can Define/Use," "Heard It," and "Don't Know" (p. 133). Figure 5.3 is an example of a modified chart that a Chinese-speaking fourth-grade ELL used to self-assess her knowledge of a list of words about eyes (see Appendix J for a reproducible version). This chart helps the student become conscious of her knowledge about the words.

Using Associations

Associations help activate students' prior knowledge about a word/concept and associate such knowledge to the word/concept under study. When students make associations about a word, they expand and deepen their knowledge about this word by learning more about the meaning of the word and its relationship to other related words. Nation (2001) lists eight different ways to make associations. In Table 5.3, I explain and give an example for each type of association.

Words	I can pronounce the word	I can explain the word	I know how to use this word	I know other forms of this word	I know this word in my language
eyebrow	✓	✓	✓		眼皮
eyelash	✓	✓	✓	eyelashes	睫毛
iris	✓				
lower eyelid	✓	✓	✓		下眼皮
pupil	✓	✓		pupils	瞳孔
sclera					
upper eyelid	✓	✓	✓		上眼皮

FIGURE 5.3. Self-assessment of words.

TABLE 5.3. Associations

Association	Explanation	Example
Finding substitutes	Using another word to replace a target word	*Adjust* for *adapt* in *The thick fur and fat in a polar bear is an example of how an animal adapts* [adjusts] *to survive its environment.*
Explaining connections	Explaining the connections in a group of related words	The concept *water cycle* is the connection for the following words: *ocean, river, evaporation, condensation, precipitation, clouds, snow, pressure, wind.*
Making word maps	Making a semantic map of a target word	
Classifying words	Using a criterion to classify a group of words (Dunbar, 1992)	Classify the following measuring devices for their function: *analog watch, bathroom scale, digital watch, electronic scale, kitchen scale, kitchen timer, room thermostat, spring balance, stopwatch, sundial,* and *thermometer*
Finding opposites	Finding an antonym for a target word	*Acid* is an antonym for *base.*
Suggesting causes or effects	Finding a cause and/or an effect for a target word/phrase (Sokmen, 1992)	Global warming *cause:* industrial pollution, car pollution, decrease in areas for forest *effect:* unhealthy air, rising sea level, extreme weather, destroyed habitats for animals
Suggesting associations	• Group 1: finding associated words for a target word, then scrambling the associations, and giving the words to Group 2 • Group 2: finding associated words for the target word • Groups 1 and 2: comparing and discussing the classification	Associations for *food chain* Group 1: *sun, water, soil, energy* Group 2: *omnivores, herbivores, carnivores* Groups 1 and 2: *decomposers, plants, animals*

(continued)

TABLE 5.3. *(continued)*

Association	Explanation	Example
Finding examples	Giving students a list of categories (e.g., sports, human digestive system, video games) Having each student choose one category or assigning one category to each student Having the student (the first student) write down on a piece of paper known words related to the category After a time limit set by the teacher, having the first student pass the paper to the next student (the second student) who will write down known words that are not on the paper Having the second student pass the paper on to the third student Repeating the same step with the rest of the class until the first student gets back his or her paper where he or she has started a list of words related to the category. Each list becomes part of a class dictionary (Woodward, 1985).	Category: Human Digestive System Student 1: *mouth, tongue, stomach, liver* Student 2: *teeth, colon* Student 3: *esophagus* Student 4: *gallbladder, pancreas, small intestines, large intestines* Student 5: *spleen, rectum*

Using Context Clues

In Haastrup's (1985, 1987, 1989) work during which L2 learners did a think-aloud to show how they had processed unknown words, he found out three sources of knowledge from which the learners had drawn: (1) *interlingual cues* from L1, or knowledge of other languages; (2) *intralingual cues* from English; and (3) *contextual cues* (context cluse) from the text or readers' general knowledge. Interlingual cues are particularly important for students whose L1 shares some commonalities with English (e.g., Spanish, French). Cognates study (see the section "Differentiated Instruction of ELLs Literate in L1" on pages) is an effective way to invite students to draw on their L1 resources in figuring out unknown words in English. Intralingual cues become visible when students have developed some morphological knowledge about English words, and about multisyllabic words in particular (see the following section, "Using Morphemic Analysis"). Context clues, useful to students, can be difficult for them, as they must have developed a good understanding of the text structure, grammar, and general world knowledge. Gunning (2008) lists eight context clues which also can be used for students to figure out academic words. In Table 5.4, I supplement an example from an expository text for each type of context clue.

While teaching context clues, it is important to focus on one context clue at a time so that students do not feel overwhelmed. It is also important to introduce first the clue that is most common, useful, and easiest to learn. For example, the context clue of explicit explanation or definition seems to be the most logical one

TABLE 5.4. Context Clues and Examples

Context clue	Example
Explicit explanation or definition	The two *which*-clauses explain what *pack ice* and *fast ice* are.
	"There are two main types of sea ice—pack ice, which forms on the surface of the open sea, and fast ice which forms between the land and the pack ice" (MacQuitty, 1995, p. 11).
Appositives	The phrase *small fish living in shallow water* is used as an appositive to explain the unknown word *blennies*.
	"Blennies, small fish living in shallow water, often rest on the bottom and hide in crannies" (MacQuitty, 1995, p. 18).
Synonyms	The phrase *sea fir* is a synonym for the unknown word *hydroid*.
	"The beautiful, flowerlike polyps of this hydroid, or sea fir, are used to capture food" (MacQuitty, 1995, p. 21).
Function/purpose indicators	The phrase *send a message to your brain* provides a clue to the unknown word *sensor* through the indication of its function.
	"When you touch something, tiny touch sensors in your skin send a message to your brain" (Bingham, 2003, p. 30).
Examples	The words *underwater mountains, plateaus, plains*, and *trenches* provide examples for the phrase *geological formations*.
	"There are underwater mountains, plateaus, plains, and trenches, making the ocean floor as complex as any geological formations on land" (MacQuitty, 1995, p. 8).
Comparison—contrast	The word *survive* is opposite to the unknown word *extinct*.
	"Some forms of life became extinct, but others still survive in the ocean today, more or less unchanged" (MacQuitty, 1995, p. 6).
Classifications	The words *towns, wards*, and *coteries* explain a classification of the social structure of prairie dogs.
	"Prairie dogs live in groups of thousands or even millions, called towns. Each town is divided into areas called wards, then into family groups called coteries" (Dalby, 2003, p. 74).
Experience	One's experience of going to beach and collecting shells and the phrase *collect shells of already dead creatures* give a clue to the unknown word *beachcombing*.
	"It is better to go beachcombing and collect shells of already dead creatures" (MacQuitty, 1995, p. 62).

to begin with, as it is most commonly used in expository texts. In addition, you need to keep in mind students' prior knowledge of the sentence content where a clue appears. It is best to use sentences with familiar content. Otherwise, you may lose the focus of instruction, spending time explaining the meaning of the sentence rather than teaching context clues.

As students become more skillful at using context clues, they need to be exposed to words for which more than one context clue can be used. To enhance the effectiveness of teaching context clues, you can incorporate a think-aloud to facilitate students verbalizing how they use one particular context clue or a combination of several clues. The think-aloud benefits other students who may not have yet mastered using one particular context clue, and now are given an opportunity to learn from the thinking process of a peer. The think-aloud further provides you with assessment data on how your students learn to use context clues.

Using Morphemic Analysis

It would be helpful and effective to incorporate teaching morphemic analysis into instruction on spelling and grammatical features of words. Morphemic analysis is related to orthography because of the three layers of English spelling: the sound or alphabet layer, the pattern layer, and the meaning layer (see Chapter 2 for details). It makes sense to teach grammatical features of words along with instruction on morphemic analysis rather than just having students complete worksheets to learn about grammatical functions of words. This approach is important to ELLs who generally lack an exposure to English language and for whom academic vocabulary poses more of a challenge. For example, after having students identify a suffix (-*tion*) added to the base word *classify*, you can ask students to figure out the parts of speech for the base word *classify* and the derivational word *classification* by exploring the position of the words in the sentences. Table 5.5 illustrates a mini-lesson that links teaching morphemic analysis to spelling and grammatical features of words (*quantities, transported, tankers, pipelines*, and *seabed*). Figure 5.4 is a form for planning a lesson with an integration of morphemic analysis, and spelling and grammatical features of words (see Appendix K for a reproducible version).

Using Morphemic Mapping

Adapted from semantic mapping (Johnson & Pearson, 1984), morphemic mapping encourages students to expand their knowledge of a morpheme by listing words derived from the morpheme and by using each word in a sentence (see Figure 5.5). The visual display of related words based on the same root (or base word) provides a support for students to observe the relationship among the words. This activity can be used as a follow-up activity for a mini-lesson on morphemic analysis like the one illustrated in Table 5.5.

(text resumes on page 136)

TABLE 5.5. Teaching Morphemic Analysis, Spelling, and Grammatical Features

Teaching step	Instructional foci
T: Another source of pollution in the ocean is an oil spill. This is the topic of the short paragraph we are about to read. I am giving you 3 minutes to read the paragraph on your own and mark any parts of the paragraph that you do not understand.	• Having students preview the text • Having students self-monitor their comprehension
T: Let's look at the first two sentences, "Oil is needed for industry and motor vehicles. Huge quantities are transported at sea in tankers, sent along pipelines, and brought up from the seabed." (MacQuitty, 1995, p. 62) What do these two sentences tell us? (*Teacher repeats this step of checking for comprehension for the rest of the text.*)	• Checking students' comprehension
T: In the second sentence, I have noted several words containing more than one morpheme. Who can tell me what a morpheme is? (*Students explain.*) T: Who can tell us the words with more than one morpheme? (*Students give the words* quantities, transported, *and* tankers.)	• Having students activate their prior knowledge on the concept • Checking students' knowledge on the concept
T: Let's look at the word *quantities.* (*Teacher writes down the word on the board.*) Can you give me other words with a similar meaning? (Students give the words *number* and *amount.*) (*Teacher writes down the words on the board.*)	• Checking students' comprehension of each word
T: Let's do some morphemic analysis with each word. Who can tell us what morphemic analysis is? (*Students respond*)	• Checking students' knowledge on the concept
T: Is there a root in *quantities*? If not, what is the base word? S1: It is a plural. T: You are right. So what is the base word? What is the suffix? Come to the board to underline the suffix and the base word. S2 underlined -*s* as the suffix and *quantitie* as the base word. T: -*S* is one of the suffixes for plural. What is the other suffix? S3: -*es*? T: That's right. Then what is the base word? Spell it for us, please. S4: *Quantiti*?	• Providing students with feedback • Guiding students to identify the suffix and the base word
T: A good try! Close. This is a very tricky word. In English, sometimes when you add a suffix to a base word, you have to change the spelling of the base word. Because the word ends in the letter *y*, it needs to be changed to the letter *i* before -*es* can be added. The base word is *quantity.* Who can give me other examples that this rule may apply to?	• Identifying and explaining the spelling rule • Inviting students to apply the rule

(continued)

TABLE 5.5. *(continued)*

Teaching step	Instructional foci
T: Let's look at this word's grammatical features. First, it is a plural noun, and used in a sentence as a . . . S5: Subject. T: Good!	• Identifying the grammatical features of the word
T: Now, let's look at the word *transported*. This is a complicated word. I am sure that you can tell the number of morphemes in the word, and each of the morphemes.	• Repeating the same steps with the word *transported*
T: Remember, a morpheme can be a word as long as it has one meaning. Look at the words in this sentence again. There are two words having more than one morpheme.	• Identifying compound words • Conducting morphemic analysis

Sentence: "Huge quantities are transported at sea in tankers, sent along pipelines, and brought up from the seabed" (MacQuitty, 1995, p. 62).

Word	Morphemic Analysis	Spelling	Grammatical Features
quantities	base word: *quantity* suffix: -es	The letter y in *quantity* is changed to i before -es is added.	a plural noun as the subject of the sentence
transported	root: *port* prefix: *trans-* suffix: -ed	no change The sound /i/ is added before the sound /d/.	a past participle as a verb in a passive voice
tankers	base word: *tank* suffix: -er suffix: -s	no change	a plural noun as the subject of the prepositional phrase *in the tanks*
pipelines	base words: *pipe, line* suffix: -s	no change	a plural noun as the subject of the prepositional phrase *along pipelines*
seabed	base words: *sea, bed*	no change	a plural noun as the subject of the prepositional phrase *from the seabed*

FIGURE 5.4. A lesson plan for morphemic analysis, spelling, and grammatical features.

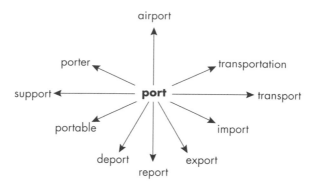

FIGURE 5.5. An example of morphemic mapping.

Focusing on Concepts

In teaching academic vocabulary, as Akhavan (2006) reminds us, we should teach concepts that words represent, not just words. The strategies of list–group–label, using analogies, concept circle, and concept of a definition map, with a focus on concepts, can be adapted to use with ELLs.

List–Group–Label

The strategy list–group–label, developed by Taba (1967), requires students to first group a list of words based on a pattern and then provide a label for each group of words (see Figure 5.6). This strategy directs students' attention to the meaning of each word, the shared meaning of related words, and a concept each group of words represent. In creating a label for a group of words, students demonstrate their understanding about the hierarchical relationship between the concept and the words representing the concept. In the example, the phrase *linear measure* is a

List	Group			Label		
				U.S. Customary System		
foot	inch	pint	ounce	Linear Measure	Liquid Measure	Weight Measure
gallon	foot	quart	pound	inch	pint	ounce
inch	yard	gallon	ton	foot	quart	pound
league	mile			yard	gallon	ton
mile	league			mile		
ounce				league		
pint						
pound						
quart						
ton						
yard						

FIGURE 5.6. An example of list–group–label.

hyponym for the words *inch, foot, yard, mile,* and *league.* In addition, students are required to use content-specific terminology. Instead of labeling the group words in the preceding example with the phrase *measurement for length,* students must use the term *linear measure.* It is more beneficial to ELLs if you encourage students to think aloud about their grouping and labeling process. Such sharing provides further assessment data for you.

Using Analogies

Word analogies have long been used for linking a similar concept to the new, unfamiliar one students are learning to aid understanding. Harmon, Wood, and Hedrick (2006) list some types of analogies:

Part to Whole (*finger : hand :: toe : foot*)
Person to Situation (*Roosevelt : Great Depression :: Lincoln : Civil War*)
Cause and Effect (*aging : facial wrinkles :: sunbathing : tan*)
Synonym (*master : expert :: novice : apprentice*)
Antonym (*naive : sophisticated :: alien : native*)
Geography (*Rocky Mountains : west :: Appalachian Mountains : east*)
Measurement (*inches : ruler :: minutes : clock*)
Example (*Folgers : Maxwell House :: Cheerios : Corn Flakes*)
Functions (*switch : lamp :: key : door*) (p. 47)

For ELLs, using analogies can be equally effective in enhancing students' understanding of a new concept when used appropriately and when you have considered several factors. First, you need to be mindful about the prior knowledge about the concept that you have assumed is familiar to ELL students. It is possible that what you think should be already in students' prior knowledge can be a brand new concept to them. If this "teacher-assumed" concept is used in an analogy, the strategy of using analogies would lose its purpose. Rather, it may confuse students more. In this example, *grapefruit : citrus fruits :: blueberries : berry fruits,* if a student does not know anything about grapefruit, he or she would have difficulty understanding this new concept (blueberries belong to the berry fruit category). A second consideration is about word choice. At times, one concept can be expressed by different words, some of which are more familiar to students than others. If you want to use an antonym analogy to facilitate students in understanding the concept of acid and base, you can use the pair *north : south,* which is easier to understand than the pair *opponent : ally.* The latter pair, however, may not be difficult for older ELLs who have some foundation in social studies.

Analogies can be used in the various stages of teaching: during preteaching of vocabulary when you assess students' knowledge about the concept and the words representing it; during teaching when you support students in mastering the concept being taught; and after teaching when you assess students' learning outcomes. After students have become familiar with analogies, they should be encouraged to make their own analogies based on learned concepts. The process of making analogies strengthens their understanding of concepts and the words representing the concepts.

Concept Circle and Concept of a Definition Map

Vacca and Vacca (2005) suggest using a circle map where students list the words related to a concept and write a sentence explaining the relationship among the words (see Figure 5.7). Beginning ELLs may use pictures to complete a concept circle. A concept of definition map challenges students to elaborate on the chosen concept (Schwartz & Raphael, 1985) (see Figure 5.8). You would have ELLs at an advanced level use this map to summarize what they have learned. While teaching a concept, you also can create this map as a visual aid to present information in an organized way and to assist students to note the relationship between elements related to a concept.

Focusing on Procedural Vocabulary

The term *procedural vocabulary* refers to vocabulary "used to establish relations in context," which often occurs in science discourse (Marco, 1999, p. 6). Procedural vocabulary often contains content and functions words, the latter signaling the relationship of the content word to other concepts or the context. For example, in the math problem *What is the smallest product of the two consecutive odd numbers?*, the phrase *the product of* is procedural vocabulary in which the content word, *product*, presents a concept, and the function word, *of*, signals a relationship between the concept *product* and the other two concepts, *consecutive* and *odd numbers*. In a study of procedural vocabulary from published scientific books and articles, Marco (1999) identifies nine relationships procedural vocabulary represents:

1. "Identity Relation": *be the same as, be equal to, share*
2. "Difference Relation": *be different from, be unlike*
3. "Inclusion Relation": *be a member of, range from*
4. "Exclusion Relation": *be absent from, lack*
5. "Process Relation": *evolve from, result in*

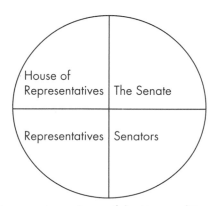

The U.S. Congress is made up of the House of Representatives and the Senate. Both senators and representatives are elected.

FIGURE 5.7. Circle map.

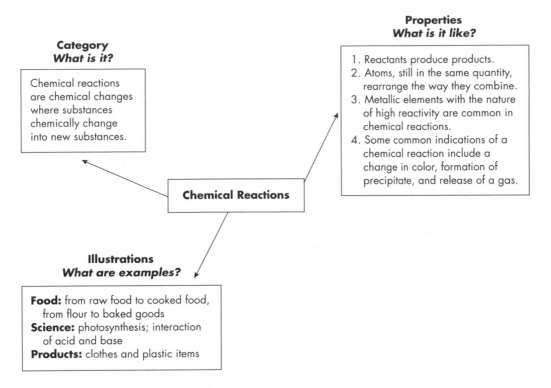

Category
What is it?

Chemical reactions are chemical changes where substances chemically change into new substances.

Properties
What is it like?

1. Reactants produce products.
2. Atoms, still in the same quantity, rearrange the way they combine.
3. Metallic elements with the nature of high reactivity are common in chemical reactions.
4. Some common indications of a chemical reaction include a change in color, formation of precipitate, and release of a gas.

Chemical Reactions

Illustrations
What are examples?

Food: from raw food to cooked food, from flour to baked goods
Science: photosynthesis; interaction of acid and base
Products: clothes and plastic items

FIGURE 5.8. A concept of definition map.

6. "Function": *be used as, be used to*
7. "Spatial Relation": *be surrounded by, extend*
8. "Relations between the concept and its physical characteristics": *in the form of, be oval-shaped*
9. "Quantity modification": *a series of, a number of* (pp. 8–17)

The importance of procedural vocabulary cannot be underestimated, as procedural vocabulary is critical in conveying complicated messages in science, math, and social studies texts. It represents a special challenge to ELLs mostly because of prepositions. If students fail to figure out a relationship based on a preposition, they may understand the concept but not its relation to the other concept(s) or the context in general. In the example *What is the smallest product of the two consecutive odd numbers?*, if students cannot figure out that the word *of* indicates a process relationship between the concept *product* and the other concepts, *the two consecutive odd numbers*, they cannot solve this math problem.

Harmon et al. (2006) describe a useful activity which promotes ELLs' learning about procedural vocabulary. In Figure 5.9, I list each step with an example. In addition to the activity described in Figure 5.9, you can designate a word wall or part of the word wall to display procedural vocabulary by categories. This makes procedural vocabulary more visible and accessible for students when they need the phrases during reading and writing.

Text: "Many people collected sea shells because of their beauty, but most shells sold in shops have been taken as living animals. If too many shelled creatures are collected from one place, such as a coral reef, the pattern of life can be disrupted" (MacQuitty, 1995, p. 62).

Step	Example
1. Identifying procedural vocabulary phrases	*because of, been taken as, are collected from, the pattern of*
2. Using each phrase in a sentence about a familiar topic	We are so happy *because of* the high scores on the tests. The boys were *taken as* slaves. The box tops *are collected from* my neighbors. I notice *the pattern of* odd number, odd number, and even number in this group of numbers.
3. Discussing the purpose of each phrase	*because of*—indicating a process *been taken as*—indicating identity *are collected from*—indicating inclusion *the pattern of*—indicating identity
4. Having students discuss each phrase in the sentence of the text and its meaning	For the sentence: *Many people collected sea shells because of their beauty, but most shells sold in shops have been taken as living animals.* Student 1: The phrase *because of* is for the process. Because sea shells are beautiful, many people want to collect them. Student 2: So this is the cause–effect process. Student 2: The phrase *taken as* indicates identity. The shells people collect are actually living animals, like mussels. They are not dead. Student 1: Just like we see on the news, so and so was taken as a hostage.
5. Reminding them to be aware of the phrases	Remember the purpose and meaning of each phrase. Apply the meaning of the phrase to the context to see if it makes sense.

FIGURE 5.9. An activity for procedural vocabulary.

Paraphrasing

Another way to enhance students' academic vocabulary is to have students paraphrase original words in a text they are reading. Paraphrasing not only facilitates students in refining their writing so that ideas are expressed more clearly and cohesively, but it also encourages them to think about the meaning and usage of words. The example provided by Nation (2001) is illustrative of English verb usage, and in particular, verbal phrases. In the original sentence, "Everybody will be helped by the changes" (p. 183), the verb phrase in a passive voice is *be helped by*. When the word *benefit* is used to paraphrase the verb *help*, the preposition *from* replaces the preposition *by* in the original sentence. That is, the paraphrased sentence, now in an active voice, is *Everybody will benefit from the changes.*

When having students paraphrase certain words in their writing, you can supply words for paraphrasing the original ones if you want to make the task less challenging, or you can have students come up with appropriate words if you want to withdraw your support. If students have use the wrong word to paraphrase an original word or use a correct word but the usage is wrong (e.g., using *benefit by* instead of *benefit from*), you can conduct a quick on-the-spot mini-lesson to draw students' attention to word meaning and usage.

Teaching Definitions

Academic vocabulary is often associated with a definition of a concept. Definitions of concepts are so important for students to understand, as they are key to the concepts under study. Regular dictionaries do not always provide a definition at the students' level of language proficiency, cognitive maturity, and background knowledge. Nation (2001) advises that teachers take the following steps:

1. Provide a clear, simple, brief explanation of a word when students first encounter it so that they are not overwhelmed by a complicated definition.

2. Explain the related meanings of the word when used in different contexts (e.g., *induction of electricity* and *induction from observations*).

3. Provide opportunities for students to experience repeated exposure to the word.

4. Teach students to recognize the different forms of definitions in texts they are reading (e.g., a definition in the form of an appositive, a definition in the form of a relative clause).

5. Prioritize the aspects of the word to be taught, beginning with its meaning (for example, explaining the meaning of the word *bacteria* is not enough; students need to know the grammatical feature of this word—*bacteria* is in the plural form of a noun. Knowing its meaning and grammatical feature, students will know how to use the word. If the word is used as a subject in a present tense, the verb should not be in a third person singular tense.).

6. Use various ways to assist students to remember the word (e.g., morphemic analysis).

7. Avoid relating the word to unfamiliar words with a similar form or to its synonyms, antonyms, and other words related to the same lexical category (e.g., students would be confused about the meaning of the target word *cumulative* when another word similar in spelling and meaning, *accumulative*, is also introduced).

Teaching Dictionary Use

In addition to learning a definition of a word from its context, students often get information about a word from a dictionary. Dictionary use is often a highly contested topic. Some advocate its use, whereas others suggest that students come up with their own definition based on their understanding of the word/concept. There is some truth to both sides. On one hand, you should encourage students to use context clues to figure out the meaning of an unknown word. One reason for this is that a dictionary does not always provide a definition that fits well with the context in which the word appears. Furthermore, a constant consultation of a dictionary while reading interrupts the flow of reading and thus affects the quality of comprehension. For example, there is no need for a student to look up the word *reflex* in this sentence: "This is a reflex action, meaning the muscles react automatically" (Bingham, 2003, p. 31). The word *meaning* signals that what follows is an explanation of the word *reflex*. The word *this* as a referent prompts the student to pay attention to the previous sentence giving one example of reflex reaction: "Under water, a baby will close a muscle to keep water out of its lungs" (p. 31).

On the other hand, some academic words appear in a context with densely packed concepts and complicated sentence structures, and the meanings of these words would be difficult for students to extract by using available context clues. In this case, looking up the words in a dictionary or at times multiple dictionaries may be helpful. Take a look at this example: "Fundamental forces and laws dictate what matter is like and how it behaves. The strongest of the four fundamental forces (the strong force) binds particles together in the nucleus of atoms" (Kerrod, 2003, p. 10). These two sentences are packed with concepts possibly difficult for students to figure out if they rely only on the context clues *fundamental forces and law, dictate, particles*, and *nucleus*. Looking up words in a dictionary would give students a quick piece of information about *particles* and *nucleus* and about the new meaning of the words with the commonly known meaning of *fundamental forces and law* and *dictate*.

You should also keep in mind several guidelines for dictionary use (Nation, 2001). One is related to the types of dictionaries accessible to students. Dictionaries with illustrations and simple language are most helpful to students in learning academic words. *Scholastic's Visual Dictionary* (Corbeil & Archambault, 1994), with 700 illustrations for 5,000 terms in 350 subjects, offers students with English equivalents for the concepts they may have learned in L1. *Scholastic Science Dictionary* (Berger, 2000), with illustrations, explains complicated science concepts in simple, clear language comprehensible to students. Many online dictionaries even allow readers to listen to the pronunciation of a target word (see Figure 7.12 for a list of online bilingual dictionaries). My favorite online dictionaries are Merriam-Webster Online (*www.merriam-webster.com*) and The Free Dictionary (*www.thefreedictionary.com*).

Second, you should teach students how to use a dictionary both receptively and productively. Nation's (2001) description of receptive and productive use of a dictionary guides teachers to identify foci in vocabulary instruction. The receptive use of a dictionary includes the following:

1. Get information from the context where the word occurred.
2. Find the dictionary entry.
3. Choose the right sub-entry. Once the correct entry has been found there may be a need to choose between different meanings and uses listed within that entry.
4. Relate the meaning to the context and decide if it fits. (pp. 285–286)

The productive use of a dictionary includes the following:

1. Find the wanted word form.
2. Check that there are no unwanted constraints on the use of the word. This step involves the skills of interpreting the dictionary style labels and codes.
3. Work out the grammar and collocations of the word. Some of this information can come from the example sentences in the dictionary.
4. Check the spelling or pronunciation of the word before using it. (pp. 287–288)

While the focus of instruction needs to be on the productive use of dictionary, you cannot assume that students have been taught and know how to use the dictionary receptively. It is necessary for you to use a few words from a text students are reading to assess students' receptive dictionary use. Based on the assessment results, you can plan needed lessons on dictionary use.

Focusing on Students' Interest and Independent Learning

Scholars with expertise in vocabulary instruction for both ELLs and non-ELLs point out the importance of student interests in their vocabulary learning (Blachowicz et al., 2006; Scarcella, 2003). When encouraging students to identify and collect words interesting to them, you motivate them to note a close connection between school learning and lifelong learning and prepare them to apply language beyond the classroom walls. Issue logs, collecting interesting words, and personal vocabulary journals are just three examples of activities that incorporate students' interests.

Issue Logs

Nation (2001) suggests use of an issue log, where a student gathers information from various sources on a topic of interest over several weeks (see Figure 5.10 for an example). Students orally share the information with a small group weekly, and every two weeks, students write a report summarizing what has been gathered. In the oral sharing and written report, students are required to use newly learned vocabulary. The issue logs prepare students for writing a final report on the topic of choice. This activity supports students in developing knowledge about the form,

Topic: Rising Gas Price				
Information		Vocabulary		
Information	Source	Word	Meaning	Forms
Adjusting to Increasing Gas Prices	Mountain View Daily	recession	declining, falling	noun synonym: depression antonym: booming
		weak	not good, downward	adjective antonym: strong
		relief	help, aid	noun synonym: aid
Text to Be Shared: The skyrocketing fuel price has pushed the weak economy into recession. To offset the fuel price, some people have bought four-cylinder cars or smaller cars. One state has used an energy relief plan by not raising tax on gas.				

FIGURE 5.10. An issue log (rising gas price).

meaning, and usage of words. Furthermore, the students' choices of topics provide an opportunity to initiate learning in their interest areas, thus motivating them to complete the task.

Collecting Words from Texts of Interests

In this activity, students collect interesting words related to content areas they are studying or in which they are interested and/or an expert. They list collected words in a word book and share the words with a peer group or the whole class once a month. You browse word books at least once a week so that each student's book is read by you at least once a month. From the collected words, you learn about the topics of students' interests and the type of words to which students are exposed. Even if some students' areas of interest seem to be unrelated to any content areas, it is possible to identify words related to academic disciplines. In a recent study about vocabulary appearing in trading cards (e.g., Pokémon and Yu-Gi-Oh, which are types of popular culture texts, not academic texts), Xu (2008b) discovered some academic vocabulary. For example, the words *more* and *by* are related to math. The words *defense* and *field* can be found in a science text. The word *resistance* may be read in a social studies text about a resistance movement or in a text about electricity. Here are some words a fourth-grade ELL collected from one issue of *National Geographic Kids: survival, survive, nutrient, fertilize, aluminum, eliminate, equestrian, data,* and *pod.*

Knowledge of words interesting to students comes in handy for you during vocabulary instruction or literacy instruction, as you can make references to what students already know. Another way to use the collected words is during vocabulary instruction when you can encourage students to refer to their word books, identifying words related to the concepts taught or the morphological or orthographic patterns of words under study. The collected words can also be used for independent practice during vocabulary instruction. For example, students can group the words and provide a label for each group in a list–group–label activity. These activities make vocabulary instruction more related to students' learning.

Personal Vocabulary Journal

Developed by Wood (1994), and Wood (2002), this strategy encourages students to develop word consciousness in reading and listening to any texts to which they are exposed in school and outside school. In the journal, students document many aspects of a word, including its definition, usage, derivational words, synonym, antonym, and parts of speech. Figure 5.11 is an example of one entry in an adapted form of personal vocabulary journal from Harmon et al. (2006). You can invite students to share their journals at least once a week (see Appendix L for a reproducible version).

The New Word: *inflict*

The Text Where I Found the Word: *Wind and Weather* (Jeunesse, 1995)

The Sentence Where I Found the Word: "Tornadoes *sometimes come in families or swarms. They can inflict terrible damage in just a few minutes.*"

The Meaning I Guessed: *cause*

The Contextual Clues I Used for Guessing: *damages*

The Dictionary Definition: *force something not nice on someone or something*

The Part of Speech: *verb*

The Base Word or Root for the Word: Latin *inflictus*

The Derivational Words: *inflicting, infliction, inflictor, inflictive*

Synonyms: *force, cause*

Antonyms: *none*

The Content Area(s) Where This Word May Be Used: *science and social studies*

The Equivalent Word in L1: *infligir (Spanish)*

The Sentence Where I Am Using This Word: *Slave owners inflicted pains on slaves.*

FIGURE 5.11. A sample of a personal vocabulary journal. Form adapted from Harmon, Wood, and Hedrick (2006, p. 140). Copyright 2006 by the National Middle School Association. Adapted by permission.

DIFFERENTIATED INSTRUCTION OF ELLS LITERATE IN L1

Using Cognates

Cummins's (1979) concept of *common underlying proficiency* (CUP) provides support for teaching cognates. Cognate study is especially beneficial for those whose L1 shares a Latin base with English (Bravo, Hiebert, & Pearson, 2007; Freeman & Freeman, 2004). In Carlo et al.'s (2004) study, researchers found that teaching Spanish-speaking ELLs how to use Spanish cognates to gain meanings of academic words enhanced their growth in vocabulary and reading comprehension. Specifically, the teacher reviewed the definition of cognates and guided students to differentiate true and false cognates. This review and brief introduction were followed by a group cognate activity including (1) reading a passage; (2) looking for English words that have Spanish cognates; (3) on a worksheet, recording each pair of the English word and the Spanish cognate; and (4) discussing each of the Spanish cognates to make sure they are true cognates (sharing the same meaning with the English words). At the end of the group activity, the teacher led the class in discussing whether the cognates were true or false cognates.

If the group cognate activity described in Carlo et al.'s study is too difficult for your students, you can try with an activity of cognate sorting (Bear et al., 2007). In this activity, students are given a set of cards with correctly and incorrectly spelled Spanish cognates (e.g., *música, musique, musik, musikk*) to sort. Here are the steps:

1. Show students picture cards and English labels for the cards.

2. Have students match each picture card with its English label.

3. Ask students if they have a card of a Spanish cognate to match one of the cards in English.

4. When a student finds a card of a Spanish cognate, have him or her pronounce the word.

5. Lead students in discussing what they have noted about the cognates and the similarities to their corresponding English words.

Another cognate activity is to have each student identify words related to one particular content area under study, find the Spanish cognates, and document the English words and Spanish cognates, including their respective derived forms. Table 5.6 shows an example of the English word *system* and its derivational words in English and Spanish.

Once students have found pairs of English words and Spanish cognates, you can display them on the word wall, and/or have students record the words in their personal word book or dictionary (Williams, 2001). It is helpful to conduct a mini-lesson on the cognates. In particular, you and the class can discuss if each found cognate is a true one or a false one; if it is a true one, discuss what a root shared by the cognate and the English word is, and what the similarities and differences in the usage are. This type of discussion is valuable in enhancing students' knowledge about word meaning, form, and usage in both languages. Refer to

TABLE 5.6. An Example of English Words and Spanish Cognates

Noun	Verb	Adjective	Adverb
system	systematize	systematic	systematically
sistema	sistematizar	sistemático	sistemáticamente

coe.sdsu.edu/people/jmora/moramodules/SpEngCognates.htm and eslbears.homestead. com/cognates.html for examples of English-Spanish cognates, and german.about. com/library/blcognates_A.htm for examples of English-German cognates. Figure 5.12 lists some examples of English-Spanish cognates related to content areas.

For students whose L1 does not share any cognates with English, they can participate in another activity where they list an L1 equivalent for a concept expressed in English. This activity encourages students to activate their prior knowledge about concepts acquired through L1 and identify any possible connections between English and L1 (in the case of cognates). Table 5.7 lists some examples of Chinese and Spanish equivalents for the geometry concepts in English.

Translating Words on a Word Wall

One simple way to encourage students literate in L1 to utilize their vocabulary knowledge in L1 is to engage them in translating words displayed on a word wall from English to L1. Each L1 equivalent can be placed next to its English word, along with a picture if needed. When referring to each word, you can encourage those literate in L1 to say the L1 equivalent and provide necessary explanation to students illiterate in L1 but proficient in L1 oral language. This process supports students in making a connection between their knowledge of words known in L1 oral language to words in written L1 and English. During the process, you and your students can consult a dictionary or a bilingual person to ensure the accuracy of translations.

Making a Bilingual Dictionary

Students' vocabulary knowledge in L1 can be further tapped through making a bilingual dictionary. Working together, students literate in the same L1 document newly learned English words, everyday or academic, and provide an L1 equivalent for each English word. A picture may be provided for each word. The dictionary can be categorized by content under study (e.g., words related to American Civil War) or by characteristics of words (e.g., words with multiple meanings). During the process of making a bilingual dictionary, you should encourage students to discuss the similarities and differences in meaning, usage, and characteristics of words in English and L1. To ensure the accuracy of each word in L1, it is necessary to advise students to consult at least one L1 dictionary or bilingual dictionary. Making a bilingual dictionary can be ongoing throughout the school year. At

A
abnormal–anormal
abolish–abolir
absolute–absoluto
abstraction–abstracción
accelerate–acelerar
acquire–adquirir
adapt–adaptar
adjust–ajustar
audience–audiencia
augment–aumentar
authentic–auténtico
author–autor
automatic–automático
autonomy–autonomía

B
balance–balanza (n), balancear (v)
basis–base
battle–batalla
benefit–beneficio (n), beneficiar (v)
biography–biografía

C
cable–cable
calculate–calcular
calendar–calendario
combine–combinar
candidate–candidato
capacity–capacidad
capital–capital
conflict–conflicto
contribute–contribuir
control–controlar
cooperate–cooperar
copy–copia
correct–correcto
create–crear

D
debate–debate
decide–decidir
declare–declarar
decline–declinar
direct–directo
district–distrito

E
effect–efecto
electricity–electricidad
element–elemento
emigrant–emigrante
empire–imperio
enemy–enemigo
essence–esencia
establish–establecer

F
facilitate–facilitar
facility–facilidad
factor–factor
falsify–falsificar
family–familia

G
gas–gas
globe–globo
gradual–gradual

H
habitual–habitual
hemisphere–hemisferio
historian–historiador
history–historia
horizontal–horizontal
hostile–hostil

I
ideal–ideal
identity–identidad
illuminate–iluminar
imperial–imperial
importance–importancia

J
jargon–jerga
judicial–judicial
judiciary–judicatura
justice–justicia
justify–justificar

K
kilogram–kilogramo

L
labor–labor (n), laborar (v)
laboratory–laboratorio
latitude–latitud
legal–legal
legislator–legislador
liberal–liberal
liberty–libertad
limit–limitar
line–línea
list–lista

M
magnitude–magnitud
mandate–mandato
manual–manual
map–mapa
mark–marca (n), marcar (v)
mediate–mediar

N
narrate–narrar
national–nacional
nationality–nacionalidad
native–nativo
necessary–necesario
necessitate–necesitar
necessity–necesidad
negative–negativo
nerve–nervio
normal–normal

O
object–objeto
objective–objetivo

oblige–obligar
obscure–obscuro
observe–observar
obstruct–obstruir
obtain–obtener
occur–ocurrir

P
Pacific–Pacífico
passive–pasivo
past–pasado

Q
quarter–cuarto

R
rare–raro
ray–rayo
reason–razonar (v)
recite–recitar
reference–referencia
refine–refinar
reflect–reflejar

S
second–segundo
senate–senado

T
tariff–tarifa
telescope–telescopio
temperature–temperatura
temple–templo
temporary–temporal
terminate–terminar
theme–tema
thesis–tesis
tolerance–tolerancia
tone–tono
traditional–tradicional
tunnel–túnel

U
ultimate–último
united–unido
unity–unidad
universal–universal
unjust–injusto
use–usar (v)
utilize–utilizar

V
vague–vago
vary–variar
vast–vasto
vehicle–vehículo
vein–vena
velocity–velocidad
verb–verbo
victory–victoria
violence–violencia
violent–violento

FIGURE 5.12. Some examples of English–Spanish cognates.

TABLE 5.7. Chinese and Spanish Equivalents for Geometry Concepts in English

English	Chinese	Spanish
circumference of circle	圆周长	la circunferencia del círculo
area of circle	圆面积	área del círculo
surface area	表面积	área superficie
volume	体积	volumen
rectangular prism	长方体	prisma rectangular
cylinder	圆柱	cilindro

the end of the year, you can either keep the completed bilingual dictionary for the next year's students or put it in the school library if there are multiple copies of a bilingual dictionary in the same L1 in your classroom. This process of dictionary making supports students in becoming more aware of their vocabulary in L1 and in English and provides you with an opportunity to learn about L1, whether you are literate in L1 or not. Further, this activity promotes students' sense of pride in L1 and self-confidence in their vocabulary knowledge.

ENGAGING FAMILIES

Students' participation in all literacy activities at school is not adequate for their development of vocabulary knowledge. Incidental learning, multiple exposures to words, and various levels of interaction with words outside school contributes, to some degree, to their vocabulary knowledge. Here are some ideas for family involvement:

> ➤ Family members observe how you teach vocabulary and how students interact with words. Provide a translator if needed.

> ➤ Family members continue reading to and with their children in L1 or in English and to discuss words in relation to the content of the book.

> ➤ Family members encourage their children to use newly learned words in oral language and writing.

> ➤ Family members discuss with students interesting L1 or English words they have heard from daily conversations and from media.

> ➤ Family members and students provide in a word book a definition, a sentence, and/or a picture for each interesting word collected from environmental print, books, or other texts.

➤ Family members and students play a game of words related to synonyms, antonyms, and multiple layers of meaning.

➤ Students share learned words with their families, explaining and using them in a sentence.

VOICE FROM THE CLASSROOM
Renee Gonzalez-Gomez
Abraham Lincoln Elementary School, Long Beach, California

As a Reading Recovery teacher in a K–5 urban elementary school with 68% of our student population as ELLs, I provide short-term literacy intervention to approximately 10 of the lowest achieving first-grade students per school year and supplemental literacy instruction to small groups of low achieving second- to fifth-grade students four days per week. The students' English proficiency ranges from beginning to early advanced levels.

I believe that ELLs possess a great capacity and strong desire to learn in English. I feel that ELLs may actually be more cognitively developed than native speaking learners because they already possess the foundations of one language. In classrooms where caring, knowledgeable, and effective literacy teachers provide instruction, ELLs can be successful. My instruction is data driven and supplements the classroom and core curriculum (Open Court). I use a variety of texts from our school's leveled library and high-quality literature. I have developed an effective lesson structure that includes word study, direct instruction with explicit modeling (comprehension skills, strategies, text structures, etc.), guided practice, and opportunities for students to listen, speak, read, and write.

Teaching academic vocabulary is a critical part of my instruction. When planning my lessons on academic vocabulary, I take into consideration all students' proficiency levels. Specifically, I make attempts to provide examples in the students' L1s (use of cognates), if possible. This allows students to link knowledge in their primary language to new learning in the second language. The use of pictures and realia is extremely valuable. I make every attempt to have the students restate the new vocabulary term in their own words and represent the new term through the use of pictures and/or symbols. I encourage student-to-student interaction because it promotes the use of language and engagement and increases learning rate (students learn so much from each other). I consistently provide opportunities for the students to encounter the new vocabulary in the reading and writing of a text. The following is an example of how I introduced the word *hibernate* to a group of second-grade ELLs.

T: (*showing the word* hibernate) Does anyone see something they know about this word?

S1: I see *hi*.

S2: I see *ate*.

S3: I know *er.*

T: Wow, you know a lot about how this word works. Now let's add two sounds that were left out (/b/, /n/) and put all of our parts together to say the word.

T AND Ss: *hi-ber-nate, hibernate.*

T: Does anyone know what our word *hibernate* means?

S1: Bears hibernate.

T: Yes, bears do hibernate. *Hibernate* means to sleep for a long period of time, days or weeks, in the winter time. (*Definition is given quickly so that students will not begin to assume other meanings of the word, given S1's sharing of his background knowledge*). Now let's write the word *hibernate* on our sheet. (*T elaborates on what it means to* hibernate *a bit more and gives a couple of examples, and then asks the students to think about the word* hibernate, *and what it means, and then get ready to share orally.*) Put your thumb up in front of you when you are ready to share what it means when animals *hibernate.*

S1: *Hibernate* means when animals sleep deep in the winter.

S2: Hibernate is when animals sleep for a long time in the winter.

T: Today we are going to read a book called *Hibernation.* As you read, you will think about what it means to hibernate and find out which animals hibernate. After we have finished reading the book, we will share what it means to hibernate with each other and then write the meaning in our own words on our sheet. We will get a chance to use the word *hibernate* in our own sentence and then draw a quick picture illustrating the word *hibernate.* (*Students read the text as the teacher "listens" to their reading. They then discuss the text.*) Now that you have read the text, and we have had a discussion, think about the word *hibernate,* and think about how you will write what it means on your sheet. When you are ready, show us your thumb so that we can share before writing. (*Students share with partners as teacher listens in.*) Who would like to share what your partner said or what you told your partner about what it means to hibernate?

S1: Hibernate means to sleep deep.

S2: She said hibernate means to sleep in the winter for a lot of days.

S3: Chipmunks hibernate in the winter because it is cold and they don't find food.

T: (*To S3*) Your sentence is good, but you didn't tell us what it *means* to hibernate.

S3: It mean to sleep.

The students complete their sheets by writing the meaning in their own words, using it in a sentence (after orally rehearsing with a partner), and drawing a picture about the word.

I often implement graphic organizers and word sorts to teach academic vocabulary. In word sorts, students categorize words with similar meanings or similar structures (affixes, base/root words). Students at a more proficient level enjoy and benefit from "playing" with English (e.g., idiomatic expressions, similes, metaphors). The following is one example of how I teach academic vocabulary to fifth-grade ELLs.

T: We have been working on Latin roots and sorting words that have a similar root in them. Today, our vocabulary word is *spectator* (*showing but not saying the word*). Does anyone see a part of this word you know?

S1: I see the Latin root *spec*.

S2: It has *or* at the end.

T: I think that with those observations we can say the whole word.

T AND Ss: *Spectator.*

T: There is a word in Spanish that looks very similar to our word *spectator* and has the same meaning. It is *espectador.* Has anyone seen or heard that word in Spanish?

S2: I heard it in Spanish, but I'm not sure what it is.

T: Someone said they saw the Latin root *spec* in the word, which means "to look" and the *or* at the end means someone who does, so the word *spectator*, as well as *espectador*, means someone who looks or watches.

S3: Like if I am watching a soccer game.

T: Yes, you are a spectator. (*Teacher continues giving more information about what* spectator *means and shows a picture of fans watching a football game.*) Now think of the word and put the meaning into your own words and then we will share with each other before writing.

The students complete the sheet, which is similar to the second-grade sheet, but they are required to include a synonym for the new word, identify the Latin or Greek root, define the word, and illustrate the word (see Figure 5.13). The students, regardless of their English proficiency levels, are engaged and enthusiastic about learning words.

If I were to offer one tip for teaching academic vocabulary for other teachers, it would be first and foremost to respect and know your students. I realize that this tip is broad and general, but ELLs are not going to be open to learning anything, especially academic vocabulary, if they do not feel respected and valued first. Before any meaningful teaching and learning can occur, an overall feeling of mutual respect and value must be established. Once this type of environment is established, you may be amazed at the amount of learning that will occur (academic vocabulary learning and otherwise!).

CONCLUSION

I began this chapter with an overview of vocabulary development, including a discussion on the characteristics of academic vocabulary. The strategies and activities for vocabulary development focus on preparing ELLs to understand and apply

Word: Spectator

Meaning: Watching an Actived but not doing the actived.

Use: The two astronauts were Spectators of outer Space.

Synonym: Watcher

Latin/Greek Root: Spec: to look

Illustrate the word:

figure 2

FIGURE 5.13. An activity with the word *spectator*.

academic vocabulary in oral and written language. The classroom examples and Ms. Gonzalez-Gomez's sharing of her teaching academic vocabulary to ELLs illustrate the importance of integrating vocabulary instruction into all components of literacy instruction, scaffolding ELLs' learning process, and building instruction on ELLs' experiences with L1 and on their interests. What has been presented in this chapter reminds us again that ELLs will develop their vocabulary knowledge and an ability to use words effectively for interpersonal and academic purposes only after they are exposed to the English language and L1 and given opportunities to apply, with proper teacher guidance, vocabulary knowledge and to develop a love for words.

CHAPTER 6

INSTRUCTION FOR READING COMPREHENSION DEVELOPMENT

In the staff lounge at Green Meadow Elementary School, several teachers of ELLs were sharing their experiences with using graphic organizers in teaching comprehension. Ms. Patel, a first grade teacher, remarked, "The beginning–middle–end story map is very helpful to my ELLs. I think my students are getting better with identifying the beginning, middle, and end part of a story." Ms. Patel's comment prompted Mrs. Gee, a third-grade teacher, to share a problem she had observed. "I agree with you on the benefits of using graphic organizers. The problem I have seen is that students rely too much on graphic organizers. Every time we read, they would ask, 'Can we do another character cluster for this book?' I think graphic organizers should aid students in the beginning, and then we need to withdraw this kind of support. They should learn how to organize ideas in their head." In support of Mrs. Gee, Ms. Temple, a fifth-grade teacher, responded, "fifth graders are required to read so much information in various subject areas, and we really can't spend much time on doing a graphic organizer for each text. I, however, do use graphic organizers a lot with several beginning level students."

The conversation among the first-, third,- and fifth-grade teachers reflects what you have been concerned about—how to best scaffold the comprehension process. For example, You may have wondered:

1. How is ELLs' reading comprehension similar to and different from that of non-ELLs?

2. How do I conduct classroom-based assessment to measure students' reading comprehension?

3. How can I scaffold my students' process of developing reading comprehension?

4. What instructional strategies and materials can I use to teach reading comprehension?

5. How can I integrate comprehension instruction into other components of literacy instruction?

DEVELOPMENT OF READING COMPREHENSION

The Process and Subprocesses of Reading Comprehension

The process of reading comprehension involves several subprocesses of which proficient readers may not be aware (Afflerbach, Pearson, & Paris, 2008; Peregoy & Boyle, 2000). Since we are helping ELLs navigate successfully through the subprocesses, it is imperative to know what readers do during each subprocess. To bring these subprocesses to our conscious level, consider two excerpts: one from a narrative text and the other from an informational book.

Excerpt 1 (Christelow, 2002)

I'm Police Detective Phineas T. Doggedly. Just call me Doggedly. I catch lowdown, no-good, chicken-chasing, pig-poaching rascals. It's an easy job because there's only one no-good rascal in this town. (p. 3)

That's the Big Bad Wolf! (p. 4)

Excerpt 2 (Simon, 1992)

The Solar System was born among the billions of stars in the Milky Way galaxy. About 4.6 billion years ago, a huge cloud of dust and hydrogen gas floating at the edges of the galaxy began to pull together to form a globe. The particles packed more and more tightly together and became hotter and hotter. Finally the enormous heat in the center of the globe set off a chain of nuclear explosions, and the sun began to shine. (p. 5)

In order to understand both texts, readers first decode words and chunk each sentence into units of phrases with meaning. For unknown words, readers may use pictures, context clues, or decoding strategies. Meanwhile, readers activate prior knowledge on the topic, make predictions, and confirm and disconfirm the predictions. Throughout the subprocesses, readers further draw on their linguistic knowledge in constructing meanings (e.g., phonics, grammar, and vocabulary). For example, the first sentence in Excerpt 1 reminds a reader of the traits (e.g., brave, smart) and responsibilities of a police officer (e.g., protecting good people and catching bad people). The connection prompts the reader to make a prediction about what might happen in the next sentence(s). The sentence on page 4 confirms the reader's prediction, which is consistent with what's written in the text. (I recommend not using the words *right* or *wrong* about a prediction. Students' prior knowledge may be different from ours and authors', and their prediction is based on what they know.) The sentence on page 4 further prompts the reader to make a connection between this book and others related to a bad wolf (e.g., *The Three Little Pigs, Little Red Riding Hood*).

Throughout the process, the reader self-monitors, including becoming aware of what has been or not been understood or misunderstood, and then using fix-up strategies, like rereading a sentence or sentences and revising predictions. While the subprocesses as described seem to be linear and sequential, they mostly happen simultaneously. However, readers who are not proficient in most subprocesses may focus on one or two subprocesses, unintentionally overlooking others. We know many struggling readers who are good decoders (word callers) but cannot comprehend much. With a lack of comprehension strategies, word callers concentrate on what they can do well at the word level, draining brain power needed for comprehending a text. On the other hand, if readers cannot decode most words in the text, they will not be able to comprehend the text as well.

The process of comprehending the text in Excerpt 2 seems similar to that of understanding the text in Excerpt 1. But the reader needs to know more in order to successfully comprehend it. Although all the words in the text are easily decoded, not all words are easy to understand. There are several content-specific words representing scientific concepts related to the solar system (*Milky Way galaxy, hydrogen gas*, and *a chain of nuclear explosions*). Furthermore, How many is "billions of stars"? What is "enormous heat"?

Comprehending both texts also requires readers to be familiar with the structure of each text. For Excerpt 1, the story structure is obvious to readers. The sentences on pages 3 and 4 state clearly the characters of this book (i.e., *I* and *the big bad wolf*), and imply the problem of the story (i.e., I want to catch the big bad wolf, who will probably run away). For Excerpt 2, the text structure, typical of expository text structure, has a mixture of several structures. The time line signals a sequence structure (i.e., *about 4.6 billion years ago* and *finally*). Embedded in this sequence structure is the cause–effect structure. If the reader recognizes one structure but not the other, the quality of comprehension will suffer. Successful readers use their knowledge of text structures to guide them in making predictions and inferences and organizing information while reading (e.g., Peregoy & Boyle, 2009).

The Text, the Learner, the Teacher, and the Context

As evidenced by preceding examples, the meaning-constructing process and subprocesses are affected by various factors. Scholars have identified four interrelated factors: (1) the text, (2) the reader, (3) the teacher, and (4) the context (Lesaux, Koda, Siegel, & Shanahan, 2006; Ruddell & Unrau, 2004; Xu, 2003b).

The Text

The linguistic and content complexity of a text can affect comprehension. At the word, phrase, and sentence levels, vocabulary, expressions (e.g., metaphorical language), relations between words, and order of words (i.e., grammar) can be a challenge to ELLs who have not mastered the English language. At the text level, variations in and embeddedness of text structures make a text more difficult to understand (as illustrated in Excerpt 2) (also see Tables 6.1 and 6.2). Within a short period of time, it is impossible for ELLs to be exposed to and understand most variations of text structures. Furthermore, even if ELLs have developed knowledge about narrative and expository text structures in L1, they have to fight against such knowledge if it causes interferences. Content complexity and a complete lack of schema or partial schema on a topic, including cultural and general knowledge, hinders comprehension.

The Reader

As illustrated with Excerpts 1 and 2, a reader needs to be equipped with word- and text-level processing skills and strategies, prior knowledge about a topic, and metacognition. Theoretically speaking, ELLs can only master these components gradually. But, in reality, they are pushed to use all these components while they are learning them. Further, readers' motivation, attitude, and self-confidence affect how well they can comprehend a text. If a student is not motivated to read a text, he or she does not feel confident about what can be accomplished, thus does not make efforts to accomplish the task. Table 6.3 summarizes the characteristics of ELLs at different proficiency levels.

TABLE 6.1. Expository Text Features and Functions

Features	Functions
Heading and subheading, table of contents	Tell a specific topic and subtopic
Appendices, sidebar text, footnotes, endnotes, captions for pictures, lists	Provide additional information
Diagrams, figures, graphs, maps	Provide additional information through visual representation
Index	Provides a location in the book for a specific set of information
Glossary	Explains terminology
Bibliography/references	Presents a set of sources from which authors have drawn information
Further readings	Provides a list of additional sources for readers
Credits/acknowledgments	Express an appreciation for others' work from which authors have drawn information
Quizzes or activities	Engage readers in exploring the topic presented in the book
Websites, CD-ROMs	Provide Internet resources

Note. From Barone and Xu (2008, p. 147). Copyright 2008 by The Guilford Press. Reprinted by permission.

TABLE 6.2. Examples of Expository Text Structure Patterns

Text structure patterns	Examples
Description	*Mysteries and Marvels of Nature* (Dalby, 2003)
	Some honey ant workers, called "honeypots", store huge amounts of nectar inside their bodies. They stay inside the nest and other workers feed them. They gradually become filled with nectar. This sugary store can be shared between all the ants in the colony when food is scarce. (p. 76)
Sequence	*365 Super Science Experiments with Everyday Materials* (Breckenridge et al., 1998)
	Stir gelatin in the cold water and let it stand one or two minutes. Then add the boiling water and stirred until all the gelatin is dissolved. Pour into 2 cups or dessert dishes. To one, add raw pineapple bits or frozen pineapple juice. To the other, add canned pineapple bits or canned juice. Put both in the refrigerator. (p. 120)
Compare and contrast	*DK Eyewitness Universe* (Kerrod, 2003)
	The Large Magellanic Cloud lies just 160,000 light-years away, a mere stone's throw in space. It is small compared with our Galaxy and is irregular in shape, as is the Small Magellanic Cloud. (p. 56)
Cause and effect	*DK Eye Wonder Human Body* (Bingham, 2003)
	What is color blindness? Your retina contains pigments that detect color. If these are not working, you will have difficulty telling some colors apart. This is known as color blindness. (p. 35)
Problem and solution	*DK Eyewitness Ocean* (MacQuitty, 1995)
	Garbage dumped at sea also kills. . . . Overharvesting has depleted many ocean animals, from whales to fishes. Even the souvenir trade threatens coral reefs. The situation is improving, however. New laws stop ocean pollution, regulations protect marine life, and in underwater parks people can look at ocean life without disturbing it. (p. 62)
A combination of description and compare and contrast	*DK Eyewitness Universe* (Kerrod, 2003)
	Saturn is made up mainly of hydrogen and helium around a rocky core, like Jupiter, but is even less dense. Indeed, Saturn is so light that it would float in water. In appearance, the planet's surface is a pale imitation of Jupiter's, with faint bands of clouds drawn out by its rapid rotation. (p. 34)

TABLE 6.3. Characteristics of Readers at Different Reading Proficiency Levels

Level	Characteristics
Beginning	• Developing concepts about print and concept of a word • Developing often fragmented understanding of a text based primarily on pictures and other visual representations (e.g., graphs, maps, and tables) • Developing some understanding of the narrative text structures and a limited understanding of the expository structures in short, simple informational books • Having no or fewer learner strategies
Intermediate	• Developing a good understanding of at-level texts based primarily on a combination of pictures and other visual representations (e.g., graphs, maps, and tables) • Developing a good understanding of the narrative text structures and some understanding of the expository text structures of longer, more complicated informational books • Developing commonly used learner strategies
Advanced	• Developing a solid understanding of texts of various genres and structures • Strengthening a good understanding of the narrative and expository text structures • Developing and using more learner strategies, including metacognition strategies

The Teacher

How well ELLs can comprehend a text in part depends on how their teachers have taught the comprehension process and learner strategies. If you often check students' comprehension by using questions from a teacher's manual and by teaching students a limited number of comprehension skills and strategies, students will not do well on comprehension. On the contrary, when you engage students in discussing the text, you provide a scaffold and help students understand that comprehension is a complicated, but an interesting process. If ELLs are supported by you throughout the process, they will be motivated to make efforts in reading.

The Context

The context seems to be less related than the text and the teacher to how well ELLs can comprehend. But, it is. For example, when you ask students to read a book and then answer all the comprehension questions without pre- and postdiscussion about the book, students might feel anxious, and their higher level of anxiety might hinder the meaning construction process. On the other hand, if students are asked to first read a book and then share with their peers their responses, they might do better with meaning construction. In a similar way, if students get to discuss the book with peers before writing their responses, the context becomes conducive to student success.

Areas of Strengths and Difficulties

ELLs at various proficiency and grade levels bring to school their experiences with oral or written L1. Their understanding of print carrying meaning and of reading for a purpose can be transferred to reading texts in English. Their developing or developed skills and knowledge needed for comprehending a text in L1 (e.g., using syntactic and semantic cues, making connections) may facilitate their understanding of how comprehension works with an English text. Furthermore, their background knowledge acquired through L1 also helps, to some extent.

ELLs are pressured to master all aspects of English simultaneously while their non-ELL peers continue making progress in comprehension. Major difficulties related to a lack of English language proficiency can occur during students' processing a text at the word, phrase, sentence, and text level. Students may be able to decode all the words, but if they lack a good understanding about the word meaning and relationships between the words (i.e., grammatical knowledge), they still cannot construct meaning successfully. For example, for the sentence *Jose gave Ming a book*, a student needs to understand that the word *Jose* is the subject of the sentence and the agent of the verb *gave*. The phrase *Ming a book* is a complete predicate. The word *Ming* is an indirect object, while the phrase *a book* is a direct object. Another way to understand the sentence is that *Ming received a book from Jose*. English grammar, necessary for meaning construction, is notoriously complicated and difficult to master (see Chapter 8). Other sources of difficulty are ELLs' lack of cultural and general knowledge, limited understanding of text structures, lack of comprehension skills and learner strategies, and limited ability to apply skills and strategies.

Goals of Instruction

A first goal of instruction is to maximize ELLs' exposure to oral and written language input (August & Shanahan, 2006; Krashen & Terrell, 1983; Peregoy & Boyle, 2009). For ELLs who lack a literate (English or L1) environment outside school, reading experiences at school may be the only source of oral and written language input. The input provided through reading aloud and various independent reading opportunities enables students to observe how language, illustration, and other text features (e.g., lists) work together to convey ideas. It is essential to have a classroom library well stocked with books of various genres, on different topics, and at different reading levels. Students will enjoy reading in a comfortable place in your classroom (see Figure 6.1).

Another goal of instruction is to prepare students to become skillful and strategic readers who can apply a wide range of learner strategies in constructing meanings while reading (August & Shanahan, 2006; Herrera & Murry, 2005; Peregoy & Boyle, 2009). Afflerbach et al. (2008) define reading skills and strategies as follows:

> *Reading skills* are *automatic actions* that result in the decoding and comprehending of texts with speed, efficiency, and fluency, usually without the reader's awareness of the components or controls involved.

FIGURE 6.1. A classroom library.

Reading strategies are *deliberate, goal-directed attempts to control and modify* the reader's efforts to decode text, understand words, and construct meanings out of text. (p. 15)

Afflerbach et al. further explain that when a strategy has been tried successfully multiple times, it needs less attention and effort from a reader. "When the strategy becomes effortless and automatic (i.e., the question 'Does that make sense?' is asked automatically, almost subconsciously, at the end of reading sentences and paragraphs), the reading strategy has become a reading skill" (2008, p. 16). The differentiation and relationship between a reading skill and strategy have implications for teaching ELLs. Teachers use instructional strategies to facilitate students in applying learner strategies which will later become skills needed for successful comprehension. For example, when you engage students in completing the K column of a KWL chart (an instructional strategy), you facilitate students' use of strategies for activating prior knowledge and connecting it to the text being read. After a lot of practice with a KWL chart, students will automatically activate prior knowledge and connect it to a text without much effort. This indicates that these learner strategies have become skills.

Closely related to the previous two goals is the goal of teaching ELLs to become motivated and engaged readers (Eskey, 2005; Freeman & Freeman, 2006a, 2006b). As Eskey (2005) puts it, a reading teacher's job is "to find a way to motivate them to read, and to facilitate their reading of whatever texts they have chosen to read or been asked to read" (p. 574). Students become more motivated to engage in a text when what is being read makes sense to them and when they enjoy the text and read for a purpose. A sense of success and enjoyment will motivate them further to read more texts. The more ELLs read, the more times they practice strategies, and the more chances they have to turn strategies into skills. Equipped with a repertoire of skills, they can read better with more challenging texts, which provide opportunities to experiment with a new set of strategies. This ongoing cycle of learning and using strategies and turning them into skills is essential for the development of skillful and proficient readers.

ASSESSING READING COMPREHENSION

Two commonly used methods to assess reading comprehension for non-ELLs are asking students to answer questions about a text and/or to retell what has been read. These two methods can be problematic when used with ELLs. For example, in order for an ELL to answer a question correctly, he or she must understand the question itself, which is itself a test of comprehension to some extent. Questions can be difficult to understand. If the student cannot understand the question, there will be less possibility of answering the question correctly. Even after the student understands the question, he or she has to rephrase or summarize what is being read and produce a response. This process deals with more than just comprehension, and it has more to do with organizing and composing thoughts. Retelling what has been read can be even more challenging for some ELLs. After surveying many teachers in my classes, I have learned that some have not spent time explicitly teaching their students (ELLs and non-ELLs) about the retelling structure. Yet, each year teachers use retelling as a method to assess comprehension. It is possible that a student has a good understanding of a text, but does not know how to organize the ideas in an acceptable retelling format. The problems with asking questions and retelling become more severe with young ELLs and older beginners, as these two methods can set them up for failure even before an assessment begins. Some explicit and embedded assessment can minimize the problems with these two assessment methods.

Explicit Assessment

Assessing Reading Comprehension in L1

If you (or someone at your school) speak your students' L1, it is better to assess students, and in particular the beginning students, in L1. Assessing reading comprehension in L1 helps you to differentiate whether the student lacks comprehension skills and strategies or whether the student is not proficient enough in English to demonstrate his or her comprehension ability. After the student has read a text in L1, you allow the student to demonstrate comprehension using visuals (e.g., pictures, graphic organizers).

Using Visuals

Students at the beginning level can have a fairly good understanding of a text because they have paid close attention to illustrations that clearly support the text and/or they have a good body of background knowledge on the topic. Yet, their limited English proficiency prevents students from demonstrating their understanding. Allowing them to use visuals helps bring out their comprehension ability. For example, after a student has read a book, you can allow the student to sequence the pictures from the book. Students can also draw pictures or fill in a graphic organizer with pictures, words, or phrases from the book. For students at the beginning level, you may use pictures to cue students during the retelling. For example, a card of a clock represents "when," and a card of a house represents "where." A set of cards with numbers 1 to 4 represents "a sequence structure" of a retelling.

Embedded Assessment

Conducting Qualitative Miscue Analysis

In analyzing the quality of miscues from oral reading, you learn if a student relied on meaning cues even when he or she was making miscues. For example, Marianne, who substituted the word *house* in the text with the miscue *home*, was using mostly a meaning cue. John, who said the word *hose* for the word *house*, was not using a meaning cue, but phonological and visual cues. Several students may make the same number of miscues, but qualitatively, their miscues can be different. Conducting a qualitative miscue analysis is a useful way to indirectly check students' comprehension (Goodman, 1973).

Directed Listening–Thinking Activity

The directed listening–thinking activity (DLTA; Stauffer, 1980a) is an instructional comprehension strategy for beginning readers. Lipson and Wixson (2009) suggest using this strategy for checking students' reading comprehension. One advantage of using DLTA with ELLs is to embed comprehension assessment in a lesson, thus lowering students' anxiety level. The other advantage is that it allows you to learn about as many students' comprehension ability as possible during the lesson. This advantage is extremely valuable to teachers who always wish to have more time for instruction and assessment. During a DLTA lesson, you read aloud a book, ask questions, prompt students to make predictions, and engage students in evaluating their predictions. You may ask the following questions:

> ➤ "What do the book title and covers tell you about the book?"

> ➤ "Can you guess (predict) what the book is going to be about? What is going to happen next?"

> ➤ "What makes you guess (predict) this? Pictures? Words? Or both pictures and words?"

> ➤ "Did you use what you know about the topic? Does another book remind you of what is going to happen? Does this book remind you of what happened to you?"

> ➤ "Is your guess (prediction) similar to what an author is saying in the book? If your guess is different from the book, how?" (Avoid using the words *right and wrong*!)

> ➤ "Why have you changed your guess (prediction)?"

You may also shorten the question or use different vocabulary to make the questions comprehensible to your students. For beginning students, you should let them draw pictures on a mini-whiteboard and then show their pictures. In this way, you can have a quick assessment about their responses to a question.

STRATEGIES AND ACTIVITIES FOR PROMOTING READING COMPREHENSION

While narrative and expository texts differ in their respective text structures and some vocabulary, a majority of strategies can be used with comprehending both types of texts. For example, you can use questioning to ask students to identify problem–solutions in a narrative text (e.g., "Who can tell me about different ways the character has tried to solve this problem?"). This same instructional strategy can be used with an expository text (e.g., "Who can share with us three major events happened during 1940s?"). However, some strategies may be more effective with a narrative text than with an expository text, and vice versa. For example, story maps are used mostly with narrative texts, and graphic organizers are used more often with expository texts.

In using instructional strategies to facilitate learner strategies, flexibility is key. When teaching a class with ELLs and non-ELLs, you may use one instructional strategy more often and longer with ELLs than with non-ELLs. For example, you may use interactive read-aloud only with ELLs at the beginning and early intermediate levels in a fifth-grade classroom. It is possible that ELLs will do well with self-monitoring while reading a narrative text, but not with an expository text. This difference may signal a difficulty in strategy transfer across different text genres. To address this difficulty, you can focus on facilitating the use of self-monitoring with a narrative text. Once students have become relatively skillful at using it, you can introduce in a direct lesson the use of the strategy with an expository text and provide students with guided and independent practices of the strategy with different expository texts.

As stated earlier, there is a close relationship between learner strategies and instructional strategies. Table 6.4 lists learner strategies adapted from the work by Chamot and O'Mallet (1994), Jiménez et al. (1996), and Jiménez (1997). Cognitive strategies help students process and construct meanings out of texts (e.g., making an inference of a sentence based on prior knowledge and foregoing text). Using metacongitive strategies, students become conscious of their own mental activities during the transaction between themselves and the text (e.g., noticing a

TABLE 6.4. Learner and Instructional Strategies for Reading Comprehension

Learner strategies	Instructional strategies

Cognitive strategies

Learner strategies	Instructional strategies
• Setting a purpose	• Interactive read-aloud
• Previewing	• Guided reading
• Activating and connecting to prior knowledge	• Asking questions
• Predicting	• Anticipation guide
• Making inferences	• Graphic organizers
• Visualizing	• Story maps
• Applying knowledge of text genre and structure	• Comprehension process motion (CPM)
• Determining important details	• KWL and KWL plus
• Organizing and summarizing ideas	• SQ3R
• Taking notes/outlining	• Cloze technique
• Using reference and resources	• Think-aloud
• Code switching	• Preview-view-review
• Using cognates	
• Transferring literacy knowledge and strategies learned from a native language	
• Translating	

Metacognitive strategies

Learner strategies	Instructional strategies
• Self-monitoring	• Interactive read-aloud
• Regulating	• Guided reading
• Applying fix-up strategies	• Anticipation guide
• Thinking aloud	• Comprehension process motion (CPM)
• Self-evaluating	• KWL and KWL plus
	• SQ3R
	• Cloze technique
	• Think-aloud

Social/affective strategies

Learner strategies	Instructional strategies
• Asking questions	• Interactive read-aloud
• Responding/providing feedback	• Asking questions
• Translating for others	• Anticipation guide
• Cooperating	• SQ3R
	• Think-aloud

difficult section of the text and then rereading the section to make better sense of it). Social/affective strategies enable students to communicate with others during an academic task (e.g., asking for clarification and making comments). Also listed in Table 6.4 is a set of instructional strategies that teachers can use to facilitate students' use of learner strategies.

Selecting Texts for Reading Comprehension Instruction

Effective instruction begins with a careful selection of texts. Texts for ELLs need to be age, content, culturally, and linguistically appropriate and not have too many difficult vocabulary words and sentence and text structures (Krashen & Terrell, 1983). Barone, Mallette, and Xu (2005) suggest considering the following factors in text selection.

Predictability

A predictable pattern book (see examples in Figure 4.4) reduces the linguistic load for ELLs, as students become familiar with a set of words, phrases, or sentences repeated throughout the book. With that, students can devote more energy to comprehending the book.

Familiarity

Familiarity with a book promotes the activation of ELLs' prior knowledge and meaningful connections between the text and their prior knowledge (e.g., other books they have read). These connections facilitate students' comprehension of content unfamiliar to them. You can enhance familiarity of books by using the following:

1. Bilingual books (e.g., *With My Brother/Con Mi Hermano* [Roe, 1991]).
2. Books reflecting native cultures (e.g., *My Name is Yoon* [Recorvits, 2003]).
3. Book with environmental print (e.g., *Detective LaRue* [Teague, 2004]).
4. Books about childhood experience (e.g., *Lunch Money* [Clements, 2005]).
5. Books adapted by children's TV shows and movies (e.g., *Harry Potter and the Sorcerer's Stone* [Rowling, 1997]).
6. Books with a same theme or on a same concept (see Figure 6.2).
7. Books written by a same author (e.g., books by Gary Paulsen).
8. Book series (e.g., Joanne Cole's *Magic School Bus* Series in picture and chapter books).

Illustration/Visual Aids

When illustrations or other visual aids (e.g., a picture with a caption) well support or supplement print, ELLs have a better chance to comprehend the text. For

Berger, M. (1999). *Can it rain cats and dogs?: Questions and answers about weather.* New York: Scholastic.
Bundey, N. (2000). *Rain and people.* Minneapolis, MN: Carolrhoda Books.
Bundey, N. (2000). *Rain and the earth.* Minneapolis, MN: Carolrhoda Books.
Carroll, C. (1996). *The weather: Sun, wind, snow, rain.* New York: Abbeville Kids.
Collins, P. (1973). *Where does all the rain go?* New York: Coward, McCann & Geoghegan.
Grazzini, F. (1996). *Rain, where do you come from?* Brooklyn, New York: Kane/Miller.
Hollander, J., & Bloom, H. (1972). *The wind and the rain: An anthology of poems for young people.* Freeport, New York: Books for Libraries Press.
Kalan, R. (1978). *Rain.* New York: Scholastic.
Peters, L. W. (1990). *The sun, the wind, and the rain.* New York: Holt.
Spier, P. (1997). *Rain.* Garden City, New York: Doubleday.

FIGURE 6.2. Books on the concept of rain.

older ELLs whose learning focuses more on subject areas, visuals in informational books can illustrate or explain a complicated concept that would be otherwise very challenging when expressed solely in words. Figure 6.3 lists some examples of informational books with supportive visuals.

Engagement

Predictability, familiarity, and illustrations/visual aids of a book tend to engage students, as students experience relatively successful reading comprehension. Engagingness of a book is further evident in how well the book invites readers to participate in the story or to gather new information to expand their existing schema about a topic. The types of books that are engaging include books with an interesting plot, books with interesting information, books allowing for making connections and predictions, and books with language play.

Adams, S. (2001). *The best book of weather.* New York: Houghton Mufflin.
Denega, D. (2004). *Let's read about Betsy Ross.* New York: Scholastic
Ehlert, L. (1988). *Planting a rainbow.* San Diego, CA: Harcourt Brace.
Gans, R. (1997). *Let's go rock collecting.* HarperCollins.
Leely, L. (2002). *Follow the money.* New York: Holiday House.
Marzollo, J. (1994). *City sounds.* New York: Scholastic.
Mccarone, G. (1995). *Cars! cars! cars!* New York: Scholastic.
Micucci, C. (1992). *The life and times of the apple.* New York: Orchard Books.
Otto, C. B. (2002). *Shadows.* New York: Scholastic.
Rockwell, A. (1986). *Fire engines.* New York: The Trumpet Club.

FIGURE 6.3. Sample informational picture books with supportive visuals.

Authenticity

The authenticity of a book is evident in how similar its language is to language used in daily oral and written communication. Books with controlled vocabulary have contrived language, an unauthentic language. It is imperative for ELLs to be exposed to books with real English language, which serves as a model for their own language output.

Additional factors to consider while selecting books are a balance between easy and hard books, and instructional foci. An easy book can be used for readers to practice or review a skill or a learner strategy. A hard book, with your guidance, may be used for students to learn a new learner strategy (e.g., self-monitoring) that cannot be accomplished with an easy book. However, a hard book should not pose too many challenges. For example, if a book has a complicated plot, it should not also have difficult vocabulary and sentence and text structures. If so, the linguistic and cognitive load is too much for students, and you will lose a focus in instruction as you have to address many difficulties the students are experiencing.

In addition, I recommend using books with different amounts of print on each page, which invite students at all levels to participate in reading. Students at higher proficiency levels can read aloud or buddy read a page with many words on one page, and students at a lower proficiency level can read along only a word, phrase, or sentence on the other page. For example, the book *Little Raccoon Catches a Cold* (Canizares, 1998) begins with a paragraph ending with an incomplete sentence: "So he hopped out of bed very quickly and—" (p. 5). The sentence is completed on page 6 with the phrase, "got dressed all by himself" (p. 6). The entire book follows this pattern. The longer phrase (*So he hopped out of bed very quickly and*) is appropriate for intermediate or advanced students to read whereas the short one (*got dressed all by himself*) is manageable by beginning readers. Other books with this varied amount of print on pages include *Miss Moo Goes to the Zoo* (Graves, 1998) and *Duck and Goose* (Hills, 2006). You may also use an (language experience approach) LEA text (see Chapter 7) as a reading text. Due to the language at students' proficiency level and the familiar content, discussing the text tends to be relevant and meaningful to students.

Modeling and Scaffolding: Interactive Read-Aloud and Guided Reading

As discussed early in this chapter, the comprehension process is complex and mostly invisible. Many students, ELLs or non-ELLs, have trouble with comprehension, not because they aren't capable of comprehension, but because they have not been taught how to comprehend. Since ELLs are dealing with English language and literacy simultaneously, it is extremely important for us to make the comprehension process visible through modeling and scaffolding. The instructional strategies of interactive read-aloud and guided reading are two appropriate strategies for this purpose.

Interactive Read-Aloud

In the read-aloud discussed in Chapter 3 (see Table 3.3), which aims to provide comprehensible input and facilitate oral language development, the teacher assumes the most responsibility for reading, asking questions, and selecting linguistic units for further discussion. To illustrate an interactive read-aloud with a focus on comprehension, I provide detailed steps related to the first reading of *Clocks and More Clocks* (Hutchins, 1970) (a narrative) (Table 6.5, pp. 170–172) and *The Life and Times of the Apple* (Micucci, 1992) (an expository text) (Table 6.6, pp.173–174). In a first reading, you model the comprehension process and use of learner strategies and invite students to try out these strategies through responding to your questions. For older ELLs, an interactive read-aloud with an expository text helps decrease the linguistic load due to the complexity and variations of text structures and complexity of multisyllabic content-related vocabulary. During the read-aloud, students can participate in discussing and responding to the text in English or L1. Although two picture books are illustrated in Tables 6.5 and 6.6, similar steps can be used with a chapter book and a longer informational book. I recommend that teachers with older ELLs at a beginning level start with picture books and then move on to easy and difficult chapter books. It is important that you guide students in revising their prior knowledge (or assumptions) about one particular category of information when needed. In doing so, you help students develop an understanding about the process of knowledge development about a topic. This point is especially important when ELLs are reading culturally specific information (for which they may have limited or even biased knowledge) and expanding their knowledge base.

An interactive read-aloud can be done with core books from a unit. It is better to use a big book version of a book for an interactive read-aloud. If a big book version is not available, you can use an ELMO document camera, which projects a text to a big screen, allowing students to see and read the print. It is not recommended that you do an interactive read-aloud with every book. The detrimental effect of this practice is that students do not get to read a book from cover to cover for enjoyment or to practice learner strategies in the context of reading.

Guided Reading

During guided reading, students continue to receive support from you, though not as much as in an interactive read-aloud, and they take more responsibility for actually reading a text. While guided reading traditionally has been used with primary grades, it can be used with upper graders. It makes sense to guide students through reading expository texts, which are often more difficult to understand. In adapting guided reading for ELLs, Cappellini (2005) suggests three types of guided lessons with different foci: (1) an emergent and early guided reading lesson focuses on talk; (2) an early fluent guided reading lesson stresses sustaining and expanding meaning; and (3) a fluent guided reading lesson emphasizes applying higher-level comprehension strategies. The prompts listed in Table 6.7 (pp. 175–176) reflect these different foci.

(text resumes on page 177)

TABLE 6.5. Interactive Read-Aloud with a Narrative Text

Steps and purposes	Text: *Clocks and More Clocks* (Hutchins, 1970)
Introducing or reviewing text features	T: Today, we are going to read a new book about clocks (*pointing at it on the front cover*). It is called *Clocks and More Clocks* (*pointing at each word*). Where do you think I can find the author's name? S1: Right there (*pointing to the author's name*). T: What about an illustrator? I only see one name on the cover. Who is the illustrator? S2: Pat Hutchins. T: How come? S3: She writed words and drawed pictures. T: She wrote the words and drew the pictures in the book (*stressing the verbs* wrote *and* drew *as a way to model the correct version of the past tense for each verb*).
Gathering information from book title and book covers	T: We all know that book covers can tell us a lot about a book. Let's look at the front cover. The title says *Clocks and More Clocks*. But how many clocks do you see on the cover? Ss: One. T: If there is only one clock on the book cover, why does the title says *Clocks and More Clocks* (*stressing the /s/ sound in the word* clocks)? S4: Pat Hutchins maked a mistake? T: Phuong said Pat Hutchins made a mistake (*stressing the verb* made *as a way to model its correct version in the past tense*). S5: She wants to give us a surprise? T: An interesting guess. Do you think the back cover of the book would tell you about more clocks? Ss: Let's see. T: (*Turning to the back cover*) Let's count how many clocks on the back cover. (*After the class counts the clocks*) How many? Ss: Four. Five. T: Let's see. We see four clocks in the house and one clock in the man's hand. So there are five clocks. Was Pat Hutchins right when she put the words *more clocks* in the book title? S5: See, she wants to give us a surprise. T: Yeah. The surprise is on the back cover. So it is always a good idea to read the book title and look at the front and back covers. They tell us something about the book. Let's see what else we can get from the book covers. Ss: A house. A tall house. Trees. The man is old . . .
Activating students' prior knowledge	T: (*Repeating students' responses*) We saw a man, an old man, some clocks, a house, and many trees. I want you to go to your brain to get something (*pointing at her head*). When you hear these words, what do these words make you think? For example, I think the man buys a new clock because the old one is broken, or because he does not like his old clock any more. Think for a moment (*pointing at her head*). Then share your ideas with your partner. Later, I will ask you to share with the class. (*Ss share with partners about what these words reminded them of.*)

(continued)

TABLE 6.5. *(continued)*

Steps and purposes	Text: *Clocks and More Clocks* (Hutchins, 1970)
Activating students' prior knowledge *(continued)*	T: Who would like to share? S6: Clock have two sticks. T: A good observation! (*Referring to the picture of the clock*) They are called hands. This clock has two hands.
Having students make predictions	T: Now you have told me what you were thinking when you heard these words. Now, who can tell us what this book is going to be about? I think this man just loves clocks, and wants more and more, just like many of you want more and more video games. Think for a moment (*pointing to her head*), and share your answer with your partner. (*Ss share with partners about their predictions.*) T: Who would like to share? S8: The man buys a new clock. He has a new house. T: That makes sense. Maybe this house has more rooms, and he wants a clock in each room. S9: His friend gave him the clock. He is very happy. T: Interesting. What makes you say that? S9: Happy face on the front cover. T: I like the way Orlando used the picture to help him make a guess. Maybe this is a story about how the clock makes the man so happy in a new house.
Previewing the book	T: I know that you are excited about this book. You want to see if your guess is the same as Pat Hutchins is telling us in the book. But first let's look at the pictures. (*Teacher lets students browse the pictures.*) You can say something about the pictures. Do you see this is a big house with lots of rooms? If you see a word you do not know, let us know. Ss: He buys another clock and put it in that room. He is crazy. He is running in his house. The clocks make him crazy. T: Here is the person, called Clockmaker. He makes clocks and knows a lot about clocks (*continuing to let the class browse the book*).
Frontloading vocabulary	T: When we are looking at the pictures, do you see any words that we should discuss before reading? (*Ss mention attic, bought, splendid, thought, kitchen, Clockmaker.*) T: Some of the words are also on my list. First, I have some words I want us to review: *bedroom, kitchen,* and *hall*. What do you know about the word *bedroom*? Ss: I sleep in my bedroom. A bed in bedroom. There are pillows, bed, and lights. T: Bedroom is where you or other people sleep (*showing a picture of bedroom*). Some of you sleep by yourself in your bedroom. Some may share a bedroom with your brother or sister. (*Teacher reviews the words* kitchen *and* hall.) T: Let's talk about another word we might not know, *attic*. Let's look at the word *attic*. Look at this picture on the front cover. The top space in a house is an *attic*. They are usually smaller than other rooms in the house. Its shape is different from other rooms in the house. Look at this picture (*referring another one in the book*). Who has an attic in their house? If you don't know, ask your parents about it and let us know tomorrow. (*Teacher explains other words.*)

(continued)

TABLE 6.5. *(continued)*

Steps and purposes	Text: *Clocks and More Clocks* (Hutchins, 1970)
Visiting previous predictions, asking questions, and making new predictions	T: Who is excited about reading this book? Looks likely everyone is! (*After reading the sentence on the first page*, One day Mr. Higgins found a clock in the attic.) This sentence makes me think of my guess. My guess is that Mr. Higgins bought a new clock. Actually, in the book, he did not buy it, but found it. So my guess is not the same as what Pat Hutchins is telling us. It is okay. But one thing I did right is use what I saw on the book cover to help me make a guess, or we can use a big word, *prediction*. Say *prediction* (*Ss repeat the word after the teacher*.) The picture does show the man is bringing a clock to his house. Who has a guess or prediction that is similar to this sentence? (*No response.*) T: It is okay. Now, let's think about what Mr. Higgins is going to do with the clock. Is he going to carry it down the hall? It does not make sense to have a clock in the attic. Every time you need to check the time, you would have to run all the way up to the attic. I think he is going to move the clock down to the living room or his bedroom. Raise your hand if you think Mr. Higgins is going to move the clock downstairs. Raise your hand if you think Mr. Higgins is going to keep the clock in the attic. S5: But he has to run from his attic to downstairs. What if he is working in the attic? T: Good thinking! So how can he solve this problem? S9: Put a clock in every room. We have a clock in every room. T: I like the way Anna used what she and her family do to help her make a guess. Let's read on to find out what Mr. Higgins is going to do with the clock.
Revisiting previous predictions	T: (*After reading the sentence on the third page, "How do I know if it's correct?" he thought.*) What do you think after you have heard this sentence? Ss: He has a problem. He is thinking. He is not happy . . . T: Mr. Higgins does have a problem. His problem is different from what we thought. What is the problem we guessed he would have? (*Ss respond.*) What is his problem Pat Hutchins is telling about in the book? (*Ss respond.*) What we did right is that we guessed Mr. Higgins has a problem. Now, we know that his problem is . . . (*Ss repeat the sentence "How do I know if it's correct?"*)
Engaging students in solving a character's problem	T: What do you think Mr. Higgins is going to do? I think he might call the Clockmaker to check on the clock. Ss: He calls his friend to check on it. He call Best Buy. He asked his Dad. . . . T: (*After reading the sentence on the fourth and fifth pages, "So he went out and bought another which he placed in the bedroom."*) An interesting way to solve the problem. Have you thought about that in your guess? Ss: It will tell him correct time. A new clock is good. T: Interesting. Can you tell us how you made this guess? S5: A new clock is more good. My new shoes are more good than my old shoes. T: That makes sense. A new clock is better than an old clock just as your new shoes are better than your old shoes. Since the clock is found in the attic, it is not new. It may not tell the correct time. So it is a good idea to buy a new clock. Let's read on to see if Mr. Higgins will have a new problem. It makes a story fun to read when a character has to solve a lot of problems. That gives us lots of chance to make guesses.

TABLE 6.6. Interactive Read-Aloud with an Expository Text

Steps and purposes	Text: *The Life and Times of the Apple* (Micucci, 1992)
Introducing or reviewing text features	T: Today we are going to read a new book about apples. It is called *The Life and Times of the Apple*. From the title and pictures on the front and back covers, what kind of book is this? S1: An informational book. T: Or we can call it an expository text (*writing the phrase* an expository text *on the board*). What does an informational book tell us? S2: It gives information. T: That's right. Like this book, it gives information about apples. It has a different purpose. A story tells a story. An informational book tells information. How else is an informational book different from a story book? S3: It has lots of pictures about information. T: Yes, it still has pictures. They tell information, too. What else? Look at the chart we have made about informational books. S4: It has a table of contents? T: Let's see if this book has a table of contents. (*Turning to the page of the table of contents*) Yes, this book has a table of contents.
Gathering information from book title, book covers, and table of contents	T: (*Referring to the table of contents*) What are these numbers for? If you need to look at the chart about informational books, that's fine. But try not to look at it. Think about the answer on your own. S4: The page number for each subtopic. T: I like the way Jordan used the word *subtopic*. The topic of the book is apples. All the things listed here are subtopics related to apples. On page 4, we can find out "The Life of an Apple." If I want to read about different ways we can use apples, which page should I go? Ss: (*After scanning the table of contents*) Page 20. (*Teacher asks for more pages.*) T: A table of contents tells us about subtopics in an informational book. Sometimes, the book covers can tell us a lot about the book. Let's look at the front cover. I see a lot of information on the cover. For example, I see food related to applies, like an apple pie, a candy apple, and apple cider, and the planting of an apple tree. What do you see? (*Ss respond with what's on the cover.*) T: That's great! The book will provide detailed information about what's pictured on the cover. Let's read the first subtopic, "The Life of an Apple."
Activating students' prior knowledge	T: Here are the two pages about "The Life of an Apple" (*showing the pages*). I want you to look at the pictures and scan the text to see if these pictures and words remind you of something related to apples. If you have found words you don't know or that are interesting, let us know. Share your ideas with your partner. T: Who would like to share? S5: I never see seeds in an apple. I always throw away the core. S6: I saw short apple trees. Never this tall like in the picture. . . .

(continued)

TABLE 6.6. (continued)

Steps and purposes	Text: *The Life and Times of the Apple* (Micucci, 1992)
Frontloading vocabulary	T: We will talk about what you know about apples and what the author, Charles Micucci, is telling us about apples. First of all, do you have any words you do not know? (*Ss mention the words* popular, continent, Antarctica, estimated, cores, chambers, horizontal, cross section, *and* pomes.) T: I also want to mention the word *family* at the bottom of page 5. It is different from the way we use it. It means a group. Like tigers, cheetahs, and bobcats belong to the cat family. Because they share a lot of similarities. This brings us to another word, *popular*. It is a little bit different from the way we use the word, like you are popular among your friends; Super Mario games are popular. What do you think it means in the sentence "The apple is one of the most popular fruit trees in the world" (p. 4)? Ss: It is common? More often? Many people like apple trees . . . T: Yes, many people like planting apple trees. They then become common trees to plant. For the words *continent* and *Antarctica*, we need to look at the map here (*directing students' attention to the map; teacher engages students in discussing the words.*) T: We have learned something about apples while discussing these words.
Inviting students to revise/ expand prior knowledge	T: Who is excited about reading this book? Looks likely everyone is! (*After reading the first sentence in the second paragraph on page 4, "An apple tree may grow to be forty feet high and live for over a hundred years."*) Remember Wei said he has seen short apple trees. His fact is correct as well. Notice the word may in this sentence. It means a possibility. It may rain, but it does not mean it is going to rain for sure. There is another sentence on page 5 that provides a specific piece of information about how tall an apple tree can grow. Who can find it? What is another word that has a similar meaning as the word *may*? S7: On page 5, . . . "It could grow to be as tall as a four story building." T: What's the word that has a similar meaning as the word *may* on page 4? Ss: *Could.* T: Yes, the word *could* has a similar meaning to the word *may*. The sentence Maria just read is another way to express a same idea, that an apple tree can grow to be very tall. When we are reading an informational book, the information we gather can be pretty much the same as we have in our brain. Sometimes the new information tells us more about a topic. Just like Wei's knowledge about short apple trees. Now he knows, and we all know, that apple trees can be short or tall. I want you to put this new information in your brains. As we read through the book, I will stop to check what you know about the subtopic and let you share if the information is new to you.

TABLE 6.7. Prompts Used in Guided Reading

Type	Narrative texts	Expository texts
Emergent and early guided reading	**Prereading (Previewing the book)** • What do the book title and covers tell you about the book? • What can you guess the book is about? Why? • What do you see from all the pictures and words? • Can you guess what's going to happen in the book? • Do you notice any words you don't know? • Can you guess the meaning of these words from the pictures? **During reading** • What made you stop? • Is your guess the same as the words in the book? Why? • How did you figure out the unknown words? • Can you read this part again? **After reading** • Which part of the book do you like most? • Which part of the book is easy for you? Which part is hard to you? Why?	**Prereading (Previewing the book)** • What do the book title and covers tell you about the book? • What do you know about the topic? • What do you see from all the pictures and words? • Do you notice any words you don't know? • Can you guess the meaning of these words from the pictures? **During reading** • What made you stop? • How did you figure out the unknown words? • Can you read this part again? **After reading** • Have you learned something new about the topic? What is it? • Which part of the book do you like most? • Which part of the book is easy for you? Which part is hard to you? Why?
Early fluent guided reading	**Prereading (Previewing the book)** • What do the book title and covers tell you about the book? • What can you predict what the book is about? • What made you predict this? • What do you see from all the pictures and words? • Do you notice any words you don't know? • Can you guess the meaning of these words from the pictures and other words around each unfamiliar word? **During reading** • What made you stop? • Is your prediction the same as the words in the book? Why? • Can you stop for a minute and tell me what you have learned so far from this book?	**Prereading (Previewing the book)** • What do the book title and covers tell you about the book? • What do you know about the topic? • What do you see from all the pictures and words? • Do you notice any words you don't know? • Can you guess the meaning from the pictures and other words around each unfamiliar word? • What other things do you need to read besides words and pictures on each page? **During reading** • What made you stop? • Is what you are reading in this book different from what you know about the topic? How? • Can you stop for a minute and tell me what you have learned so far from this book?

(continued)

TABLE 6.7. *(continued)*

Type	Narrative texts	Expository texts
Early fluent guided reading *(continued)*	• How did you figure out the unknown words? • Can you read this part again with expression? After reading • Did you change your predictions throughout the book? Why? • Do any words sound, look, and mean something like words you know? • Which part of the book do you like most? • Which part of the book is easy for you? Which part is hard for you? Why? • Can you tell me the story in a few sentences? • Is the book similar to what you have read or heard?	• How did you figure out the unknown words? • Can you read this part again with expression? After reading • Have you learned something new about the topic? What is it? • Do any words sound, look, and mean something like words you know? • Which part of the book do you like most? • Which part of the book is easy for you? Which part is hard for you? Why? • Can you tell me what you have learned from this book in a few sentences? • Is the book similar to what you have read or heard?
Fluent guided reading	Prereading (Previewing the book) • What can you predict the book is about? • What made you predict this? • If you don't understand some words, phrases, or sentences, what will you do? During reading • What made you stop? • What strategies have you used so far in reading this part? • Can you stop for a minute and tell me what you have learned so far from this book? • How did you figure out the unknown words? • Can you read this part again with expression? After reading • Did you change your predictions throughout the book? Why? • Which part of the book do you like most? • Which part of the book is easy for you? Which part is hard for you? Why? • What strategies did you use most while reading this book? • Can you tell me the story in a few sentences? • Is the book similar to what you have read or heard?	Prereading (Previewing the book) • What do you know about the topic? • If you don't understand some words, phrases, or sentences, what will you do? During reading • What made you stop? • What strategies have you used so far in reading this part? • Can you stop for a minute and tell me what you have learned so far from this book? • How did you figure out the unknown words? • Can you read this part again with expression? After reading • Have you learned something new about the topic? What is it? • Which part of the book do you like most? • Which part of the book is easy for you? Which part is hard for you? Why? • What strategies did you use most while reading this book? • Can you tell me what you have learned from this book in a few sentences? • Is the book similar to what you have read or heard?

Setting Purpose: Asking Questions and Anticipation Guide

After students have experienced teacher modeling, they need to practice reading skills and strategies. One important component of the comprehension process is to set a purpose for reading. When a reader has a clear purpose, he or she will be more likely to work toward that goal. Otherwise, reading can become another set of language exercises. Although the purpose of any instruction is tied very closely to curricular standards which sometimes may make no sense to students at all, you can use instructional strategies to help students note or develop a purpose. Asking questions before reading and the use of an anticipation guide can achieve this purpose.

Asking Questions

Asking students questions before reading is not a new instructional strategy (Duke & Pearson, 2002). What is new is that when used with ELLs, you do not ask only questions provided by your teacher's manual. Rather, you allow students to ask questions related to a reading selection. In so doing, despite linguistic challenges they may face, students will connect well with reading a selection as they have a more authentic purpose for finding an answer to each question. As shown in Figure 6.4, Mrs. Martinez, a first-grade teacher, had her students ask questions during a unit on Native Americans, and then summarized all the information learned from the unit in a graphic organizer. She and the students checked off the questions for which students had found answers in the unit readings. For the unanswered questions, the students would read more books to find answers. For Mrs. Martinez's students, what made reading and gathering information purposeful and authentic was a cycle of asking questions, reading to find answers, answering questions, and reading more to find unanswered questions. This cycle can be adapted even for

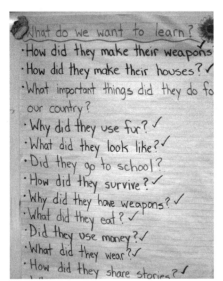
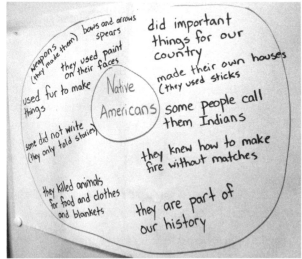

FIGURE 6.4. Asking and answering questions.

very beginning students. You can supply a picture or L1 word next to each question in English, and the answers can include English, L1, and/or pictures.

As students become more skillful at generating questions, you need to help students speed up their reading process. For example, you can encourage students to ask questions in their head before reading. In the beginning, you may have students share their questions before reading and ask them again after reading if they were able to find answers from the text or from inferences based on the textual clues. Gradually, you do not have students share their questions before reading, but after reading they would share how they located answers to their questions and what questions were unanswered. Of course, for students who take a longer time to learn how to generate questions before reading, your continued support is crucial.

Anticipation Guide

A widely used instructional strategy in content-area reading for non-ELLs, the anticipation guide (Readence, Bean, & Baldwin, 2004), can be easily adapted for ELLs. In an anticipation guide, you would follow these steps:

1. Read a selection of text and identify key concepts.
2. Make statements related to the identified key concepts.
3. Present the statements to students.
4. Discuss the statements with students (e.g., agree or disagree; true or false; yes or no).
5. Have students read the selection.
6. Have students discuss the statements again and use evidence from the selection to support their opinion about each statement.

Because you and students discuss each statement, students get a chance to connect their prior knowledge to the topic of the text and to possibly challenge what they have known about the topic. This process is particularly important for ELLs when what they know about a topic is limited or inaccurate (e.g., culturally and socially related information). Through this process, students read for the authentic purpose of checking facts in the text against their pre-existing knowledge about a topic. Figure 6.5 shows an example of an anticipation guide used with a selection about insects in a fifth-grade classroom. For older ELLs at the beginning level, you may modify an anticipation guide by adding pictures to each statement to enhance students' understanding of the statements.

Providing Visual Support: Graphic Organizers, Story Maps, and Comprehension Process Motion

Graphic Organizers and Story Maps

Graphic organizers and story maps aim to make the abstract, invisible comprehension process visible and concrete through a display of content from a text. For stu-

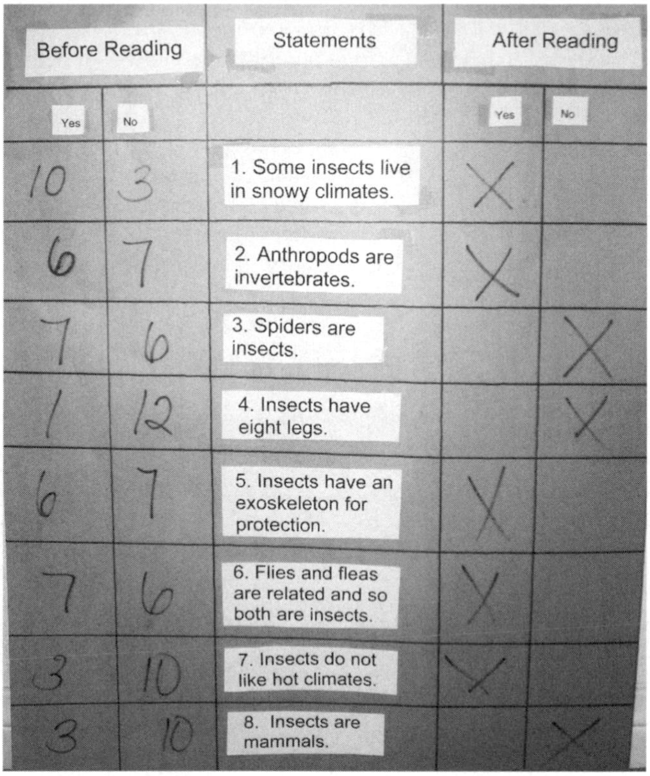

Before Reading		Statements	After Reading	
Yes	No		Yes	No
10	3	1. Some insects live in snowy climates.	X	
6	7	2. Anthropods are invertebrates.	X	
7	6	3. Spiders are insects.		X
1	12	4. Insects have eight legs.		X
6	7	5. Insects have an exoskeleton for protection.	X	
7	6	6. Flies and fleas are related and so both are insects.	X	
3	10	7. Insects do not like hot climates.	X	
3	10	8. Insects are mammals.		X

FIGURE 6.5. An example of an anticipation guide.

dents who partially comprehend a text, such a display supplies additional information that students would otherwise have missed. Furthermore, graphic organizers and story maps teach students how to organize ideas extracted from a text based on a text genre and structure. For example, ideas from an expository text about the westward movement in the 19th century are generally organized in sequence on a time line. In Figure 6.6, I show some examples of graphic organizers and story maps and comment on each example about its benefits to ELLs.

Graphic organizers are supportive of students' learning, but you need to make a decision as to when to use or not to use them and which ones to use. For example, once students have mastered the beginning–middle–end structure of a narrative text, a beginning–middle–end story map should not be used. You should focus on developing students' in-depth understanding of the story elements. For example, you can use a character cluster or a Venn diagram for comparing two characters in the story as a way to assist students in increasing their comprehension of the characters. It is possible that you may use different types of graphic organizers and story maps with different groups of students, depending on their comprehension ability.

(text resumes on page 182)

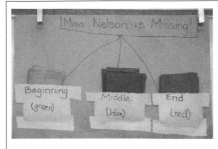

Ms. Snow, a second-grade teacher, had her students list in a beginning–middle–end story map important events that happened throughout the story *Miss Nelson Is Missing* (Allard, 1977). Instead of having each student complete a story map, she had each student write events on three cards of different colors. Then she invited her students to read and discuss what was written about the beginning, middle, and end of the story. This example illustrates a step beyond a beginning–middle–end story map, making it easier to focus on events that happened in each stage of a story. It also makes it easier for the teacher to assess students' comprehension ability by checking the content on the cards.

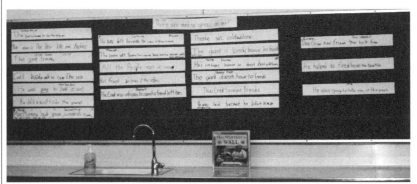

Mrs. Falcone, another second-grade teacher, had used a beginning–middle–end story map with her class. After reading *MacMurtrey's Wall* (Sutherland, 2001), Mrs. Falcone decided to remove the actual frame of a beginning–middle–end story map. She had each student write down on a sentence strip one event from the story. Then she guided the class to arrange the sentence strips based on the events that happened in the beginning, middle, and end of the story. This example shows that removing the actual frame of a story map serves as a way to push students to rely less on visual clues for a story structure and to internalize as much as possible about the structure.

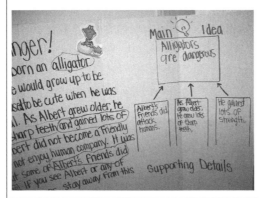

Ms. Stone, a third-grade teacher, used a short text with a mixture of narrative and expository text structures to teach students how to form a main idea with supporting details from a text. The enlarged text makes it possible for her students to identify and discuss specific details supporting the main idea.

(continued)

FIGURE 6.6. Samples of graphic organizers and their benefits.

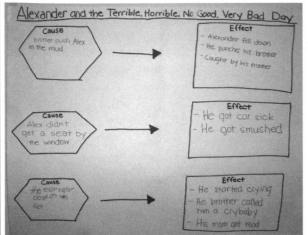

Ms. Truman, a second-grade teacher, used a cause–effect graphic organizer with the book *Alexander and the Terrible, Horrible, No Good, Very Bad Day* (Viorst, 1972) to familiarize her students with the cause–effect text structure, which is more common in expository texts. With the graphic organizer with a narrative text, Ms. Truman helped students develop some prior knowledge related to the concept of cause and effect. Thus, students would potentially have less difficulty with understanding a cause–effect structure in an expository text.

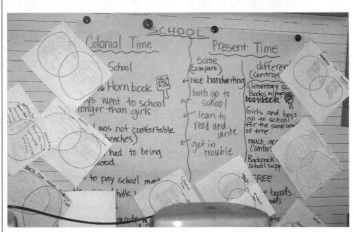

Ms. Park, a fourth-grade teacher, had her students compare and contrast schools during the colonial time and the present time. She first presented a chart with three columns (Colonial Time, Same, Present Time), and then had her students complete a Venn diagram for the comparison. Later, her students shared their comparisons, and Ms. Park recorded students' responses on the chart. This example illustrates the use of Venn diagram as a tool to engage students more in active participation.

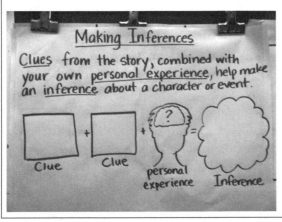

Mrs. Perkins, a fourth-grade teacher, used this Making Inferences chart to remind her students of what is needed to make an inference. During her teaching, whenever she noted that her students had a problem making inferences, she would refer them to the chart. This chart helped her students gain independence in developing skills.

FIGURE 6.6. *(continued)*

Comprehension Process Motion

Block, Parris, and Whiteley (2008) have developed a kinesthetic comprehension strategy, comprehension process motion (CPM), which can be easily adapted by teachers of ELLs. They describe CPMs as "kinesthetic hand placements and movements that portray the visual and physical representations of abstract, unseen comprehension processes such as finding main ideas, inferring, making predictions, and clarifying" (p. 461). For example, in teaching a main idea, you can use a paragraph that can be tracked by students while you are reading it (e.g., from a big book, or enlarge it if it is from a book of regular size). The main idea of CPM includes the following motions:

1. Bend your left arm and hold it horizontally in front of the chest with left hand pointing to the right.

2. Hold the right hand vertically under the left arm at the right side of the left arm (close to the finger tips of the left hand).

3. Every time a detail sentence is read, move the right hand a little bit toward the left side of the left arm.

4. Repeat step 3 for all the detail sentences.

5. At the end of reading the paragraph, the right hand should be at the far left side of the left arm.

Block et al. (2008) suggest telling students that "each time you read a detail sentence your mind moves forward, collecting and adding all the single facts together" (p. 463). For motions related to making predictions, inferring, and clarifying, see the work by Block et al. (2008). CPMs seem appropriate for ELLs at all levels as they provide visual support in addition to linguistic support. For beginners, you can provide your students with complete support by demonstrating the motions and saying the direction. For intermediate or advanced students, you just do the motions, serving as a reminder for students.

Facilitating the Application of Learner Strategies: KWL and KWL Plus Chart, SQ3R, and Cloze Technique

As discussed earlier in this chapter, there is a close relationship between instructional strategies and learner strategies. You can use one specific instructional strategy to help students develop one or two specific learner strategies. For example, when you use an anticipation guide, you facilitate students' use of several learner strategies. Before reading, students activate prior knowledge and connect to prior knowledge while making a judgment on each statement, and thus set a meaningful purpose for themselves. After reading, students check and discuss the statements and provide evidence from the reading to support their judgment of each statement. There is a group of instructional strategies that facilitate students in applying multiple learner strategies. Some examples include KWL and KWL Plus chart,

SQ3R, and cloze technique. The use of these instructional strategies is important in that they nudge students to orchestrate several learner strategies to assist the comprehension process, an ability of a proficient, strategic reader.

KWL and KWL Plus Chart

Since its introduction (Olga, 1986), the KWL chart has been used primarily with expository texts, but it can be used equally effectively with a narrative text. Figure 6.7 shows a KWL chart on *The Stray Dog* (Simont, 2001). Ms. Burton, a first-grade teacher, had her students first look at the front and back covers of the book and then tell the class what they knew about the book. She recorded students' responses in the K column. Next, based on the covers and their prior knowledge, the class asked questions, which Ms. Burton recorded in the W column. After they had finished reading the book, Ms. Burton guided students to complete the L column. For each column, students applied different learner strategies. For the K column, the learner strategies were activating and connecting to prior knowledge and making inferences; for the W column, students used the strategies of setting a purpose for reading and making predictions; for the L column, the learner strategies included noticing, sequencing, and summarizing important details, making inferences, and self-monitoring. A KWL Plus chart allows your students to ask more questions about a topic that they have read about. In particular, the Plus column serves as a way to encourage students to read more on the topic again for the purpose of finding answers to questions listed in the Plus column.

KWL and KWL Plus charts offer students opportunities to experiment with orchestrating multiple learner strategies in a structured, supportive way. Due to the nature of KWL and KWL Plus charts, I want to caution their use with beginners who can be overwhelmed by a need to apply multiple learner strategies while they are still in the process of becoming familiar with each learner strategy. If a

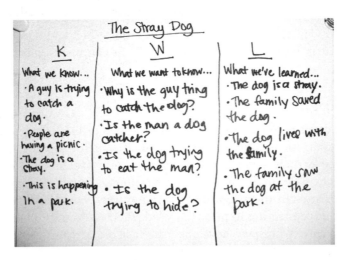

FIGURE 6.7. KWL chart.

KWL chart is used with beginners, you must provide a great deal of modeling and scaffolding and focus only on one column per day or even longer.

SQ3R

SQ3R is another instructional strategy that engages students in using multiple learner strategies while reading an expository text. The steps of SQ3R provide a scaffold for ELLs by breaking down a text into multiple sections, by having students revisit each section multiple times, and by encouraging students to read independently.

S: Survey headings, subheadings, and other information accompanying the text (e.g., illustrations, tables, figures). This step allows students to get an overview of the reading and activate and connect to prior knowledge. ELLs need to be taught what to scan and what not to scan.

Q: Change the headings and subheadings into questions. After this step, students have gained a sense of purpose as they need to find answers to the questions. (This part is also a meaningful grammar exercise for transforming statements into interrogative sentences.)

R: Read the text. During this step, students apply different learner strategies, assisting them to comprehend the text.

R: Recite an answer to each question. Students may write down their answers. During this step, students use learner strategies to help them identify, sequence, and summarize important details related to each question. This step also serves as an informal assessment for students. Not being able to answer questions may signal partial comprehension or misunderstanding of the text. This situation prompts students to become more conscious during the rereading and pay attention to difficult parts of the text. When you spot wrong or incomplete answers, you can offer needed assistance.

R: Review the text by answering the questions and summarizing important ideas in oral or written language. ELLs can share their responses with their peers.

Cloze Technique

The comprehension process requires a reader to use some or all of the phonological, syntactic, semantic, and/or pragmatic cueing systems. As a strategy, cloze technique facilitates a reader to use these cueing systems while thinking about an appropriate word to fill in a blank in a sentence. Further, students rely on learner strategies to help them figure out missing words in the cloze text (e.g., making inferences, connecting to prior knowledge). Traditionally, cloze technique is used with students who have developed at least basic reading comprehension skills. However, with some modifications, it can be used with primary-grade students. It is better to create a cloze text from books students have read. An appropriate choice of books includes predictable books with repeated patterns across pages, books with one or two sentences on each page, and books with illustrations supporting the text.

For example, you can make a cloze text out of a big book by covering up words you would like students to fill in. In the book *Insect Picnic* (Rockwell, n.d.), each page introduces one insect and describes what it does and where it lives: for the first insect, "a cricket singing in the grass" (p. 2); for the second insect, "bees buzzing in the flowers" (p. 4). The sentences about a cricket and bees are well supported by the pictures. When students are asked to fill in the missing word after the phrase *on a green, green* in the sentence *A caterpillar was chewing on a green, green* _____ from page 6, they need to apply their prior knowledge about the sentence patterns learned from pages 2 and 4 (i.e., an insect doing an action in _____). The picture helps students figure out the missing word (*leaf*). The word *a* in the phrase *a green, green*, which is a syntactic cue, gives students another clue for the word *leaf*, not *leaves*.

Whether the cloze text is a narrative text or an expository text and whether you are using a cloze text with late beginning students or advanced students, you should accept all synonyms and engage students in a discussion about these synonyms. Through the discussion, you can make an invisible thinking process of comprehension visible, helping students better understand how vocabulary and comprehension are closely related and how the meaning of one word can change depending on the context where it appears. For example, in a cloze text adapted from the book *A Picture Book of Benjamin Franklin* (Adler, 1990), students may use the word *made* for the missing word in the second sentence of the paragraph, "Benjamin always had lots of ideas. When he was still a young boy, he _____ swimming paddles that fit over his hands and helped him swim faster" (n. p.). You can direct students' attention to the first sentence in the paragraph. However, it may not lead students to think about the word *invented*. If this is the case, you would accept the word *made* for the time being. As students read through the whole text and learn more about Benjamin Franklin, you should remind students of the inventions he made, and then prompt students to consider the word *invented* to replace the word *made*. Furthermore, you explain to students that these two words are synonyms. The word *made* is not a wrong word, but the word *invented* is a more appropriate word to fit the sentence. The discussion and negotiation about words help ELLs to apply oral language, vocabulary knowledge, comprehension skills, and learner strategies. During the process, ELLs experience how different components of the English language and their linguistic proficiency and ability work together in constructing meaning.

Promoting Metacognition: Think-Aloud

Metacognition is a reader's awareness of his or her thinking process when reading and comprehending a text. When a reader thinks aloud, he or she verbalizes an abstract and invisible comprehension process. As a strategy, a think-aloud facilitates students to develop an awareness about their use of learner strategies. In particular, the awareness is related to declarative knowledge (e.g., What is the learner strategy?), procedural knowledge (How do I use this strategy?), and conditional knowledge (When should I use this strategy?). These three types of knowledge are crucial to the development of strategic and skilled readers. A think-aloud can be used with students at all proficiency and grade levels. For example, during a modeled reading, when you say to your kindergartners, "I look at the book cover and see a picture of flowers, birds, and children who are not wearing winter clothes. I guess that this story most likely happened during the spring." you verbalize the process of using picture clues to help with making an inference. Later, you invite the students to share how they make an inference or a prediction about the text and discuss with them what has been used for an inference or a prediction (e.g., prior knowledge, context clues, pictures).

In selecting a text for a think-aloud, Krashen's (1985) comprehensible input *i* + 1 level applies. A text needs to be not too difficult to comprehend, but challenging enough to require students to use multiple learner strategies. The think-aloud example in Table 6.8 shows students the interrelationship between comprehension, vocabulary, and prior knowledge and experience.

The steps for a think-aloud include:

1. Model a think-aloud with one section of a text. Use language comprehensible to students at an appropriate speed (not too fast, not too slow). Consider the word choice, sentence structure, and prior knowledge students need in order to understand the modeling. At the end of the think-aloud, highlight the cueing systems, context clues, and learner strategies that aided comprehension.

2. Provide guided practice where students in a group first do a think-aloud with the second section of the text using the Think-Aloud Guide (see Appendix M), and then share the think-aloud with the class. Comment on students' use of cueing systems, context clues, and learner strategies, highlighting effective ones and offering suggestions for less effective ones.

3. Have each student do a think-aloud with a third section of the text using the Think-Aloud Guide (see Appendix M). Then have each student share the think-aloud with the group peers or with the class. Comment on students' use of cueing systems, context clues, and learner strategies, highlighting effective ones and offering suggestions for less effective ones.

4. Repeat, if needed, steps 1 to 3 or 2 to 3 multiple times with other sections of the text.

I have found that not finishing the whole text during steps 1 to 4 is very motivating and engaging to students. Since they have developed some background knowledge about the text, they are eager to finish the text on their own because they want to find out more about the story or additional interesting facts about a topic. A by-product of a think-aloud is the student motivation and excitement it generates, which is a driving force for ELLs to overcome difficulties during the comprehension process of the text.

TABLE 6.8. Think-Aloud with an Expository Text

Text	Think-aloud
What Do Plants and Animals Need? Plants and animals need certain things. They must have food, water, and **oxygen**. They must not be too hot or too cold. They must be safe. And, they must **reproduce**. Plants do this with seeds. Animals have babies. (Sanchez, 2008, p. 5).	"Plants and animals need certain things. They must have food, water, and **oxygen**." At the end of the second sentence, I see the word *oxygen* written in bold. It must be an important word. I am going to read on to see if the next sentence will give me some clues to the meaning of this word. "They must not be too hot or too cold." This sentence does not explain the word *oxygen*. But it does remind me that feeling too hot or too cold has something to do with the air. Maybe the word *oxygen* means air. Now I remember that we have talked that any living thing needs food, water, and air. So the word, *oxygen* means air. Here is another word, *reproduce*, written in bold, and it must be a special word. But this word has a special part we call a prefix, *re-*. Remember, I often ask you to reread a book. The part *re-* in the word, *reread*, is a prefix, meaning "again." So the word *reproduce* means produce again. But what does it actually mean? I am going to read the next sentence to see if it helps me figure out the meaning of this word. "Plants do this with seeds." So plants make seeds—that is what the word *reproduce* means? I am going to read on. "Animals have babies." When a dog gives birth to puppies, the dog reproduces. So when I was born, my parents reproduced. I just did a think-aloud for you. I told you what I was thinking while reading this paragraph, including how I got the meaning of two words, *oxygen* and *reproduce*. I used some learner strategies: 1. I read the sentence following the word *oxygen* and the word *reproduce* to see if the sentence following those words gave me a clue to the meaning of each word. 2. I made an inference about air from the sentence "They must not be too hot or too cold." 3. I made a connection to my background knowledge about what living things need and about reproducing in dogs and humans. 4. I analyzed the word *reproduce* and connected the part *re-* with the same part in the word *reread*. I hope that while you are doing a think-aloud, you can try a few of the things I just did.

DIFFERENTIATED INSTRUCTION FOR ELLS LITERATE IN L1

For ELLs literate in L1, it is essential to tap into their knowledge of the comprehension process and the use of learner strategies. If you are literate in L1, or if someone from the students' community can volunteer in the classroom, an interactive read-aloud can be done with a book in L1, and students can respond to the book in L1. If students are reading books in English, they are given a choice to respond to or summarize what they have read in English or in L1. This is especially useful for students at the beginning level whose English proficiency and comfort level may prevent them from demonstrating in English what they understand about the text.

Freeman and Freeman (2006b) suggest an instructional strategy called preview–view–review, which can be applied to teaching comprehension.

1. *Preview.* A bilingual teacher, bilingual aide, or bilingual student provides an overview of a comprehension lesson. For example, an overview may be about the content of a book to be read in the lesson, steps involved in a learner strategy, and visual aids (e.g., pictures, graphs, realias) related to the content of lesson.

2. *View.* Teach in English the comprehension strategy with a focus on one area of comprehension (e.g., scanning a text, visualizing).

3. *Review.* The bilingual teacher, a bilingual aide, or a bilingual student works with students in a small group and reviews what has been covered in the lesson through various activities (e.g., responding to the book, summarizing the main ideas).

The preview-view-review strategy allows you to tap into students' knowledge and learner strategies based on reading L1 and makes a text in English manageable for students who are still developing basic reading skills in English.

ENGAGING FAMILIES

Like other components of literacy development, mastery of reading comprehension does not occur within a short period of time. Families can help their children apply and strengthen their reading comprehension skills and learner strategies by reading to and with children and discussing with them what is being read.

> Each family establishes a daily routine of reading for at least 20 minutes.

> Help families locate resources in L1 that they can read to and with their children.

> Families make different types of reading materials (print and nonprint) available to students.

> Family members (if literate in L1) read to or with their children narrative and expository texts in L1 (depending on students' interests) and discuss the content through sharing a response to the text, making comments, and questioning.

> Family members watch with their children an episode of a TV show (with captions on) or a movie in L1 or in English, and discuss it with the children.

> Family members observe you during a comprehension lesson and make an attempt to imitate at least one step demonstrated in the lesson (e.g., preview a text by showing the student the pictures).

> Students read a text with siblings or neighbors' children and turn it or part of it into a play or a short review of the text. They then share the play or the review with families in the neighborhood.

> Family members have students explain what is written in a manual for a video game and demonstrate the steps of how to play a game.

> Family members and students keep a reading log in which they document book titles, interesting or useful quotes (which students later can imitate in their own writing), vocabulary, and literary devices (e.g., metaphor).

VOICE FROM THE CLASSROOM

Camille Wilson
John Muir Academy, Long Beach, California

I have worked as a bilingual teacher and as a Title I teacher with linguistically and culturally diverse students since 1980. I am currently teaching first grade with 25% of my 20 students as designated ELLs with Spanish or Tagalog as L1. I enjoy working with ELLs. I believe it is a huge benefit to be bilingual, biliterate, and bicultural, and I value the rich culturally and linguistically diverse backgrounds my ELLs bring with them. I want my classroom to be a place where all children feel appreciated and honored for who they are and the strengths they already have when they arrive at my door.

Open Court and Write from the Beginning are the literacy programs at my school. I use the sheltered instruction observation protocol (SIOP) model (Echevarria et al., 2008) to guide my instruction. For example, I tell and *write* the content and language objectives for the students. I provide visual aids to provide comprehensible input. When I teach vocabulary, an essential component of comprehension, I say and *write* the vocabulary word on the board. Furthermore, I use technology to support my vocabulary teaching by finding pictures at the website *www. picsearch.com*. I model examples and nonexamples of the vocabulary words. For the word *feathers*, I would show a picture of a bird that has feathers. Then, I show students a nonexample such as a picture of a snake with scales or a cat with fur. I provide English language learners lots of opportunities to interact with their peers and learn from them. Partners complete a graphic organizer such as a circle map listing words that have something to do with a bird. Students can interact together and learn from each other.

When asking comprehension questions before, during, or after reading the text, I consider the proficiency level of students. I often provide various levels of linguistic frames to scaffold my student's access to the academic language required for higher-level comprehension. For example, I have my students use comprehension sticks during a comprehension lesson (see Figure 6.8). My students hold up a comprehension stick with the appropriate icon when I or a classmate use a particular strategy. The comprehension sticks can also be used by the students themselves

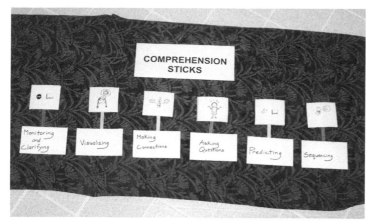

FIGURE 6.8. Comprehension sticks.

to determine which strategy or skill would lend itself to better comprehension. For example, before reading the text, I have my students sit on the rug and I give them two different comprehension sticks, visualizing and monitoring/clarifying. We first review these two comprehension strategies. Then, during the reading of a text, I model visualizing and monitoring/clarifying. I ask them, "Show me what comprehension strategy I'm using. How do you know?" This activity, in particular, promotes a good discussion and fosters students' use of metacognitive strategies.

A mainstay of my comprehension instruction for ELLs is to have plenty of opportunities for them to interact with their peers in meaningful ways. I also like to use poetry, a short, playful text to promote reading comprehension. One activity with poetry and partners was especially successful. I gave the students a poem entitled "Wren" from *Playing with Poems: Word Study Lessons for Shared Reading, K–2* (White, 2008). We read the poem together. Then, sitting with a partner, students tried to figure out what a wren was, using clues from the poem (e.g., *perched on a peg, you can teach me how to fly* and *Wren stretched her wings*). In pairs, students discussed together what they thought a wren was and gathered clues from the poem to support their guess. Finally, after we discussed their ideas and came to a consensus, students drew a picture to go with the poem to show what they understood from the poem.

In closing, I hope the following tips will prove helpful when teaching reading comprehension to ELLs: (1) Use literature personally relevant to the students; (2) consider prior knowledge required to build better comprehension; (3) differentiate questions based on language proficiency levels; (4) use graphic organizers to teach comprehension skills (e.g., compare and contrast, sequencing, and cause–effect); (5) include books written in L1 in your classroom library; (6) provide linguistic frames at different proficiency levels to support students when responding to comprehension questions; and (7) remember that a student's L1 is a strength upon which we build literacy instruction rather than a deficiency to eliminate.

CONCLUSION

In this chapter, I began with a discussion of the comprehension process and sub-processes and various factors that affect ELLs' comprehension. Further, I encouraged teachers to consider, in teaching reading comprehension, the strengths ELLs' bring to understanding an English text and the difficulties they may experience during the process. The strategies and activities for fostering reading comprehension, though similar to those used with non-ELLs, are effective only when teachers have considered criteria for text selection, provided needed modifications and scaffolding, and encouraged students to participate in small-group and whole-class discussions about what is being read. I hope you have benefited from reading about the classroom examples illustrating strategies and activities and goals of instruction for reading comprehension. Ms. Wilson's account of teaching comprehension reflects the goals of comprehension instruction. Her seventh tip for other teachers powerfully highlights one aspect of the essence of this book—valuing students' strengths.

CHAPTER 7

INSTRUCTION FOR WRITING DEVELOPMENT

Before the beginning of the school year, teachers of ELLs at Mountain View Elementary School gathered to analyze the writing assessment data from the previous year's state test. The teachers noted a pattern across grade levels—students did better in individual components of writing (e.g., identifying and correcting run-on sentences; identifying supporting details for a topic sentence) than actual writing (i.e., timed writing on a given topic). Ms. Gibson and Mrs. Chang identified another challenge for their fourth graders who were able to write a good introduction and a detailed body, but unable to conclude a piece in an effective way. Teachers at the primary grades (kindergarten, first, and second grade) felt frustrated with the overwhelming challenge for them and for their students. Mrs. McCarthy explained, "My first graders did not want to write because they could not find words to express ideas. After I told them it is okay to use pictures to express ideas, some students started using pictures. But others were still into the idea of using only words in writing." Ms. Gutierrez pointed out that her third graders need more writing practice in class, but that there is not enough class time for this type of practice.

This scenario sounds so familiar to teachers of ELLs. Writing seems to be difficult for teachers to teach and for students to learn and master. Teachers often ask questions like these:

1. How can I get students interested in writing and motivated to write?
2. Should I wait to teach writing until my students have developed oral English proficiency?
3. How can I conduct classroom-based assessment to measure ELLs' writing proficiency?
4. What instructional strategies can I use to teach writing?
5. How can I balance having students revise and having them edit their own writing?

192

In this chapter, I provide an overview of writing development, highlighting the areas of strengths and difficulties ELLs possess. Following that, I discuss ways to assess writing. The next section focuses on strategies and activities for teaching writing to students at various levels. Finally, I share ideas for engaging families in supporting their children's writing development. To conclude this chapter, Ms. Hilary Shuler, a fifth-grade teacher, shares her experience of teaching writing.

DEVELOPMENT OF WRITING

It is a common misconception that ELLs can write only after having developed oral proficiency. Research, however, has shown that ELLs are capable of expressing their thoughts even if they are still developing knowledge in grammar, vocabulary, and oral language (Fitzgerald, 2005; Hudelson, 1984; Samway, 1993; Taylor, 2000). Kamil and Bernhardt (2004) recognize a unique benefit that writing offers ELLs: "Writing affords children the opportunity to demonstrate their knowledge without being inhibited by the time constraints of immediate oral performance and the social constraints of needing to look and sound like 'the other kids'" (p. 33).

In writing, students may use environmental print, symbols, words, phrases, and expressions acquired at school and outside school (Mora-Flores, 2009; Samway, 2006) (See Figure 7.1, pp. 194–195). Literature has indicated that the writing development of ELLs is similar to that of non-ELLs (August & Shanahan, 2006; Edelsky, 1982; Fitzgerald & Amendum, 2007). The process of writing development for non-ELLs is also nonlinear, developmental, and complex (Calkins, 1983; Freeman & Freeman, 2009; Graves, 1983; Hudelson, 1984; Samway, 1987, 2006). While students go through similar developmental stages of writing, the ways of going through the stages vary from student to student. One student may stay at one stage longer than another stage; another student may move back and forth between two stages. Table 7.1 (p. 196) lists characteristics of ELL's writing at the beginning, intermediate, and advanced levels (California State Board of Education, 1999; Samway, 2006; TESOL, undated).

The complexity of writing development is further evident in various factors involved in ELLs' writing, including linguistic and contextual knowledge (e.g., classroom writing instruction, motivation, and self-confidence) (Samway, 2006). Table 7.2 (p. 197) summarizes the factors mentioned by Samway (2006) and those I feel are important.

Areas of Strengths and Difficulties

Students bring some strengths to learning how to write. For example, ELLs with some literacy experience in L1 understand, to some extent, the functions and conventions of writing and the process of communicating ideas with others through a written text. Such knowledge facilitates their learning how to write in English.

Beginning (kindergartners)

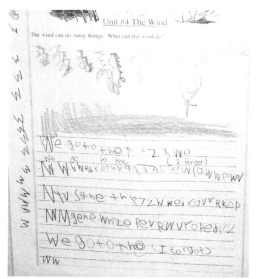

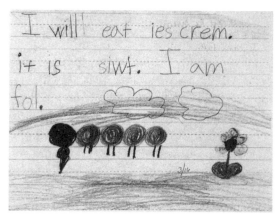

Intermediate (third grader)

All About Me

Do you want to know about me? I live with my Mom, Dad, sisters and grandma. I play with my family. My family is fun.

My favorite Hobby is watching TV. I watch TV on weekends. My favorite show is Sponge Bob, Because it make me laugh. I watch with my siter.

My school subect is Math. Math is fun because I am good at it. I think that 3rd grade math is easy because I understand all of it.

My dream is to become a Doctor. Being a Doctor is fun. I like Math and science. I like help people that are sick.

I want Miss Johnston to know that I am funny and smart. I like making people laugh.

(continued)

FIGURE 7.1. Writing samples.

Advanced (fourth grader)

Frindle

Nick Allen is a character in the book Frindle. His hair is red, has blue eyes and he is in 5th grade and he was an expert at asking the delaying questions. He felt excited when he made up a new word and he felt nervous when the lady went to his house and felt happy when Mrs. Granger didn't scream and talked to him nice. He says in class "I dropped my frindle," and read an article to the whole class. He asks Mrs. Granger if he can have the letter that he signed. Nick Allen thinks of making up a new word, making a letter to Mrs. Granger and was behaving bad during class. Nick Allen acts silly during class, sometimes he acts nice and sometimes he is mean to Mrs. Granger. Nick Allen is one of the main characters in the book Frindle.

FIGURE 7.1. *(continued)*

Even for ELLs with limited literacy experiences in L1, their general knowledge about the functions and conventions of language fosters an awareness of functions of writing, and structures and rules governing a language.

One salient difficulty for ELLs at various proficiency levels results from their limited or developing knowledge about English language, and in particular, the areas of grammar, vocabulary, and orthography. For students whose L1 is very different from English, their challenges are more than those whose L1 is similar to English. For example, an ELL with Farsi as L1 has to learn to write from left to right rather than from right to left as in Farsi. Students may produce a sentence based on a word order in L1. A second area of difficulty is ELLs' background knowledge about a topic. Older ELLs may know more than younger ELLs, but their knowledge, and in particular knowledge related to culture, may be insufficient or incorrect as well.

TABLE 7.1. Stages of ELLs' Writing Development

Stages	Characteristics
Beginning	• Conveying a simple idea (often very personal) • Drawing pictures and/or scribbling (symbols like letters and words) • Copying or spelling the English alphabet or familiar words (e.g., environment print, words learned, words posted in the classroom) along with pictures • Using formulaic language (e.g., *It is _____. I like _____*.) along with pictures • Writing phrases and simple sentences with the presence or absence of pictures • Possibly mismatching print, symbols, and scribbling, and pictures • Having legible or illegible handwriting • Making an attempt at using appropriately common, simple punctuation (e.g., period), capitalization (e.g., *I*, proper names), and word spacing • Producing many errors in the areas of syntax, semantics, and orthography that hinder communication
Intermediate	• Conveying an elaborated, mostly focused idea • Following structures of narrative texts often (e.g., fairy tale) and/or attempting to follow structures of expository texts (e.g., cause and effect) • Drawing pictures (if needed) to accompany print • Using more appropriate words from everyday English • Using more complex formulaic language (e.g., *I like _____ because _____*.) • Using simple, compound, and maybe complex sentences • Experimenting with sentence variety • Having legible writing more often • Using appropriately varied punctuation (e.g., comma, exclamation point) and capitalization (e.g., name of a book) more often • Producing some errors in the areas of syntax, semantics, and orthography that hinder communication
Advanced	• Conveying a complex, focused idea or multiple, focused ideas on a wide range of topics • Following text structures of narrative (e.g., personal narrative) and expository texts (e.g., biography, persuasion) • Using more appropriate advanced and varied vocabulary (e.g., multisyllabic words; content-specific words) from everyday and academic English • Using more, varied compound and complex sentences and other advanced sentence structures • Incorporating literary devices (e.g., figurative language) • Using appropriately more advanced punctuation (e.g., apostrophe 's, hyphen) and capitalization • Producing few errors in the areas of syntax, semantics, and orthography that may not hinder communication

Note. See Figure 7.1 for writing samples.

TABLE 7.2. Factors Involved in ELLs' Writing

Factors	Explanation
Language	Syntax, semantics, pragmatics, morphology, orthography
Context	• Writing topic and genre (familiarity vs. unfamiliarity) • Purpose of writing (assessment driven vs. meaning driven) • Approaches to writing instruction (accuracy and mechanics focused vs. meaning focused; writing curriculum; writing as a process vs. writing as a product) • Classroom culture (high anxiety vs. low anxiety)
Learner	• Reading and writing experience and literacy level in L1 and English • Knowledge of the writing process • Background knowledge in content areas and about the world in general • Self-confidence, motivation • Willingness to take risks
Community	• Print presence (limited vs. a lot) • Literacy practices in public places and in families (limited vs. a lot)

Text structure is an area that cannot be overlooked. Among narrative and expository text structures, structure variations are endless and inconsistent (Freeman & Freeman, 2009). It is not easy for students to learn about these variations from their readings and then apply them to their own writing. For students literate in L1, learning process is further complicated by the possible interferences from L1 and its discourse structure. In other languages, a text structure may not be in a linear order as in English (Kaplan, 1966; Kaplan & Ramanathan, 1996).

Goals of Instruction

A reader is likely to be engaged in a good book with an interesting topic, as it often provides the reader with instant pleasure. On the contrary, fewer people are fond of writing, because it is a laborious, lengthy process and does not provide instant pleasure for the writer. Given that, the primary goal for writing instruction for ELLs is to motivate them to write and help them develop an enjoyment of writing. To achieve this goal, students need to have opportunities to write about something relevant to and familiar to them (Freeman & Freeman, 2009; Graves & Rueda, 2009; Samway, 2006). Levitt (2009) suggests "experiences they can dissect and analyze" (e.g., a family trip) (p. 9). When students have a lot to say about a topic, they have a better chance to produce a piece of writing with substance and in an acceptable form for a genre. Students' sense of success further boosts their self-confidence, which in turn motivates them to meet challenges that may occur in future writing. It is common sense that nobody wants to try something again at which they are not good (Guthrie & Davis, 2003) and which makes the doer experience failure and frustration.

A second goal of writing instruction is for students to become familiar with the writing process, a nonlinear, recursive one. Writing is not practiced as just spelling words on a piece of paper. Rather, it involves these steps: brainstorming and organizing ideas and careful planning; drafting a piece; revising the written piece for clarity, cohesion, and effectiveness; editing to correct mechanical errors; and sharing the written piece with others. The only way for ELLs to learn about the process is for them to go through each stage of the writing process with scaffolded assistance from their teachers. Thus, a process-focused approach to writing instruction is helpful to ELLs (Fitzgerald & Amendum, 2007; Kendall & Khuon, 2006; Samway, 2006).

A last goal of writing instruction is for students to become skillful at writing for daily communication and academic purposes (Freeman & Freeman, 2009; Samway, 2006). We fail to prepare students to survive in a society if they are not taught how to write for communicating with others in their daily life (e.g., writing a thank-you note). Of equal importance is for students to learn how to write for academic purposes, a type of writing essential for their academic success. To achieve this daunting goal, it is imperative for teachers to make a close connection between teaching reading and writing of narrative and expository texts. After being exposed to and having received instruction on various types of text genres, students have a better chance to develop their writing skills through imitating, practicing, and internalizing the English language at the word, phrase, paragraph, and text level. Freeman and Freeman (2009) remind us that it is never too early to introduce students to expository texts in their readings.

ASSESSING WRITING DEVELOPMENT

Assessment data from standardized tests are not usually available before the end of the school year, thus making these data less useful for teachers who try to modify instruction to address the needs of individual students before the end of the school year. Teachers conduct explicit assessment where a student is asked to write something about a topic and embedded assessment where a student's writing samples related to content areas (e.g., a summary piece on the Civil War unit; a thank-you letter) are analyzed. In assessing students' strengths and needs, teachers analyze and compare and contrast data from both types of assessments. Figure 7.2 shows three pieces of writing from a second grader in the early intermediate level that yield strengths and needs in various ways.

Explicit Assessment

In an explicit assessment, a student writes on a topic either of his or her choice or on a topic given by you, and you document the student's strengths and needs (see Appendix N). When conducting explicit assessment, you need to consider three questions: (1) Will a student choose topic of interest or will a student be given a

Writing on a Topic Chosen by the Student: A Letter to Santa Claus
(The teacher had modeled the format of a letter.)

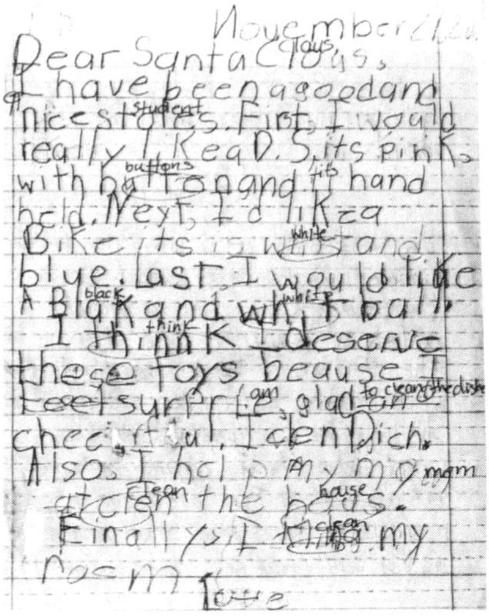

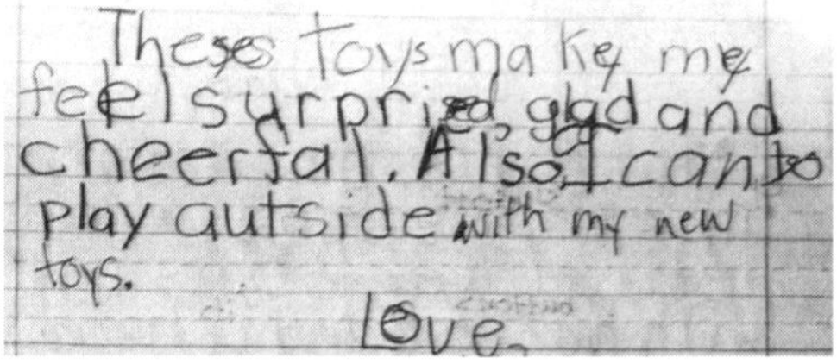

Writing on a Topic Given by the Teacher:
What Do You Like to Do and Where Do You Like to Go in Your Free Time?

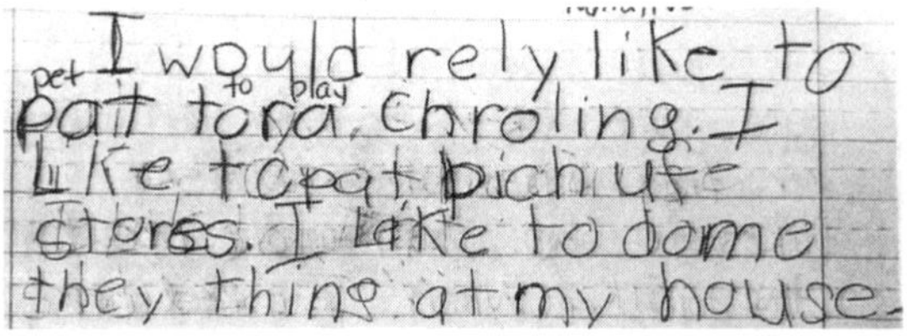

Writing on a Topic under Study: Cats

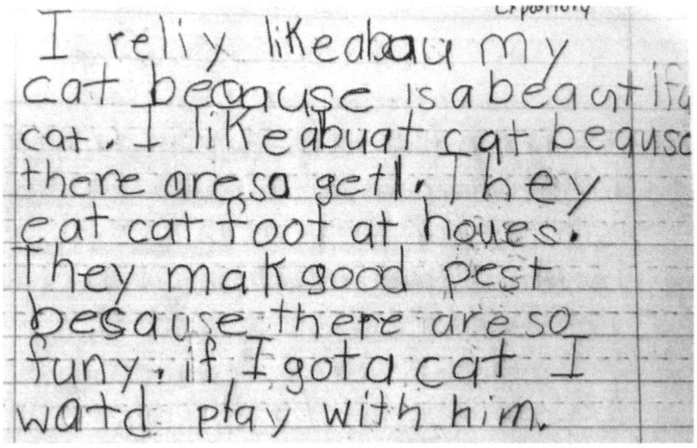

FIGURE 7.2. Three pieces of writing.

topic to write? (2) Should the topic be familiar or unfamiliar to a student? (3) How much time should a student be given for completing the writing? There needs to be a balance between giving students a prompt to write about and allowing students to choose their own topics. As shown in the first sample (with a free choice) and the second sample (written in response to a teacher's prompt) in Figure 7.2, different strengths and needs are obvious. Allowing a student to choose a topic increases the possibility that the student has enough information about it and is interested in it. These advantages can decrease the possibility that a writing test becomes a measure of the student's knowledge about a topic, not his or her writing and language skills. On the other hand, students do need to have an experience with writing on a given topic, because that is how they will be assessed on a standardized test. It is also important to assess an ability to write a narrative and an informational piece. As shown in Figure 7.2, the student seems to be better at writing a letter than just a narrative and information.

The factor of time allocation for writing cannot be overlooked. Time constraints can result in pressure for students, thus increasing their anxiety level. In allocating the amount of writing time for ELLs, you should consider a student's proficiency level. Beginning ELLs may need more time to brainstorm and piece all elements together while later intermediate and advanced ELLs who are familiar with the writing routine may take less time with prewriting and actual writing. Furthermore, prior knowledge, formal schooling with L1, and personality are important factors. For example, an ELL with limited general knowledge and with L1 different from English needs more time for composing and may do better with writing a topic of free choice.

Embedded Assessment

In embedded assessment, you collect at least two pieces of writing students completed during literacy tasks (e.g., a response to a book) for an analysis of strengths and needs (see the third sample in Figure 7.2). Data from embedded assessment can shed light on how well the student uses writing for various purposes. Some students may do well on explicit assessment but not on actual writing, whereas others may be skillful at conveying ideas related to a content area but have trouble writing about a topic given by you. Using data from both explicit and embedded assessment, you will obtain a relatively holistic picture of the student's writing ability.

STRATEGIES AND ACTIVITIES FOR PROMOTING WRITING

The guiding principle for ELL writing instruction is to teach students the process of writing rather than just having students produce a piece of writing. When the perspective of the writing process is adopted, teachers "create situations in which writing is a natural way to communicate" (Freeman & Freeman, 2006, p. 156). That is, students need learn to write and write to learn for authentic and meaningful purposes. The following is a summary of the elements of effective writing instruction Freeman and Freeman (2006b, p. 159) identify:

1. Teachers model and scaffold the process of choosing a topic for students.

2. Teachers encourage students to choose topics related to their own experience and write for an authentic purpose.

3. Students make reading–writing connections in choosing topics to write.

4. Students keep an updated list of topics for future writing.

5. Students understand writing as a process from a draft to a final version.

6. Students have access to texts of various genres and resource books while going through the writing process.

7. Students are allowed to use invented spelling.

8. Students share their writing and receive feedback relevant to their needs.

These elements for effective writing instruction are reflected in the strategies and activities presented in the following section (see Table 7.3).

Varying Instruction for Different Types of Writers

Although ELLs go through a similar set of stages in their writing development, there is much difference in the process taken by individual students. In order to scaffold writing instruction for individual ELLs, writing lessons should be based on students' needs as shown through a careful analysis of students' writing samples (Kendall & Khuon, 2006). Based on their experience of working with ELLs at various grade and proficiency levels, Kendall and Khuon (2006) identify nine types of writers and suggested possible ways to help each type of writer. In Table 7.4, I list Kendall and Khuon's nine categories of writers and include Kendall and Khuon's and my own suggestions for instructional foci for each type of writer.

Herrera and Murry (2005) suggest scaffolding writing in content area by differentiating the expectations for students at different proficiency levels. For example, the expectations of writing a persuasive paragraph are as follows. The expectations for newcomers who cannot participate in any English assessment include (1) "List reasons using isolated words"; and (2) "Incorporate ordinal numbers and transitions (*next, then*) with the words from the generated list." Beginners are expected to (1) "List reasons using phrases/simple sentences"; and (2) "Incorporate ordinal numbers and transitions (*next, then*) with phrases from the generated list." Expectations for intermediate students include (1) "List reasons using simple sentences"; and (2) "Incorporate the generated sentences into a highly structured paragraph frame." Advanced students are expected to (1) "List reasons using more complex sentences"; and (2) "Incorporate the generated sentences into a paragraph frame with transitional signals" (p. 271).

(text resumes on page 204)

TABLE 7.3. Proficiency Levels, Instructional Foci, and Strategies and Activities for Writing Instruction

Proficiency level	Instructional foci	Strategies and activities
Beginning	• Providing comprehensible input for writing ideas and developing a general and linguistic knowledge base through oral and written language activities (e.g., talks, read-aloud) • Teaching students to convey a simple idea • Teaching conventions of writing through modeling and scaffolded practice • Encouraging risk taking in composing in a form of print, pictures, and/or symbols and in spelling • Encouraging students to use learned words, phrases, and sentences in writing • Making reading and writing connections • Introducing students to the writing process	• Varying instruction for different types of writers • Using mentor texts • Providing opportunities to write various text genres • Composing morning message/daily news and Language Experience Approach (LEA) • Interactive writing • Connecting writing with reading • Writers' workshop
Intermediate	• Providing comprehensible input for writing ideas, expanding the general and linguistic knowledge base, and developing knowledge of text structure of various genres through oral and written language activities (e.g., sharing) • Teaching students to convey an elaborated idea with clarity, focus, and cohesion in a paragraph or multiple paragraphs • Teaching conventions of writing through modeling and scaffolded practice • Encouraging students to use a variety of words and sentences from everyday and academic English • Making reading and writing connections • Engaging students in the writing process	• Varying instruction for different types of writers • Using mentor texts • Providing opportunities to write various text genres • Connecting writing with reading • Writers' workshop
Advanced	• Providing comprehensible input for expanding the general and linguistic knowledge base and knowledge of text structures of various genres through oral and written language activities (e.g., discussion, independent reading) • Teaching students to convey a complex idea or multiple ideas with clarity, focus, and cohesion in multiple paragraphs • Teaching conventions of writing through the writing process (e.g., text structure) • Teaching students various text genres • Requiring students to use everyday and academic English in composing • Making reading and writing connections • Helping students become skillful with the writing process	• Varying instruction for different types of writers • Using mentor texts • Providing opportunities to write various text genres • Connecting writing with reading • Writers' workshop

TABLE 7.4. Instructional Foci for Different Types of Writers

Types of writers[a]	Instructional foci
Writers who don't write	• Motivating writers • Inviting writers to choose topics to write about • Creating a low-anxiety environment • Allowing writers write in L1
Writers whose writing is difficult (or impossible) to read	• Having writers read the writing back to inform you what is written • Having writers draw a picture to express intended ideas • Having someone speaking L1 translate the writing if there is much code switching or if writing is done in L1
Writers whose writing does not make sense	• Having writers ask themselves the question, "Does this make sense?" • Having writers work with partners and ask each other the same question
Writers who never revise	• Having writers reread their work (preferably aloud) to note confusing, unclear ideas, or awkward use of diction and sentence structures • Having others read writers' work • Having writers discuss their work with partners who will provide constructive feedback
Writers who edit only a little, if at all	• Scaffolding the editing process, focusing on capitalization, punctuation, grammar and usage, sentence variety, and spelling • Having writers reread their work to note the impact of mechanics errors on meaning
Writers who take forever to finish	• Dividing the writing assignment into small tasks • Setting reasonable deadlines • Rewarding writers for completing each small task
Writers who always write about the same topic	• Reading aloud to writers to expand their knowledge base • Having writers read texts of different genres and on different topics • Having writers share texts they have read or written • Integrating writing into content areas • Having writers document in a writer's notebook interesting ideas they have found
Writers who find it difficult to get organized and come up with ideas	• Using graphic organizers to help writers organize their thoughts • Having writers document in a writer's notebook interesting ideas they have found
Writers who struggle, really struggle, with spelling	• Teaching spelling as part of the writing workshop • Teaching spelling strategies • Developing writers' knowledge about English spelling • Discussing similarities and differences between English and L1 spelling

Note. Kendall and Khuon (2006).

Using Mentor Texts

Mentor texts have been a powerful tool for teaching students about the craft of writing (Dorfman & Cappelli, 2007; Ray, 2006). Dorfman and Cappelli (2007) define mentor texts as "pieces of literature that we can return to again and again as we help young writers learn how to do what they may not yet be able to do on their own"; as "our coaches and our partners as we bring the joy of writing to our students"; and as texts that "help students and teachers continually reinvent themselves as writers" (pp. 2–3). You can identify mentor texts from a basal reader anthology and/or from supplementary books interesting to students.

Dorfman and Cappelli (2007) suggest considering these factors in selecting a mentor text: personal connection to the text, text connection to curricular standards and students' needs, a balance of genres, and diversity issues. Before selecting mentor texts for ELLs, three more factors need to be taken into consideration: students' background knowledge of the topic (Cummins, 2000; Kendall & Khuon, 2006), the complexity of the language used in the text (Kendall & Khuon, 2006), and the ways a book can support students' writing (Kendall & Khuon, 2006). If students lack prior knowledge of the topic, they may enjoy the text less due to a possible difficulty in comprehending the text. This holds true if the language of the text is beyond students' proficiency levels. Furthermore, a mentor book may become less valuable and useful if it does not provide a good model for a genre students are learning or will be learning to write.

There are many benefits of using mentor texts for ELLs (Freeman & Freeman, 2009; Kendall & Khuon, 2006; Samway, 2006). Reading and discussing mentor texts provides opportunities for students to explore author's craft. This type of comprehensible input from familiar texts contextualizes their learning about the craft of writing. Mentor texts can contribute to students' growth and expansion in knowledge about the world in general and about content areas, including social and cultural knowledge. The growth and expansion of knowledge prepares students for writing, as they have more choices for writing topics. Perhaps the most important benefit mentor texts offer students is an opportunity to examine text structures of different genres so that they later can imitate a specific text structure for a specific genre in their own writing. This opportunity is particularly crucial when students are learning to write an expository text (e.g., argument and persuasion). Table 7.5 lists the benefits of mentor texts, and Table 7.6 (p. 206) shows some examples of books, illustrating some of the benefits mentor texts offer.

Here are the steps I have developed based on the suggestions and guidelines by Dorfman and Cappelli (2007), Kendall and Khuon (2006), and Samway (2006).

Choosing a Mentor Book

> Select or have students select a mentor text that is age, content, and language appropriate.

> If students are allowed to choose a book, a collection of mentor texts should be available in the classroom library. The collection should include books by the same author on the same topic or different ones; books on different topics; books

---

TABLE 7.5. Benefits of Mentor Texts

Obtaining ideas for writing and expanding knowledge base
- Personal experiences with family, friends, nature, and events (e.g., family gathering; travel)
- Information about various subjects (e.g., environment)
- Cultural and social information (e.g., a cultural celebration)

Studying author's craft
- Diction (e.g., strong adjectives, verbs, and nouns)
- Sentence variety (e.g., a balance of long and short sentences; use of simple, compound, complex, and compound complex sentences)
- Literary devices (e.g., figurative language, personification, hyperbole)
- Content presentation (e.g., showing not telling; creating suspense)

Exploring text structure of genres
- Narrative text structures (e.g., elements of a story)
- Expository text structures (e.g., compare and contrast)
- A combination of narrative and expository text structures

---

reflecting students' cultures and/or languages; books with males and females as characters; and bilingual books.

➢ Texts other than fiction and nonfiction (e.g., photo essays, question/answer books, diaries, and concept books) are good models for writing specific genres (Hadaway, Vardell, & Young, 2004). Some high-quality magazines include *Kids Discover* (*www.kidsdiscover.com*), *National Geographic Kids* (*www.nationalgeographic. com/ngkids*), *National Geographic Explorer* (*magma.nationalgeographic.com/ngexplorer/*), *Sports Illustrated for Kids* (*www.sikids.com*), and *Time for Kids* (*www.timeforkids.com*).

Reading and Discussing the Book

➢ Read to and/or with students or have students read the book by themselves.

➢ Discuss the book with students to make sure that they can comprehend the content.

➢ Guide the discussion through teacher and student questioning, thinking aloud, sharing responses to the book, and making text-to-self, text-to-text, and text-to-world connections.

Selecting Instructional Foci from the Book

➢ Identify an element or elements from the book for whole-class or small-group instruction (e.g., effective use of action verbs; metaphor; a descriptive text structure).

TABLE 7.6. Benefits of Mentor Texts Illustrated with Children's Books

Obtaining ideas for writing and expanding knowledge base

Tom (dePaola, 1993)

- Tomie dePaola describes interesting childhood experiences (e.g., visiting his grandparents, helping out in the grandparents' grocery store). This book provides students with some ideas to write about their own childhood experiences.

The Tiny Seed (Carle, 1987)

- Eric Carle describes a life cycle of a tiny seed in the format of a story. The book can serve as a model for presenting information in a narrative format.

Studying author's craft

WOW! It's Great Being a Duck! (Rankin, 1997)

- Joan Rankin introduces a unique main character in the opening sentence. "*Lillee was the last born, the last to hatch, and the* smallest *and* skinniest" (n. p.).
- The author uses onomatopoeic words to make the story alive (e.g., *crack, crash, plomp*).

Weather Words and What They Mean (Gibbons, 1990)

- Gail Gibbons uses pictures and words to explain weather words (e.g., drawing curved lines and leaves to show "Wind is air in motion" [n. p.]).
- The author uses everyday words to explain weather words (e.g., "Drizzle is when raindrops are very small" [n. p.]).

Exploring text structure of genres

A Picture Book of Benjamin Franklin (Adler, 1990)

- David Adler writes a short biography of Benjamin Franklin in chronological order, but he varies the way that each specific time period is mentioned. For example, in the first half of the book, Franklin's age is emphasized (e.g., "Benjamin began school when he was eight years old" [n. p.]). Toward the end of the book, specific years are given as they are historically important (e.g., "Benjamin Franklin returned to the colonies in 1775, soon after the beginning of the American Revolution" [n. p.]).

Our Solar System (Simon, 1992)

- Seymour Simon uses a mixture of description, cause and effect, and compare and contrast structures to present information about the solar system.

➢ In choosing an element or elements, consider students' strengths and needs and curricular standards (see Table 7.7 for a sample). For example, to address a writing standard (showing not telling in writing a narrative), you should select several books with varied plot and language (e.g., vocabulary, sentence structure) at various difficulty and interest levels. The selected books should illustrate specific ways to describe a plot (e.g., an effective use of words, literary devices, and sentence structures).

TABLE 7.7. A Sample of Instructional Foci for Using Mentor Texts

Language
- Diction: effective use of parts of speech (e.g., verbs, nouns); synonyms
- Figurative language (e.g., idioms, metaphors)
- Literary devices and propaganda techniques

Structure

At the paragraph level
- A topic sentence of a main idea/thesis with supporting details
- Cohesion within a paragraph and between paragraphs through the use of referents, conjunctions, prepositional phrases, transitional words and phrases, nominalization, and clauses (see grammatical knowledge section in Chapter 8 for each concept)

At the text level
Narrative text
- Story elements
- Different ways a story is told (e.g., beginning, middle, and ending)
- Functions of illustration
- Author's style and purpose

Expository text
- Text structure of description, sequence, compare and contrast, cause and effect, problem solution, and persuasion
- Different ways information is presented (e.g., a combination of different text structures)
- Functions of visual texts (e.g., pictures, graphs, lists, diagrams)
- Functions of supplementary information (e.g., endnotes and footnotes, sidebar texts, glossary, appendices)
- Author's style and purpose

Poetry
- Poetic structure of rhymed verse, free verse, and patterned verse
- Author's style and purpose

Discussing a Selected Element

➢ Discuss with students about how a selected element helps an author convey meaning more effectively. For example, in Joanne Cole's Magic School Bus series, a mixture of narrative and expository text structures makes information on various science topics more interesting to read, as if readers were reading a story about the characters' adventure in a world of science. In *Too Many Tamales* (Soto, 1993), Soto begins with an opening paragraph about the setting of Christmas. The opening allows readers to activate their prior knowledge about the holiday in the Latino culture and to predict a possible storyline.

➢ Have students choose one example of the selected element from the book, discuss it in a small group or with a partner, and share the discussion with the class.

➢ Record on chart paper examples selected by the students and comment on the examples. For example, you can direct students' attention to identified powerful verbs (*glared, studied*, and *observed*) whose meaning is similar to a common verb, *see*, in *WOW! It's Great Being a Duck* (Rankin, 1997). "She *glared* at his furry legs. She *studied* his LONG TAIL. She *observed* his sharp snout" (n. p., emphasis added).

Inviting Students to Imitate an Identified Element

➢ Have students work with a partner to apply the element by imitating it. For example, imitating the question–answer format in Bill Martin's (1983) *Brown Bear, Brown Bear, What Do You See*, students create an I spy book (e.g., *Jose, Jose, What do you spy? I spy a little brown bird looking at me.*)

➢ Comment on students' imitations. For example, in the above response to the question, the student used two adjectives rather than one as in Martin's book.

Encouraging Students to Apply Learned Elements

➢ Remind students of discussed and imitated elements before any types of writing (e.g., free journal writing, writing for a content area).

➢ Share with the class students' writings with elements incorporated.

Providing Opportunities to Write Various Text Genres

Reading, discussing, and imitating mentor texts allow students to access comprehensible input of various text structures. But this type of exposure is not an adequate condition for ELLs to develop writing proficiency in everyday and academic literacy. They need to have opportunities in class and outside class to write different genres of texts (Freeman & Freeman, 2006b; Mora-Flores, 2009; Peregoy & Boyle, 2009; Samway, 2006). Such writing experiences prepare students with language and literacy skills needed for achieving academic success and later for becoming productive members of society. Figure 7.3 lists text genres that you can integrate into your curriculum and encourage students to write. Figure 7.4 is an example of mixed genre writing that Ms. Cervantez was modeling for her first graders.

Composing Morning Messages and the Language Experience Approach

Writing morning messages and the language experience approach (LEA) are two strategies for helping young English-speaking children learn about how speech is written down, how ideas are expressed in a written text, and how conventions of print are used (Calkins, 1994; Stauffer, 1980b). Literature on literacy instruction for ELLs has indicated that these two strategies can serve a similar purpose (Fitzgerald & Amendum, 2007; Manyak, 2008). In writing a morning message, you demonstrate the conventions of print (i.e., concepts about print, grammar, and

Advertisement	Memoir
Argument	Myth
Article (for a newsletter or newspaper)	Note
Autobiography	Outline
Biography	Personal narrative
Book jacket	Persuasion
Brochure	Photo essay
Cartoon/comic strips	Play script (e.g., Readers' Theater)
Collage	Poem (free or patterned verse)
Diary	Poster (e.g., movie, wanted)
Editorial	Questionnaire
E-mail	Recipe
Expository text (e.g., cause and effect)	Report
Fable	Response to literature
Fairy tale	Review (of a book, a movie, or a video game)
Glossary	Song
Greeting card	Speech
Haiku	Story (different genres)
Instruction (e.g., how to play a video game)	Summary
Journal (e.g., dialogue, double-entry)	Survey
Letter	Time line
List	Translation
Map	

FIGURE 7.3. Text genres.

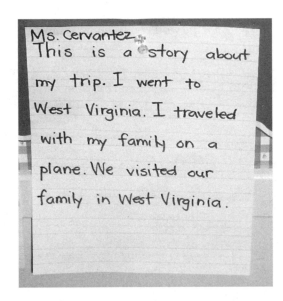

FIGURE 7.4. An example of mixed genre writing.

punctuation), formulaic language (e.g., *Today is Tuesday January 15th, 2008. We will _____.*), and letter–sound correspondence (see Figure 7.5). This modeling also allows students to receive comprehensible input and observe the process of composing. Further, students learn from each morning message about a daily routine, which gives students a sense of what is expected for the day (Barone & Xu, 2008). Once students become familiar with the procedure of morning message, they can be responsible for telling you what to write for the message. Toward the third semester of the school year, you can invite students, working in groups or in pairs, to write a morning message.

In writing an LEA text, you demonstrate more than in a morning message. You use questions to guide students in constructing a short text based on an experience. Students are challenged to formulate an idea and construct sentences for it. During the process, they experiment with English. Older ELL at the beginning level benefit from LEA if the content for LEA focuses more on a content area they are learning (e.g., steps for conducting an experiment or solving a math problem; a summary of an article on a historical event). LEA activities can be carried out across a week.

Day 1

1. Provide students with an experience so that they will have something to say (e.g., a trip to a local library; a five-senses activity with apples).

2. You and students talk about the experience. If needed, you prompt students with questions. For example, *What did we do first, second, and last? What is the name of the library? What did we do in the library? How does your apple taste? How does your apple smell?*

3. Record on chart paper each sentence given by the students. If needed, you can prompt students with questions for clarification and for reminding students of the experience. If a student's speech is hard to understand, have the student draw

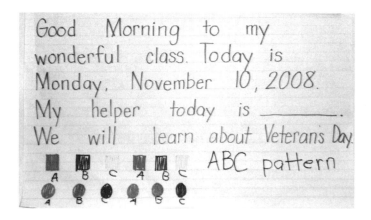

FIGURE 7.5. An example of a morning message.

a picture on the board, and you supply a word for the picture. If a student speaks in L1, have other students translate. If impossible, have the student draw a picture. Pointing at each word, you read with students a finished sentence before working on the next sentence. Many scholars have recommended writing down whatever students say to you in LEA, including grammatically unacceptable errors (Kendall & Khuon, 2006; Morrow, 2005). The reason is that meaning, not form, of what students try to convey is more important at this stage. Furthermore, you want to cultivate a low-anxiety environment so that students participate actively in their language production. Dictated texts at a students' proficiency level become comprehensible materials for revision and editing (Nessel & Dixon, 2008).

4. Read with students the finished sentences, pointing at each word.

5. You and students come up with a title for the dictated text. It is easier to do so at the end of the dictation than in the beginning of the dictation, as based on what's written, students can come up with a title that reflects a main idea of the dictated text.

6. You word process the dictated text and prepare a hard copy for each student.

Day 2

1. You and students read the dictated text on chart paper multiple times.

2. You comment on the text and make suggestions for improving the text if students are ready to do so. For example, you could say, "I like the describing words you used in the story. I wonder if we can use another word for the word, *fun*. This word is used too many times. It gets boring to read the same word again and again." If students are not ready, inviting students to revise the content of the text can be done later (e.g., a few weeks later).

Day 3

Engage students in reading and grammar activities (see Chapters 6 and 8).

Day 4

1. Work with a small group of students at the same proficiency level. Comment on the linguistic patterns and words used in the text that are comprehensible to the students.

2. Have students imitate the discussed patterns and use target words in sentences.

Day 5 and the Following Week(s)

Have students compose their own piece about the experience, using the target linguistic patterns, words, and pictures (if needed).

Interactive Writing

Like composing a morning message and an LEA text, interactive writing is an approach for helping beginning students learn about writing (Button, Johnson, & Furgerson, 1996; Pinnell & McCarrier, 1994). On the other hand, in interactive writing, you release most of the responsibility of composing to students who write a letter, a word, a few words, or a sentence. As the name of this approach suggests, there is much interaction between you and the writer and between the writer and his or her peers in the audience. This type of interaction is crucial and helpful to students' developing knowledge about an oral–written language connection and about the process of constructing and conveying meaning. During the interaction, it is natural for you and the writer to think-aloud about conveying ideas and applying phonics rules.

Mrs. Barlow, a kindergarten teacher with ELLs at the beginning and early-intermediate levels, used interactive writing (in addition to morning messages) on most days of the week. She focused on helping students write only one sentence related to their life experience during each interactive writing session. Before writing, she first posted a blank sentence strip on the board. During writing, she wrote on the space above the sentence strip each letter of a word after a student told her about the letter and before the student came up to the board to write it. This modified step modeled how to write letters. Later in the year, Mrs. Barlow would not write the letters of the word first for her students. Table 7.8 documents how in early November Mrs. Barlow guided students through the process of writing the sentence *We go to the farm*. During a follow-up activity, Mrs. Barlow cut out each word while saying it as a way to teach word boundary and sight words. Later, one student was chosen to draw a picture representing the sentence, a way to direct students' attention to the meaning of the written sentence (see Figure 7.6, p. 215).

Connecting Writing with Reading

As discussed in the section on using mentor texts, a connection between reading and writing needs to be stressed in writing instruction and made explicit to ELLs. To scaffold ELLs' writing, you should seize every opportunity to make reading–writing connection. In a fourth-grade class, Ms. Vuoso wrote down the key vocabulary and main ideas from a reading on the dust bowl. She then modeled for her students how to write a summary by using the key words and including the main ideas (Figure 7.7, p. 215). Other ways to connect writing with reading include the following:

- ➢ Writing a response to a book
- ➢ Rewriting a book (e.g., with a different ending, from a different perspective, with a setting of a student's home country, in a native language)
- ➢ Writing a review of a book

(text resumes on page 216)

TABLE 7.8. The Process of Interactive Writing

Steps	Interactive writing by Mrs. Barlow's class
Activating prior knowledge about phonics	The class began with students' singing a phonics song as a review of letter sounds; they did actions while singing.
Activating prior learning experience	T: We have been writing about where friends go and what friends do. (*T shows each sentence and points at each word while reading each sentence.* We go to the park. We go to the circus.)
Choosing a sentence to write	T: Tell us where friends go. S1: We are going to the race car. T: You mean the speedway. We go to the speedway. S2: We are going fishing. T: Where do you go fishing? S2: The pond. T: We go to the pond. S3: We go to the farm. (*Several students say, "We go to the farm."*) T: I have heard several times *We go to the farm.* Let's write *We go to the farm.*
Repeating the chosen sentence	T: Let's clap the sentence *We go to the farm.* (*Ss and T say the sentence, clapping each word.*) T: Let's squeeze our belly to it. (*Ss say the sentence, squeezing their belly for each word.*) T: Let's pull one ear to it. (*Ss say the sentence, pulling their ears for each word.*)
Counting the number of words in the sentence	T: Let's count the words in the sentence. (*Ss say the words aloud, counting with their hands.*)
Writing the sentence	T: (*Pointing at the blank sentence strip posted on a small white board*) Let's read *We go to the farm* (*moving the pointer across the strip as if each word were written on it*). T: (*Pointing at the middle of the strip*) Do I start our sentence here? Ss: No. We start up there (*pointing at the beginning space on the strip*). T: Right. We start here (*pointing at the beginning space on the strip*). What is the first letter in *We.* Ss: W. (*T writes the letter w on the space above the sentence strip. Then T draws a name stick from a can and shows the stick to Ss.*) Ss: Miguel. T: Miguel, come up here. Write *W.* (*Miguel writes the letter W.*) See how Miguel is writing *W* on the line. What is the next letter in *We*?

(continued)

TABLE 7.8. *(continued)*

Steps	Interactive writing by Mrs. Barlow's class
Writing the sentence *(continued)*	Ss: *E.* T: Letter *e,* that's right. (*T writes the letter* e *on the space above the sentence strip.* [T continues to call different students to the board.]) (*Jorge writes the letter* e *after the letter* w *on the sentence strip.*) T: What's the next word? Ss: *Go.* T: What's first letter in the word *go?* Ss: *G.* T: Do I squish *go* into *We?* Ss: No. We need finger space. (*T writes the letter* g *on the space above the sentence strip.*) (*Milton writes the words* go *and* to *on the sentence strip.*) T: Let's read what we have written. Ss: (*T pointing at each word*) *We go to.* T: Raise your hand if you know how to spell the word *the.* This word is tricky. *The* is a sight word. We see and use this word a lot. We need to spell all the letters together. (Adriana writes the word *the.*) T: (*Pulling out the sight word card for* the) See, Adriana knows how to spell *the.* Let's read the words. (*Pointing at each word, T leads Ss in reading the words* We go to the.) T: What is our next word ? Ss: *Farm.* T: What is the beginning letter of the word *farm.* Ss: *F.* (*T writes the letter* f *on the space above the sentence strip.*) (*Jose writes the letter* f *on the sentence strip.*) T: The next sound is tricky, /ar/ Ss: Letter r. T: Remember Carlos's name, /ar/ *a-r* (*pointing at the display of student names on the wall*)? The /ar/ sound in the word *farm* is spelled just like the /ar/ sound in Carlos's name (*pointing at the display of Carlos's name*). (*Maria writes the letters* ar, *and Juan writes the letter* m.) T: Let's read. Ss: (*T pointing at each word*) *We go to the farm.* T: Did we write all of our words in the sentence? Ss: Yes. We need to put a period. (*T puts a period at the end of her model sentence.*) (*Jan puts a period at the end of the sentence on the strip.*)

(continued)

TABLE 7.8. *(continued)*

Steps	Interactive writing by Mrs. Barlow's class
Reading the written sentence	T: With a whisper voice, read the sentence (*T pointing at each word; T stopping at the word* to, *but some Ss read on*) My pointer is still at the word *to*. How come you are reading the word *the*? Let's read again. (*Ss read the sentence again.*) (*T repeats this step several times to make sure that Ss are reading each word, not memorizing the sentence.*)
Extending interactive writing to journal writing	T: In your journal, you are going to write one sentence about one place friends can go together. Use the words we've learned. Where do we find these words? Ss: Over there (*pointing at the wall where sentences written during the previous interactive writing activities are posted*).

FIGURE 7.6. An example of interactive writing.

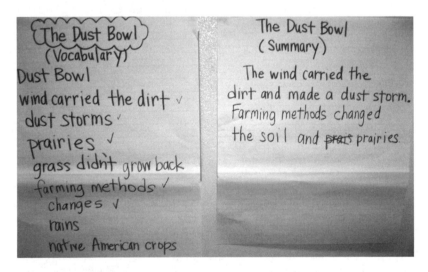

FIGURE 7.7. An example of reading–writing connections.

> ➤ Writing a summary on readings on a topic or from a unit

> ➤ Writing a script based on one or more parts of a book or a whole book that has been read

> ➤ Revising and editing one's own writing after reading it aloud or silently

> ➤ Writing comments and providing suggestions for revision and editing on a peer's paper

Writers' Workshop

Scholars have suggested the use of Writers' Workshop with ELLs (e.g., Freeman & Freeman, 2009; Kendall & Khoun, 2006; Mora-Flores, 2009; Samway, 2006). While many strategies and activities effective with non-ELLs can be used with ELLs, some modifications are still necessary. For example, newcomers, whose English writing instruction during L1 schooling (if any) might be equivalent to grammar exercises, need much more time to get acquainted and comfortable with the writing process. Families of these newcomers also need to be informed of the writing process, which may be contrary to their beliefs about writing instruction and their own experiences with learning to write during their schooling.

Prewriting

The goal of prewriting is to get students to gather information for writing.

1. *Choosing a topic.* If students are to choose their own topic, you should encourage them to pick a topic that is interesting to them, and possibly to readers of their writing, and about which they know enough to write. They can pick a topic from their writer's notebook or from what they have learned from a mentor text. If a topic for writing is assigned, you need to make sure that students have enough information to write about the topic.

2. *Setting purpose and identifying audience.* Inform students of the purpose of writing (e.g., sharing your weekend experience) and the audience (e.g., the peers who will listen to the story).

3. *Identifying text structure for the writing.* Model or remind students of the text structure they are to use (e.g., a personal narrative). If needed, refer students to the mentor texts containing the structure. Students who are developing an understanding of the structure can follow a graphic organizer reflective of the structure.

4. *Brainstorming and organizing ideas for the topic.* Students can obtain ideas for writing from various print and Internet texts. I recommend these websites providing content-specific information: eFieldtrips (*www.efieldtrips.org*), Online Expeditions (*www.globalschoolnet.org/gsnexpeditions*), New York Times Learning Network (*www.nytimes.com/learning/*), and How Stuff Works (*www.howstuffworks. com*). For beginning students and students with limited knowledge on the writing topic, you should engage students in activating prior knowledge and provide them with background knowledge through discussing ideas and key vocabulary.

After gathering information, students narrow down to a focus on the topic.

Students use an appropriate graphic organizer or a story map for organizing ideas for one particular genre (e.g., a flow chart for a narrative with a chronological order or an expository text with sequential order) (see *www.eduplace.com/ graphicorganizer/* and *www.teachervision.fen.com/graphic-organizers/printable/6293. html?detoured=1* for different types of graphic organizers). Beginning writers can use pictures to present ideas for writing. An important part of the brainstorming process is discussing a selected topic with the whole class (see Table 7.8 for the beginning part of interactive writing), with a small group, or with a partner. For students at the speech preproduction and early preproduction (if literate in L1), the use of L1 should be encouraged. You should pay attention to older ELLs literate in L1 who may organize their ideas in the way ideas are expressed in L1. If this occurs, conduct a mini-lesson again with the students about an English text structure.

5. *Revising generated ideas.* Students revise generated, organized ideas if needed.

Drafting

In the drafting stage, students focus on writing ideas down in sentences and paragraphs in a cohesive way. Beginning and early intermediate students may compose with a mixture of print and pictures, in L1, or code switch. It is helpful to allow some students to focus on one part of writing at a time (e.g., the setting of a story; an introduction in an expository text) (Mora-Flores, 2009) so that writing becomes a manageable, less overwhelming task to them. It is imperative for you not to correct any type of error in student writing at this stage. This way students are encouraged to express a flow of ideas in written language in a low-anxiety environment.

Revising

One way to achieve revising for "purpose, clarity, and effectiveness" (Mora-Flores, 2009) is to have students share their writing. To lower their anxiety level, you can begin with having students share with a buddy and move on to sharing with a small group of students, and later with the whole class. To guide the students through the peer-revision process, you can ask some guiding questions (see Figure 7.8) if the writing is orally shared with a group or the whole class or provide them with a peer-revision and editing form (see Appendix O for a reproducible form) if a piece of writing is read by a peer (Freeman & Freeman, 2009; Mora-Flores, 2009; Samway, 2006). For students at an advanced level, a strategy of guided revision is a way to scaffold the revision process. In guided revision (see Figure 7.9), a teacher uses general, not specific, questions to prompt students at an advanced level to think about the flow and details of ideas, diction, sentence structure and variety, text structure, clarity, and cohesion. It is okay to delay the revision process

1. What do you like most about this ________ (e.g., story, book review, advertisement, report)?

2. Do you understand everything in this ________ ? If not, which part?

3. What are the words the writer uses effectively?

4. What are the sentences the writer uses effectively?

5. What are the literary devices the writer uses effectively?

6. What suggestions can you offer the writer for making this ________ better?

FIGURE 7.8. Guiding questions.

Iron Maiden

I am going to write about a band called Iron Maiden. It is ~~o.k~~ one of my favorite bands. The bands genre is heavy metal. It is a band from the 70's that started producing songs around 1975. The music was inspired by some ~~of the~~ rock bands from the 70's. Three of the bands were The Rolling Stones, The Beatles and Led Zeppelin. The band members are Steve Harris, Bruce Dickinson, Dave Murray, Adrian Smith, Janick Gers, and Nicko ~~Brian~~ Brain.

What I like about this band is that it made ~~good~~ great songs. The singer has a loud and hard voice and when I hear their music it makes me feel energetic. The band has a great singer and two excellent guitar players. The lead guitarist ~~Bruce Dickinson~~ Steve Harris knows how to play the guitar fast and energetic and loudly and the other guitarist ~~Steve Harris~~ Dave Murray knows how to make the song sound ~~better~~ more interesting. Because they know how to play the drums and the guitar and bass.

When I hear their songs I feel energized and I feel like running until the song ends. My favorite songs are Killers, ~~The Assassin~~, The Evil that Men Do, and the Number of the beast ~~Women in Uniform~~.

They have their own website called IronMaiden.com. You can download and listen to their music from their website. You could see their tours and when they could play live. In addition by being a member of their website, You could get discounts to see them in concert live. Also you join you receive free clothing and other Iron Maiden supplies like one album and bumper stickers. They will mail it directly to your home. In conclusion is one of my favorite band because they awesome music.

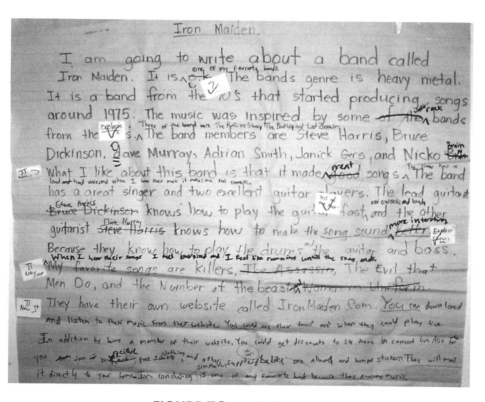

FIGURE 7.9. Guided revision.

for beginning writers until a few weeks later when students have developed more knowledge about writing a particular genre.

Another way to teach students to focus on meaning of their writing is to have them write like a reader. Writing like a reader stimulates students to put themselves in the position of a reader of their piece. This is a good strategy to be integrated into the revising and editing stages of the writing process. In helping students write like a reader, you can use questions to prompt students to think like a reader. For example, *What did you try to say in this sentence? Is your sentence clear or confusing to a reader? What can you change in this sentence so that meaning is clear?* Figure 7.10 shows one example of a draft and a revision by a first-grade ELL at an advanced level who was prompted by her teacher to write like a reader.

To support students during the revising process, you should allow students to focus on one aspect of writing. For example, if the sentences are lacking in details and liveliness (telling rather than showing), you should work with the student on expanding and/or paraphrasing sentences (see Chapter 8 for details), or using some literary devices (e.g., metaphors). If the content of writing is not well organized, it is necessary to have the student check what has been written in a graphic organizer to determine whether the brainstormed ideas are organized based on the text structure of a particular genre. If not, the brainstormed ideas need to be reorganized.

Throughout the revising process, it is easy for both you and students to lose track of focusing on the meaning and to get sidetracked to correcting grammatical and spelling errors. Given that, you need to remind students to focus on making meaning clear during the revising stage and to correct mechanical and conventional errors during the editing stage. Errors need to be viewed by teachers and their students as "something to celebrate, as it indicates that students are active learners—they are using what they already know about print to construct and

Draft	Mexico I like to go to Mexico. I saw some kids playing. I heard them screaming. I felt happy because I get to play to play tag. I get to play tag. I love Mexico because I get to play tag!
What do I need to change? (after teacher's prompt)	• An unclear idea (*I saw kids playing.* [playing what?]). • Repetition of the idea (*because I get to play to play tag.*). • Need to use an exclamatory point to show my strong feeling (*I get to play tag.*) • A mixed use of verb tense (*I felt happy because I get to play to play tag. I get to play tag.*).
Revision	I like to go to Mexico. I saw some kids playing tag outside. I heard them screaming. I felt happy because I got to play tag with the kids. I got to play tag with them! I love going to Mexico because I get to play tag!

FIGURE 7.10. An example of writing like a reader.

refine understandings about how written language works in another language" (Samway, 2006, p. 58). If errors hinder communication, you can guide the student to look at errors in relation to what is being expressed. For example, the word *casa* in the phrase *in my casa* can be left for a later discussion (during a conference or a mini-lesson). However, a phrase such as *at my* deserves immediate attention, as the error interferes with meaning construction. This error may be due mostly to the student's lack of an English word or a careless mistake. If the former, you can suggest that the student draw a picture after the word *my* to indicate an intended meaning. You can then supply a corresponding English word.

Editing

An ELL's piece of writing may have errors ranging from grammar to usage to spelling. Teachers of ELLs often feel overwhelmed by the number and types of errors in writing. It is important for you and students to focus on errors that hinder communication and errors whose correct forms are part of grade-level curricular standards. Teachers should also consider the interferences from L1. Once types of errors are identified, focused editing can begin. For example, after reading a paragraph by a fourth grader at early intermediate level whose errors fortunately have not hindered communication (Figure 7.11), the teacher identified these focal areas for editing based on the grade-level curricular standards and those the student should have mastered in a previous grade level: (1) adding appropriate punctuation for the paragraph; (2) changing some sentence structures (e.g., . . . *and I sow some of my frinds wen it was Hallowen*); and (3) correcting spelling of many words (e.g., *wen* for *when*, *sow* for *saw*). To support ELLs during the revising and editing process, you make writing resources (e.g., an English dictionary, a thesaurus, dictionaries of synonyms and spelling, and bilingual dictionaries) available to students (see Figure 7.12).

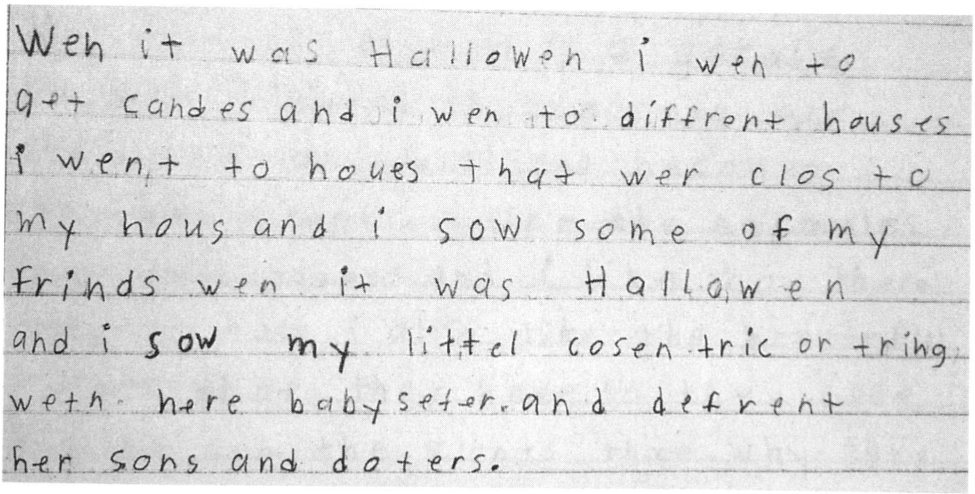

Wen it was Hallowen i wen to
get candes and i wen to diffrent houses
i went to houes that wer clos to
my hous and i sow some of my
frinds wen it was Hallowen
and i sow my littel cosen tric or tring
weth here babyseter. and defrent
her sons and doters.

FIGURE 7.11. A writing sample.

- Your Dictionary.Com (*www.yourdictionary.com*)
  An online English dictionary allows you to look up words in other languages (Chinese, French, German, Italian, Hindi, Japanese Korean, and Russian, and Spanish).
- Merriam-Webster Online (*www.m-w.com*)
  The online version offers other resources (e.g., word of the day, word games).
- Word Central (*www.wordcentral.com*)
  An online word resource for young students includes a thesaurus, buzzwords, games, and puzzles. Students can compose a verse through a template.
- Roget's II: The New Thesaurus (*education.yahoo.com/reference/thesaurus*)
- Reverso Dictionary (*dictionary.reverso.net/english-synonyms*)
- Synonym.com (*www.synonym.com*)
- Chinese–English Dictionary (*www.mandarintools.com/worddict.html*)
- Farsi–English Dictionary (*www.farsidic.com/F2E*)
- Hmong-English Dictionary (*www.hmongdictionary.com*)
- Japanese-English Dictionary (*www.englishjapaneseonlinedictionary.com*)
- Korean-English Dictionary (*www.ectaco.co.uk/English-Korean-Dictionary*)
- Spanish-English Dictionary (*www.spanishdict.com*)
- Vietnamese-English Dictionary (*vdict.com*)
- Dictionaries at freedict.com (*www.freedict.com/onldict/dan.html*)

FIGURE 7.12. Writing resources.

Publishing

This is an exciting stage for you and students. Sharing with peers and students from other grades is one way to publish students' writing. Here are other ways:

➢ Compiling individual students' writings into a class book and housing the book in a classroom or school library

➢ Compiling writings related to one topic or unit from each student into a book and sending the book home to share with each student's family

➢ Translating a student's writings into L1 and compiling the writing into a book to share with the family. Students literate in L1 from the same class or from other grades may complete this task as a group project.

➢ Publishing students' work on the Internet via online projects, such as Newsday (*www.globalschoolnet.org/gsnnewsday*) and Letters to Santa (*www.globalschoolnet.org/gsnsanta*)

Throughout the writing process, teacher–student conferences, mini-lessons, and sharing are other three important components. You can conduct individual or group conferences to address difficult areas and to guide students through the process. Conferencing with ELLs is critical, because it provides students with opportunities to talk for a real purpose (their writing purpose) and enables you to learn about what works and what does not work with each student (Samway, 2006). Questions, difficulties, and confusions that emerge from conferences can become the topics for mini-lessons (see Figure 7.13 for a mini-lesson on a expository text structure, a topic, and subtopics). This type of on-the-spot, ongoing mini-lesson

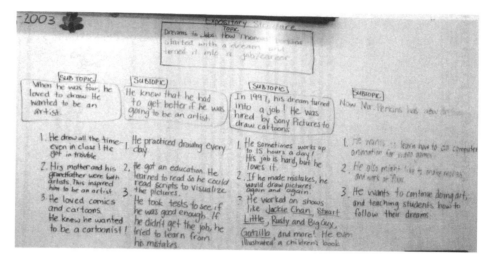

FIGURE 7.13. A mini-lesson on topic and subtopic.

helps address students' needs in a timely manner. Finally, it is valuable to students if they have an opportunity to share their in-progress or completed work throughout the writing process. Sharing, like think-alouds, creates another meaningful learning context for students. Mora-Flores (2009) suggests including in sharing "new strategies, words, ideas, or techniques" a writer used and "reflecting on being a writer" (p. 7). One more thing to keep in mind is that it is common for students to go through the stages of the writing process at different paces. To make Writers' Workshop more manageable, you can have each student keep track of the stage at which he or she is (see Figure 7.14).

FIGURE 7.14. Keeping track of the writing stages.

DIFFERENTIATED INSTRUCTION FOR ELLs LITERATE IN L1

ELLs literate in L1 bring to the classroom a body of knowledge about written language and about content areas acquired through L1. This type of knowledge can be tapped to facilitate transfer in writing skills and strategies from L1 to English. Working with this group of ELLs, the first important step is to let them know how much their native language is valued in your classroom. This can be done through such ways as allowing them to write, read, and speak in L1 and share interesting aspects of L1. Here are more ideas for this group of students:

➤ Have students form pen pals with their peers in their home country and write to each other in English and/or in L1.

➤ Have students translate their own and their peers' writing into L1 so that family members can read about their children's writings.

➤ Have students at an intermediate or advanced oral proficiency level assist you during the writing process (e.g., working with their newly arrived peers or peers at a beginning level).

➤ Have students at an intermediate or advanced oral proficiency level share with the class and you the similarities and differences between English and L1.

ENGAGING FAMILIES

It may be challenging to engage families in supporting their children's development of English writing skills, as family members may not be skillful at composing in English. However, it is still possible and very important to engage families.

➤ Family members (if literate in L1 or English) read books in L1 or English to and with students and discuss the books read. Knowledge of how L1 or English is used in books helps students develop a general knowledge about how language is used to convey ideas.

➤ Family members (if literate in L1 or English) write with students functional texts in L1 or English (e.g., a thank-you card, a holiday greeting, a shopping list).

➤ Family members contribute to an entry in a cultural and expert journal that rotates among each family throughout a school year; contribute words to a letter page on a class L1 alphabet book; and write about L1 idioms in an idiom book (Barone & Xu, 2008).

➤ Family members (if literate in L1 or English) dictate students' oral story in L1 or English (e.g., a retelling of a book, an account of an event) and read together the dictated text.

➤ Family members (if illiterate in L1) talk and discuss topics of interest in L1, which helps their children expand general knowledge (e.g., concepts) and vocabulary that would be useful for their composing.

➢ Students share with family members their writing in L1 or English about their day at school.

➢ Students write about social, cultural, and family events and share the pieces with other classmates and families in the neighborhood.

➢ Students and family members together keep a writing notebook at home, documenting anything interesting (including words) they have discovered.

➢ Family members assist you in helping students during the writing process.

VOICE FROM THE CLASSROOM
Hilary Shuler
Dr. Theodore T. Alexander Jr. Science Center School, Los Angeles, California

Recess is a time for students to take a break from the rigor of the classroom. While it is usually a time of joy and excitement, on occasion conflicts arise. A couple of times a week I am approached by students who have had some conflicts while playing basketball, soccer, or jumping rope. The involved students meet with me and try to use persuasion to prove to me that their perspective of the situation is the correct description of events. Witnesses are called by both parties of students in an attempt to strengthen their argument. Upon returning to class everyone involved completes a conflict form detailing their perspective of the situation in their last effort to persuade me to side with their viewpoint. During lunch, I read the conflict forms, and each time I encounter the same dilemma. The students' writing lacks detailed descriptions and is laden with structural and grammatical mistakes. Further, their writing lacks the persuasive quality that is so clearly evident in their oral descriptions. Continuously I would ask myself, Why do these trends occur? What can I do to help my students become stronger writers? It was imperative that I seek out strategies to help my students improve their expository writing.

I work at an affiliated charter K–5 elementary school with a focus on a math, science, and technology. Each year my class is composed predominantly of ELLs ranging from emergent students having no verbal English and relying on nonverbal responses to students nearly fluent in all areas of English. Typically, my students are partially proficient in reading, writing, listening, and speaking. Like non-ELLs, ELLs are capable of learning and developing critical thinking skills, need time to connect their prior knowledge with new information, and engage in critical thinking activities in content areas to broaden their understanding of newly acquired skills or concepts. They cannot be limited to instruction in only reading/language arts and math, as it will impede their ability to fully function in the society.

The affiliated charter status of my school allows me to integrate content across the curriculum to help students make connections in order to meet state standards. While Open Court and Into English! are the district-mandated programs for literacy and English language development, our school has adopted Lucy Calkins's Writers' Workshop (a mini-lesson, a writing block, and an author's chair) to supplement the writing portion of Open Court.

Upon working with my students during Writers' Workshop, I discovered a cause for the trend I had noticed in their conflict forms. My students needed modeling, scaffolding, and explicit instruction in the different forms of writing, with an emphasis on expository writing. In order to help them develop their skills as writers, I use the lesson structure from the writing section of Into English! as a guide. For each writing piece, I create a communication guide (containing sentence starters) for the students to use as a model (Figure 7.15; also see Figure 7.16 for a student writing sample.) I first model how to complete the guide orally and through writing using simple, elaborated, and complex responses reflecting the various proficiency levels. Students then practice using the communication guide by orally completing the sentences with a classmate. Once they have practiced using the guide orally, they move on to the writing application. In addition, I make sure to have a variety of text models available in the classroom and try to incorporate a hands-on activity prior to any writing piece so that students can develop the necessary vocabulary and content knowledge.

To help my students develop their persuasive writing skills, I created a unit with social studies content. Students began the unit by building background knowledge about persuasion and developing an argument. Integrated into the unit is a WebQuest lesson, *The Power of Persuasion*, which I developed and focused on developing the language of an argument. Students navigated through four different tasks: (1) developing an understanding of the vocabulary by defining key terms; (2) observing historical and present-day advertisements that use persuasion to sell their product or sway their viewer; (3) analyzing the advertisement to determine

---

Dr. Seuss wrote *Bartholomew and the Oobleck* (Seuss, 1949) to _____ (author's purpose) readers.

The story takes place in _____ (time and place).

_____ and _____ are the main characters in the story.

_____ is (describe) _____.

_____ is (describe) _____.

A conflict arises when _____.

_____ tries to solve this problem by _____.

Also, _____ tries to _____.

Finally, the problem is solved when _____.

From reading this story, Dr. Seuss wanted us to learn _____.

FIGURE 7.15. Sample communication guide for a story summary.

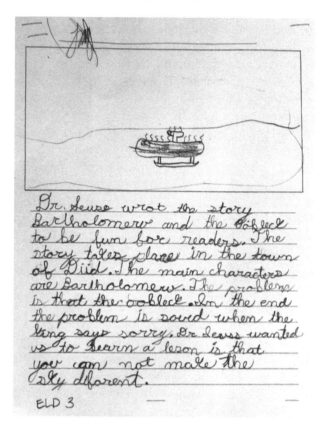

FIGURE 7.16. A piece of narrative writing based on the communication guide in Figure 7.15.

what the creator was trying to persuade people to do or think and identifying techniques used to evoke persuasion; and (4) choosing a topic and establishing a point of view. Students then researched traits of a character from their popular culture interests (e.g., *The Simpsons, Batman,* and *High School Musical*). The last step was to use gathered evidence to create a poster that would persuade their peers to agree with their point of view about the character.

The WebQuest was just the beginning of the persuasion writing unit. The next step was for students to apply persuasion to social studies content by assuming the role of a historian. Students learned the skills of and language used by a historian. Then, they applied these skills to the topic of explorers. Using fiction and secondary and primary sources, students gathered information about Christopher Columbus's exploration west from Spain and analyzed the exploration from the perspective of the Native Americans as well as Columbus himself. Once a wide range of evidence had been gathered, students wrote a persuasive newspaper article establishing their viewpoint about the character traits of the explorers. A communication guide was used to help ELLs structure their arguments (see Figure 7.17; also see Figure 7.18 for a student writing sample). Further, peer-to-peer discus-

A hero is _____.
On the other hand, a villain is _____.
In my opinion, the Spanish Explorers were _____.
First, _____.
This shows they were because _____.
Second, _____.
This also proves they were _____ because _____.
Further, _____.
Again, this proves they were _____ because _____.
In conclusion, the evidence proves that the Spanish Explorers were _____
_____.

FIGURE 7.17. Sample communication guide for persuasive writing (basic format).

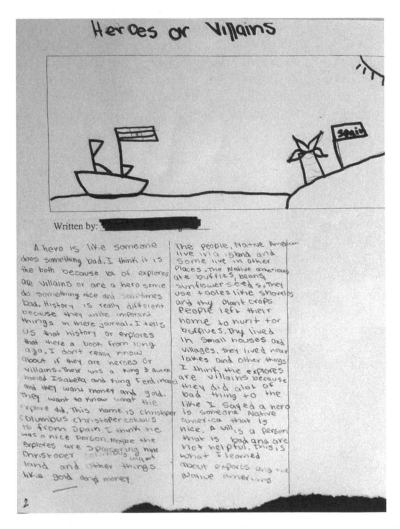

FIGURE 7.18. A piece of expository writing based on the communication guide in Figure 7.17.

sion and assistance were encouraged in students' creating a persuasive argument. During all of these activities, students were highly engaged in utilizing a variety of skills and strategies in reading, language arts, listening, and speaking. Further, I noticed an immediate improvement in their writing skills. Conflicts still arise during recess. My students are still asked to complete a conflict form documenting their perspective of the situation in their last effort to persuade me to side with their viewpoint. Now, however, the writing is more descriptive, persuasive, and free of some grammatical and structural errors.

Teaching writing in the content areas can be challenging. Whenever possible, look for cross-curricular connections to help ELLs make connections between prior knowledge and concepts being introduced. Build upon students' prior knowledge. If it is lacking or insufficient, help students build knowledge necessary for success by incorporating a variety of engaging background-building activities. Once background knowledge has been developed, use sentence frames or starters in the form of a communication guide to help students develop oral and written language. Give students time to practice using the communication guide orally before expecting them to write. Allow for discussion, drawing, and student-to-student interaction before writing, so that students can develop necessary vocabulary. Background building, modeling, multiple practices, and communication guides are just some of the strategies that I discovered would help my students become stronger writers.

CONCLUSION

The goals of writing instruction for ELLs are no different from those for non-ELLs. However, as illustrated in the teaching examples reflective of the strategies and activities in this chapter, teachers' thoughtful modifications and scaffolding are crucial to ELLs' successful experiences with learning to write and writing to learn. Again, I cannot stress enough the value of integrating writing into all curricular areas and of getting students interested in writing and motivating them to write. What Ms. Shuler shared manifests the powerful impact that a teacher can make on students' attitudes toward writing and on their writing performance. Ms. Shuler has reminded us to engage students in learning about the purpose and conventions of writing, thus enabling them to witness a close connection between writing and their personal lives.

CHAPTER 8

INSTRUCTION FOR GRAMMAR

During the first week of the school year, the fourth-grade teachers at Pacific View Elementary School discussed their students' writing performance on a state writing test. Many teachers noted that the students' scores in the section of written and oral language conventions continued to be lower than other sections (e.g., phonics). As teachers compared the scores of ELLs to those of non-ELLs, they noted a larger gap. Mrs. Nguyen expressed her frustration, "We spent a lot of time teaching grammar, and kids did a lot of exercises. Their scores are still low." "I think kids did not internalize what we taught them," added Mr. Johnson. "They can do pretty well on the exercise, but they are not able to use their knowledge in their writing." Other teachers nodded to agree with Mrs. Nguyen and Mr. Johnson. Ms. Kim reminded her colleagues, "Many ELLs are so confused with English grammar. In writing, some students translated their thoughts from L1 to English." Ms. Hsu brought up another issue, "Maybe it is not a good way to teach grammar only as a subject, and it should be part of reading, writing, and oral language." Mr. Gunn suggested, "It seems important to find new, different ways to teach grammar."

The discussion among the fourth-grade teachers about their students' grammatical knowledge may sound familiar to you. You and your colleagues may have also experienced the frustration of not seeing your hard work on grammar instruction pay off during the standardized testing and in your students' speaking and writing. You may ask these questions:

1. What type of knowledge about grammar do I need to know?
2. How can I conduct classroom-based assessment to evaluate ELLs' grammatical knowledge?
3. How can I help ELLs apply grammatical knowledge to reading, writing, and oral language?
4. How can I address the interferences from L1 while teaching grammar?
5. How can I motivate and engage students in their learning of English grammar?

These questions may prompt you to think about teaching grammar in a way different from the way many of us were taught (pencil-and-paper exercises of "drill and kill"). In this chapter, I begin with a brief introduction to elements of grammar that we need to know and that students need to master, areas of strengths and difficulties ELLs possess, and goals of instruction. Following that, I present different ways to assess students' grammatical knowledge. In presenting strategies and activities for grammar instruction, I provide a detailed procedure for each one. Then, you will read about how to seek support from students' families to facilitate students' growth in grammatical knowledge. To conclude this chapter, Ms. Maritza Magana, a sixth-grade teacher, shares with you her experience of teaching grammar.

GRAMMATICAL KNOWLEDGE

It is vital for teachers to have a good knowledge of English grammar, whose extensive discussion is beyond the scope of this chapter. The following books are useful in refreshing our memory about English grammar: *Eats, Shoots & Leaves* (Truss, 2003), *Grammar for Teachers* (DeCapua, 2008), *The Elements of Style* (Strunk & White, 2000), and *The King's English: A Guide to Modern Usage* (Amis, 1997). Appendix P summarizes the components of English grammar. The following section focuses on some unique features of academic grammar (phrasal structure, sentence structure, grammatical features of words, and use of modal auxiliaries), a body of knowledge critical to ELLs' literacy development (Scarcella, 2003; Schleppegrell; 2004; Zwiers, 2008).

Phrasal Structure

Similar to ordinary English, academic text is full of phrases (e.g., *result in, result from, in accordance with*) (Nation, 2001; Scarcella, 2003). The use of correct collocation (the way words are combined) is an indication of fluency in language use. For example, in the sentence *The political leaders bickered over the election results*, the verb *bicker* has to be followed by the preposition *over* not by other prepositions (e.g., *at, about,* and *for*). Another feature of phrasal structure is nominalization, the process of turning a verb into a noun and having the resulting noun act as a subject or an object of a sentence (Zwiers, 2008). Nominalization condenses an explanation of a concept and its relationship to other concepts by using fewer words, making the concept more abstract. The sentence *Memorization of the multiplication table before taking a test would speed up solving multiplication and division problems* entails a relationship of a condition (*if you memorized the multiplication table before taking a test*) and an outcome (*you would be fast at solving multiplication and division problems*). Such a relationship, hidden due to nominalization, is more difficult for students to detect than a straightforward complex clause with a conditional clause, like this one: *If you memorized the multiplication table before taking a test, you would be fast at solving multiplication and division problems.*

A third feature of phrasal structure is that present or past participles are used to compact a long sentence. In the sentence *After analyzing the problem, you should formulate an equation by using several algebra concepts*, the two present participles, *analyzing* and *using*, compact the sentence through the elimination of one subordinating clause, *after you have analyzed the problem*, and through the reordering the verb phrases. The sentence with *by using several algebra concepts* has a clear focus on the action, *formulate an equation*.

Sentence Structure

The sentences of academic language often have long, complex patterns, passive voices, figurative language, and advanced use of punctuation (Scarcella, 2003; Schleppegrell, 2004; Zwiers, 2008). The complex clauses include the following:

> ➤ A compound sentence with an embedded complex sentence (e.g., "They [distant suns] always appear as tiny, faint pinpricks of light, but if you traveled trillions of miles to look at them close up, you would find that they are huge, bright bodies like the Sun" [Kerrod, 2003, p. 42]).

> ➤ A complex sentence (e.g., *Salts are conductors of electricity because they are composed of metallic elements having positive charges and nonmetallic elements having negative charges.*)

> ➤ A complex sentence with an embedded complex sentence (e.g., *After the water is boiled, it produces steams that can be used as a powerful force to operate an engine, like the one on a steam train.*)

Every time a complex sentence is used, a hierarchical relationship between ideas in each clause is suggested. ELLs must first understand each idea expressed in each clause and then figure out the relationship among the ideas. Consider the sentence about distant suns. The misconception about the size of distant suns expressed in the first clause is contrasted with the scientific fact about their sizes expressed in the second clause. In the second clause, the condition for learning about the truth about the size is expressed in a conditional subordinating sentence, and the outcome based on the stated condition is expressed in the independent clause.

Passive voices is another salient feature of academic language. Texts of specialized disciplines, particularly in science and math, often focus on the outcome or an object of an action rather than an agent of an action. In the sentence *Neptune is surrounded by seven satellites*, the object of the verb *surround* (Neptune) rather than the subject of the verb (*seven satellites*) is the focus of the sentence.

Similar to its function in narrative texts, figurative language in academic English is used to help describe or explain abstract concepts. Figurative language can hinder students' comprehension of concepts if they cannot figure out the figurative meaning. To understand the sentence *The seeds of war had been growing for decades* (Davis, 2003, p. 136), students must first have a clear concept about a seed and its role in the life cycle of a plant. Otherwise, the metaphor of seeds does not help readers understand that there are more than one cause of the war and that the causes started a while ago.

Punctuation

Punctuation marks in academic language are used to make an explanation of a concept more explicit. Consider the use of commas in this sentence: "Farmers were also at the mercy of things they couldn't control, including railroad rates, monopolies that made farm machinery, and loans from eastern banks" (Davis, 2003, p. 122). The first comma introduces the second half the sentence, which offers an explanation for *things they couldn't control*. Less frequently used punctuations marks in ordinary English, like semicolons, colons, and dashes, become more common in academic English. The dash in the sentence "They came at the height of a huge flood of newcomers—more than 30 million between 1820 and 1920—to the United States" (Davis, 2003, p. 123) is used to emphasize the appositive for a huge flood of newcomers.

Areas of Strengths and Difficulties

ELLs, even those at the beginning levels, bring to learning about English grammar some strengths. One strength is their understanding of general grammatical concepts common in all languages (e.g., parts of speech). For example, although a subject–object–verb order in a Korean sentence is different from a subject–verb–object order in an English sentence, the concepts of word order and the relationship between sentence meaning and word order are the same for both languages. Hence, a Korean-speaking ELL can transfer an understanding of word order to his or her learning about English word order. Additionally, strategies for learning L1 grammar can also be transferred to learning English grammar. For example, after students have learned a new grammatical rule, they can apply and evaluate it, and discover exceptions to it.

The areas of difficulties result from two sources. One source is the interferences from L1. For example, Spanish-speaking ELLs can confuse the meaning and usage of the prepositions *in, on,* and *into,* as there is not much difference between them in Spanish. The concept of modal auxiliaries, for example, is completely new to ELLs speaking many Asian languages. Even for students whose language is similar to English (e.g., Spanish, German, French), verbal phrases can be different from their L1 and difficult to master. The other source is the grammatical features nonexistent in L1, which take ELLs longer to understand and apply after being exposed to it. ELLs speaking some Asian languages do not remember to use an article before a countable noun and add *-s* or *-es* to a countable noun for its plural form.

Goals of Instruction

One goal of instruction is for students to understand English grammar through exposure to listening, speaking, reading, and writing, rather than through an approach of drill-and-kill grammar exercises. Similar to learning about other aspects of English literacy, students need to have some level of familiarity, background knowledge, and experience with what they are going to learn. For example, before students are able to understand, recognize, and use different types of sentences, they need to at least have heard or read these types of sentences in oral and written language. Otherwise, grammar instruction on sentence types becomes less relevant to students. This type of exposure can occur only when students are immersed in a language- and print-rich classroom environment.

Another instructional goal is to prepare students to understand and apply grammar across all areas of literacy. To achieve this goal, we need to conceptualize and plan grammar instruction in a way different from how grammar has been taught in the past. Benjamin and Oliva (2007) advise us to think of "grammar instruction as closely related to language play" and "to see you and your students take risks, wrestle with uncertainties, argue over changing rules, and splash around in the fun of language" (p. xiii). Furthermore, they invite us to think of "grammar as a resource model":

> If you think of grammar as a resource model, you're thinking of it as a way of understanding how you can get language to do what you want it to do. You are thinking of how you can make your language beautiful as well as functional, unobtrusive as well as powerful, efficient as well as thorough. You are thinking of grammar *rhetorically*. (p. 23)

Viewing grammar as a resource model allows us to go beyond delivering isolated grammar instruction for the sake of teaching grammatical rules. Rather, we are treating grammar as an integral part of literacy instruction and making grammar instruction "lively, challenging, and fun" for students (Benjamin & Oliva, 2007, p. xvii). This perspective is especially important when it comes to teaching ELLs about English grammar, as ELLs' "growth in English proficiency develops globally, not linearly" (Andrew, 2006, p. 322). The ultimate goal for grammar instruction is for students to develop a body of grammatical knowledge and an ability to apply such knowledge in oral and written communication. To that end, grammar instruction is best done within a framework of reading and writing workshop (Atwell, 1998; Calkins, 1994, 2001) where there is an integrated teaching of oral language, reading, writing, and vocabulary.

ASSESSING GRAMMATICAL KNOWLEDGE

Classroom-based assessment provides data from students' performance in oral and written language. Figure 8.1 is an example of documenting what a student knows and does not know in various elements of grammar (see Appendix Q for a reproducible version). In identifying a student's needs and determining instructional foci, you should triangulate data from multiple sources of assessment and consider differences between English and L1. Haussamen, Benjamin, Kolln, and Wheeler (2003) summarizes nine areas of possible differences with eight areas related to

Date	Category	Subcategory	Example (Source)	Instructional Foci
10/2/2007	Verb	Phrasal Verb	*He looked to his dog.* (journal)	commonly used phrasal verbs (e.g., *look at, listen to, watch out*)
11/9/2007	Determiner	Article	*I read book.* (oral sharing)	• indefinite articles (*a, an*) • definite article (*the*) • the differences between indefinite and definite articles

FIGURE 8.1. Documenting students' needs and instructional foci.

grammar. The differences related to grammar include gendered nouns in L1; no articles in L1; different forms for a plural form; different word order in a sentence; antecedent and pronoun agreement; the use and location of a preposition in a sentence; no inflection in L1; and different written conventions. Since grammatical knowledge is reflected more in its actual usage in oral and written language, the four types of classroom-based assessment discussed below are all embedded assessments.

Exploring Students' Oral Output

One powerful informal tool to assess students' knowledge of grammar is to listen to and observe students' oral output during various classroom activities. This knowledge includes the aspects of grammar students have mastered, are developing, or are confused about. For example, when a kindergartner said in a show-and-tell, "This is a picture. Me and brother playing the beach," the student demonstrated some level of understanding of the concept of a sentence as demonstrated in the production of first sentence. The second sentence, however, shows that the student lacked a complete understanding in the concept of a subject (*me* instead of *I*), a verb (*playing* instead of *were playing*), and a prepositional phrase (*the beach* instead of *on the beach*). The grammatical errors of the second sentence may also result from an interference from L1.

While it is impossible to conduct this type of observing and listening for every ELL in a classroom, you can focus on a few children per day or per week. The observation and listening can be done in various settings: individually (e.g., show-and-tell), in a group (e.g., paired work on word sorts), and with the whole class (e.g., responding to what is being read aloud or what has been read). Use Appendix Q to document each student's knowledge of grammar.

Analyzing Students' Miscues from Oral Reading

Different from exploring students' oral output, analyzing students' miscues from oral reading allows you to learn about the student's grammatical knowledge

TABLE 8.1. Examples of Miscues

Student text	Student's oral reading	Miscue	Syntactically acceptable	Syntactically unacceptable
1. *I am happy.*	"I am hop."	*hop*		X
2. *I am happy.*	"I am hopping."	*hopping*	X	
3. *I am happy.*	"I am glad."	*glad*	X	

through syntactically acceptable and unacceptable miscues. In the examples listed in Table 8.1 (Barone & Xu, 2008), all three students read the same sentence, *I am happy*, but their miscues revealed grammatical knowledge at different levels. Student 1 used a verb, *hop*, to replace an adjective, *happy*, making the new sentence meaningless and grammatically wrong. Student 2, however, showed some level of understanding of present progressive tense by using *hopping* to replace *happy*, though the meaning of the new sentence is different from the original one. Unlike Student 1 and Student 2, Student 3 demonstrated a good understanding of the sentence structure by producing a new sentence that was grammatically and semantically acceptable.

The data shown in Table 8.1 can help you plan a targeted instruction for the student and others who share a similar need. For example, Student 1 was confused between an adjective and a verb and had limited knowledge about the structure of a linking verb (*am*) + adjective (*happy*). If you were the teacher of Student 1, after triangulating data from other sources, you might plan to focus instruction on parts of speech and sentence structure with a linking verb.

Exploring Students' Writing

Students' writing has long been considered a good source for assessing grammatical knowledge. Consider one sample from a fourth-grade student at a beginning level (see Table 8.2). In addition to the spelling issues, the sample reflects the student's lack of knowledge in several areas of English grammar, which suggest several instructional foci.

TABLE 8.2. A Writing Sample and Possible Focal Areas for Grammar Instruction

Writing sample	Instructional focus
I went to my auts house this wekeh She has 25 dogs and there were cute because there were littel like rats So I weht insied and there were a lot of bird and cats and ants so I went outside So I went back home.	• Simple sentence • Punctuation (i.e., period) • Possessive noun (e.g., *auts* for *aunt's*) • Plural (e.g., *bird* for *birds*)

Exploring Students' Difficulties in Reading Comprehension

When students experience difficulty in reading comprehension, we tend to first think about the following factors as possible causes: prior knowledge of a topic, knowledge of text structure, decoding ability, and vocabulary. Grammatical knowledge, seldom a factor taken into consideration, can actually be a source of difficulty.

Consider the first sentence in the opening paragraph of the book *Floss* (Lewis, 1992): "Floss was a young Border collie who belonged to an old man in a town" (n. p.). The *who* relative clause tells readers about Floss's owner, and the prepositional phrase *in a town* informs where Floss's owner lived. If a student does not understand the function of the relative clause and the prepositional phrase and their relationship to the main clause, *Floss was a young Border collie*, it is not an easy task to extract meaning from the sentence. For ELLs whose L1 does not have a similar sentence structure, an interference from L1 would make comprehension more difficult.

Grammatical knowledge plays an even more important role in the comprehension of informational texts. Consider this sentence from *Life in the Deserts* (Baker, 1990): "A surprising variety of plant and animal life struggles to survive the harsh conditions of the desert and many people call it their home" (p. 4). The present participle *surprising* serves as a modifier for *a variety of*. The infinite verb *to survive* tells readers the purpose of the verb *struggle*. The pronoun *it* stands for *the desert*. If a student cannot figure out these syntactic relationships of different parts in the sentence, the student would find it difficult to develop a complete understanding of the sentence.

To identify the difficulties caused by limited grammatical knowledge, you can have students underline or write down the sentences that are difficult for them. During a conference with a small group of students who share similar difficulties, you can have them tell you why the sentences are difficult and check off the non-grammar related factors (e.g., prior knowledge, vocabulary). After the conference, it will not be too hard for you to identify the grammatical sources of difficulty and then plan needed, focused lessons to address the difficulties.

STRATEGIES AND ACTIVITIES FOR PROMOTING GRAMMATICAL KNOWLEDGE

Table 8.3 lists all the strategies that reflect an integrated approach to grammar instruction. Some strategies are appropriate for students at all levels while others are useful for students at a certain level. Each strategy targets one or more aspect of grammatical knowledge.

Using Mentor Texts and Everyday Texts

Mentor texts, as discussed in Chapter 7, are used for helping students with writing. There is an increasing attention to using mentor texts (Angelillo, 2002; Dean,

TABLE 8.3. Proficiency Levels, Instructional Foci, and Strategies and Activities for Grammar Instruction

Proficiency level	Instructional foci	Strategies
Beginning	• Concept of word, phrase, and sentence • Singular and plural nouns, possessive pronouns • Contractions • Declarative, imperative, exclamatory, and interrogative sentences • Correct word order in a sentence • Correct use of various parts of speech (e.g., nouns, verbs) • A period, exclamatory point, and question mark	• Using mentor texts and everyday texts • Using children's books on grammar • Using follow-up activities in LEA and interactive writing • Cloze technique • Using Internet resources
Intermediate	• Correct subject–verb agreement • Pronouns, adjectives, compound words, and articles • Past, present, and future verb tenses • Regular and irregular verbs • Coordinating conjunctions • Simple and compound sentences • Combining sentences with appositives and verb, adjective, adverb, and prepositional phrases • Multiple functions of comma and use of parentheses and apostrophes	• Using mentor texts and everyday texts • Reading like a writer • Using children's books on grammar • Using follow-up activities in LEA and interactive writing • Expanding sentences • Combining sentences • Paragraphing sentences • Cloze technique • Using Internet resources
Advanced	• Prepositional phrases, appositives • Independent and dependent clauses • Conjunctions • Correct use of easily confused verbs • Modifiers and pronouns • Complex and compound complex sentences • Indefinite pronouns • Present perfect, past perfect, and future perfect tenses • Compound subjects and verb agreement • Advanced use of colons	• Using mentor texts and everyday texts • Reading like a writer • Using children's books on grammar • Expanding sentences • Combining sentences • Paragraphing sentences • Cloze technique

2008; Ehrenworth & Vinton, 2005; Topping & Hoffman, 2006) and everyday texts (e.g., newspapers, magazine articles, advertisements) for teaching conventions of writing, mechanics, and grammar (Angelillo, 2002; Ray, 2006; Topping & Hoffman, 2006). When used for grammar instruction, everyday texts foster students' understanding of how language is used in their lives outside school, thus making grammar instruction more relevant. Table 8.4 shows some examples of using texts of various genres to teach specific grammatical points.

As discussed in Chapter 7, in selecting mentor texts, you should consider various factors: personal connection to the text, the text's connection to curricular

---

TABLE 8.4. Examples of Mentor Texts and Everyday Texts

Text	Genre	Grammatical points and examples
The Missing Mitten Mystery (Kellogg, 2000)	Narrative	1. Contraction (*Let's*) 2. Possessive noun (*Ralph's*) 3. Exclamatory sentence (*Wow!*) 4. Modal verb ("It <u>would</u> be easier to grow new ones!") (n. p.) 5. Verb tenses (present, past, perfect, future, and progressive) ("I <u>haven't seen</u> your mitten, Annie") (n. p.).
. . . If You Lived When There Was Slavery in America (Kamma, 2004)	Expository	1. Complex sentences (with subordinating conjunctions *when* and *since*) ("<u>When</u> the United States became a new nation in 1783, half a million people in the country were slaves") (p. 6). 2. Relative/adjective clause ("A slave is someone <u>who is owned by another person</u>") (p. 6). 3. Noun clause ("The Declaration of Independence says <u>that 'all men are created equal'|</u>") (p. 6).
Albertson's ad (a grocery store)	Advertisement	1. Adjective (<u>*fresh boneless*</u> *beef*) 2. Verb (<u>*buy*</u> *one* <u>*get*</u> *one free*) 3. Adverb (*save* <u>*instantly*</u>) 4. Exclamatory point (*3 Days Only!*) 5. Period (*oz.*)

---

standards and students' needs, a balance of genres, diversity issues (Dorfman and Cappelli [2007], background knowledge of the topic, and the complexity of the language in the text. The steps for using mentor texts include the following:

1. Select or have students select a mentor text or everyday text that is age, content, and language appropriate and interesting.

2. Read with students or have students read the text.

3. Apply instructional comprehension strategies to help students construct meanings from the text (e.g., think-aloud, questioning, discussing). If you are using a text that students have comprehended well, you may skip this step.

4. Identify a grammar point related to the grade-level standards and/or students' needs.

5. Discuss with students the identified grammar point.

6. Have students participate in guided and independent practices of applying the grammar point in oral and written language (e.g., making up or writing a sentence using one particular grammar point, identifying from other texts one particular grammar point).

Table 8.5 shows one example of how a first-grade teacher used the mentor text *Brown Bear, Brown, What Do You See?* (Martin, 1983) to teach these grammar points: an interrogative sentence, descriptive words, and the order of a subject and verb in a sentence.

Instruction with mentor texts can be differentiated for ELLs at different levels by the focus of grammatical points, texts used, and scaffolding used. For example, for a fourth grader at the beginning level, books like *Brown Bear, Brown Bear*

TABLE 8.5. Grammar Instruction with a Mentor Text for First Graders at the Beginning Level

Focus of grammatical point
1. Interrogative sentence
2. Descriptive words
3. Order of subject and verb in a sentence

Text
Brown Bear, Brown Bear ,What Do You See? (Martin, 1983)

Scaffolded practice
1. Ms. Gunn wrote the sentence *What do you see?* on the board and drew a picture of an eye under the word *see*.
2. Ms. Gunn read the sentence, pointing at her own eye when reading the word *see*, and emphasizing the rising tone.
3. She then had the students repeat after her the sentence, pointing at their eyes when they read the word *see*.
4. She had some students come to the board and read the sentence, pointing at each word and at their eyes for the word *see*.
5. Ms. Gunn referred back to the book and invited the class to read with her the first sentence of the book *Brown Bear, Brown Bear, What do you see?* and the part *What do you see?* throughout the book. She then read the sentence in response to the question (*I see a red bird looking at me*), emphasizing a flat tone.
6. Ms. Gunn wrote down each response on the board.
7. She underlined the words, *I*, *see*, and *red* (and other adjectives).
8. She invited the class to read the whole book with her, pointing at her eye and colored animals in the book when reading the corresponding words.
9. After modeling the question—answer sequence, Ms. Gunn had her students ask her the question *Teacher, Teacher, What do you see?* and she responded with *I see you looking at me*.
10. She asked individual students *What do you see?* and wanted the students to respond, *I see you looking at me*.

Guided practice
1. She had the class work in pairs, with one student asking the question [Mary] *What do you see?* and the other responding to the other, *I see you looking at me*.
2. She then had each pair share their question and answer.

Independent practice
1. For homework, she had each student practice the question—answer pattern with his or her sibling(s) and/or family members.

(see Table 8.5) might not be age and content appropriate. It is helpful to use easy informational books about familiar concepts (e.g., *Rain* [Kalan, 1978]) to teach the basic elements of grammar (e.g., prepositional phrases such as *on the green grass*). Easy informational books with familiar content will not embarrass older students.

A mentor text or everyday text in a big print version (e.g., a big book) is better than one with a regular size, because you can talk about grammatical points with the examples illustrated in the book for the whole class to see. You can later invite students to demonstrate what they have learned about the grammatical points. Thus, the use of big books is not limited just to kindergarten and first-grade classrooms. For example, with older students, you can use highlighting tape to draw students' attention to a grammatical point on a page (e.g., different ways to use a comma).

Reading Like a Writer

From the perspective of a resource model, grammar instruction is considered an integral part of studying author's craft (Angelillo, 2002; Benjamin & Oliva, 2007; Dean, 2008). Reading like a writer promotes students' awareness of how authors effectively use and manipulate language to best convey intended meaning. This strategy can be used after the strategy of using mentor texts and everyday texts. For example, students can conduct a grammar hunt (Haussamen et al., 2003) where they identify effective sentences reflecting various aspects of grammar, state the purpose that an author intends, and then imitate the sentences (see Table 8.6). During the process, your guidance focuses on providing students with texts of high-quality writing, reminding students of learned grammatical points, and offering opportunities for students to share what has been "hunted."

TABLE 8.6. Examples of Reading Like a Writer

Text	*Olivia* (Falconer, 2000)	*Moosetache* (Palatini, 1997)
Grammatical point Example	Appositive "Olivia lives with her mother, her father, her brother, her dog, <u>Perry</u>, and Edwin, <u>the cat</u>"(n. p.).	Ellipse "And their cooking was hot, hot . . . hot!" (n. p.)
Meaning of the grammatical point	Adding detail to a noun or a proper noun *Perry* is the name of *her dog*. *Edwin* is *the cat*.	Adding an emphasis Their cooking is very hot, and the author had to say the word *hot* many times.
Sentence I can make by using the grammatical point	*I like to play with Maria, Jose, Ming, a new student, and Adam, my neighbor.*	*The test is hard, hard . . . hard!*

Using Children's Books on Grammar

One group of children's books has a specific focus on different elements of English grammar (see Figure 8.2). These books are valuable for grammar instruction, because the pictures that accompany the text make a talk about grammar interesting and engaging. You can use these books in a similar way that you would use regular children's books, but with a step further. That is, you can include an explanation and/or discussion on the grammar elements.

In selecting children's books on grammar, you do need to be mindful of students' prior knowledge about English grammar and about the topic of a chosen book. The books in Cleary's series, with short, simple sentences, are more appropriate for students at a late beginning and early intermediate levels. For example, *A Mink, A Fink, a Skating Rink* (Cleary, 1999) begins with a sentence of definition about a noun on a page preceding the title page: "Noun: A word that names a person, animal, place, or thing" (n. p.). The first two pages of the book explain what a noun actually is: "Hill is a noun. Mill is a noun. Even uncle Phil is a noun" (n. p.). Heller's series, full of longer sentences with varied structures, would not be too difficult for students at an intermediate and higher level. For example, *Mine, All Mine: A Book about Pronouns* (Heller, 1997) begins with a sentence highlighting the important role of pronouns by stating "*PRONOUNS take the place of nouns . . . so we don't have to say . . . 'Mike said Mike walked Mike's dogs today. Mike walked Mike's dogs a long, long way'*" (n. p.) Both series, however, explain a target part of speech in an explicit way with many examples. Here are some steps for using these books:

1. Read aloud the book or have students read silently if they can.

2. Discuss the content, focusing on comprehension. Otherwise, the book is no different than the grammar workbook. For example, while reading "Hill is a noun. Mill is a noun. Even Uncle Phil is a noun" (n. p.) from *A Mink, A Fink, a Skating Rink* (Cleary, 1999), you can point at the picture representing each noun. For the sentence "Nouns can sometimes be quite proper, like Brooklyn Bridge, or Edward Hopper, London, Levis, Pekinese—Proper nouns name all of these" (n. p.), you can explain with a picture showing each proper noun. You can tie your explanation to students' experiences (e.g., their names, the name of their home country).

3. You and students identify examples of a grammatical point, and you write the examples on the board. Some examples from *A Mink, A Fink, a Skating Rink* (Cleary, 1999) include *hill, mill, Phil, gown, crown, Brooklyn Bridge, Edward Hopper, London, Levis,* and *Pekinese.*

4. Engage students in categorizing examples according to the definition of a grammar point you have presented. In the example of *A Mink, A Fink, a Skating Rink* (Cleary, 1999), you want students to group the listed examples into a noun category for person, place, animal, and thing.

5. Have students add other examples to each category by orally telling you or writing down these examples in their notebook. This step is crucial in help-

Parts of Speech

Beller, J. (1984). *A-B-Cing: An action alphabet*. New York: Crown.

Burningham, J. (1986). *Cluck baa, jangle twang, slap bang, skip trip, sniff shout, wobble pop*. New York: Viking.

Cleary, B. P. (1999). *A mink, a fink, a skating rink: What is a noun?* Minneapolis, MN: Carolrhoda Books.

Cleary, B. P. (2000). *Hairy, scary, ordinary: What is an adjective?* Minneapolis, MN: Carolrhoda Books.

Cleary, B. P. (2001). *To root, to toot, parachute: What is a verb?* Minneapolis, MN: Carolrhoda Books.

Cleary, B. P. (2002). *Under, over, by the clover: What is a preposition?* Minneapolis, MN: Carolrhoda Books.

Cleary, B. P. (2003). *Dearly, nearly, insincerely: What is an adverb?* Minneapolis, MN: Carolrhoda Books.

Cleary, B. P. (2004). *I and you and don't forget who: What is a pronoun?* Minneapolis, MN: Carolrhoda Books.

Heinrichs, A. (2004). *Adjectives*. Chanhassen, MN: Child's World.

Heinrichs, A. (2004). *Prepositions*. Chanhassen, MN: Child's World.

Heinrichs, A. (2004). *Pronouns*. Chanhassen, MN: Child's World.

Heinrichs, A. (2004). *Verbs*. Chanhassen, MN: Child's World.

Heller, R. (1987). *A cache of jewels and other collective nouns*. New York: Grosset & Dunlap.

Heller, R. (1988). *Kites sail high: A book about verbs*. New York: Grosset & Dunlap.

Heller, R. (1989). *Many luscious lollipops: A book about adjectives*. New York: Grosset & Dunlap.

Heller, R. (1991). *Up, up and away: A book about adverbs*. New York: Grosset & Dunlap.

Heller, R. (1995). *Behind the mask: A book about prepositions*. New York: Grosset & Dunlap.

Heller, R. (1997). *Mine, all mine: A book about pronouns*. New York: Grosset & Dunlap.

Heller, R. (1998). *Fantastic! wow! and unreal!: A book about interjections and conjunctions*. New York: Grosset & Dunlap.

Hoban, T. (1973). *Over, under & through, and other spatial concepts*. New York: Macmillan.

Hoban, T. (1991). *All about where*. New York: Greenwillow Books.

McMillan, B. (1989). *Super, super, superwords*. New York: Lothrop, Lee & Shepard.

Neumeier, M., & Glasser, B. (1985). *Action alphabet*. New York: Greenwillow.

Pulver, R. (2007). *Nouns and verbs have a field day*. New York: Holiday House.

Rotner, S. (1995). *Action alphabet*. New York: Atheneum.

Schneider, R. M. (1995). *Add it, dip it, fix it: A book of verbs*. Boston: Houghton Mifflin.

Shierman, V. (1981). *M is for move*. New York: Dutton.

Terban, M. (1984). *I think I thought and other tricky verbs*. New York: Clarion.

Punctuation

Anders, T. (2000). *Punctuation pals*. Fallbrook, CA: Alpine.

Donohue, M. R. (2008). *Penny and the punctuation bee*. Morton Grove, IL: Albert Whitman.

Petty, K. (2006). *The perfect pop-up punctuation book*. New York: Dutton.

Pulver, R. (2003). *Punctuation takes a vacation*. New York: Holiday House.

Truss, L. (2006). *Eats, shoots & leaves: Why commas really do make a difference!* New York: G. P. Putman's Sons.

Truss, L. (2008). *Twenty-odd ducks: Why every punctuation mark counts!* New York: G. P. Putman's Sons.

Truss, L. (2007). *The girl's like spaghetti: Why you can't manage without apostrophes!* New York: G. P. Putman's Sons.

FIGURE 8.2. Children's books about grammar.

ing students make a connection between the grammatical point they are learning and what they already know. Furthermore, this step provides an opportunity for students to feel confident about their developing knowledge about English and its grammar.

Using Follow-up Activities in LEA and Interactive Writing

LEA (Stauffer, 1980b) and interactive writing (McCarrier, Pinnell, & Fountas, 1999), as discussed in Chapter 7, are two instructional strategies used with primary-grade students to develop their writing ability. Both strategies can be effective tools for teaching grammar. During LEA, you usually write down what is being said by students, even grammatically incorrect sentences. A few weeks later, you can engage students in follow-up activities focusing on grammatical points as reflected in grammatically unacceptable sentences in the LEA text.

One activity directs students' attention to grammatically wrong sentences. After dictating all sentences from students, you read the text with students. If you spot any grammatically wrong sentences, you use questioning to prompt students to rethink their sentences and to encourage them to revise the sentences. For example, for the sentence *Yesterday, we visit a pumpkin patch*, you might say, "Good, you used the word *Yesterday*. It tells us our field trip happened yesterday. If the field trip happened yesterday, can we still use the word *visit*?" If the class does not respond, you can scaffold further by providing two choices. "Should we use *visit* or *visited*?"

For this activity, it is important for you not to choose too many grammatically incorrect sentences and prompt students to make a change. In so doing, you may make students feel less competent, a feeling that will do more harm than good. Rather, you should choose the grammatically incorrect sentences related to the grammar points being taught and related to curricular standards. Through this approach, you reinforce a grammatical concept beyond a grammar lesson and help students understand that grammar lives in a text with meaning, not in isolation.

Another activity is to use an LEA text for grammar exercises. The advantage of using such a text is students' familiarity with the text content and the language used in the text. Thus, students can focus more on the grammar elements. In this activity, after an LEA text is produced, you type it up and print a copy for each student in the class. For a grammar exercise, students identify words about people, animals, places, and things (nouns), describing words (adjectives), action words (verbs), different types of sentences, or punctuation marks. Figure 8.3 shows one example of an LEA text with most nouns circled and adjectives underlined by a first-grade ELL at the later beginning and early intermediate proficiency level. Remember to focus on one grammar point at a time. The student circled adjectives a few weeks later when instruction on adjectives began.

During interactive writing, there is constant interaction between the student who is writing and the audience who is helping the writer with spelling and reminding the writer about the grammatical rules (e.g., word spacing, capitalization, punctuation, and word order). The process of interactive writing has a strong element of embedded grammar instruction. During the process of producing the

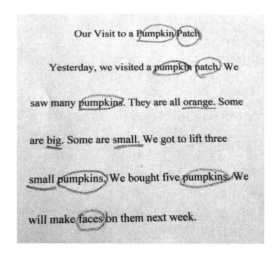

FIGURE 8.3. Nouns and adjectives in an LEA text.

sample in Figure 8.4, Ms. McBride prompted her kindergartners about the following grammatical elements: capitalization, possessive pronouns (*my*), contractions (*I'm*), punctuation (*period*), and a simple sentence pattern (subject + verb + object: *I like me.*). It is also important for teachers not to prompt students too often about varied components of grammar. Too many prompts, however, may disrupt the flow of composing.

Expanding Sentences

Noguchi (1991) states that the native-like abilities ELLs need to develop are closely related to their knowledge about sentences. Noguchi explains five different types of abilities.

1. The ability to distinguish a grammatical sentence from an ungrammatical one.
2. The ability to produce and understand an infinite number of new sentences of potentially infinite length.

FIGURE 8.4. Interactive writing: "I Like Me."

3. The ability to recognize ambiguous sentences: e.g., *My mother hates boring guests.*
4. The ability to recognize synonymous sentences: e.g., *Alice and Tom washed the car* versus *The car was washed by Alice and Tom.*
5. The ability to recognize the internal structure of sentence: e.g., *Julia is eager to help* versus *Julia is easy to help.* (pp. 65–66)

Expanding sentences is a strategy that helps students develop and strengthen their syntactic knowledge about sentences and improve the quality of sentences produced in their oral and written communication. The following are the suggested steps for teaching students how to expand sentences by adding specific details about the content.

Selecting Sentences

The sentences selected need to be at students' proficient level. It is best to obtain them from children's books students have read. Many children's books for K–2 students have relatively simple sentence structures and content that appeals to students. An example of this type of sentences is from *The Cheerios Counting Book* (McGrath, 1998), "You can count cereal" (n. p.). Sentences from students' writing can be another source for the exercise of expanding sentences. You, however, need to avoid choosing grammatically incorrect sentences, which would keep you busy instructing students on how to revise grammatically incorrect sentences into grammatically correct ones.

Providing Scaffolding

Once a sentence has been chosen, you use the *wh* questions (*who, what, where, when, how, why*) to assist students in including different areas while expanding the sentence. For example, the sentence *You can count cereal* (McGrath, 1998) repeats several times throughout the book. Mrs. Hsu guided her fourth graders through the process of expanding the sentence, including making a meaningful connection to reading comprehension:

T: Now let's look at the *wh* questions on the whiteboard. We will go through each one to see if the sentence can help us get an answer to the question. First, the *who* question. Does the sentence tell us *who*?

S1: Yes. *You.*

T: Yes. Next, does the sentence tell us *what*?

S2: Yes, *count cereal.*

T: That's right. *Can count cereal.* We need to put the word *can* in the response. Now we come to the *where* question. Does the sentence tell us *where*?

Ss: No.

T: The sentence does not tell us where *you can count cereal.* I am circling the word *where* so that we know we need to add information to the sentence about *where.* Let's look at the *when* question. Does the sentence tell us *when*?

Ss: No.

T: That's right. I am circling the word *when*. Next, does the sentence tell us *how*?

S3: No.

T: I am circling the word *how*. Finally, does the sentence tell us *why*?

Ss: No.

T: Now I have a question for you. Why do you think the author of this book left out the information about *where*, *when*, *how*, and *why*? Each sentence we say or write has its own purpose. What's the purpose of this sentence in the book?

S4: Children can count. They count cereal from one to one hundred.

T: Yes. Actually, where and when you can count is not important in the book. Let's look at the *how* question. The pictures in the book show that you count one by one. But it does not tell us to count aloud or count silently. The response to the *why* is actually the purpose of this book, learning to count to one hundred. Now we will do a fun activity. I would say, "Maria counted the fruit loops in her spoon one by one to see how many loops are red, blue, and yellow." Let's check if my sentence has answered all the *wh* questions. (*Mrs. Hsu underlines the word* Maria *and writes* who *under it. She repeats the same step for the phrases* counted the fruit loops [what], in her spoon [where], one by one [how], *and* see how many loops are red, blue, and yellow [why].) Now, I want you to work with a buddy to expand the sentence. Your sentence needs to have an answer to each of the *wh* questions.

When working with students at an advanced level, you can guide students to expand a simple sentence into a compound or a complex sentence. For example, the main sentence Mrs. Hsu said, "Maria counted the fruit loops in her spoon one by one to see how many loops are red, blue, and yellow." can be expanded into a complex sentence if Mrs. Hsu adds a *when* dependent clause: *when she was eating fruit loops first time*.

Engaging Students in Sharing and Discussing

After students have produced expanded sentences, you have them share and discuss the sentences, a process permitting you to informally assess students' thinking process and allowing students to learn from peers. You may provide students with questions to frame the discussion. Some examples of questions are: Does the sentence have all the answers to the *wh* questions? What do you like most about your sentence? How can your peer make the sentence better?

Engaging Students in Independent Practice

Independent practice of expanding the sentences needs to be an integral part of the writing process. Students can create a sentence workbook. Weekly, students can choose at least five sentences from their own writing and expand these sentences to make them more specific and detailed. Once a week, students share the sentences from their workbook, and you check the workbook to assess their knowledge.

Combining Sentences

Similar to the purpose of expanding sentences, combining sentences helps students improve the quality of output in oral and written language by applying a variety of sentence structures. Sentence variety, particularly common among academic texts and even complicated narrative texts, is one of the characteristics of academic grammar. Students will produce better sentences in their own writing only after they have practiced writing a variety of sentences. The same steps are involved in teaching how to combine sentences as those used for expanding sentences: selecting sentences, provide scaffolding, engaging students in sharing and discussing, and engaging students in independent practice. Furthermore, the following additional steps are necessary.

Identifying a Focus

Longer sentences with complex sentence structures are more common in expository texts than narrative texts. It is more challenging to combine sentences into a longer one with grammatically accepted structure and semantically intact meaning. Given that, before having students combine several sentences into one, you need to engage students in studying model sentences with complex structure structures in mentor texts. In particular, the study should focus on compound and complex sentences and sentences with participle structures (e.g., *Having discovered a new tool to measure the volume of oxygen, the scientist decides to test the tool on different types of gas*).

Reviewing Adverbial Subordinators

When two sentences are combined into a complex sentence, an adverbial subordinator (a subordinating conjunction) is needed to connect a main clause with a subordinating sentence. If students are not familiar with the subordinators, it is difficult for them to combine two sentences into one syntactically and semantically acceptable sentence. DeCapua (2008) categorizes the subordinators, which signal various relationships between two simple sentences, into the categories of condition, contrast, manner, place, reason, result, and time. The following is a list of subordinators under DeCapua's categories but in the order from the most common to the least common in English: (1) time (*after, as, before, since, until, when, while*); (2) place (*where, wherever*); (3) condition (*if, unless*); (4) result (*so, so that*); (5) reason (*because, since*); (6) manner (*as if, like*); and (7) contrast (*although, even though, though, while, whereas*) (p. 433).

Reviewing adverbial subordinators should be done in conjunction with studying model sentences from mentor texts and everyday texts. After studying each category of model sentences, students can make up their own sentences using one subordinator from the category. Teachers need to be aware of areas of difficulty. For example, the use of the word *since* for a reason relationship (*Since he is sick, he couldn't get the work done on time*) and for a time relationship (*Since the beginning of this month, she has read 10 books*) deserves a lengthy discussion with students. You may also direct students' attention to the differences, though subtle, between *although, even though*, and *though*.

Dissecting a Model Sentence

After identifying a model sentence for one particular category (i.e., compound sentences, complex sentences, or sentences with participle structures), you and students "dissect" the sentence into a main sentence (a main idea) and a part with supplementary information. For example, for the sentence, *Reading too quickly through the text, she missed some details*, the main sentence is *she missed some details*, and the part with supplementary information offering the cause for the effect as stated in the main sentence is *Reading too quickly through the text*. Dissecting a model sentence fosters students' understanding of a relationship between a main clause and a subordinate sentence. Such an understanding is crucial to sentence combining, which links ideas together. You repeat this process with all categories of sentences, though it is better to focus on one category at a time so that students are not confused or overwhelmed.

Paraphrasing Sentences

Like expanding and combining sentences, paraphrasing sentences allows students to produce quality writing. What is unique about paraphrasing sentences is that this is an ability students in upper grades critically need for various projects (e.g., an author study, a research report) for which they extract information from multiple sources and turn authors' words into their own words without losing the original meaning. If students lack an ability to paraphrase sentences, they will probably end up excessively quoting authors' words or distorting authors' original intent in their paraphrased sentences. Developing this ability is a big challenge for ELLs, because they may translate an original sentence from English to L1, paraphrase it in L1, and then translate the paraphrased sentence from L1 to English. The translation process may cause students to produce a paraphrased sentence with a meaning different from the original one, and even worse, with a structure reflective of L1 syntactic interference.

Although paraphrasing sentences is not an easy skill to develop, it can be taught as part of grammar instruction. Paraphrasing sentences is a good exercise for students for applying their grammatical knowledge (e.g., sentence structures, tenses, and verbal and noun phrases). As with teaching expanding and combining sentences, teacher modeling, discussing, and guided and independent practice are important steps in teaching paraphrasing. There are additional steps as well:

Providing Students with Prompts

Students could be at a loss as to how to paraphrase a sentence. By providing students with prompts, you lay out the guideline and expectation for the paraphrased sentences. The prompts may be in a question format. For example, How can you use a different sentence structure to make the meaning of the sentence clear?

> *Example*: I stopped reading.
>
> *Intended meaning*: I stopped what I was doing and started to read.
>
> *Paraphrased sentence*: I stopped to read.

Another way to prompt students is for them to go through a checklist to see which elements of grammar can be used for paraphrasing the sentences. The checklist may include the following:

> ➤ Variety of sentence structures (simple, compound, complex, and compound complex)
> ➤ Active versus passive voices
> ➤ Phrases (noun, verb, and preposition)
> ➤ Variety of punctuation

Discussing the Relationship between Sentence Structure and Meaning

In English, sentences sharing the same underlying meaning can have different structures. For example, Sentence 1, *Jim gave Maria a book*, Sentence 2, *Jim gave a book to Maria*, and Sentence 3, *Maria was given a book by Jim*, all have the same meaning, though their respective structures are different. Sentence 1 has a subject + indirect object + direct object structure. Sentence 2 has a subject + direct object + indirect object structure. Sentence 3 has a passive voice structure. During teaching how to paraphrase sentences, you engage students in discussing how the meaning of an original sentence can be intact while the structure of the original sentence is transformed into a new structure (i.e., the preceding three sentences) and how the meaning of an original sentence can be altered while the structure of the original sentence is transformed into a new structure (e.g., *Jim gave Maria a book* vs. *Jim was given a book*). Such discussion can be scaffolded with prompting questions: Does the paraphrased sentence share the same meaning as the original sentence? If not, what is the meaning of the paraphrased sentence? Why is the meaning different?

Discussing the Quality of Paraphrased Sentences

Helping students develop an ability to produce high-quality paraphrased sentences is as important as helping them understand the relationship between sentence structure and meaning. Teachers can foster this ability through discussing the quality of paraphrased sentences. For example, here are two paraphrased versions of the sentence, "They [distant suns] always appear as tiny, faint pinpricks of light, but if you traveled trillions of miles to look at them close up, you would find that they are huge, bright bodies like the Sun" (Kerrod, 2003, p. 42):

1. *Distant suns always look like tiny, faint pinpricks of light. However, they look huge and bright, just like the Sun, if after traveling trillions of miles, you get a closer look at them.*

2. *Distant suns are always tiny, faint pinpricks of light. When you travel trillions of miles, you get closer to them. You will find that they are just like the Sun, huge and bright.*

Version 1 is better paraphrased as it maintains the original meaning, a contrast between how distant suns look like from a distance and how they actually look like close up. The student demonstrates a command of verb phrases (i.e., *after traveling trillions of miles*). While version 2 maintains the original meaning, its structure seems choppy, But the use of the appositive *huge and bright* after the noun phrase *the Sun* is good. While discussing the quality of paraphrasing, you help students understand the relationship between having grammatical knowledge and producing better sentences, an important element of good writing.

Cloze Technique

Cloze technique (Taylor, 1953) has been recommended for use with ELLs to teach them how to apply their linguistic, cultural, and general knowledge to the process of supplying missing words in a text (Chamot & O'Malley, 1994; Echevarria, Vogt, & Short, 2008). Barone and Xu (2008) further suggest using cloze technique for students to practice applying their grammatical knowledge. You can take out certain categories of words (e.g., modal verbs) or words serving certain grammatical functions (e.g., subordinating conjunctions). Words related to grammatical features may include (1) parts of speech; (2) plurals; (3) subordinating conjunctions (e.g., *when, after, because, while, as*); (4) present participles (inflectional endings) (e.g., *flowing* in the phrase *the volcano with flowing lava*); (5) past participles (inflectional endings) (e.g., *inflicted* in the phrase *the torture and pain inflicted on the slaves*); (6) derivational words (e.g., *-tion* in *evolution*); and (7) collocations (e.g., *against* in the phrase *discriminate against*). Table 8.7 shows four examples, with the first three from Barone and Xu's book.

While cloze technique is often used with upper-grade students, you may use it with young ELLs at the late beginning level. It is better to select a text familiar and comprehensible to students. Otherwise, students will struggle with the text content and lose focus on using their grammatical knowledge. Or they may be able to fill in the words but fail to understand the text. Both situations are not what you want your students to experience.

This strategy can also be used with expository texts (see the last two examples in Table 8.7). In making a cloze out of an expository text, pay attention to the following:

1. Select a text with a topic familiar to students. You may write up a summary of a topic, including the grammatical features students are expected to master.

2. Avoid deleting any words in the beginning sentences, which are often related to background information on the content of the text.

3. Focus on one or two grammatical features so that students can practice these features.

4. Provide students with an easy text during the initial use of the cloze technique, when students learn how to complete a cloze.

5. Increase the difficulty level of a cloze text by using a longer text, focusing on several grammatical features, and deleting more key vocabulary.

TABLE 8.7. Cloze Texts

Purpose	Cloze Text
Adjectives	*Brown Bear, Brown Bear, What Do You See?* (Martin, 1983) Brown bear, brown bear, what do you see? I see a red bird looking at me. Red bird, _____ bird, what do you see? I see a _____ duck looking at me. _____ duck, _____ duck, what do you see? I see a _____ horse looking at me. (n. p.)
Verbs	*I Like Me!* (Carlson, 1988) I have a best friend. That best friend is me! I do fun things with me. I draw beautiful pictures. I ride fast! And I _____ good books with me! I _____ to take care of me. I _____ my teeth. (n. p.)
Past tense	*The Little Yellow Chicken* (Cowley, 1996) The little yellow chicken thought he'd have a party. He said to his friends, "Will you help me do the shopping?" His friends _____ at him. "Hop it!" _____ the frog. "Buzz off!" _____ the bee. And the big brown beetle _____, "Stop bugging me!" So the little yellow chicken _____ shopping by himself. (pp. 2–3)
Subordinating conjunctions	*. . . If You Lived When There Was Slavery in America* (Kamma, 2004). Since the United States became a nation in 1783, half a million people in the country were slaves. Most of them were farmworkers in the South. A slave is someone _____ is owned by another person. Slaves were forced to work their whole lives without pay. _____ a slave was thought of as a piece of property—like a cow or a chair—owners were allowed to do whatever they wanted with their slaves. They could whip them, sell them, or even work them to death. (p. 6)
Prepositions	*Rain Forest Babies* (Darling, 1996) The rain forest is full of bugs. They are creeping and crawling on the vines and bushes. They're flying _____ the treetops. Look high. Look low. Look anywhere, and you will see insects. They are there even when you can't see them. Whole armies of bugs hide _____ tree bark or _____ tunnels _____ the forest floor. (n. p.)

Note. Adapted from Barone and Xu (2008, p. 232). Copyright 2008 by The Guilford Press. Adapted by permission.

At the completion of a cloze text, you should engage students in a class, group, or individual discussion in which you encourage students to think aloud about the process of supplying the words and offer feedback on their thinking process. Such a discussion is valuable because it yields information for you about how well students have mastered the targeted grammatical features and offers students an opportunity to learn from their peers.

Using Internet Resources

The Internet offers a variety of resources for grammar instruction and exercises. Schoolhouse Rock Lyrics (*www.schoolhouserock.tv*) has a YouTube video for parts of speech. The YouTube site (*www.youtube.com*) houses various video clips on grammar instruction. Other websites with grammar exercises include English Club (*www.englishclub.com/grammar/index.htm*), Interesting Things for ESL Students (*www.manythings.org/e/grammar.html*), The OWL at Purdue (*owl.english.purdue.edu/owl/resource/611/01*), and ESL Quiz Center (*www.eslcafe.com/quiz/#grammar*). The Online Writing Lab (OWL) at Purdue University (*owl.english.purdue.edu/handouts/interact/index.html*) allows students to take online grammar and punctuation exercises, submit their answers online, and receive immediate feedback. Another example is Dave's ESL Café (*www.eslcafe.com*) where there are grammar exercises. You can have students work on online exercises and print out the answers and feedback, and then have a mini-lesson with students if needed.

While many online exercises provide immediate feedback on an exercise, your guidance cannot be overlooked. You might take turns working with a group of students on an Internet exercise, observing and offering assistance if needed. The questions students ask and behaviors they display during the exercise will provide you with some data regarding students' grammatical knowledge. During one of my research studies, I observed a group of fifth graders complete the modal verb quiz from Dave's ESL Café. When they got to the item _____ *you help me?*, there was not a consensus in the group about which modal verb (*May, Shall,* or *Will*) was appropriate to fill in the blank. Most thought the word *shall* was not appropriate. Some chose the word *may*, as it was close to the meaning of the word *can*. One student thought that the word *will* was the correct answer. Their teacher, Mrs. Adams, seized this teachable moment.

T: Jose, tell us why you chose the word *will*.

Jose: I don't know. *Will* sounds right in the sentence.

Fang: We say, *Can you help me? May* and *can* are similar. So I think we should use *may*.

T: Good that you all told us the reason. Fang, you are right. We do say, *Can you help me?* But we don't say, *May you help me?* We say, *May I help you?* I know it is very confusing. In the context of the sentence, *will* is the best choice.

At the end of my observation on that day, Mrs. Adams told me that she was planning a review lesson on modal verbs. Had she not observed the group, she would not have known the students' confusion about the modal verbs *may, can,* and *will* and the reasons for such a confusion.

DIFFERENTIATED INSTRUCTION FOR ELLs LITERATE IN L1

Using Children's Books on Grammar

In using children's books on grammar with ELLs, you can engage students literate in L1 in two more activities. In one activity, you have them compare and contrast the similarities and differences in a grammar point between English and L1. The comparison of differences will make students become more aware of possible L1 interferences and a new grammatical element in English they must master. For example, students speaking Chinese, Japanese, or Korean might note capitalization of proper nouns in English, which does not exist in their L1.

For late intermediate to advanced students literate in L1, you can have them write about how writers use punctuation marks in L1 and English effectively to convey the precise meaning of a sentence. Before having students do so, you can introduce students the book *Twenty-Odd Ducks: Why Every Punctuation Mark Counts!* (Truss, 2008). On pages side by side throughout the book, Truss illustrates how a punctuation mark placed in a different position in a sentence can produce different meanings. For example, when the sentence *How many shoes do you need* ends with an exclamation point, it is a declarative sentence. This same sentence, once ended in a question mark, is just an interrogative sentence. On the back of the book, Truss provides an explanation for each pair of sentences with the same words, but two different sets of punctuation marks. With this model, you can have students identify sentences from their reading books in L1 and English, explain the purpose of the punctuation marks used in the sentences, compare and contrast the use of punctuation marks in L1 and English, and discuss a changed meaning that may occur if another punctuation mark replaces the original one.

Identifying and Discussing Linguistic Interferences

Since paraphrasing often involves transforming sentence structures, there is a high possibility that L1's interferences will occur. For example, a Spanish-speaking ELL may paraphrase the sentence *You would find that they are huge, bright bodies like the Sun* as *You will find that they are just like the Sun huge and bright*. In this case, the student used a Spanish grammatical rule (i.e., an adjective comes after its modified noun). If a comma is used after *the Sun*, it is acceptable in English: *the Sun, huge and bright*.

It is important for ELLs literate in L1 to become aware of L1 interferences in paraphrasing English sentences. When noting grammatically unacceptable or awkward sentences, you cannot treat these sentences as those just with grammatical errors. Rather, you need to try to identify possible L1 interferences. In this case, your knowledge of L1 becomes crucial. Having limited knowledge of L1 grammar, however, should not prevent you from identifying the interferences. For example, you can ask questions to prompt students to think about if they are applying L1 grammar in paraphrasing or not. Here are some examples of questions: Did you translate this original sentence into your native language, paraphrase it, and then translate it back to English? Did you use your native language grammar in your paraphrasing? Does this paraphrased sentence have something related to your native language grammar?

The discussion on L1 interferences promotes students' awareness of the similarities and differences between English and L1 grammar. During this process, teachers also benefit from learning more about L1 grammar in a contextual and meaningful way. I strongly suggest that teachers document what is being discussed in the format shown in Table 8.8. What is documented in the table can be shared with students, and if necessary, you can make a poster and put it on the class wall so students can refer to it during writing and grammar activities.

Using Bilingual Texts

Bilingual texts, used for grammar instruction, allow ELLs literate in L1 to witness a similar or different way that an idea is expressed in L1 and English. A text in which L1 and English appear side by side on a page makes it possible for students to compare and contrast sentence by sentence. However, you do need to remind students that a text in one language cannot always be translated into another language without a loss of its original ideas, writing style, and tone, among other elements. You then encourage ELLs to examine the differences (if any) in grammar between English and L1. Table 8.9 lists one sentence from an English–Chinese text and one from an English–Spanish text and the differences in grammar structure between English and the two native languages.

Spanish bilingual texts are relatively easy to obtain through public libraries and the Internet. Several websites offer bilingual books in other languages. The website Language Lizard: Inspiring Kids through Language (*www.languagelizard. com/SearchResults.asp?Cat=1660*) has books written in 50 languages. The International Children's Digital Library (*www.icdlbooks.org*) offers free electronic books written in many native languages. While bilingual books are good for grammar instruction, books written in L1 also offer students the resources to review their knowledge about L1 grammar, knowledge useful for developing metalinguistic awareness of similarities and differences in English and L1.

ENGAGING FAMILIES

Engaging families is particularly important for ELLs whose L1 is very different from English. Families can provide you with valuable resources about L1 grammar and assist their children in learning English grammar. Family members may have had a learning experience with grammar as purely drill-and-kill exercises. Given that, you can invite parents to observe you teach grammar with an integration of all aspects of literacy.

> ➤ Encourage family members to attend ESL parent classes to learn about English grammar.

> ➤ Invite family members to several lessons to observe how you teach students to read like a writer and write like a reader.

> ➤ Invite family members (if literate in L1 or in English) to come to class to share their knowledge about the similarities and differences in grammar between English and L1.

> ➤ Ask family members (if literate in L1 or in English) to create posters

TABLE 8.8. Interferences of L1 Grammar

Original sentence	Paraphrased sentence	L1	Interference	Instructional focus
You would find that they are huge, bright bodies like the Sun	*You will find that they are just like the Sun huge and bright*	Spanish	An adjective comes after a noun.	Position of an adjective in relation to a noun
if you traveled trillions of miles to look at them close up	*if trillions of miles you traveled and them closely look at*	Korean	An object comes before a subject and verb.	Subject–verb–object order in a sentence

TABLE 8.9. Examples of Differences in Grammar Structure between English–Chinese and English–Spanish

Text	English sentence	L1 sentence	Differences
Illustrated Children's English–Chinese Dictionary (Zhang, 2003)	"The plane flew above the clouds" (p. 1).	飞机在云层上方飞行。	1. The location of the prepositional phrase *above the clouds* • <u>English</u>: at the end of the sentence • <u>Chinese</u>: in the middle of the sentence, just before the verb, *flew*
Half-Chicken (Ada, 1995)	"Then Half-Chicken decided that it was time for him to leave the ranch" (n. p.).	*Entonces, Mediopollito decidió que había llegado la hora de abandonar la hacienda.*	1. The use of comma • <u>English</u>: no comma after the word *Then* • <u>Spanish</u>: there is a comma after the word *Then* 2. Subject–verb order • <u>English</u>: *it was time to . . .* • <u>Spanish</u>: has arrived (*había llegado*) the hour (*la hora*) 3. Prepositional phrase *for him* • <u>English</u>: the phrase is before the action verb, *to leave the ranch* • <u>Spanish</u>: the word *de* before the word *abandonar* reflects the third person singular.

outlining the similarities and differences in grammar between English and L1.

➢ Encourage family members to complete with their children a weekly or monthly mini-project (e.g., grammar hunt in various texts for examples illustrating a grammar point being taught).

➢ Encourage family members to inform you of their children's oral output that sounds awkward, or grammatically incorrect.

VOICE FROM THE CLASSROOM
Maritza Magana
Leona Jackson School, Paramount, California

"I don't get it!" Unfortunately, these words are too common for some of my ELLs. As a fairly new teacher, hearing these words worried me. Although I felt I graduated from a teacher education program prepared, the lack of experience and trying to stay on the pacing guide often clouded my mind. Now with a few years of teaching upper elementary under my belt, I have discovered that letting my students utter "I don't get it" is not a bad thing, but an indicator that reminds me to stop and question the explanations, strategies, and opportunities that I have provided my students.

Although my philosophy of teaching has evolved with experience in the classroom, the basics still remain the same. Providing my students with as much literacy interaction and practice as possible will support their reading, writing, speaking, and listening development. Since most of my students are ELLs, it is important that the strategies I use daily support their learning. Currently, in my sixth-grade assignment in a 4–8 school, I have been given the flexibility to use *Time for Kids* and supplemental material within the curriculum of Into English and English at Your Command. In teaching language arts, English language development, and social studies, I am consistent with the use of strategies to support ELLs. For example, when student are reading any text, I stress the use of reading with correct expression, intonation, and decoding words. With writing, students are also expected to write in complete sentences with proper punctuation. Although a quick review of literacy expectations and examples are provided, specific strategies are primarily addressed during language arts.

I have found that the most effective way for me to differentiate instruction with grammar is by working with small groups. For ELLs, I generally provide direct instruction of a grammar skill before the initial lesson with the whole class. For example:

T: Today, we are going to learn how to extend sentences by adding adjectives. You will be working with a partner to extend his or her sentences by using two adjectives. Who knows what an adjective is and how they can make our writing better?

S: Adjectives are describing words.

From this point, I would brainstorm a few adjectives and write them down so that all students could see them. Then on a white board, I would write a simple sentence, such as *I bought a car.*

T: Who can give me an adjective before the word *car* to give more detail about the car?

S: *Red*

T: Great! Let's read our new sentence, *I bought a red car.*

The students and I would continue to add adjectives to a few more sentences. Then, I would transition students into working with a partner.

T: Now you are going to work with a partner to add adjectives to each other's sentences.

Students would take turns writing sentences and extending them with adjectives. Lastly, students would create a sentence with at least two adjectives to demonstrate that they have understood the concept and then share their extended sentences and identify the adjectives in the sentences.

After the small-group lesson, students would reunite with the whole class, and I would deliver a lesson on the grammar skill that was introduced in the small group. Within the next few days, I would pull my small group again to reassess the lesson. I would model with an example and have students independently create a sentence using the grammar concept that they have learned. I would continue to pull students into small groups to work on various grammar skills until they have received about 80% mastery.

Another strategy that I have found useful in teaching grammar is A–B partners. A–B partners allow for two students to work together on various activities and engage in oral practice. For instance, within a week, student work in pairs to read a *Time for Kids* article, select unknown vocabulary, answer questions in complete sentences, and complete graphic organizers. After students have finished writing and responding to questions about the article, they pass their paper to their partner to extend their response sentences. Following that step, the students collaborate to review sentences and check for one grammar item at a time (e.g., first checking on capital letters, then adding adjectives, and so on). This activity allows students who have participated in a small group to practice what they learned as well as serve as support for other students. Working with a partner has allowed my students to feel more confident with their answers and improve their reading, writing, speaking, and listening aptitude.

Overall, teaching grammar or any area of literacy can be a challenge, but it is important to remember that teaching is not the teacher talking, but providing students with meaningful opportunities to learn.

CONCLUSION

The overview of English grammar in the beginning of this chapter has reminded teachers of grammar's abstract, complex, and irregular nature. Given that, drill-and-kill type of grammar exercises are not conductive to ELLs' development of English grammatical knowledge, not to mention an ability to apply such knowledge for interpersonal and academic purposes. Viewing grammar as a resource model, an approach I have advocated in this book, enables teachers to infuse teaching grammar into all aspects of literacy instruction. In so doing, teachers make grammar come alive, connected to learning in subject areas, reading, and writing. I hope the strategies and activities illustrated with classroom examples presented in this chapter and Ms. Magana's sharing will add to your teacher toolbox of grammar instruction.

Reflection on Modifications of Instructional Strategies and Materials

Date:			
Name of an ELL/a Group of ELLs:			
Need(s) of an ELL/a Group of ELLs:			
Strategy		Material	
Modifications	Why?	Modifications	Why?
Reflections			
What Works?	What Does Not Work?	Possible Further Modifications	

From *Teaching English Language Learners: Literacy Strategies and Resources for K–6* by Shelley Hong Xu. Copyright 2010 by The Guilford Press. Permission to photocopy this appendix is granted to purchasers of this book for personal use only (see copyright page for details).

Similarities and Differences between English and L1

Linguistic Systems	Similarities between English and _____	Differences between English and _____
Writing System • Alphabetic versus Nonalphabetic • Concepts about Print		
Phonology • Phonological Concepts • Syllable Patterns • Phonological Rules		
Orthography • Sound or Alphabet Layer • Pattern Layer • Meaning Layer		
Semantics • Lexical Semantics • Sentential Semantics • Pragmatics		
Syntax • Word Level • Sentence Level • Transformation		
Morphology • Free Morphemes • Bound Morphemes • Morpheme Complexity		

Student Errors and Possible Explanations for the Errors

Student Error	L1s	Possible Explanation for the Error

Instructional Focus Based on Interferences

Student Name	L1	Interference	Instructional Focus
			1. 2. 3.

Oral Language Assessment Chart (Say Something and Oral Retelling)

Student Name:	Date:

Topic: (or Book Title)

Expressed Ideas

Linguistic Patterns Used	
Effective or Acceptable Ones	Less Effective or Unacceptable Ones

Diction	
Effective or Acceptable Ones	Less Effective or Unacceptable Ones

Average Length of a Sentence

Plan for Instruction

Conversation Assessment Chart

Student Name:	Date:
Topic:	

Expressed Ideas

Linguistic Patterns Used	
Effective or Acceptable Ones	Less Effective or Unacceptable Ones

Diction	
Effective or Acceptable Ones	Less Effective or Unacceptable Ones

Average Length of a Sentence

(continued)

Conversation Assessment Chart *(page 2 of 2)*

Turn Taking

Prompts Provided

Plan for Instruction

Anecdotal Record Form

Student Name:	
Setting (e.g., playground, small-group activity)	Content (e.g., discussing a book, playing basketball)
Standard	
Date: Record: Example: Date: Record: Example: Date: Record: Example:	

(continued)

Anecdotal Record Form *(page 2 of 2)*

Peers with Whom the Student Is Interacting (Name(s) and Proficiency Level)

Strengths:

Needs:

Plan for Instruction

Factors to Consider in Selecting Books for Read-Aloud

Factors	Questions to Ask	Frequency of Presence		
Background Knowledge	Do students have adequate background information on the topic?	Often	Sometimes	Seldom
	If no, can an activity for activating background knowledge be helpful?	Often	Sometimes	Seldom
	Does the book reflect students' culture?	Often	Sometimes	Seldom
	Does the book reflect students' experiences?	Often	Sometimes	Seldom
Linguistic Load	Are there sentence structures that are difficult for students?	Often	Sometimes	Seldom
	Are there words that are unfamiliar to students?	Often	Sometimes	Seldom
	Is there figurative language (e.g., metaphors, similes, idioms)?	Often	Sometimes	Seldom
Linguistic Quality	Is the language natural in rhythm and flow?	Often	Sometimes	Seldom
	Is the language predictable?	Often	Sometimes	Seldom
	Is the language contrived with a purpose of controlling vocabulary?	Often	Sometimes	Seldom
	Is the book bilingual?	Often	Sometimes	Seldom
Picture Quality	Do pictures support the print?	Often	Sometimes	Seldom
	Do pictures supplement the print?	Often	Sometimes	Seldom
	Are there pictures that are confusing to students?	Often	Sometimes	Seldom
Appeal of the Book	Does the topic of the book interest students?		Yes No	
	Is the title of the book catchy?		Yes No	
	Do the pictures on the book covers appeal to students?		Yes No	

Fluency Assessment Chart

Student Name:				Text Title:			

Date	Words per minute (wpm)	Fluency Rubric *Directions*: Circle the parts applied to the student's oral reading.					
			Self-Monitoring	Accuracy	Speed	Phrasing	Expression
		Nonfluent	No self-correction of errors	Below 90%	Many pauses Many repetitions Choppy	Word-by-word reading	No expression No attention to punctuation
		Average Fluent	Some self-correction of errors	90–94%	Some pauses Some repetitions Relatively smooth	Mixed phrasing with some word-by-word reading	Mostly appropriate expression Attention to most punctuation
		Fluent	Appropriate self-correction of errors	95–100%	Few pauses Few repetitions Smooth	Chunking words into meaningful units	Appropriate expression Attention to punctuation

Spelling and Sound Patterns of the Miscues

Self-Assessment of Words

Words	I can pronounce the word	I can explain the word	I know how to use this word	I know other forms of this word	I know this word in my language

A Lesson Plan for Morphemic Analysis, Spelling, and Grammatical Features

Sentence:			
Word	Morphemic Analysis	Spelling	Grammatical Features

Personal Vocabulary Journal

The New Word:

The Text Where I Found the Word:

The Sentence Where I Found the Word:

The Meaning I Guessed:

The Context Clues I Used for Guessing:

The Dictionary Definition:

The Part of Speech:

The Base Word or Root for the Word:

The Derivational Words:

Synonyms:

Antonyms:

The Content Area(s) Where This Word May Be Used:

The Equivalent Word in L1:

The Sentence Where I Am Using This Word:

Think-Aloud Guide

☐ Preview the text (title, headings, subheadings, illustration, graphs, tables, figures, captions).

☐ Activate prior knowledge.

☐ Connect prior knowledge to the text.

☐ Set a purpose.

☐ Make inferences.

☐ Make predictions.

☐ Apply knowledge of text genres and structures.

☐ Question about words, phrases, and sentences.

☐ Use cognates.

☐ Visualize what is being read.

☐ Connect what is being read to what has been read.

☐ Self-monitor comprehension through summarizing what has been read.

☐ Apply fix-up strategies.

Writing Strengths and Needs

Student Name:			Date:		

Check All That Apply:
☐ Writing on a self-selected topic:
☐ Writing on a given topic:
☐ Writing related to content:

Elements of Writing	Questions to Consider	Frequency of Presence		
Ideas	Does the writing have a clear focus?	Often	Sometimes	Seldom
	Are there supporting details for each topic sentence or thesis statement?	Often	Sometimes	Seldom
	Are multiple ideas well connected?	Often	Sometimes	Seldom
Diction	Does the student use appropriate, specific words to convey meaning?	Often	Sometimes	Seldom
	Does the student use a variety of words to convey a similar meaning? (e.g., the words *exciting* and *interesting* for the word *fun*)	Often	Sometimes	Seldom
	Does the student use only known or short words?	Often	Sometimes	Seldom
	Does the student code switch?	Often	Sometimes	Seldom
Sentence Structure and Variety and Text Structure	Does the student use a variety of sentences?	Often	Sometimes	Seldom
	How often does the student use simple sentences?	Often	Sometimes	Seldom
	How often is the structure of simple sentences correct?	Often	Sometimes	Seldom
	How often does the student use compound sentences?	Often	Sometimes	Seldom
	How often is the structure of compound sentences correct?	Often	Sometimes	Seldom
	How often does the student use complex sentences?	Often	Sometimes	Seldom

(continued)

Writing Strengths and Needs *(page 2 of 2)*

Elements of Writing	Questions to Consider	Frequency of Presence		
Sentence Structure and Variety and Text Structure *(continued)*	How often is the structure of complex sentences correct?	Often	Sometimes	Seldom
	Are sentence structures reflective of interferences from L1?	Often	Sometimes	Seldom
	Does the narrative have a beginning, middle, and end?	Often	Sometimes	Seldom
	Does the expository text have an introduction, body, and conclusion?	Often	Sometimes	Seldom
	Does the writing have all the elements of a text structure of a particular genre?	Often	Sometimes	Seldom
	Does the student use cue words for a particular text structure (e.g., *similar to* for comparison and *on the contrary* for contrast)	Often	Sometimes	Seldom
Spelling	Does the student use invented spelling?	Often	Sometimes	Seldom
	Does invented spelling interfere with conveying meaning?	Often	Sometimes	Seldom
	Does the invented spelling reflect interferences from L1?	Often	Sometimes	Seldom
	Does the student write only words he or she can spell correctly?			
Punctuation	Does the student use punctuation properly?	Often	Sometimes	Seldom
	Does the student use varied punctuation effectively?	Often	Sometimes	Seldom
Capitalization	Does the student use capitalization properly?	Often	Sometimes	Seldom

Plan for Instruction

Peer-Revision and Editing Form

☐ Read through your peer's writing without making any oral or written comments.

☐ Read through the directions for the writing (if applicable).

☐ Read through your peer's writing again without making any oral or written comments.

☐ Read your peer's writing *and* make oral or written comments related to the *content*. Use the following questions to guide you to focus on what your peer has done well *and* what he or she needs to improve.

☐ 1. Does the writing have all components specified in the directions (i.e., the prompt) and for the genre of the writing (e.g., text structure)? If not, what is missing?

☐ 2. Does your peer's writing include enough information for each component? If not, which component(s) need(s) more detail?

☐ 3. Do you understand the idea(s) expressed in your peer's writing? If not, why?

☐ 4. Are the paragraphs well connected to express one or several ideas? If not, why?

☐ 5. Does your peer use appropriate and effective vocabulary? If not, why?

☐ 6. Does your peer use appropriate and effective literary devices? If not, why?

☐ 7. What impresses you the most about your peer's writing?

☐ Read your peer's writing and make oral or written comments related to the *grammar and spelling*. Use the following questions to guide you to focus on what your peer has done well *and* what he or she needs to improve.

☐ 1. Do all or most sentences follow correct English grammar? If not, why?

☐ 2. For sentences that do not follow correct English grammar, is the meaning of the sentences confusing/unclear to you or still clear to you?

☐ 3. Does your peer spell all or most words correctly? If not, why?

☐ 4. For misspelled words, can you guess them? If not, why?

☐ 5. What impresses you the most about your peer's use of English grammar and spelling?

☐ Discuss with your peer your written comments on his or her writing.

A Summary of Components of English Grammar

Component	Category	Subcategory and Example
Parts of Speech	Noun	Common noun (*book*) Proper noun (*California*) Concrete noun (*student*) Abstract noun (*democracy*) Countable noun (*desk*) Uncountable/mass noun (*water*) Collective noun (*committee*)
	Verb	*Forms* Action verb (*visit*) Linking verb (*be*) Auxiliary verb (*have* visited) Modal verb (*may* visit) Transitive verb (*He hit the ball.*) Intransitive verb (*He cried.*) Regular verb (*visit, visited*) Irregular verb (*go, went, gone*) Phrasal verb (*look at*) *Tenses* Present tense (*They go to school every day. He goes to school every day.*) Past tense (*He went to the store yesterday.*) Progressive tense (*He is reading a book.*) Future tense (*He will/is going to read the book.*) Perfect tense (*He has read the book. He will have read the book by this weekend. He had read the book before he went to visit his classmate.*) *Mood* Indicative (stating something) (*The school starts at 8:00 a.m.*) Imperative (expressing commands or requests) (*Watch out!*) Subjunctive (expressing unreal conditions or wishes) (*If I were you, I would talk to the boss. I wish that I were there to help you fix the car.*) *Voice* Active (*The teacher gave each student a book.*) Passive (*Each student was given a book by the teacher.*)
	Adjective	(*happy*)

(continued)

Component	Category	Subcategory and Example
Parts of Speech *(continued)*	Adverb	*(happily)*
	Pronoun	Personal pronoun (*I, he*) Possessive pronoun (*my, yours*) Demonstrative pronoun (*this, these*) Relative pronoun (*which, whose* used in a relative clause) Interrogative pronoun (*what, who*) Indefinite pronoun (*each, none*) Reflexive pronoun (*myself, oneself*)
	Preposition	*(in, on)*
	Conjunction	Coordinating conjunction (*and, or, but*) Subordinating conjunction (*because, although*) Correlative conjunction (*both . . . and . . . , either . . . or . . .*) Pronoun as conjunction (*that, who, what*) Compound conjunction (*on one hand, on the other hand*)
	Interjection	*(oh, hooray)*
Phrases	Noun Phrase	As a subject, an object (*A book is a good gift.*) As an appositive (*My favorite color, deep blue, is present throughout this picture.*)
	Verb Phrase	Infinitive (*To read everyday is good for you.*) Gerund (*Reading everyday is good for you.*) Present participle (*Reading too quickly through the text, she missed some details.*) Past participle (*He had a shocked look on his face.*)
	Prepositional Phrase	*(at school, in the afternoon)*
	Absolute Phrase	*(Summer break being over, teachers were getting ready for a new school year.)*
Sentences	Components	Subject (*He is a good student. A well-written book is a good gift. The doorbell and cell phone rang at the same time.*)
		Predicate (*She is happy now. He has read the book. He is reading the book. He might read the book.*)
		Direct object (*Jim gave Maria a book.*)
		Indirect object (*Jim gave Maria a book.*)
		Subject complement (*The leaves turned yellow. She became a teacher a year ago.*)
		Object complement (*The parents named their baby Adam.*)

(continued)

Component	Category	Subcategory and Example
Sentences *(continued)*	Types	simple sentence (subject + predicate) (*He read a book. He is a good student. She may come.*)
		Compound sentence (independent clause + independent clause) (*I teach in the United States, and my best friend teaches in Canada.*)
		Complex sentence (dependent clause + independent clause) (*When I was five years old, I started reading books.*)
		Compound–complex sentence (*When I was young, I loved reading books and my older sister enjoyed exploring nature. When I was young, I love reading books that had suspenseful plots.*)
Agreement	Subject–Verb Agreement	*He reads books every day. They read books every day. She is a good girl. They are good girls.*
	Pronoun–Antecedent Agreement	*She likes her new roommate. They enjoyed their new class. The dog wagged its tail.*
Determiner	Articles	Indefinite article (*a, an*) Definite article (*the*)
	Pronouns	*See Pronouns*
	Numbers	(*the three pigs*)
Modifier	Restrictive	(*The book that you read last week is very interesting.*) (*The book The Three Little Pigs is funny.*)
	Nonrestrictive	(*The book, which you read last week, is very interesting.*) *That book, The Three Little Pigs, is funny.*)
Inflection	Noun	Plural (*books, oxen*)
	Verb	Tenses (*See Verbs*)
	Adjective	Comparative (*happier, more beautiful*) Superlative (*happiest, most beautiful*)
	Adverb	Comparative (*more easily*) Superlative (*most easily*)

(continued)

A Summary of Components of English Grammar *(page 4 of 4)*

Component	Category	Subcategory and Example
Punctuation	Comma	(*Mary, my aunt, read me books when she visited me.*)
	Period	(*I enjoyed the book.*)
	Question mark	(*Do you like the book?*)
	Quotation marks	(*The boy yelled, "Be quiet!"*)
	Exclamatory point	(*What an interesting book!*)
	Apostrophe	(*John's essay is excellent.*)
	Hyphen	(*This is a well-written book.*)
	Colon	(*The teacher bought her students these two books:* The Three Little Pigs *and* The True Story of the Three Little Pigs.)
	Semicolon	(*Gary Paulson is Jan's favorite author; Dav Pilkey is my favorite.*)
	Ellipsis	(*The student kept saying, "I am thinking, I am thinking, . . . "*)

Documenting Students' Needs and Instructional Focus

Date	Category	Subcategory	Example (Source)	Instructional Focus

REFERENCES

Adams, M. J. (1990). *Beginning to read: Thinking and learning about print.* Cambridge, MA: MIT Press.

Afflerbach, P., Pearson, P. D., & Paris, S. (2008). Skills and strategies: Their differences, their relationships, and why it matters. In K. Mokhtari & R. Sheorey (Eds.), *Reading strategies of first- and second-language learners* (pp. 11–24). Norwood, MA: Christopher-Gordon.

Akhavan, N. (2006). *Help! My kids don't all speak English: How to set up a language workshop in your linguistically diverse classroom.* Portsmouth, NH: Heinemann.

Alegria, J., Pignot, E., & Morais, J. (1982). Phonetic analysis of speech and memory codes in beginning readers. *Memory and Cognition, 10,* 451–456.

Amis, K. (1997). *The king's English: A guide to modern usage.* New York: St. Martin's Griffin.

Anderson, R. C., & Nagy, W. E. (1992). The vocabulary conundrum. *American Educator, 16,* 14–18, 44–47.

Andrew, L. (2006). *Language exploration and awareness: A resource book for teachers* (3rd ed.). Mahwah, NJ: Erlbaum.

Angelillo, J. (2002). *A fresh approach to teaching punctuation.* New York: Scholastic.

Anthony, A. R. B. (2008). Output strategies for English-language learners: Theory to practice. *Reading Teacher, 61,* 472–482.

Atwell, N. (1998). *In the middle: New understandings about writing, reading, and learning* (2nd ed.). Portsmouth, NH: Heinemann.

Au, K. H. (2002). Multicultural factors and the effective instruction of students of diverse backgrounds. In A. E. Farstrup & S. J. Samuels (Eds.), *What research has to say about reading instruction* (3rd ed., pp. 392–413). Newark, DE: International Reading Association.

August, D., Calderón, M., & Carlo, M. (2000). *Transfer of skills from Spanish to English: A study of young learners.* Washington, DC: Center for Applied Linguistics.

August, D., & Shanahan, T. (Eds.). (2006). *Developing literacy in second-language learners.* Mahwah, NJ: Erlbaum.

Barone, M. D., Mallette, M., & Xu, S. H. (2005). *Teaching early literacy: Development, assessment, and instruction.* New York: Guilford Press.

Barone, M. D., & Xu, S. H. (2008). *Literacy instruction for English language learners pre-K–2.* New York: Guilford Press.

Bear, D. R., Helman, L., Templeton, S., Invernizzi, M., & Johnston, F. (2007). *Words their way with English learners.* Upper Saddle River, NJ: Prentice Hall.

Bear, D. R., Templeton, S., Invernizzi, M., & Johnston, F. (2008) *Words their way: Word study for phonics, vocabulary, and spelling instruction* (4th ed.). New York: Allyn & Bacon.

Benjamin, A., & Oliva, T. (2007). *Engaging grammar: Practical advice for real classrooms.* Urbana, IL: National Council of Teachers of English.

Blachowicz, C., & Fisher, P. (2006). *Teaching vocabulary in all classrooms* (3rd ed.). Upper Saddle River, NJ: Merrill Prentice Hall.

Blachowicz, C., & Fisher, P. (2007). Best practices in vocabulary instruction. In L. B. Gambrell, L. M. Morrow, & M. Pressley (Eds.), *Best practices in literacy instruction* (3rd ed., pp. 178–203). New York: Guilford Press.

Blachowicz, C. L. Z., Fisher, P. J. L., Ogle, D., & Watts-Taffe, S. (2006). Theory and research into practice: Vocabulary: questions from the classroom. *Reading Research Quarterly, 41,* 524–539.

Block, C. C., Gambrell, L. B., & Pressley, M. (Eds.). (2002). *Improving comprehension instruction.* San Francisco, CA: Jossey-Bass.

Block, C. C., Parris, S. R., & Whiteley, C. S. (2008). CPMs: A kinesthetic comprehension strategy. *Reading Teacher, 61,* 460–470.

Block, C. C., & Pressley, M. (2007). Best practices in teaching comprehension. In L. B. Gambrell, L. M. Morrow, & M. Pressley (Eds.), *Best practices in literacy instruction* (3rd ed., pp. 220–242). New York: Guilford Press.

Boyd-Batstone, P. (2004). Focused anecdotal records assessment: A tool for standards-based, authentic assessment. *Reading Teacher, 58,* 230–239.

Bravo, M. A., Hiebert, E. H., & Pearson, P. D. (2007). Tapping the linguistic resources of Spanish-English bilinguals: The role of cognates in science. In R. K. Wagner, A. E. Muse, & K. R. Tannenbaum (Eds.), *Vocabulary acquisition* (pp. 140–156). New York: Guilford Press.

Button, K., Johnson, M., & Furgerson, P. (1996). Interactive writing in a primary classroom. *Reading Teacher, 49,* 446–454.

California Department of Education. (2006). *Top 10 languages spoken by ELLs 2005–2006.* Retrieved April 20, 2007, from data1.cde.ca.gov/dataquest.

California State Board of Education. (1999). *English-language development standards for California public schools.* Sacramento, CA: Author.

California State Board of Education. (2007). *Reading/language arts framework for California public schools* (rev. ed.). Sacramento, CA: Author.

Calkins, L. (1983). *Lessons from a child: On the teaching and learning of writing.* Portsmouth, NH: Heinemann.

Calkins, L. (1994). *The art of teaching writing* (New ed.). Portsmouth, NH: Heinemann.

Calkins, L. (2001). *The art of teaching reading.* New York: Addison-Wesley.

Cappellini, M. (2005). *Balancing reading and language learning.* Portland, ME: Stenhouse.

Carlo, M. S., August, D., McLaughlin, B., Snow, C. E., Dressler, C., Lippman, D. N., et al. (2004). Closing the gap: Addressing the vocabulary needs of English-language learners in bilingual and mainstream classrooms. *Reading Research Quarterly, 39,* 188–215.

Carlo, M. S., August, D., & Snow, C. E. (2005). Sustained vocabulary-learning strategies for English language learners. In E. H. Hiebert & M. Kamil (Eds.), *Teaching and learning vocabulary: Bringing research to practice* (pp. 137–153). Mahwah, NJ: Erlbaum.

Carrillo, M. (1994). Development of phonological awareness and reading acquisition: A study in Spanish language. *Reading and Writing, 6,* 279–298.

Cazden, C. (2001). *Classroom discourse: The language of teaching and learning.* Portsmouth, NH: Heinemann.

Chamot, A. U., & O'Malley, J. M. (1994). *The CALLA handbook: Implementing the cognitive academic language learning approach*. New York: Addison-Wesley.

Collier, L. (2008, March). The importance of academic language for English language learners. *The Council Chronicle*, 10–13.

Collier, V. P. (1995). *Acquiring a second language for school*. Washington, DC: National Clearinghouse for Bilingual Education.

Cummins, J. (1979). Linguistic interdependence and the educational development of bilingual children. *Review of Educational Research, 49*, 222–25l.

Cummins, J. (1986). Empowering minority students: A framework for intervention. *Harvard Educational Review, 56*, 18–35.

Cummins, J. (1989). *Empowering minority students*. Covina: California Association for Bilingual Education.

Cummins, J. (2000). "This place nurture my spirit": Creating contexts of empowerment in linguistically diverse schools. In R. Phillipson (Ed.), *Rights to language: Equity, power, and education* (pp. 249–258). Mahwah, NJ: Erlbaum.

Cummins, J. (2003). Reading and the bilingual student: Fact and friction. In G. García (Ed.), *English learners reaching the highest level of English literacy* (pp. 2–23). Newark, DE: International Reading Association.

Cunningham, A. E. (2005). Vocabulary growth through independent reading and reading aloud to children. In E. H. Hiebert & M. Kamil (Eds.), *Teaching and learning vocabulary: Bringing research to practice* (pp. 45–68). Mahwah, NJ: Erlbaum.

Cunningham, P. M. (2008). *Phonics they use* (5th ed.). New York: Allyn & Bacon.

Davis, F. B. (1944). Fundamental factors of comprehension in reading. *Psychometrika, 9*, 185–197.

Davis, F. B. (1972). Research on comprehension in reading. *Reading Research Quarterly, 7*, 628–678.

Dean, D. (2008). *Bringing grammar to life*. Newark, DE: International Reading Association.

DeCapua, A. (2008). *Grammar for teachers: A guide to American English for native and non-native speakers*. New York: Springer.

Delgado-Gaitan, C. (2001). *The power of community*. Denver, CO: Rowman & Littlefield.

Diaz-Rico, L. T., & Weed, K. Z. (2006). *The crosscultural, language, and academic development handbook: A complete K–12 reference guide* (3rd ed.). New York: Allyn & Bacon.

Dorfman, L. R., & Cappelli, R. (2007). *Mentor texts: Teaching writing through children's literature, K–6*. Portland, ME: Stenhouse.

Dressler, C., & Kamil, M. L. (2006). First- and second-language literacy. In D. August & T. Shanahan (Eds.), *Developing literacy in second-language learners* (pp. 197–238). Mahwah, NJ: Erlbaum.

Duke, N. K., & Pearson, P. D. (2002). Effective practices for developing reading comprehension. In A. E. Farstrup & S. J. Samuels (Eds.), *What research has to say about reading instruction* (pp. 205–242). Newark, DE: International Reading Association.

Dunbar, S. (1992). Developing vocabulary by integrating language and content. *TESL Canada Journal, 9*, 73–79.

Dutro, S., & Moran, C. (2003). Rethinking English language instruction: An architectural approach. In G. García (Ed.), *English learners: Reaching the highest level of English literacy* (pp. 227–258). Newark, DE: International Reading Association.

Dyson, A. H. (2003). *The brothers and sisters learn to write: Popular literacies in childhood and school cultures*. New York: Teachers College Press.

Echevarria, J., Vogt, M., & Short, D. J. (2008). *Making Content Comprehensible for English Learners: The SIOP Model* (4th). Boston: Allyn & Bacon.

Edelsky, C. (1982). Writing in a bilingual program: The relationship of L1 and L2 texts. *TESOL Quarterly, 16,* 211–228.

Edelsky, C., & Jilbert, K. (1985). Bilingual children and writing: Lessons for all of us. *Volta Review, 87*(5), 57–72.

Edwards, P. A. (2004). *Children's literacy development: Making it happen through school, family, and community involvement.* New York: Allyn & Bacon.

Ehrenworth, M., & Vinton, V. (2005). *The power of grammar: Unconventional approaches to the conventions of writing.* Portsmouth, NH: Heinemann.

ERIC Clearinghouse on Languages and Linguistics. (2000). *What elementary teachers need to know about language.* Washington, DC: Author. (EDO-FL-00-06 NOVEMBER 2000) Retrieved January 22, 2007, from *www.cal.org/resources/digest/digest_pdfs/0006fillmoresnowwhat.pdf.*

Eskey, D. E. (2005). Reading in a second language. In E. Hinkel (Ed.), *Handbook of research in second language teaching and learning* (pp. 563–579). Mahwah, NJ: Erlbaum.

Farrell, T. S. C. (2006). *Succeeding with English language learners: A guide for beginning teachers.* Thousand Oaks, CA: Corwin Press.

Fillmore, L. W. (2000). Loss of family languages: Should educators be concerned? *Theory into Practice, 39,* 203–210.

Fillmore, L. W., & Snow, C. E. (2000). *What teachers need to know about language.* Washington, DC: ERIC Clearinghouse on Languages and Linguistics. Retrieved March 25, 2007, from *faculty.tamu-commerce.edu/jthompson/Resources/FillmoreSnow2000.pdf.*

Fisher, D., & Frey, N. (2003). Writing instruction for struggling adolescent readers: A gradual release model. *Journal of Adolescent & Adult Literacy, 46,* 396–405.

Fitzgerald, J. (1995). English as a second language instruction in the United States: A research review. *Journal of Reading Behavior, 27,* 115–152.

Fitzgerald, J. (2005). Multilingual writing in preschool through twelfth grade: The last 15 years. In C. A. MacArthur, S. Graham, & J. Fitzgerald (Eds.), *Handbook of writing research* (pp. 337–354). New York: Guilford Press.

Fitzgerald, J., & Amendum, S. (2007). What is sound writing instruction for multilingual learners? In S. Graham, C. MacArthur, & J. Fitzgerald (Eds.), *Best practices in writing instruction* (pp. 289–307). New York: Guilford Press.

Fitzgerald, J., Amendum, S. J., & Guthrie, K. M. (2008). Young Latino students' English reading growth in all-English classrooms. *Journal of Literacy Research, 40,* 59–94.

Fitzgerald, J., & Graves, M. F. (2004). *Scaffolding reading experiences for English language learners.* Norwood, MA: Christopher-Gordon.

Fitzgerald, J., & Noblit, G. (2000). Balance in the making: Learning to read in an ethnically diverse first-grade classroom. *Journal of Educational Psychology, 92,* 3–22.

Folse, K. S. (2004). *Vocabulary myths: Applying second language research to classroom teaching.* Ann Arbor: University of Michigan Press.

Freeman, D. E., & Freeman, Y. S. (2004). *Essential linguistics: What you need to know to teach reading, ESL, spelling, phonics, and grammar.* Portsmouth, NH: Heinemann.

Freeman, D. E., & Freeman, Y. S. (2006a). Teaching language through content themes: Viewing our world as a global village. In T. Young & N. L. Hadaway (Eds.), *Supporting the literacy development of English learners: Increasing success in all classrooms* (pp. 61–78). Newark, DE: International Reading Association.

Freeman, Y. S., & Freeman, D. E. (2006b). *Teaching reading and writing in Spanish and English in bilingual and dual language classrooms* (2nd ed.). Portsmouth, NH: Heinemann.

Freeman, Y. S., & Freeman, D. E. (2009). *Academic language for English language learners and struggling readers.* Portsmouth, NH: Heinemann.

Freeman, Y. S., Freeman, D. E., & Mercuri, S. (2002). *Closing the achievement gap.* Portsmouth, NH: Heinemann.

Ganske, K. (2006). *Word sorts and more.* New York: Guilford Press.

García, G. E. (1991). Factors influencing the English reading test performance of Spanish-speaking Hispanic children. *Reading Research Quarterly, 26,* 371–392.

García, G. E. (2000). Bilingual children's reading. In M. L. Kamil, P. B. Mosenthal, P. D. Pearson, & R. Barr (Eds.), *Handbook of reading research* (Vol. 3, pp. 813–834). Mahwah, NJ: Erlbaum.

García, G. E., McKoon, G., & August, D. (2006). Synthesis: Language and literacy assessment. In D. August & T. Shanahan (Eds.), *Developing literacy in second-language learners* (pp. 583–624). Mahwah, NJ: Erlbaum.

Gee, J. P. (2003). *What video games have to teach us about learning and literacy.* Hampshire, England: Palgrave-Macmillan.

Genesee, F., Geva, E., Dressler, C., & Kamil, M. L. (2006). Synthesis: Cross-linguistic relationships. In D. August & T. Shanahan (Eds.), *Developing literacy in second-language learners* (pp. 153–174). Mahwah, NJ: Erlbaum.

Genesee, F., Lindholm-Leary, K., Saunders, B., & Christian, D. (2006). *Educating English language learners: A synthesis of research evidence.* New York: Cambridge University Press.

Geva, E., & Genesee, F. (2006). First-language oral proficiency and second-language literacy. In D. August & T. Shanahan (Eds.), *Developing literacy in second-language learners* (pp. 185–195). Mahwah, NJ: Erlbaum.

Gibbons, P. (2002). *Scaffolding language, scaffolding learning: Teaching second language learners in the mainstream classroom.* Portsmouth, NH: Heinemann.

Goldenberg, C., Rezaei, A., & Fletcher, J. (2005, May). *Home use of English and Spanish and Spanish-speaking children's oral language and literacy achievement.* Paper presented at the annual convention of the International Reading Association, San Antonio, TX.

Gonzáles, N., & Moll, L. (1995). Funds of knowledge for teaching in Latino households. *Urban Education, 29,* 443–471.

Gonzáles, N., Moll, L., & Amanti, C. (2005). *Funds of knowledge: Theorizing practice in households, communities, and classrooms.* Mahwah, NJ: Erlbaum.

Goodman, K. S. (1973). Miscues: Windows on the reading process. In K. S. Goodman (Ed.), *Miscue analysis* (pp. 3–14). Urbana, IL: ERIC Clearinghouse on Reading and Communication Skills and the National Council of Teachers of English.

Goodman, Y. (1985). Kidwatching: Observing children in the classroom. In A. Jaggar & M. Smith-Burke (Eds.), *Observing language learners* (pp. 9–18). Urbana, IL: National Council of Teachers of English and Newark, DE: International Reading Association.

Graham, S., MacArthur, C. A., & Fitzgerald, J. (Eds.). (2006). *Best practices in writing instruction.* New York: Guilford Press.

Graves, A. W., & Rueda, R. (2009). Teaching written expression to culturally and linguistically diverse learners. In G. A. Troia (Ed.), *Instruction and assessment for struggling writers: Evidence-based practices* (pp. 213–242). New York: Guilford Press.

Graves, D. H. (1983). *Writing: Teachers and children at work.* Portsmouth, NH: Heinemann.

Graves, M. F. (1987). The roles of instruction in fostering vocabulary development. In M. C. McKeown & M. E. Curtis (Eds.), *The nature of vocabulary acquisition* (pp. 165–184). Mahwah, NJ: Erlbaum.

Graves, M. F. (2006). *The vocabulary book.* New York: Teachers College Press.

Graves, M. F., & Watts-Taffe, S. M. (2002). The place of word consciousness in a research-based vocabulary program. In A. E. Farstrup & S. J. Samuels (Eds.), *What research has to say about reading instruction* (pp. 140–165). Newark, DE: International Reading Association.

Gregory, G. H., & Kuzmich, L. (2005). *Differentiated literacy strategies for student growth and achievement in grades K–6.* Thousand Oaks, CA: Corwin Press.

Gunning, T. (2008). *Creating literacy instruction for all students in grades 4–8* (2nd ed.). New York: Allyn & Bacon.

Guthrie, J., & Davis, M. (2003). Motivating struggling readers in middle school through an engagement model of classroom practice. *Reading and Writing Quarterly, 9,* 59–85.

Haastrup, K. (1985). Lexical inferencing—a study of procedures in receptions. *Scandinavian Working Papers on Bilingualism, 5,* 63–87.

Haastrup, K. (1987). Using thinking aloud and retrospection to uncover learners' lexical inferencing procedures. In C. Faerch & G. Kasper (Eds.), *Introspection in second language research* (pp. 197–212). Clevedon, UK: Multilingual Matters.

Haastrup, K. (1989). *Lexical inferencing procedures, Part 1 and Part 2.* Copenhagen, Denmark: Handelshojskolen i Kobenhavn.

Hadaway, N. L., Vardell, S. M., & Young, T. A (2004). *What every teacher should know about English language learners.* Boston, MA: Allyn & Bacon.

Haggard, M. R. (1986). The vocabulary self-collection strategy: Using student interest and world knowledge to enhance vocabulary growth. *Journal of Reading, 29,* 634–642.

Halliday, M. A. K., & Hasan, R. (1976). *Cohesion in English.* London: Longman.

Halliday, M. S. K. (1975). *Learning how to mean.* New York: Elsevier.

Harmon, J. M., Wood, K. D., & Hedrick, W. B. (2006). *Instructional strategies for teaching content vocabulary, grades 4–12.* Westerville, OH: National Middle School Association and Newark, DE: International Reading Association.

Harris, K. R., Graham, S., Mason, L. H., & Friedlander, B. (2008). *Powerful writing strategies for all students.* Baltimore, MD: Brookes.

Haussamen, B., Benjamin, A., Kolln, M., & Wheeler, R. S. (2003). *Grammar alive!: A guide for teachers.* Urbana, IL: National Council of Teachers of English.

Herrell, A. (2000). *Fifty strategies for teaching English language learners.* Upper Saddle River, NJ: Prentice Hall.

Herrera, S. G., & Murry, K. G. (2005). *Mastering ESL and bilingual methods.* New York: Allyn & Bacon.

Holmes, B. C., & Roser, N. L. (1987). Five ways to assess readers' prior knowledge. *The Reading Teacher, 40,* 646–649.

Horwitz, E. K. (2008). *Becoming a language teacher: A practical guide to second language learning and teaching.* Boston: Allyn & Bacon.

Houk, F. A. (2005). *Supporting English language learners: A guide for teachers and administrators.* Portsmouth, NH: Heinemann.

Hudelson, S. (1984). Kan yu ret an rayt en Ingles: Children become literate in English as a second language. *TESOL Quarterly, 18,* 221–238.

International Reading Association. (2000). *Excellent reading teachers: A position statement of the International Reading Association.* Retrieved March 29, 2003, from *www.reading.org/ downloads/positions/ps1041_excellent.pdf.*

International Reading Association. (2001). *Second-language literacy instruction: A position statement of the International Reading Association.* Retrieved April 15, 2006, from *www. reading.org/downloads/positions/ps1046_second_language.pdf.*

International Reading Association. (2003). *Investment in teacher preparation in the United States.* Retrieved April 15, 2006, from *www.reading.org/downloads/positions/ps1060_ teacher_preparation.pdf.*

Jiménez, R. T. (1997). The strategic reading abilities and potential of five low-literacy Latina/o readers in middle school. *Reading Research Quarterly, 32*, 224–243.

Jiménez, R. T. (2004). More equitable literacy assessments for Latino students. *The Reading Teacher, 57*, 576–578.

Jiménez, R. T., García, G. E., & Pearson, P. D. (1996). The reading strategies of bilingual Latina/o students who are successful English readers. *Reading Research Quarterly, 31*, 90–112.

Johns, J. J. (2005). *Basic reading inventory* (9th ed.). Dubuque, IA: Kendall/Hunt.

Johnson, D. D., & Pearson, P. D. (1984). *Teaching reading vocabulary*. New York: Holt, Rinehart, & Winston.

Juel, C., Griffith, P. L., & Gough, P. B. (1986). Acquisition of literacy: A longitudinal study of children in first and second grade. *Journal of Educational Psychology, 78*, 243–255.

Kamil, M. L., & Bernhardt, E. B. (2004). The science of reading and the reading of science. In E. W. Saul (Ed.), *Crossing borders in literacy and science education* (pp. 123–139). Newark, DE: International Reading Association and Arlington, VA: National Science Teachers Association.

Kaplan, R. B. (1966). Cultural thought patterns in intercultural education. *Language Learning, 16*, 1–20.

Kaplan, R. B., & Ramanathan, V. (1996). Audience and voice in current L1 composition texts: Some implications for ESL student-writers. *Journal of Second Language Writing, 5*(1), 21–34.

Kendall, J., & Khuon, O. (2006). *Writing sense: Integrated reading and writing lessons for English language learners K–8*. Portland, ME: Stenhouse.

Krashen, S. (1981). *Second language acquisition and second language learning*. New York: Prentice Hall.

Krashen, S. (1982). *Principles and practice in second language acquisition*. Oxford, UK: Pergamon Press.

Krashen, S. (1985). *The input hypothesis: Issues and implications*. New York: Longman.

Krashen, S., & Terrell, T. (1983). *The natural approach: Language acquisition in the classroom*. Englewood Cliffs, NJ: Alemany/Prentice Hall.

Kress, J. E. (2008). *The ESL/ELL teacher's book of lists* (2nd ed.). San Francisco, CA: Jossey-Bass.

LaCelle-Peterson, M., & Rivera, C. (1994). Is it real for all kids? A framework for equitable assessment policies for English language learners. *Harvard Educational Review, 64*, 55–75.

Lenski, S. D., Ehlers-Zavala, F., Daniel, M. C., & Sun-Irminger, X. (2006). Assessing English-language learners in mainstream classrooms. *The Reading Teacher, 60*, 24–34.

Lesaux, N., Koda, K., Siegel, L., & Shanahan, T. (2006). Development of literacy. In D. August & T. Shanahan (Eds.), *Developing literacy in second-language learners* (pp. 75–122). Mahwah, NJ: Erlbaum.

Lesaux, N., & Siegel, L. (2003). The development of reading in children who speak English as a second language. *Developmental Psychology, 39*, 1005–1019.

Levitt, M. (2009). *Putting everyday life on the page: Inspiring students to write, grades 2–7*. Thousand Oaks, CA: Corwin Press.

Li, G. (2004). Perspectives on struggling English language learners: Case studies of two Chinese-Canadian children. *Journal of Literacy Research, 36*, 31–72.

Lipson, M. Y., & Wixson, K. K. (2009). *Assessment and instruction of reading and writing difficulties: An interactive approach* (4th ed.). Boston: Allyn & Bacon.

Mallozzi, C. A., & Malloy, J. A. (2007). Second language issues and multiculturalism. *Reading Research Quarterly, 42*, 430–436.

Manis, F. R., Lindsey, K. A., & Bailey, C. E. (2004). Development of reading in grades K–2 in Spanish-speaking English-language learners. *Learning Disabilities Research & Practice, 19*, 214–224.

Mansukhani, P. (2002). The explorers club: The sky is no limit for learning. *Language Arts, 80*, 31–39.

Manyak, P. C. (2008). What's your news?: Portraits of a rich language and literacy activity for English-language learners. *Reading Teacher, 61*, 450–458.

Marco, M. J. L. (1999). Procedural vocabulary: Lexical signaling of conceptual relations in discourse. *Applied Linguistics, 20*(1), 1–21.

Martin, J. R. (1992). *English text: System and structure*. Philadelphia: Benjamins.

McCarrier, A., Pinnell, G. S., & Fountas, I. (1999). *Interactive writing: How language and literacy come together, K–2*. Portsmouth, NH: Heinemann.

Meier, D. R. (2004). *The young child's memory for words: Developing first and second language and literacy*. New York: Teachers College Press.

Moats, L. C. (2000). *Speech to print: Language essentials for teachers*. Baltimore, MD: Brookes.

Moll, L. C. (1998). Turning to the world: Bilingual schooling, literacy, and the cultural mediation of thinking. In T. Shanahan & F. V. Rodriguez-Brown (Eds.), *47th yearbook of the National Reading Conference* (pp. 59–75). Chicago, IL: National Reading Conference.

Moll, L. C., Amanti, C., Neff, D., & González, N. (1992). Funds of knowledge for teaching: Using a qualitative approach to connect homes and classrooms. *Theory into Practice, 31*, 321–141.

Mora-Flores, E. (2009). *Writing instruction for English learners*. Thousand Oaks, CA: Corwin Press.

Morrow, L. (2005). *Literacy development in the early years: Helping children read and write* (5th ed.). Boston: Allyn & Bacon.

Nagy, W., McClure, E., & Mir, M. (1997). Linguistic transfer and the use of context by Spanish-English bilinguals. *Applied Psycholinguistics, 18*, 431–452.

Nagy, W., & Scott, J. (2000). Vocabulary processes. In M. L. Kamil, P. B. Mosenthal, P. D. Pearson, & R. Barr (Eds.), *Handbook of reading research* (Vol. 3, pp. 269–283). Mahwah, NJ: Erlbaum.

Naslund, J. C. (1990). The interrelationships among preschool predictors of reading acquisition for German children. *Reading and Writing, 2*, 327–360.

Nation, I. S. P. (2001). *Learning vocabulary in another language*. Cambridge, UK: Cambridge University Press.

National Council of Teachers of English. (2006). *NCTE Position paper on the role of English teachers in educating English language learners*. Retrieved May 25, 2007, from *www.ncte.org/about/over/positions/category/div/124545.htm?source=gs*.

National Reading Panel. (2000). *Teaching children to read*. (National Institutes of Health NIH Pub No. 00-4754). Washington, DC: Author.

Nessel, D. D., & Dixon, C. N. (2008). *Using the language experience approach with English language learners*. Thousand Oaks, CA: Corwin Press.

Neuman, S. B., & Roskos, K. (1990). Play, print, and purpose: Enriching play environments for literacy development. *Reading Teacher, 44*, 214–221.

New London Group. (1996). A pedagogy of multiliteracies: Designing social futures. *Harvard Educational Review, 66*, 60–92.

Noguchi, R. (1991). *Grammar and the teaching of writing*. Urbana, IL: National Council of Teachers of English.

Ogle, D. (1986). K–W–L: A teaching model that develops active reading of expository text. *Reading Teacher, 39*, 564–570.

Palincsar, A., & Brown, A. (1984). Reciprocal teaching of comprehension-fostering and monitory activities. *Cognition and Instruction, 1*, 117–175.

Paratore, J. R., Melzi, G., & Krol-Sinclair, B. (2003). Learning about the literate lives of Latino families. In D. M. Barone & L. Morrow (Eds.), *Literacy and young children: Research-based practices* (pp. 101–118). New York: Guilford Press.

Peregoy, S. E., & Boyle, O. F. (2000). English learners reading English: What we know, what we need to know. *Theory into Practice, 39*, 237–247.

Peregoy, S. E., & Boyle, O. F. (2005). *Reading, writing, and learning in ESL: A resource book for K–12 teachers* (4th ed.). New York: Allyn & Bacon.

Peregoy, S. E., & Boyle, O. F. (2009). *Reading, writing, and learning in ESL: A resource book for K–12 teachers* (5th ed.). New York: Allyn & Bacon.

Pinnell, G., & McCarrier, A. (1994). Interactive writing: A transition tool for assisting children in learning to read and write. In E. Hiebert & B. Taylor (Eds.), *Getting reading right from the start* (pp. 149–170). Needham Heights, MA: Allyn & Bacon.

Pressley, M., Mohan, L., Fingeret, L., Reffitt, K., & Raphael-Bogaert, L. (2007). Writing instruction for engaging and effective elementary settings. In S. Graham, C. MacArthur, & J. Fitzgerald (Eds.), *Best practices in writing instruction* (pp. 13–27). New York: Guilford Press.

Ray, K. W. (2006). *Study driven: A framework for planning units of study in the writing workshop*. Portsmouth, NH: Heinemann.

Rea, D. M., & Mercuri, S. P. (2006). *Research-based strategies for English language learners*. Portsmouth, NH: Heinemann.

Readence, J. E., Bean, T. W., & Baldwin, R. S. (2004). *Content area reading: An integrated approach* (8th ed.). Dubuque, IA: Kendall/Hunt.

Roberts, T. A. (2008). Home storybook reading in primary or second language with preschool children. *Reading Research Quarterly, 43*, 103–130.

Rothenberg, C., & Fisher, D. (2007). *Teaching English language learners: A differentiated approach*. Boston: Allyn & Bacon.

Ruddell, R. B., & Unrau, N. J. (2004). Reading as a meaning-construction process: The reader, the text, and the teacher. In R. B. Ruddell & N. J. Unrau (Eds.), *Theoretical models and processes of reading* (5th ed., pp. 1462–1521). Newark, DE : International Reading Association.

Samway, K. D. (1987). Formal evaluation of children's writing: An incomplete story. *Language Arts, 64*, 289–298.

Samway, K. D. (1993). This is hard, isn't it?: Children evaluating writing. *TESOL Quarterly, 27*, 233–258.

Samway, K. D. (2006). *When English language learners write*. Portsmouth, NH: Heinemann.

Saville-Troike, M. (1984). What really matters in second language learning for academic achievement? *TESOL Quarterly, 18*, 199–219.

Scarcella, R. (2003). *Academic English: A conceptual framework*. Technical Report 2003-1. Berkeley: The University of California Linguistic Minority Research Institute.

Schleppegrell, M. J. (2004). *The language of schooling: A functional linguistics approach*. Mahwah, NJ: Erlbaum.

Schleppegrell, M. J., & Colombi, M. C. (Eds.). (2002). *Developing advanced literacy in first and second languages*. Mahwah, NJ: Erlbaum.

Schmidt, P. R., & Finkbeiner, C. (Eds.). (2006). *The ABC's cultural understanding and communication: National and international adaptations.* Greenwich, CT: Information Age Publishing.

Schwartz, R. M., & Raphael, T. E. (1985). Concept of definition: A key to improving students' vocabulary. *Reading Teacher, 39,* 198–205.

Shanahan, T., & Beck, I. (2006). Effective literacy teaching for English-language learners. In D. August & T. Shanahan (Eds.), *Developing literacy in second-language learners* (pp. 415–488). Mahwah, NJ: Erlbaum.

Short, D. J. (1993). Assessing integrated language and content instruction. *TESOL Quarterly, 27,* 627–656.

Skilton-Sylvester, E. (2002). Literate at home but not at school: A Cambodian girl's journey from playwright to struggling writer. In G. Hull & K. Schultz (Eds.), *School's out: Bridging out-of-school literacies with classroom practice* (pp. 61–90). New York: Teachers College Press.

Slavin, R. E., & Chueng, A. (2003). *Effective reading programs for English language learners: A best-evidence synthesis.* Baltimore: Johns Hopkins University, Center for the Education of Students Placed at Risk.

Snow, C. E., Burns, M. S., & Griffin, P. (Eds.). (1998). *Preventing reading difficulties in young children.* Washington, DC: National Academy Press.

Snow, M., & Brinton, D. (1997). *The content-based classroom: Perspectives on integrating language and content.* New York: Longman.

Sokmen, A. J. (1992). Students as vocabulary generators. *TESOL Journal, 1,* 16–18.

Soltero, S. W. (2004). *Dual language: Teaching and learning in two languages.* Boston: Allyn & Bacon.

Stanovich, K. E. (1986). Matthew effects in reading: Some consequences of individual differences in the acquisition of literacy. *Reading Research Quarterly, 21,* 360–406.

Stauffer, R. (1980a). *Directing the reading-thinking process.* New York: Harper & Row.

Stauffer, R. (1980b). *The language experience approach to the teaching of reading* (2nd ed.). New York: Harper & Row.

Street, B. (1995). *Social literacies: Critical approaches to literacy in development, ethnography and education.* London: Longman.

Strickland, D. S., & Morrow, L. M. (Eds.). (1989). *Emerging literacy: Young children learn to read and write.* Newark, DE: International Reading Association.

Strunk, W., & White, E. B. (2000). *The elements of style* (4th ed.). New York: Longman.

Sundem, G., Krieger, J., & Pikiewicz, K. (2008). *10 languages you'll need most in the classroom.* Thousand Oaks, CA: Corwin Press.

Swain, M. (2005). The output hypothesis: Theory and research. In E. Hinkel (Ed.), *Handbook of research in second language teaching and learning* (pp. 471–483). Mahwah, NJ: Erlbaum.

Swales, J. (1990). *Genre analysis: English in academic and research settings.* Cambridge, UK: Cambridge University Press.

Taba, H. (1967). *Teacher's handbook for elementary social studies.* Reading, MA: Addison-Wesley.

Tabors, P. O., & Snow, C. E. (2001). Young bilingual children and early literacy development. In S. B. Neuman & D. K. Dickinson (Eds.), *Handbook of early literacy research* (Vol. 1, pp. 159–178). New York: Guilford Press.

Taylor, D. M. (2000). Facing hardships: Jamestown and colonial life. In K. D. Samway (Ed.), *Integrating the ESL standards into classroom practices: Grades 3–5* (pp. 53–81). Alexandria, VA: Teachers of English to Speakers of Other Languages.

Taylor, W. L. (1953). Cloze procedure: A new tool for measuring readability. *Journalism Quarterly, 30*, 415–453.

Teale, W. H. (1984). Reading to young children: Its significance for literacy development. In H. Goelman, A. A. Oberg, & F. Smith (Eds.), *Awakening to literacy* (pp. 110–121). Portsmouth, NH: Heinemann.

Teale, W. H. (2003). Reading aloud to young children as a classroom instructional activity: Insights from research and practice. In A. van Kleeck, S. A. Stahl, & E. B. Bauer (Eds.), *On reading books to children: Parents and teachers* (pp. 114–139). Mahwah, NJ: Erlbaum.

TESOL. (2001). Position statement on language and literacy development for young English language learners. Alexandria, VA: Author. Retrieved May 3, 2007, from *www.tesol.org/s_tesol/bin.asp?CID=32&DID=371&DOC=FILE.PDF.*

TESOL. (2003). Position paper on high-stakes testing for K–12 English-language learners in the United States of America. Alexandria, VA: Author. Retrieved January 10, 2007, from *www.tesol.org/s_tesol/bin.asp?CID=32&DID=375&DOC=FILE.PDF.*

TESOL. (2005). Position paper on assessment and accountability of English language learners under the No Child Left Behind Act of 2001 (Public Law 107-110). Alexandria, VA: Author. Retrieved January 10, 2006, from *www.tesol.org/s_tesol/bin.asp?CID=32&DID=4720&DOC=FILE.PDF.*

TESOL. (2006a). Position statement on the diversity of English language learners in the United States. Alexandria, VA: Author. Retrieved February 10, 2007, from *www.tesol.org/s_tesol/bin.asp?CID=32&DID=7212&DOC=FILE.PDF.*

TESOL. (2006b). TESOL Revises pre-K–2 English language proficiency standards. Alexandria, VA: Author. Retrieved October 10, 2008, from *www.tesol.org/s_tesol/sec_document.asp?TrackID=&SID=1&DID=5349&CID=1186&VID=2&RTID=0&CIDQS=&Taxonomy=False&specialSearch=False.*

TESOL. (undated). What does the research tell us about how many years of instruction English language learners need to become proficient in academic reading? Retrieved March 20, 2008, from *www.tesol.org/s_tesol/cat_tapestry.asp?TRACKID=&SID=1&VID=268&CID=1588&DID=8745&RTID=0&CIDQS=&Taxonomy=False&specialSearch=False#yearsinstruction.*

Topping, D., & Hoffman, S. (2006). *Getting grammar: 150 new ways to teach an old subject.* Portsmouth, NH: Heinemann.

Truss, L. (2003). *Eats, shoots & leaves.* New York: Gotham.

Uribe, M., & Nathenson-Mejía, S. (2008). *Literacy essentials for English language learners: Successful transitions.* New York: Teachers College Press.

Vacca, R. T., & Vacca, J. L. (2005). *Content area reading: Literacy and learning across the curriculum* (8th ed.). New York: Allyn & Bacon.

Valdez-Pierce, L., & O'Malley, J. M. (1992). *Performance and portfolio assessment for language minority students.* Washington, DC: National Clearinghouse for Bilingual Education.

Vukelich, C., Christie, J., & Enz, B. (2007). *Helping young children learn language and literacy* (2nd ed.). Boston: Allyn & Bacon.

White, Z. R. (2008). *Playing with poems: Word study lessons for shared reading, K–2.* Portsmouth, NH: Heinemann.

Williams, J. (2001). Classroom conversations: Opportunities to learn for ESL students in mainstream classrooms. *Reading Teacher, 54*, 750–757.

Wood, K. D. (1994). *Practical strategies for improving instruction.* Westerville, OH: National Middle School Association.

Wood, K. D. (2002). Differentiating reading and writing lessons to promote content learning.

In C. C. Block, L. B. Gambrell, & M. Pressley (Eds.), *Improving comprehension instruction* (pp. 155–180). San Francisco: Jossey-Bass.

Woodward, T. (1985). From vocabulary review to classroom dictionary. *Modern English Teacher, 12*, 29.

Xu, S. H. (2003). The learner, the teacher, the text, and the context: Sociocultural approaches to early literacy instruction for English language learners. In D. M. Barone & L. M. Morrow (Eds.), *Literacy and young children: Research-based practices* (pp. 61–80). New York: Guilford Press.

Xu, S. H. (2008a). *Exploring academic vocabulary in trading cards.* Unpublished manuscript.

Xu, S. H. (2008b). *Exploring types of environmental print (EP) as a community resource for teaching.* Unpublished manuscript.

Xu, S. H., & Rutledge, A. L. (2003). "Chicken start with Ch!": Kindergartners talk about print through environmental print. *Young Children, 58*(2), 44–51.

Yopp, H. K., & Stapleton, L. (2008). Conciencia fonémica en español (Phonemic awareness in Spanish). *Reading Teacher, 61*, 374–382.

Yopp, H. K., & Yopp, R. H. (2000). Supporting phonemic awareness in the classroom. *Reading Teacher, 54*, 130–141.

Zwiers, J. (2008). *Building academic language: Essential practices for content classrooms, grades 5–12.* San Francisco: Jossey-Bass.

CHILDREN'S BOOKS CITED

Ada, A. F. (1995). *Half-chicken.* New York: Bantam Doubleday Dell Books for Young Readers.

Ada, A. F. (1997). *Gathering the sun: An alphabet in Spanish and English.* New York: Lothrop, Lee & Shepard.

Adams, S. (2001). *The best book of weather.* New York: Houghton Mufflin.

Adler, D. A. (1990). *A picture book of Benjamin Franklin.* New York: Holiday House.

Allard, H. (1977). *Miss Nelson is missing.* Boston: Houghton Mifflin.

Anders, T. (2000). *Punctuation pals.* Fallbrook, CA: Alpine.

Aylesworth, J. (1992). *Old black fly.* New York: Henry Holt.

Baker, A. (1994). *Black and white rabbit's ABC.* New York: Larousse, Kingfisher, Chambers.

Baker, J. (1991). *Window.* New York: Greenwillow Books.

Baker, J. (2004). *Home.* New York: Greenwillow Books.

Baker, L. (1990). *Life in the deserts.* London: Two-can Publishing.

Banks, K. (2006). *Max's words.* New York: Farrar, Straus & Giroux.

Banyai, I. (1995). *Zoom.* New York: Viking.

Beller, J. (1984). *A-B-Cing: An action alphabet.* New York: Crown.

Berger, M. (1999). *Can it rain cats and dogs?: Questions and answers about weather.* New York: Scholastic.

Berger, M. (2000). *Scholastic science dictionary.* New York: Scholastic.

Bingham, C. (2003). *DK eye wonder human body.* New York: DK.

Blake, Q. (1996). *Clown.* New York: Holt.

Breckenridge, J., Mandell, M., Fredericks, A. D., & Loeschnig, L. V. (1998). *365 super science experiments with everyday materials.* New York: Sterling.

Briggs, R. (1978). *The snowman.* New York: Random House.

Bundey, N. (2000a). *Rain and people.* Minneapolis, MN: Carolrhoda Books.

Bundey, N. (2000b). *Rain and the earth*. Minneapolis, MN: Carolrhoda Books.

Burningham, J. (1986). *Cluck baa, jangle twang, slap bang, skip trip, sniff shout, wobble pop*. New York: Viking.

Calmenson, S. (1993). *It begins with an A*. New York: Hyperion Books for Children.

Canizares, S. (1998). *Little Raccoon catches a cold*. New York: Scholastic.

Carle, E. (1973). *I see a song*. New York: Crowell.

Carle, E. (1976). *Do you want to be my friend?* New York: HarperCollins.

Carle, E. (1987). *The tiny seed*. Natick, MA: Picture Book Studio.

Carle, E. (1993). *Today is Monday*. New York: Scholastic.

Carle, E. (1997). *From head to toe*. New York: HarperCollins.

Carlson, N. (1988). *I like me*. New York: Viking.

Carlson, N. (1997). *ABC, I like me*. New York: Viking.

Carroll, C. (1996). *The weather: Sun, wind, snow, rain*. New York: Abbeville Kids.

Christelow, E. (2002). *Where's the big bad wolf?* New York: Clarion Books.

Cleary, B. P. (1999). *A mink, a fink, a skating rink: What is a noun?* Minneapolis, MN: Carolrhoda Books.

Cleary, B. P. (2000). *Hairy, scary, ordinary: What is an adjective?* Minneapolis, MN: Carolrhoda Books.

Cleary, B. P. (2001). *To root, to toot, parachute: What is a verb?* Minneapolis, MN: Carolrhoda Books.

Cleary, B. P. (2002). *Under, over, by the clover: What is a preposition?* Minneapolis, MN: Carolrhoda Books.

Cleary, B. P. (2003). *Dearly, nearly, insincerely: What is an adverb?* Minneapolis, MN: Carolrhoda Books.

Cleary, B. P. (2004). *I and you and don't forget who: What is a pronoun?* Minneapolis, MN: Carolrhoda Books.

Clements, A. (2005). *Lunch money*. New York : Simon & Schuster.

Cole, J. *Magic school bus series*. New York: Scholastic.

Collins, P. (1973). *Where does all the rain go?* New York: Coward, McCann & Geoghegan.

Corbeil, J-C., & Archambault, A. (1994). *Scholastic visual dictionary*. New York: Scholastic.

Cowley, J. (1996). *The little yellow chicken*. Bothell, WA: Wright Group.

Crews, D. (1980). *Truck*. New York: Greenwillow Books.

Crews, D. (1984). *School bus*. New York: Greenwillow Books.

Dalby, E. (2003). *Mysteries and marvels of nature*. New York: Usborne.

Darling, K. (1996). *Rain forest babies*. New York: Walker Publishing Company.

Davis, K. C. (2003). *Don't know much about American history*. New York: HarperCollins.

DeGross, M. (1994). *Donavan's word jar*. New York: HarperCollins.

De Zutterm H. (1993). *Who says a dog goes bow-bow?* New York: Doubleday.

Denega, D. (2004). *Let's read about Betsy Ross*. New York: Scholastic.

dePaola, T. (1978). *Pancakes for breakfast*. New York: Harcourt Brace.

dePaola, T. (1993). *Tom*. New York: Putnam.

Donohue, M. R. (2008). *Penny and the punctuation bee*. Morton Grove, IL: Albert Whitman.

Drescher, H. (1987). *The yellow umbrella*. New York: Bradbury Press.

Ehlert, L. (1988). *Planting a rainbow*. San Diego, CA: Harcourt Brace.

Ehlert, L. (1989). *Eating the alphabet: Fruits and vegetables from A to Z*. San Diego, CA: Harcourt.

Falconer, I. (2000). *Olivia*. New York: Atheneum Books for Young Readers.

Falwell, C. (1998). *Word wizard*. New York: Clarion Books.

Feder, J. (1995). *Table, chair, bear: A book in many languages*. New York: Houghton Mufflin.

Fleischman, P. (2004). *Sidewalk circus*. Cambridge, MA: Candlewick Press.

Gans, R. (1997). *Let's go rock collecting*. HarperCollins.

Garza, C. L. (1996). *In my family/En mi familia*. Danbury, CT: Children's Press.

Gibbons, G. (1990). *Weather words and what they mean*. New York: Holiday House.

Graves, K. (1998). *Miss moo goes to the zoo*. New York: Scholastic.

Grazzini, F. (1996). *Rain, where do you come from?* Brooklyn, New York: Kane/Miller.

Heinrichs, A. (2004a). *Adjectives*. Chanhassen, MN: Child's World.

Heinrichs, A. (2004b). *Prepositions*. Chanhassen, MN: Child's World.

Heinrichs, A. (2004c). *Pronouns*. Chanhassen, MN: Child's World.

Heinrichs, A. (2004d). *Verbs*. Chanhassen, MN: Child's World.

Heller, R. (1987). *A cache of jewels and other collective nouns*. New York: Grosset & Dunlap.

Heller, R. (1988). *Kites sail high: A book about verbs*. New York: Grosset & Dunlap.

Heller, R. (1989). *Many luscious lollipops: A book about adjectives*. New York: Grosset & Dunlap.

Heller, R. (1991). *Up, up and away: A book about adverbs*. New York: Grosset & Dunlap.

Heller, R. (1995). *Behind the mask: A book about prepositions*. New York: Grosset & Dunlap.

Heller, R. (1997). *Mine, all mine: A book about pronouns*. New York: Grosset & Dunlap.

Heller, R. (1998). *Fantastic! wow! and unreal!: A book about interjections and conjunctions*. New York: Grosset & Dunlap.

Hills, T. (2006). *Duck and goose*. New York: Schwartz & Wade Books.

Hoban, T. (1973). *Over, under & through, and other spatial concepts*. New York: Macmillan.

Hoban, T. (1986). *Shapes, shapes, shapes*. New York: Morrow.

Hoban, T. (1987). *26 letters and 99 cents*. New York: Greenwillow Books.

Hoban, T. (1990). *Exactly the opposite*. New York: Greenwillow Books.

Hoban, T. (1991). *All about where*. New York: Greenwillow Books.

Hollander, J., & Bloom, H. (1972). *The wind and the rain: An anthology of poems for young people*. Freeport, New York: Books for Libraries Press.

Hopkins, L. B. (1990). *Good books, good times*. New York: HarperCollins.

Hutchins, P. (1970). *Clocks and more clocks*. New York: Macmillian.

Jeunesse, G. (1995). *Wind and weather*. New York: Scholastic.

Kalan, R. (1978). *Rain*. New York: Greenwillow Books.

Kalan, R. (1981). *Jump, frog, jump*. New York: Greenwillow Books.

Kamma, A. (2004). *. . . If you lived when there was slavery in America*. New York: Scholastic.

Kelley, M. F. (2006). *Buz words: Discover words in Pairs*. Morgan Hill, CA: April Arts Press.

Kellogg, S. (2000). *The missing mitten mystery*. New York: Dial Books for Young Readers.

Kerrod, R. (2003). *DK Eyewitness Universe*. New York: DK.

Kightley, R. (1986). *Opposites*. New York: Little, Brown.

Leely, L. (2002). *Follow the money*. New York: Holiday House.

Lehman, B. (2004). *The red book*. Boston: Houghton Mifflin.

Lewis, K. (1992). *Floss*. Cambridge, MA: Candlewick Press.

Lillie, P. (1993). *When this box is full*. New York: Greenwillow Books.

Liu, J. S. (2002). *Yellow umbrella*. La Jolla, CA: Kane/Miller.

Lobel, A. (1981). *On market street*. New York: Greenwillow Books.

Lyne, A. (1997). *My name is . . . A*. Dallas, TX: Whispering Coyote Press.

MacQuitty, M. (1995). *DK eyewitness ocean*. New York: DK.

Martin, B., Jr. (1983). *Brown bear, brown bear, what do you see?* New York: Holt, Rinehart & Winston.

Martin, B., Jr. (1991). *Polar bear, polar bear, what do you hear?* New York: Holt, Rinehart & Winston.

Martin, B., Jr., & Archambault, J. (1989). *Chicka chicka boom boom*. New York: Simon & Schuster.

Marzollo, J. (1994). *City sounds*. New York: Scholastic.

Marzollo, J. (1998). *How kids grow*. New York: Scholastic.

Mccarone, G. (1995). *Cars! cars! cars!* New York: Scholastic.

McCully, E. A. (1987). *School*. New York: Harper & Row.

McGinley, P. (1948). *All around the town*. Philadelphia: J. B. Lippincott.

McGrath, B. B. (1998). *The cheerios counting book*. New York: Scholastic.

McMillan, B. (1989). *Super, super, superwords*. New York: Lothrop, Lee & Shepard.

McPhail, D. (1989). *Animals A to Z*. New York: Scholastic.

Micucci, C. (1992). *The life and times of the apple*. New York: Orchard Books.

Miranda, A. (1997). *To market, to market*. San Diego: Harcourt.

Neumeier, M., & Glasser, B. (1985). *Action alphabet*. New York: Greenwillow Books.

Numberoff, L. (1985). *If you give a mouse a cookie*. New York: Harper & Row.

Numberoff, L. (1991). *If you give a moose a muffin*. New York: HarperCollins.

Numberoff, L. (1998). *If you give a pig a pancake*. New York: HarperCollins.

Numberoff, L. (2000). *If you take a mouse to a movie*. New York: HarperCollins.

Numberoff, L. (2002). *If you take a mouse to school*. New York: HarperCollins.

Osborne, M. P. (2005). *Magic tree house: Carnival at candlelight*. New York: Scholastic.

Otto, C. B. (2002). *Shadows*. New York: Scholastic.

Palatini, M. (1997). *Moosetache*. New York: Hyperion Books for Children.

Pallotta, J. (1998). *The boat alphabet book*. Watertown, MA: Charlesbridge.

Pallotta, J. (1998). *The flower alphabet book*. Watertown, MA: Charlesbridge.

Peters, L. W. (1990). *The sun, the wind, and the rain*. New York: Holt.

Petty, K. (2006). *The perfect pop-up punctuation book*. New York: Dutton.

Pulver, R. (2003). *Punctuation takes a vacation*. New York: Holiday House.

Pulver, R. (2007). *Nouns and verbs have a field day*. New York: Holiday House.

Rankin, J. (1997). *Wow! It is great being a duck*. New York: Simon & Schuster.

Recorvits, H. (2003). *My name is Yoon*. New York: Farrar, Straus & Giroux.

Rockwell, A. (1986). *Fire engines*. New York: The Trumpet Club.

Rockwell, A. (n.d.). *Insect picnic*. Columbus, OH: Macmillan/McGraw-Hill.

Roe, E. (1991). *With my brother/Con mi hermano*. New York: Macmillan.

Rogasky, B. (1994). *Winter poems*. New York: Scholastic.

Rohmann, E. (1994). *Time flies*. New York: Crown.

Root, P. (1998). *One duck stuck*. Cambridge, MA: Candlewick Press.

Rotner, S. (1995). *Action alphabet*. New York: Atheneum.

Rowling, J. K. (1997). *Harry Potter and the sorcerer's stone*. New York: Scholastic.

Sanchez, C. (2008). *Amazing plants and animals*. Carson, CA: Lakeshore Learning Materials.

Schneider, R. M. (1995). *Add it, dip it, fix it: A book of verbs*. Boston: Houghton Mifflin.

Schotter, R. (2006). *The boy who loved words*. New York: Schwartz & Wade Books.

Seuss, Dr. (1949). *Bartholomew and the oobleck*. New York: Random House.

Seuss, Dr. (1957). *The cat in the hat*. New York: Random House.

Seuss, Dr. (1968). *The foot book*. New York: Random House.

Seuss, Dr. (1986). *The cat in the hat comes back*. New York: Beginner Books.

Shannon, G. (1995). *Tomorrow's alphabet*. New York: Greenwillow Books.

Shaw, N. (1991). *Sheep in a shop*. Boston: Houghton Mifflin.

Shaw, N. (1992). *Sheep out to eat*. Boston: Houghton Mifflin.

Shaw, N. (1997). *Sheep trick or treat*. Boston: Houghton Mifflin.

Shierman, V. (1981). *M is for move*. New York: Dutton.

Sierra, J. (2000). *There's a zoo in room 22*. Orlando, FL: Harcourt Brace.

Simon, N. (1954). *Wet world*. New York: Candlewick Press.

Simon, S. (1992). *Our solar system*. New York: HarperCollins.

Simont, M. (2001). *The stray dog*. New York: HarperCollins.

Slate, J. (1996). *Miss Bindergarten gets ready for kindergarten*. New York: Dutton.

Soto, G. (1993). *Too many tamales*. New York: Putnam.

Spier, P. (1983). *Christmas*. Garden City, NY: Doubleday.

Spier, P. (1997). *Rain*. Garden City, New York: Doubleday.

Spinelli, J. (1990). *Maniac Magee*. New York: Little, Brown.

Sutherland, M. (2001). *MacMurtrey's wall*. New York: H. Abrams.

Taback, S. (1997). *There was an old lay who swallowed a fly*. New York: Viking.

Teague, M. (2004). *Detective LaRue: Letters from the investigation*. New York: Scholastic.

Terban, M. (1984). *I think I thought and other tricky verbs*. New York: Clarion.

Truss, L. (2006). *Eats, shoots & leaves: Why, commas really do make a difference!* New York: G. P. Putman's Sons.

Truss, L. (2007). *The girl's like spaghetti: Why you can't manage without apostrophes!* New York: G. P. Putman's Sons.

Truss, L. (2008). *Twenty-odd ducks: Why every punctuation mark counts!* New York: G. P. Putman's Sons.

Viorst, J. (1972). *Alexander and the terrible, horrible, no good, very bad day*. New York, Atheneum.

Walsh, E. S. (1989). *Mouse paint*. Orlando, FL: Harcourt Brace.

Weitzman, J. P. (1998). *You can't take a balloon into the metropolitan museum*. New York: Dial Books for Young Readers.

Weitzman, J. P. (2000). *You can't take a balloon into the national gallery*. New York: Dial Books for Young Readers.

Wells, R. (1997). *Bunny cakes*. New York: Dial Books for Young Readers.

Wells, R. (2004). *Max's first word*. New York: Viking.

Wiesner, D. (1991). *Tuesday*. New York: Clarion Books.

Wiesner, D. (1998). *Fire fall*. New York: Lothrop, Lee & Shepard.

Wiesner, D. (1999). *Sector 7*. New York: Clarion Books.

Wiesner, D. (2006). *Flotsam*. New York: Clarion Books.

Williams, L. (1986). *The little old lady who was not afraid of anything*. New York: HarperCollins.

Wilson, A. (1999). *Magpie magic: A tale of colorful mischief*. New York: Dial Books.

Wood, A. (2001). *Alphabet adventure*. New York: Scholastic.

Yolen, J. (2003). *How do dinosaurs get well soon?* New York: Scholastic.

Zhang, D. (2003). *Illustrated children's English-Chinese dictionary*. Beijing, China: Foreign Language Teaching and Research Press.

INDEX

"*f*" following a page number indicates a figure; "*t*" following a page number indicates a table.